three

From beginning to end

A novel by

LYNN BROWN

Three **by Lynn Brown**

Copyright © 2017 by Lynn Brown

First printing 2017

ISBN-13:978-0692925058

Cover design and production:
Mike Inks, mlidesign.co

Published by LAB Publishing

Visit:
www.threethebook.com

"And now these three remain:
faith, hope and love. But the greatest of these is love"

1 Corinthians 13:13

To Greg, Max and Anna
The three of you are the best part of my life …

Acknowledgments

My deepest thanks to …

Kirkland Fire Department Aid 24, Engine 25. Northshore Fire Department Engine 51, Engine 57, Aid 51, Rescue 51, Battalion 51. Shoreline Fire Department Medic 65, Medical Support Officer 6. Redmond Fire Department Medic 23. Bothell Fire Department Truck 42. Airlift Northwest and American Medical Response. The incredible medical staff at Harborview and Seattle Children's Hospitals. All those that prayed and supported our family during this time, the anonymous gentleman that helped Max after he crawled out of the car and then brought a stuffed animal to Anna at Harborview, my sisters Ann and Teensie for flying to my side and taking care of our family and home, Cedar Park Christian School, Tracy Harrison for reading *Three* three times and offering her input and support, Mike Inks for his gift of design and creativity in the visuals for *Three,* and my editor Lynne Pearson for reading and re-reading my book to get it ready for print.

I would also like to thank my mom and dad for raising their three daughters with strength, humor and a sense of purpose. These are much needed characteristics to rely on as we journey through our adventures in life.

three

From beginning to end

Chapter One

"God keep you all in His loving arms as He cares for you"
— Clare and Barbara Herman

I love you. A hug and a kiss? Eyeballs? Have a great day at school.

These are remembering words I repeat to our kids every morning before they pull out of our driveway to begin their short drive to high school. Even if their eyes are rolling and they look at me with that "I don't want to talk to you" expression, I still say these words and mean them from the depths of my soul.

The I love you, speaks for itself. I have made sure to say I love you once, if not multiple times a day from the moment they drew their first breath. I do love them. They will never know how much until they have their own children. Saying I love you should be easy. It is for me and I want those three beautiful words to be easy for them to repeat to their families.

A hug and a kiss, are the words I say before I grab them, and wrap them in my arms, only to give them a little kiss on the side of their head. Much to their chagrin, they can't escape my embrace. Lord knows some mornings they've tried.

Eyeballs; this is a reminder for them to look into my eyes when I tell them I love them so they not only hear it, they see it. Eye contact reveals the truth. They are loved.

Have a great day at school is my way of wishing that their school day is loaded with work, fun, and laughter. Of course, this is not always the case with two teenagers, but it is an attempt to start their day with a positive thought. Saying it makes me feel better, even though there is rarely a reply.

Sending them off with these four messages is so important to me, that if I miss them before they leave the house, I call the passenger to inform both of them that I love them and to have a great day. Again, not always met with a warm welcome, but at least I put it out there.

One beautiful, slightly chilly fall morning in October, Max and Anna back out of the driveway while I stand waving goodbye, with a towel wrapped around my wet hair, full makeup on, wearing jeans and a bathrobe. Looking around our yard, I notice my garden perennials are beginning to die back and the fall aster is in full bloom, shooting color into a dying season of summer flowers. I love this house. We live in a two-story cottage that we have painted Cape Cod gray with bright white trim. We have surrounded the house with colorful flowers and a white picket fence. I never like to leave our house and I am always glad to get home.

But, today is Tuesday and a workday for me. It's time for me to go inside, finish getting dressed, and dry my hair. On Tuesday and Thursday mornings I teach preschool at our church, Epiphany Lutheran. Greeting the smiling faces on a room full of three-year-old children is always a welcome treat when raising two teenagers at home. I have to be in my classroom by 8:30 am and ready for my preschool class by 9:00 am. If I haven't showered before the kids leave for school, my morning becomes a frantic race against time. And, if I can't leave a few minutes early, it means I can't stop and get my Starbucks soy latte with a dollop of whipped cream! This is a special little treat I allow myself as the mother of two teenagers. I like to believe I earn it.

Well, this morning, by the grace of God, I am almost ready for the day. Entering the house through the laundry room, I am stopped by two of our four-legged family members. "Ah," I laugh, "are you two waiting for some attention?" I reach down to give Sammy dog a rub on the head and look into the eyes of Jazzy cat to say hello. These two are a pair. Not only do we love them dearly, but they love each other. They even look alike! Both of them are black and white, which happens to be perfect, because they complement our home's décor. That was not planned!

"Okay guys, I've gotta get going. Move aside." Jazz turns and lumbers off to lie in the sun somewhere. Sammy, my shadow, follows me upstairs. I whip the towel off my head, hang it up, put the leave-in cream rinse in my hair, comb out the tangles and pull out the blow dryer. Here I go. A great blow dryer is known by its deafening blast that drowns out all other sounds while in use. If it's not incredibly loud and forceful, it's not doing its job. Many phone calls and dog barking alerts have been missed because the only thing I hear is the roar of the blow dryer at work.

"Ten minutes," I tell myself. It takes me ten minutes to dry my hair. I only put the dryer down for a few seconds a couple of times in order to get through this drying routine.

"Almost done, just the bangs left," I mention to Sammy who is curled up on the floor next to me. The moment I set the dryer down, I hear the phone ringing.

Greg had left before the kids this morning for a meeting in Seattle. He has his own marketing company and also works for an advertising agency three days a week in downtown Seattle. Normally he works from home on Tuesdays and Thursdays. This morning I'm home alone and I rush to pick up the call. I always answer the phone when I'm home. We don't have caller ID and I always assume it's important.

I pick up the receiver and answer with my usual "Hello."

It's 7:50 am. Slowly and carefully Max says, "Mom, we've been in an accident and Anna is hurt."

I do not miss a beat and ask Max "Where are you?"

He says, "We are at the top of the hill."

"Okay," I say, "I will be right there."

I am not panicking, but need to get in the car, take care of business and get to my kids. I quickly and methodically rush through my routine by throwing my bathrobe off and putting on a cream turtleneck and black cardigan sweater. I actually ask myself what fabric will be comfortable in case I am in these clothes for a while. I grab Jazzy cat and put him in the garage, put Sammy in the kennel and put the clip in the gate to make sure the kennel is locked so he cannot escape, turn the house alarm on and lock the door, get into the car and back out of the garage leaving the garage door open a bit so the kitties can get in and out for food and water.

I pull out of the driveway and head down our street. Stop. Turn left. I am trying to drive safely along our short but winding road. Stop. Turn left up Holmes Point Drive to head up to the top of the hill. Holmes Point is a beautiful neighborhood. I love living here. We are surrounded by two parks, a lake and fabulous neighbors we have known for twenty-two years. I am comfortable here.

Coming around the first bend, I see a large construction truck ahead of me. Having driven this road thousands of times, I know I am trapped. Holmes Point is a very curvy, winding two-lane road that can be dangerous on any given day for walkers, bikers, pedestrians, and cars.

"Okay," I say out loud, "don't follow too close. We're okay." The truck can barely get any speed going up the hill and I can't pass him. As I look around in frustration, I fumble for my cellphone and call Greg. He answers. Thank you, God.

"The kids have been in a car accident," I tell him in a small high voice.

"They're at the top of the hill. I'm on my way."

Urgently he responds, "Are they okay?"

I quickly reply, "Max called and said Anna's hurt. That's all I know. I will call you back when I get to the top of the hill." Thank God, he answered. We hang up knowing we will reconnect in a matter of minutes.

Then I call my dear friend Lisa Brackett. I have known Lisa since Anna was three and Max was five. She started out as our day care provider. Lisa is my church buddy and my dear, unselfish friend. We shop together, laugh together, and raise teenagers together. She lives eight minutes from me.

"Please answer," I repeat to myself. I know Lisa's routine. Every Tuesday morning Lisa walks with her neighbors and her dog. Even, if by chance she is home, Lisa rarely answers the phone.

I wait. Her phone is ringing. Then I hear her familiar voice. "Hello." Thank God.

"Lisa," I quickly spit the words out "Max and Anna have been in a car accident at the top of the hill. I talked to Greg, he's in Seattle and I am en route to the accident."

Lisa does not hesitate and responds immediately with, "I am on my way." Lisa will run out of the house naked if she needs to. That is who she is and that is what I love about her.

Finally, I am approaching the top of the hill. As the truck in front of me comes to a stop at the light, I pull off to the right shoulder into the one spot at the top of Holmes Point where I can park and leave my car. It is open and waiting for me to pull in, park, and get to my kids. As I pull over, I slam the car into park before I have completely stopped and hear a loud grind as the car jerks to a stop and I turn off the ignition.

In one continuous movement, I grab my cellphone, call Greg, jump out of the car, lock the doors, and look up into the intersection in front of me. I see red. I see red vehicles. I see emergency vehicles. I do not see Max's baby blue Ford Explorer. "Oh," I think, "the kids must be on the other side of the intersection." "Good, Anna probably has only minor injuries." Red fire trucks and aid cars continue to stream in. All I can see is a large white truck. It seems fine, just sitting in the middle of the road. With car keys in my left hand, I am standing still at the entry to the intersection when my eyes fix on a small patch of baby blue metal. Slowly my mind catches up with my vision and it is now that I am able to see the whole picture. Baby Blue, as Max and Anna affectionately refer to the Explorer, is on its side with the driver's side leaning against a huge, metal traffic pole. The black, blank spot I had been staring into was the under belly of Baby Blue. My worst fears are realized as my left hand begins to twist side to side, keys thrashing wildly, and I scream, "Those are my kids." I run into the intersection. Thank the Lord all traffic has stopped as I barely glance from side to side to make sure I can run across.

I am running to Maxie. There he is on the curb, sitting all by himself. My sandy-blond-haired son with a big heart and a wonderful smile is all alone. The brother, the son, the driver. He is very quiet. I hug him and give him a kiss and ask him if he is okay.

"Yes," he says quietly, "Go see Anna, she's hurt." Okay, Max is okay. And he wants me to go to Anna. I hand Max the phone so he can talk to Dad. I run around the white truck and past all the red vehicles. Then I see my beautiful baby girl. She is trapped. Her tall frame is dangling from her seatbelt inside the car on the passenger side. Her face is obscured by her long brown hair. The passenger side door is completely smashed inward surrounded by twisted and distorted metal from the car frame. The windshield is still attached to the frame, yet looks like a rolling hill of cracked glass. The driver's headrest is resting behind the huge metal light pole and the roof is caved in. How did they survive? I fix my eyes on Anna. Her legs and arms are moving. I say thank you to God. I feel covered in faith. Faith that Anna is okay. I have no tears. I rush up to the Explorer with firemen and medics everywhere.

A woman comes up behind me and asks, "Are you the mom?"

"Yes." I am the mom. I am the mom who loves these kids more than life itself and right now is steeped in faith knowing I have no control. I am unsure, calm, panicked, and scared all at the same time. She says she is a nurse from the doctor's office across the street and wants me to know what she has observed. She says, "She is moving her legs and arms. That's good."

I ask, "What about her head?"

She looks at me and replies, "That I can't tell you."

There are firemen trying to get Anna out through the passenger window. The windshield is still in the car and I lean toward the car and call Anna's name and tell her I love her and I am here. She is physically moving but not mentally engaged. She gives me no reply or sign of having heard me. Nothing.

I run back to Max. He is obviously dazed and he puts his arm around my shoulder. This is where those hugs and kisses come in. My son is comfortable with "I love you" and with hugs and kisses. We never know when we may need to call on those comforts. This is one of those times. As Max rests against me, a female paramedic notices us and realizes Max had been in the accident. She immediately and with great authority yells out. "Has anyone helped this boy?" What am I thinking? Of course, Max needs help. "Help!" my mind is screaming, but no words come out.

Within seconds, medics descend on Max with a neck brace and questions. "Max, I am going to check on Anna and I'll be back." I run around the white truck and red vehicles to Anna. As I look up, I see Lisa running towards the accident scene. She's here. She's with Max. She's on the phone with Greg. Thank you, God.

With my eyes taking in the wreckage, I notice my neighbor Scott Blackburn is standing off to the side of the accident. We are both watching frantically as the firemen are trying desperately to get Anna out of the car. I have a moment. It is one of those moments when you can take a small breather to let out your emotions before digging back in to be strong in order to help others stay strong. I fly into Scott's arms. Scott is a big guy. He scoops me up and holds me for just enough time for me to cry and then say something about Anna. He says, "I know." What a great neighbor and man. Scott releases me and I go back to check on Anna. They are still trying to get her out of Baby Blue. I run over to Max.

As I approach the curb where Max had been sitting, I see a fireman stretching yellow tape all around the area. Max is now on a stretcher with a neck brace and lots of medics surround him. He is on the other side of the tape and I cannot reach him. I can't even talk to him. As I am looking at the back of the fireman, I notice the name "Pratt" is written across his uniform.

I half scream "That's my son, where are they taking him?" The fireman turns around and looks at me. It is Josh Pratt, the father of one of my preschool kids from the previous year. Great family, all of us teachers loved them. Mr. Pratt had come to the preschool in his fireman outfit to show and teach the kids what a fireman looked like in gear so they would never be afraid during a fire. I had met and seen Mr. Pratt on many occasions at school. Thank you, God.

"Mr. Pratt, it's Mrs. Brown, where are they taking my son?"

He helps me. He turns and calls to the medics that are preparing to load Max into the ambulance. Looking back to me, he says, "Harborview. They are taking him to Harborview Medical Center in Seattle." Harborview is the premier trauma center in a five-state radius. There is no place better. Max will be checked out by the most thorough emergency room team in the state. Thank you.

I head over to see Anna. They are still trying to get her out of Baby Blue. I see two firemen on top of the passenger door and more standing by. Anna's legs and arms are moving but they cannot get her out. The windshield has been removed. There are lots of people standing around watching. I notice a crowd has gathered at the gas station on the corner. A fireman keeps telling me to move back. I almost trip on the windshield which is lying on the ground. It is cracked and shattered yet still in one twisted piece. Lisa is with me and still has Greg on the phone. She is giving him a play-by-play of what is happening. Miraculously, Greg is only a few blocks from Harborview in Seattle and is heading there now to meet the ambulance when they bring Max in. He will be there. Max will not be alone. Thank you, God.

Then, I see this piece of machinery that looks like a generator. It is in front of Baby Blue. As Lisa and I back away, there is a fireman yelling, "Power!" The machine roars to life and I realize they are trying to cut Anna out of the car with the Jaws of Life. I can't watch this. I can't bear it. I run back to see Max being loaded up and leaving.

I never see them pull her out. In the few seconds it takes to send my baby boy off in an ambulance, the firemen have cut Anna out of the car, put her on a stretcher, strapped a huge stabilizing brace around her neck, and prepared her for the ambulance ride.

One of the medics approaches and says, "She is going to Inglemoor High School in the ambulance. From there, she will be airlifted to Harborview Medical Center." These are terrifying words to digest. Airlift and Harborview. I'm numb.

Lisa and I watch while Anna is loaded into the back of the ambulance. The moment that ambulance door closes, we are ready to go. Surrounded by yellow tape, busy firemen, red vehicles, debris, and two totaled trucks, I begin to realize this journey is just beginning.

A large, fully geared fireman approaches me from inside the tape and says, "What can I do for you?" He and his crew have just rescued my children from a horrible car accident and I am so amazed with them and he wants to know what he can do for me?

I look into his eyes and tell him, "Nothing."

As this wonderful human being turns away, I say, "Oh!" He immediately turns back towards me. "You can pray for my kids."

He replies, without hesitation, "I can do that."

At that moment, Lisa looks at me and says, "Let's go." Simultaneously we run around the outside of the accident scene to get to Lisa's car. Lisa is a godsend. Really. We run past the yellow tape, past the red emergency vehicles, past the white truck, past Baby Blue, and past the crowd of people. We throw ourselves into Lisa's van. She backs out of the parking stall, puts the car into drive, and we head to Harborview.

We are underway. The only thing I can think of is that my kids need help. Greg is on his way to Harborview and he will be there when they both arrive. I pick up my cellphone and call Cedar Park Christian School. This is where my kids have gone to school since Max started 5th grade and Anna started 3rd grade. I love this school. Max is now a senior, the cocaptain and point guard on the basketball team. He has lots of friends and is a good student. Anna is a sophomore. She was the only freshman last year to make the girls varsity basketball team and they are counting on her this year. She is a hard worker, a good student, and she loves basketball. And boys.

The phone is ringing. I have to listen to the prerecorded message before I can punch in the extension to the high school office. The receptionist picks up and I ask for Debbie Angell. I have known Debbie for years. Debbie and her husband Scott have two sons, both of whom played little league baseball with Max when Greg was coaching. Theirs is a wonderful family. Good people. Debbie is also the assistant to Garron Smith, our high school principal. I need to let Cedar Park know my kids have been in a horrible car accident and we need their help. We need prayer.

Debbie picks up. I blurt out, "Debbie, this is Lynn Brown. Anna and Max have been in a car accident. Max is on his way to Harborview in an ambulance and Anna is being airlifted to Harborview."

Debbie is so calm. She listens and then repeats everything I tell her. I want her to know what we need. I say "Debbie, what we need now is prayer."

She says, "Okay." I am so grateful to know I can go so many places to have people pray for my kids and Cedar Park is at the top of that list.

I need to talk to Greg. I call Greg and see how he is doing and to find out if he is at Harborview yet. Greg is a great dad and I know he is having a very tough time. I am glad that he was not at the accident scene and that he is near Harborview. This is the best possible scenario for parents, one at each end to help each other through this accident and be there for the kids.

Greg picks up his phone immediately. "Hi, where are they?"

I reassure him, "They are on their way. Will you do me a favor?" Without waiting for his response, I continue, "Please get a hold of Deb Fly. I don't have her number with me." Deb's husband, Guy, is a fraternity brother of Greg's. I know Greg has Guy's cell number in his phone.

"Okay," Greg says, "I will call Guy right now and ask him to call Deb."

"Thanks. We are on our way and I will see you soon."

When I first met Deb, she and Guy were already married and had two kids. That was more than twenty years ago. Deb has more medical experience than anyone I know. She was an emergency room nurse at Harborview for twenty-five years and is currently working for the American Heart Association at Harborview. Deb and I have traveled together, had weekend getaways together, dinners and celebrations together, and have been friends since the moment we met. We share the same birthday and I love her. She is knowledgeable and a voice of reason. God places people in our lives for many reasons. Today I know one of the reasons why Deb is my friend.

Next, I call my big sister Ann Bowen. Ann and her husband Gene have a son Dane and a daughter, Jordyn. There have been many phone calls from me to Ann about parenting and situations she's already lived through. Their daughter Jordyn is four years older than Anna and those two girls are like two peas in a pod. Ann always has great advice.

It's ringing. Ann answers and I quickly give her a brief outline of this morning's accident and where I am right now. She immediately asks "Do you want me to fly up to Seattle?"

"Not yet" I respond. Ann lives in Las Vegas where all three of us sisters were raised. I'm not sure what is going on with our kids and I won't ask Ann to leave home to come up here unless I need her. Ann recently retired after teaching junior high for thirty years. She loved her job and her students, but is thoroughly enjoying retirement and doesn't need to drop everything to come up here. Part of me holds the fear that if Ann has to fly up here, this situation is more serious than I can admit right now. I need facts. I want Ann to pray for my kids and hope that she will. I ask.

I then call my little sister, who we affectionately refer to as Teensie. She lives in Decatur, Alabama with her husband Fred Marschner. Teensie and her family have lived in Alabama for years. She has fireflies, rattlesnakes, tornados, and other southern specialties that I have only heard about. Teensie does not pick up. I decide not to leave a message about what is going on. This is way too alarming and I don't want to scare her, so I just hang up.

My friend Nancy Plenert is next. I am still under control, thank you

God. I have known Nancy since 1980. We started out as department managers at the Bon Marche (now Macy's). I had women's sportswear and Nancy had The Cube which was the junior department. We worked, lunched, and played together, got promoted together, became buyers and then sales reps together. Our lives paralleled each other. We saw boyfriends come and go and supported each other in a way only your girlfriends can do. Nancy introduced me to Greg. She is fabulous. Nancy is fun, smart, and energetic. I don't know anyone who does more in one day than Nancy, and always makes it sound effortless.

Nancy's phone is ringing. Quickly I hear, "This is Nancy."

"Nancy, the kids have been in a car accident and Max is in an ambulance on his way to Harborview and Anna is being airlifted to Harborview."

Nancy doesn't ask any questions. She immediately responds, "Do you want me to come to Harborview?"

"No, that's okay, I will keep you posted." But, I ask if she will pray for my kids. "Yes," she says. Nancy will pray.

Now, I must call Stacey McAllister so she can contact our prayer group, Faithful Hearts. God is so good. Stacey is my friend and neighbor. She and her husband Craig, moved into the neighborhood when their two boys were little. A few years later, they had their baby girl. We have been friends since they moved in and they are neighbors we can always count on. Stacey is one of the most reliable women I know and if she says she is going to do something, count on it getting done.

Stacey picks up and I tell her what has now become my message. Pray. Pray. Pray. Stacey says she will contact everyone immediately to get the prayers started. I know the Faithful Hearts will start praying almost before I hang up the phone.

Pam Allen. This is when I lose it. Pam and her husband Brian live across the street from us. We were building our house when Pam was pregnant with their first child, Alee. We were both pregnant with boys at the same time. Our first baby, their second. Brad Allen is Max's best friend. They have been best friends since birth. Brad and Max have a friendship that has surpassed all expectations. They have shared nannies, played every sport imaginable together, read Harry Potter repeatedly together and gone to school together since preschool. This is truly a unique friendship and right now I need Brad to be at the hospital with Max. Pam is at work and I dial her number from memory. Ringing.

Pam picks up. I can no longer control myself. I start screaming and crying into the phone. Pam says calmly "Lynn, I cannot understand you."

I try to steady myself enough to explain what has happened. When I finally get the story out I ask Pam if she can pick up Brad from Cedar Park and get him to Harborview. There is no hesitation. "Yes, I will leave right now and take him to Harborview." I know Pam. At this very second, she is tying up loose ends and preparing to leave work to go get Brad. Max will have his best friend in his greatest time of need. Thank you, God.

Okay, the ball is rolling. Lisa is carefully maneuvering us through rush hour traffic and trying to get me there as fast as humanly possible. I-5 is packed, we are at a crawl and I am about ready to go crazy. I am praying and talking and praying and talking. We are getting closer. Finally, we are in the vicinity, but there is lots of construction around Harborview. Lisa sees a place to stop and let me out of the car so I can run to the nearest entrance. It is the corner right across the street from the emergency vehicle entrance. I jump out of the car and run up to the large glass doors. They won't open, I can't get in. Then, I see an ambulance driver sitting in the front seat of his ambulance. I sprint up to him and bang on his window yelling "My kids were just brought in." Without saying a word, he leaps out of his cab and runs over to the glass doors. He does something I can't see and the wide glass doors part, allowing me into the emergency entrance. I will never forget what this stranger did for me.

It takes only a few seconds to find my family. Greg, at 6'2" is hovering over Anna's gurney in a draped-off section in the emergency rooms. Anna is intubated and restless. I look at my baby girl. Her arms are strapped down to the side of the bed and she has a hard-plastic piece of medical equipment down her throat. Her chin and neck are bound by a huge stabilizing neck brace that allows no head movement.

Dan Ursino, our emergency room nurse must see the look on my face and explains, "The tube allows her to breath freely and keeps her from throwing up and choking on her own vomit. They intubated her on the flight."

The hair near her right eye is matted with blood. I can't see blood anywhere else. Anna is trying to free her arms from the straps and is thrashing her legs around. She is very agitated. She is not mentally together. She has a head injury. We don't know yet what other injuries she has sustained nor do we know the extent of her head injury. God is with us. I know we are going to be okay. Greg and I stand by her side and talk to her. Her nurse, Dan, is a gift. He is telling us everything that he and the doctors are doing, and is very positive about Anna. Nurse Dan has a family of his own with young kids.

Greg looks up and says, "Max is just across the aisle in the last draped-off room." I run over to check him. Flinging the drape aside I see Max's long, athletic, body lying on a stiff board. They must have brought him into the hospital on the same stiff board he was put on at the accident scene. He is wearing a neck brace and lying very still. He looks completely unharmed. In my heart, I know he will be okay physically. I am so glad he is at Harborview. I am so thankful he is here with us.

"Are you okay?" I ask him.

"I'm fine," he says. This is a typical teenage boy response which tells me nothing. Then he quickly asks, "How's Anna?" followed by, "When can I get off this board and get rid of this neck brace?" It's good to hear his voice. He asks again, "How's Anna?" She is his biggest concern. This is difficult. Anna is just a few feet away from him and she is not okay.

"Max, how did you get out of Baby Blue?" I wonder.

He looks and me and relaxes his body ever so slightly. "I crawled out through the driver's window. Someone helped me when I got out," he said "Then I called you. But, that's all I remember." I can't even imagine what he must be feeling.

The doctor comes back in and reports her findings. "Max has a concussion and glass embedded in his right hand."

Max quietly says to me, "My eye hurts."

I turn to the doctor who has stepped a few feet away and mention this to her while the medical team readies themselves and Max to remove the embedded glass. I watch as they remove the glass and put two stitches in Max's right hand. Then with a little flashlight, the doctor looks into his eye, pulls back the eyelid and pours green liquid into the eye. A moment later she reexamines Max's eye with a magnifying glass. "Scraped cornea." she announces. There is no glass is his eye. Thank you God.

Max immediately says, "Go check Anna."

"Okay, Maxie," my back is to him when I finish my sentence, "I'll be back."

I dash over to Anna's curtained room. She is surrounded by Greg, Nurse Dan, and Deb Fly. Deb has arrived and is standing next to Anna's head at the top of the gurney. Thank God, she's here. I look down at Anna. She is still intubated. To see my baby girl with this apparatus covering her mouth and extending down into her throat scares me to death.

"Hi Deb," followed immediately with, "What if she throws up. Can she breathe?"

Deb and Nurse Dan simultaneously respond with, "She is and always was, breathing on her own. Even if she did throw up, it would not go into her lungs with this tube in place."

I simply can't wrap my mind around that. Greg stands across the bed from me. Both of us have absolutely no experience with anything like this. We know nothing.

Anna's heart rate is in constant fluctuation. I don't understand. It scares me. Hearts are important.

"Is there a problem?" I ask Nurse Dan.

"No," he says, "This is perfectly normal under these circumstances."

As I reach down to hold her hand, Anna becomes very agitated about the multiple rings she loves to wear on her fingers. Her fingers are swollen and the rings are really bothering her. With her arms strapped down, she keeps flailing her hands around. She can't talk. This is her communication.

Nurse Dan knowingly hands me a tube of lubricant and says, "Here, take the rings off."

I apply the lubricant gently to her fingers and slide the rings off. She is calmer. But she is not right. Anna is moving her chin around and trying to get the neck brace off and the tube out of her throat. She is tied down and cannot remove anything. We are waiting for a specific doctor to come remove the tube. Anna throws up. I am scared to death, a little panicked actually. Again, Deb and Nurse Dan reassure me as they suck out the vomit with a syringe, that this is not abnormal and she is fine.

Greg and I stand next to Anna and take turns running over to talk to Max. We are a strong team. No tears, no time for a breakdown. We are here to save our family. We are both gleaning as much information as we can from Nurse Dan and Deb, while waiting for doctors to appear.

Finally, the doctor comes in to take out the intubation tube. I cannot watch.

"I am going to check Max. He wants to know how Anna is," I tell Greg, "I'll be back in a minute." Greg nods. Greg is amazingly calm with everything. He is calm with Max and Anna as we dart from room to room to reassure our kids and each other. Greg is a good man.

I look at Max. "How is Anna?" is the first thing he asks me.

"They're taking the tube out of her throat right now." I see relief on his face.

"I'm really uncomfortable on this board with this neck brace on. I need to go to the bathroom," he says.

Max sounds more like himself. We know he is physically okay, but I am worried about him mentally. Since he's somewhat of a nonverbal guy who keeps everything in, I'm not sure what is going on in his mind. He is naturally very worried about his little sister.

"Go check on Anna," he barks at me. I nod my head and scramble back to the other draped room.

The tube is finally out of her throat. She is much more comfortable. But, Anna is still trying to get the neck brace off and is tucking her chin under the chin rest which holds her head still. We all tell her why it is on and not to move her chin under the rest. She listens and relaxes. Within minutes she is trying to move her chin under again, and we have to tell her to relax. She relaxes. She is not right.

Our pastor comes in. We don't know him well. He's new and is an interim pastor for our church while we search to replace our retired pastor. Pastor Craig Patterson is very warm and kind. He is also very calming and has come to say a prayer with us. I am glad to have Pastor Craig here. This is quite an introduction to the Brown family.

Family members start to arrive in the waiting room and want to come see Anna. We can only have a few people back at a time, so Pastor Craig leaves to attend to those in the waiting room. Gramma and Grandpa, Greg's parents, come in to see their granddaughter and talk to Greg and me. They don't really say anything to Anna because she is not responsive in a way we are all used to. Normally we cannot stop her from talking. Gramma and Grandpa only stay a few minutes with Anna and then walk across the hallway to see Max. As they leave Anna's room, Greg's youngest brother Doug, and his wife Becky enter the room.

Becky cries. Becky is one of the nicest people you will ever meet and is always looking on the bright side of life. We talk for a few minutes. Doug and Becky have twins, Andrew and Emily. They are great kids and love to hang out with their older cousins Max and Anna. I can see in Becky's eyes she is looking at Anna as though Anna was her own daughter and the anguish is unmistakable. They also stay only a few minutes and then go to visit Max. Greg's middle brother Rick is waiting to come in and enters as Anna's room clears out. Rick is a volunteer fireman on Vashon Island. He has assisted and witnessed a number of accidents and is very encouraging about Anna's condition. Greg and I are so glad the family has come to see the kids. As our relatives leave, Greg and I stand at Anna's bedside with Deb and Nurse Dan.

Nurse Dan is so encouraging. And Deb. Having Deb with us is a huge blessing. Deb has put her life on hold to rush over here to be with us, forgoing her weekly scheduled massage appointment as well as any other commitments in her life. Deb always puts others first. She insists I eat something and offers to go get a sandwich for me from the cafeteria. I cannot eat a thing. Ignoring my lack of interest, Deb leaves for the cafeteria to get a sandwich for me anyway. She's as stubborn as I am.

Greg and I stand by Anna's bed side and talk to Nurse Dan. A doctor comes in and announces he wants Anna readied for a CAT scan. We don't know what her internal injuries are and now that the tube is out of her throat, the doctor wants to look at her brain and her body. Within minutes, Anna is wheeled out of the emergency room leaving us standing and waiting for her return and the results of her CAT scans.

Chapter Two

"You can know that God's Angels were with them"
— Jayne Vitulli

"Lynn, people need to see you. You need to go out to the waiting room." Greg pleads as I stand waiting for Anna's return.

"Okay," I nod. He's right. This is the best time to go. Max is fine and I let him know I will be right back. Greg is staying with Max as I venture away from the emergency rooms.

Down the halls and winding around to get out of the private areas for the wounded of heart and body, I walk towards the waiting room. What I see when I arrive is overwhelming. I am momentarily overcome with emotion as I gasp in surprise. Wall to wall people have gathered to be with our family and help us though this. Max's friends, Anna's friends, our friends, and family. Well over fifty people in this waiting room. All faces full of tears and hope. I see Nancy with tears streaming down her face as we reach to each other and hug. Pam and Brian Allen are both there with Brad in tow to be with Max. Max's friend Andy Bangs and his dad are there. Mr. Bangs is crying. Lamont Franklin, Max's basketball coach is there along with teammates and good buddies Josh Orrico and Riley Bettinger. Anna's friends Candice Whipple, Amie Rippeteau, and Kayla White are there, standing next to Lisa's daughter Katy. Lisa is sitting in a chair with her husband Murray standing by her. Pastor Craig is there along with Heather Ulrich, our education coordinator, whom I have known and worked with for years. There are so many people I see and so many prayers being said. Hugs, hugs and more hugs. This is amazing. God is so good.

There is also a tall young man standing near me that I do not recognize. He is carrying a teddy bear in his arms. Pam introduces me to him and I discover that he is the man that helped Max at the accident scene. He is here at Harborview with a teddy bear for Anna. This is amazing. I hug him and thank him and ask Pam to please get his name. What a wonderful person to help my family and to bring hope to the hospital.

Pam and Brian are amazing neighbors. It is around lunchtime now and they have ordered tons of pizza for everyone in the waiting room. As kids and adults wait, they are being fed and loved by each other and our neighbors. Pastor Craig leads us in prayer. So much hope for Max and Anna in this room. This is not about being an athlete, a good student or a classmate. This is about loving your friends and it is the true meaning of living.

"Well" I tell them all, "Max is doing fine. He has a concussion, corneal abrasion, and some stitches in his right hand. But he is okay. Anna is having some tests. She has a head injury. That is all we know right now. I cannot tell you what it means to have you here. Thank you all for coming and for praying." It is so wonderful to see this amazing support for our kids. However, I feel an urgent need to get back to the emergency room.

"I have to go back now," I tell them. They all understand.

As I turn to leave, Pam gently reminds me "I brought Brad with me to be with Max."

"Oh, good," I respond. I almost forgot about my request.

I turn to Brad who stands waiting to escort me, "Okay, let's go."

I see Josh out of the corner of my eye and call out, "Josh, why don't you come too." The two boys and I leave the waiting room together. Hopefully, the staff will let them into Max's little cubby. As the three of us head down the winding hallway, we are quiet. We enter the private area and I scoot Brad and Josh into Max's curtained-off room. Brad walks towards Max, leans over the bed and hugs him. Josh also hugs Max. Max smiles. This is so good for him. The boys are talking quietly and know they can't stay long. I leave to go across to Anna's stall.

Anna enters on her gurney. The doctor is with her and has films and results for us. Deb arrives with a chicken salad sandwich that I cannot eat. One bite makes me feel nauseous and I put the sandwich back into its plastic container. "Sorry," I say to Deb. She understands. I feel bad she spent $6.00 on a sandwich no one will eat. I will have to reimburse her later.

The doctor puts film up on the lighted board across from Anna's gurney.

"Intraventricular hemorrhage. Her brain is bleeding." These are the first words out of his mouth.

Then he adds, "It appears to be a small bleed, but there will be more CAT scans over the next twenty-four hours to determine if the bleeding continues or stops." Deb and Nurse Dan look closely at the scan. Deb points to the bleeding area on the film so we can see what the doctor is referring to.

"Anna also has a C2 lateral mass fracture," he continues, "The fracture will be evaluated by the surgical team, but will probably heal itself." That is what I hear him say.

There's more. "She also has a spleen laceration, bilateral renal lacerations and a right pulmonary artery contusion." The biggest problem is the brain bleed. I understand him to say the other injuries will most likely heal themselves and not require any surgery. None the less, this is very frightening. The doctor leaves.

Thank God Deb is there. She explains all of this to us with Nurse Dan staying right next to Anna. Deb is navigating us through one of the toughest times of our lives and I couldn't be happier having her as our advocate. She is my friend and one of the most loyal people I can think of.

As all of this new information sinks in, I focus on the bleeding brain. The next CAT scan will be in a few hours and will tell us if the bleeding has stopped, is continuing or is getting worse. I know everyone is praying for Anna and Max. I know Anna is in good hands and I want so desperately to protect her and bring her back to herself. While it is hard to be here, I don't want to be anywhere else. I will help both kids through this and I know we are going to be okay. I am not sure what is ahead for our family, but I trust my gut feeling, as well as Nurse Dan and Deb. We will be okay and Anna will be fine. They continue to tell us she is doing well. Nurse Dan says she is going to be okay.

While we are standing next to Anna's bed and trying to take all of this in, a head pops around the corner of the drape.

"Are you Lynn Brown?" he asks quickly.

"Yes, I am Lynn Brown," I say.

"I'm a nurse in the hospital and I can't stay. I'm not supposed to be here because of the privacy laws, but my sister, Vicky, called and wanted me to check on you and your family," he explains.

Vicky is my hairdresser and a good gal. I met her at the gym and she lives just a few minutes from us. We often have the opportunity to talk about God, our kids and our husbands. She is such a wonderful friend and I so appreciate Vicky sending her brother to me. This is a time for reassurances and regardless of the privacy laws, I am honored that he and his sister are thinking about us.

"Tell Vicky thank you. We're doing okay. And, thank you for coming." We both smile as he quickly withdraws his head from the room and disappears around the corner. Wow, I think, friends everywhere. Thank you.

The doctor swings in and announces, "Anna is stabilized and we are ready to move her into the intensive care unit." Deb smiles. The reality is we will be with Nurse Dan a little longer, at least until ICU is ready to receive her. Nurse Dan has been great. Part of me wants to stay right here in the emergency room with Nurse Dan at Anna's bedside constantly. I know that's not the way it works, but it's a comforting thought.

Deb and I stand by her bedside waiting while Greg heads over to check on Max and make sure Josh and Brad have gone back to the waiting room.

"Max is ready to go," Greg announces upon his return to Anna's little room, "He has been thoroughly checked out, he's off the stiff board he was brought in on, and he has been cleared by the doctor to be released. His stitches are in his hand, his eye is okay, and he's ready to leave."

It's my turn. I walk over to Max's little stall and help him get his belongings organized. Max and I decide we are going to go to the waiting room and let our caring and worried friends see him and love on him. He needs it, we need it, and the people in the waiting room need it. It is good therapy for all. Greg can stay with Anna while I walk Max over to the waiting room. Good plan.

Max is quiet when we stop by Anna's stall. He sees her and talks to her for a minute. She is unable to respond and he knows she is not right. He just needs to see her. We don't stay long. It is very hard on Max. He feels responsible for Anna and regardless of how this accident happened, Max loves his sister and would never do anything to hurt her. Now, he may bug and tease her beyond belief as siblings two years apart do, but when no one is paying attention, they still creep into each other's rooms to lie around and discuss the state of their high school lives. They are competitive with each other for grades and sports, but relate in a way only a brother and sister can. He loves her and she loves him.

Because Anna's injuries are so much more severe than Max's, we have focused a lot of time on trying to help and figure out what is going on with Anna. Max has not had the same attention. Thank you, God, that they both did not need this attention. Max's driver side of the car was crushed and resting on a pole and I am not sure yet how he made it through this. I am just so thankful that he has minor physical injuries. But, I am worried about his emotional injuries and want to make sure he is alright. I will have to talk to Greg about this after Max leaves the hospital. But, for now, I want to take him to see his friends and let his healing begin.

We leave Anna and enter the winding hall on our way to the waiting room. Max is quiet and very hard to read. Max keeps his thoughts to himself most of the time. This is very hard for me. I talk a lot. Max would probably call it babbling, as most seventeen-year-old boys would, yet as his mom, I continue to try to break through and communicate. This day is different. I do not babble and just want him to be okay.

"We're almost there. You okay?" I ask.

"Yeah," he responds quietly.

Max walks into the waiting room with his head cast slightly downward. He does not like to have attention focused on him. Everyone smiles and stands up, so glad to see a survivor. Then the most fabulous thing happens. Max's friend Josh strides across the room until he is standing face to face with Max. Josh carefully places his hands on Max's head, just above his ears, and tilts Max's head forward. He kisses Max on the forehead. That says it all. Max lifts his head and smiles. It is so beautiful to see this wonderful friend, fellow athlete, and God loving young man lift Max up so he can relax in this huge crowd of friends and family. This relief also gives the long-waiting crowd permission to leave the hospital and head home to their loved ones. They have been here for hours and Harborview was not sure what to do with so many guests in the waiting room. It was unusual. At one point, security asked if some of them could leave to make room for the families of other patients. No one left, they just moved around.

Max talks for a little bit to everyone in the room. This has been a stress filled day and Max is tired. He wants to go back to collect his things, see Anna and then go home. I will not be going home and Greg will be here far into the night.

I am searching the crowd for Pam. Ah, there she is and I head toward her. "Of course," says Pam, reading my mind. Pam is going to take Max home and keep him at her house until Greg comes to get him later tonight. The Allens are the best. Max will be with Brad and I know they will take good care of him. He did have a concussion, so we talk about watching him and checking to make sure he stays awake. Pam assures me she will watch over him with the best of care. I know she will because I know Pam.

Greg and I feel comforted that Max has left the hospital and is in the Allens' care. We are, however, concerned about the state of Max's mental health.

"I'm calling Steve Call," Greg says calmly.

That's a great idea, I think and respond with a loud, "Yes!"

Steve is not only a friend, but he has been Max's AAU basketball coach for years. Steve is a clinical psychologist and counselor, who has known and coached Max since he was a little boy in grade school. Steve's son Jordan has played basketball with Max ever since they could dribble. Steve took Max and their basketball team Eastside Magic to Nationals in Tennessee when Max was going into the ninth grade. Steve is an outstanding individual and Max has always had a great deal of respect for him.

"This is perfect," I say excitedly. Greg calls Steve.

Steve already knew about the accident and said he would drive over to the Allens' house this evening to talk with Max. More help. Thank you.

At the Allens', Pam gets Max and Brad fed and comfortably settled into Brad's room. Then a stream of teammates and school friends arrive to see Max. Some call and some just show up. Bill Bettinger, Riley's dad and Cedar Park's athletic director stops by. Bill treats Max like his own son. Bill loves to watch Max play basketball and he just simply loves Max. He is a wonderful, caring man and I know Max is glad to see him. Also arriving is Max's basketball coach, Lamont Franklin. Lamont is a great coach for Max and was a point guard himself. Cedar Park is fortunate to have him. All of this is good for Max and we are, again, so thankful for all of the people helping us and loving our kids. This kind of support speaks to the goodness of our friends and neighbors and their willingness to reach out and inconvenience themselves to help others.

Steve Call arrives and takes Max aside to spend a little time talking with him. Steve knows Greg and I are worried about how Max is feeling inside and are waiting to hear the results of his conversation with Max.

"Max is fine," reports Steve, "Max is very worried about Anna, but he has a healthy outlook and is okay."

What a relief. This is such good news because when you have a child that does not communicate his feelings, you never know what they are thinking or going through. At times, I have felt that the only way to get anything out of Max would be if I reached my hand in and pulled out the words!

Around 8:30 pm, two more friends call and want to see Max. Pam knows Max is getting tired but she wants to let these kids see Max so everyone can feel better. Pam says yes, knowing she will be kicking everyone out shortly. Brad, however, does not like so many people bothering Max. Brad thinks it is getting to be too much and Max needs to be left alone. Max tells Brad that it's okay and that he is fine. I love the fact that Brad is with Max. He is so protective of Max and such a great friend. Those two are great kids and will have a friendship that will see them through many chapters in their lives.

Finally, everyone is gone and Max has the opportunity to rest. He is so tired. He doesn't complain. I am sure he is thinking about Anna lying in her hospital bed. As he is finally in a comfortable place he is very familiar with, Anna is being prepared to be moved to the intensive care unit.

Chapter Three

"Our second miracle Anna, is in ICU"
— Greg Brown

We are learning the most interesting things. The sort of information that is good to know, yet better when it has been experienced by someone else. Like secondhand knowledge. However, I would not want any parent to have to experience this. So, I guess it is best that Greg and I go through this trial because we have a strong faith and lots of faithful friends. I really don't know where we would be right now if it were not for our faith. Prayers are a very important part of our life and today, prayer is walking us through this life crisis.

Anna is being wheeled up to the intensive care unit and the doctors want to do another CAT scan before she is settled in. Then they want her to have a third CAT scan at 4:00 am. That will give us the opportunity to see if the brain has stopped bleeding, which is what we are all praying for. No one has talked to us about what we will do if the brain continues to bleed. You know, I think that's good because we need to keep the facts in the present and the doctors here at Harborview know what to do if we have continuous bleeding.

As we roll Anna into the intensive care unit, the look and feel of the room is very much like the emergency room. The rooms are separated by curtains, though there appears to be more space between patients. When we reach our final destination, the gurney stops and Anna is lifted onto a hospital bed and secured. Anna is fitful and restless and still not mentally engaged or fully aware of what is going on around her. Oh, it is so hard to see her like this. So far, all the doctors, Nurse Dan and Deb have told us only positive outcomes for her. But, it is her brain and it is bleeding. Yet, a sense of peace continues to envelop me. Thank you.

We meet our nurse who will be with Anna all night. She will also be with me all night because I will be sleeping in the small cot next to Anna's bed. I set my purse down and watch Anna. I immediately get a sense of this nurse. She is young, bossy, and a touch abrasive. Maybe she's irritated I'm staying. Too bad. But, I do remind myself, she wouldn't be at this great hospital if she wasn't a good nurse.

Greg and I are silent. Just sitting and watching. Waiting.

Our nurse seems surprised, as am I, when the head nurse pops in. She introduces herself to Greg and I while leaning over Anna and tucking her blankets in real tight. I love that she is caring for my baby girl. She is very upbeat and makes us feel better about where we are and what will happen to Anna. We are so thankful she came in and, at the same time, a little perplexed to see her. She did not go to any other patients, but what do we know? She's probably just checking on the new arrival.

Another head pops into our curtained off room. She draws back the curtain and reveals herself in full scrubs, hat and all.

"Hi, I am Zach's mom," she says. I am completely dumbfounded. I have absolutely no idea who this woman is.

"Zach from school," she adds. Still, this is not registering with me. I am drawing a complete blank.

Greg turns to me and says, "Lynn, your preschool."

Finally, the light goes on and I know who she is. She is the mom of one of my preschool kids. Zach came into our program a few weeks late and I haven't taught him that long. Both his parents are anesthesiologists and apparently, his mom works at Harborview. I have no idea how she knows about Anna, but I think it is so wonderful of her to take the time to track us down and come see how we are doing. She only stays for a moment and then rushes off to continue her evening.

"That was really nice of her to come by," I whisper to Greg.

"Yeah, it was," Greg says. We both look at Anna and are truly thankful so many people care.

We take a look at our watches and realize it is about 10:00 pm. It's late.

"I need to get home and get Max," Greg says.

"Yeah, you do," I agree. Greg does need to go. He's got to pick up Max from the Allens and get the two of them comfortable at our house. He will also have to take care of our three kitties and get Sampson from Scott and Kim Blackburn. The Blackburns are dog people and had gone over in the middle of the day and taken Sammy out of the kennel and kept him at their house with their two boys and two dogs. We have such great neighbors. There's no doubt Sammy is in good hands and having a blast with the boys. I am also confident he is asleep on one of the boys' beds, possibly snoring.

"I'll be back early in the morning," he quietly says before he bends over and kisses Anna, "Goodnight Schmoo."

I settle onto my little cot, watching Anna breathe. I'm thankful. This is the best situation we could have right now. Greg will be home with Max and I will be right next to Anna. I find myself being in the moment. It's quiet. This is reality. I'm dealing with it. We're all okay.

The curtain quietly slides back and the nurse says, "You have visitors." She sees the confusion on my face. Not only is it late, but Anna can't have visitors in intensive care. "They are outside in the hall," she smiles.

"Okay," I nod and get up to venture out to the hallway.

When I emerge from the doors of the intensive care unit, I see the scared and worried faces of Anna's soccer coach Mark Gauger, his daughter Kelsi, my friend Kathy Bartoli, her daughter Talia and Loni Rotter with her daughter Stephanie. All people we have known for years. These girls all play on the same soccer team, the Jaguars, and Mark has been their coach since they were in grade school. The girls have known each other forever. Anna and Talia actually went to preschool together. Even though they do not go to the same school now, they hang out together and love each other. We all try not to cry. I hug each of them.

Then I see Wendy Legat and her daughter Lindsay. They are from Cedar Park. They love Anna, too. Lindsay was Anna's first friend when Anna transferred to Cedar Park in the third grade.

How truly great it is that these wonderful friends have come to support Anna and our family.

"We had to come," I hear, "We could not sit at home. We needed to be here."

Wow! They had to come. These are good people.

As difficult as it is, I give them an update of Anna's condition and let them know she is still not herself. I'm not sure who this is harder on, the parents who understand what this must be like or the kids who are scared to death for Anna.

Then, out of nowhere dashes Mrs. Schmoll. She was Anna's 4th grade teacher at Cedar Park. I am so surprised to see her here this late. When Anna had Mrs. Schmoll as a teacher, I was the room mom. Actually, I am always the room mom for both kids and I love that job! Anyway, at the beginning of the school year, Mrs. Schmoll was having a hard time with Anna. She thought Anna was being disrespectful and she didn't understand some of Anna's behavior. When this came to light, Mrs. Schmoll and I had a conversation about Anna.

I remember saying, "Anna is not a wallflower, never will be a wallflower and I don't want her to be a wallflower. Anna speaks her mind and is very black and white about herself and her thoughts. She is outgoing and does not possess a submissive bone in her body. She is a unique girl and has a hearty spirit." What I didn't tell Mrs. Schmoll is that I know this is the truth because the apple doesn't fall far from the tree. Sometimes these characteristics are a good thing. Sometimes not so much. But, it is reality.

Mrs. Schmoll was very understanding. From that point on, she and Anna enjoyed a fun relationship. It was a wonderful year for both Anna and me.

Mrs. Schmoll hands me a present and says, "This is for Anna."

Then she says something to me I will never forget, "Of any student I have ever had, Anna radiated life. She sparkled." This comment means so much to me, that in that moment, I realize the life Anna leads affects so many people. Here is Mrs. Schmoll who hasn't been a teacher at Cedar Park for years, is now selling real estate, heard about the accident this morning and is here at Harborview at 10:00 p.m. to honor Anna. Wow. As quickly as she dashed towards me, Mrs. Schmoll turns and leaves. I think she does not want to interfere, but wants to show her love for Anna. That is really special. I am so thankful.

Before the rest of the group leaves, Coach Mark tells me to give Anna a message. He says, "Tell Bags to get better." Bags is a nickname that had been given to Anna when she had gone on vacation with Coach Mark, Kelsi and their family. One of the girls had decided since Anna's last name is Brown, she must be in some fun, teenage humor kind of way, related to the local Brown Bag Café. Thus, Anna should be called Bags as a tribute to the commonality of the names. Only teenage girls on a vacation could come up with this and have it stick.

Kathy Bartoli also has a message which happens to be from her husband Corby. Corby is a teddy bear of a guy and a huge football fan. Corby wants to make sure to tell Anna he "wants Urlacher back on the field." Anna is unforgiving on the soccer field and Corby is comparing her to Brian Urlacher, a middle linebacker in the NFL.

These comments remind me who Anna is and the inner strength she possesses. She doesn't give up. She's a fighter. I pray she's fighting her best fight right now.

We all give our last hugs and goodbyes as the hallway begins to clear out and each family makes their way out of the hospital and back to their homes. What an uplifting night.

Turning to go back to Anna, I see Candice and Debbie Whipple standing quietly and alone. Candice had been in the waiting room at the hospital earlier this morning. I am surprised to see her here again, but her heart is broken and she needs to see her friend that she loves. Candice is one of Anna's best and funniest friends. Her sense of humor and laughter is what has bonded these two like glue. Debbie, Candice's mom, has driven her down here at night for Candice to be near Anna. I hug both of these fine people.

"I'm not supposed to take anyone into Intensive Care," I tell Candice. I know she came here to see Anna. She needs to see Anna. The look on her face says it all.

"Okay, come on," I whisper, hoping we don't get caught. Then I do something unusual. I break a rule. I sneak them in to see Anna. This is truly unauthorized.

Before we reach her bedside, I warn Candice and Debbie about her.

"She's heavily drugged and will not recognize or acknowledge you. She's not herself," I confirm. They nod. Candice just wants to see her. She softly walks into Anna's room and slowly snuggles up to the side of Anna's bed. There is no response from Anna, but Candice whispers to her. I don't know if Anna hears her, but I do know Anna loves Candice and that they are inseparable at school. Candice tries to holds back the tears as they quietly fall from her eyes. She is so sad. But, I know she will pray hard for Anna. Candice and Debbie are strong Christians and good-hearted people. They pray.

Minutes later, I walk them back out to the hallway and thank them so much for coming. Sneaking Candice in was a good idea and I am glad I did it. They are safe people. I retreat back to Anna's room and get comfortable on my cot.

Our nurse walks into the room. Thank goodness she wasn't here a few minutes ago. I doubt she would have let Candice and Debbie come in.

"I am going to tell the doctor I don't think Anna needs to have her 4:00 am CAT scan," she announces.

This young gal is getting on my last nerve. I love and respect nurses. However, in this case, I think it is best to let the neurologist make the decisions. I also think it is vitally important to find out if Anna's brain is still bleeding. Fortunately, I soon discover, the doctor does not listen to her advice and the CAT scan is still set for 4:00 am. Thank you.

"The doctors come between 5:00 am and 6:00 am. If you want to talk to them, this is when you should do it. You will hear them coming," she says as a matter of fact.

Well, that's good information to have. I do know that Harborview is a teaching hospital and when rounds are made, doctors are accompanied by a group of residents and medical personnel. Since there are quite a few of them, it only makes sense that you can hear the loud slapping of shoes around the hospital.

Before I put my head down, I look up at my baby girl with her head resting on her pillow. I just want to smother her with kisses and hold her. Like when she was a baby. Hold her tight and make sure she's okay. I begin to pray. I pray a prayer of thanks. Then I pray for help. This is when something changes. And this is when my extraordinary conversation with God begins.

I love God. I thank my grandmother Mamaw for planting that seed. Even though we lived hundreds of miles from her and saw her infrequently, she left an imprint on me. God was important to her. God and Bibles were part of her daily life. She wrote in her Bibles and recorded family history in the front pages of her favorite Bible. As we speak, Mamaw's Bibles sit in a corner case at the end of our upstairs hallway, guarding the kids' bedrooms.

My first remembrance of going to a church was when I was a small child. I was walking outside the church on an uneven sidewalk with my mom and her mom, Mamaw, when I tripped and skinned my knee. Although Mamaw was a regular church member, our family did not attend any church on a regular basis, or on any basis. We went to church rarely. Yet, throughout my life I have turned to God. I used to specifically talk to God and thought, since he was the head guy and Jesus was second in command, I needed to go straight to the man in charge. It wasn't until Greg and I had kids that we started attending church regularly and I discovered who Jesus is. God, Jesus, and the Holy Spirit have been with me now for years. And I know they are with me tonight.

I believe in the promises of God. I believe in miracles. I feel God with me at this very moment. I talk to God and God talks back. Do I hear a booming voice coming from above? No. Do I see a bright light with voices speaking to me? No. What I do have, that no one can ever take away from me, is a dialogue with God that continues throughout the night. I am not asleep. I am not dreaming. I am awake. We are in constant communication. I ask a question; I get an answer. I say a prayer; I get an answer. The answer comes before I have completed my thought. I know that not only was God with my kids this morning, He has been with us all day and is now comfortably resting with Anna and me in Anna's room. I feel Him here; I see His work and I thank him for being and staying with us. I ask him to help Anna. I know He will, just as I knew at the scene of the accident that He had sent angels to wrap themselves around Max and Anna to protect them from the cold grip of death. He saved my family today. I am not really sure what all happened this morning and right now it doesn't matter. What does matter and what I do know is that we have been shown a lot of grace and love from our maker. He was there. My conversation with God is something I know I will always have and it is one more reason to be thankful.

Throughout the night, Anna jars herself awake and her body twitches. Every time she moves or moans, I jump up off the cot and look at her. It feels like it did when we first brought her home from the hospital and she slept next to me in the bassinet my mom had bought for us. I remember peering over the bed constantly to see if she was breathing. Well, this is so similar. She is moving and moaning constantly and I have to look at her. Moms don't really sleep during a crisis. They lie waiting, available at a second's notice.

Around 4:00 am the medical people come in and work with the nurse to get Anna ready to go to her CAT scan. They wheel her out and I wait. Because I know she is with doctors, nurses, and attendants, I can rest for a few minutes.

It is so quiet in the intensive care unit. I have lots to think about and lots of time to think. My mom comes to mind. Mom died nine days after Anna was born. The morning of Anna's birth, Mom sat up in her rented hospital bed and did a crossword puzzle. She wanted an update every hour. I think it was because she had been here when Max was born. He was an emergency C-section after hours of labor. Mom said she knew something was wrong and she was very worried. Her worry may have had something to do with my own birth. I had been an emergency C-section at a time when babies didn't always make it. But, for the last month of my pregnancy with Anna, Mom was on hospice care at home and had pretty much been out of it until the day she knew I was going to be induced. We were inducing because my doctor said Anna was 'fully cooked' and the doctor knew we were racing against time to try to make sure Anna met Mom before she died. As soon as Anna was born and Mom knew everything was okay, she slipped back into her comatose state. When Anna was five days old, with doctors' approvals, we flew to Las Vegas so Mom could see Anna. Again, the day she knew we were coming, she sat up in bed and waited. Mom was able to hold Anna. Mom looked at me and said, "She's beautiful." Mom died four days later. I still miss her. I know she's in this hospital somewhere right now.

Then I think about my dad. Dad has Alzheimer's. But, he's doing great and has a terrific companion, Dottie. Dottie keeps him busy and they have had some wonderful years together. Dad gave Max and Anna the Ford Explorer, Baby Blue. That gift saved my kids' lives. Had they been in a smaller car, well, I don't even want to think about it. I can't tell Dad what's going on right now, even though Ann told Dottie. It would upset him and throw him off balance. I am going to wait. When I do tell him, I think I will tell him how his gift saved Anna and Max from sure death. Dad will remember that and he will like that he was able to help. My dad is a good-hearted person and preached safety to us our whole lives. If it weren't for the Alzheimer's, I know Dad would be here.

I hear the wheels of the gurney. Here she comes. Our nurse is with her and they put Anna back in her bed, adjust her pillows and get her comfortable. Anna is still not mentally engaged.

I look at my beautiful little girl and want to gather her up and will her to respond to me. But, she is easily agitated and I don't want to overstimulate her. So, I just give her a kiss when I can and watch her slide in and out of sleep.

"So," I ask our nurse, "what are the results." The CAT scan results had been instantly available when Anna had her first two scans. I am anticipating immediate feedback.

"I don't know," she says, "you will have to wait until the doctors come in and ask them. The results will come up on the computer at some point, but the doctors will tell you."

I may slug this gal. I don't believe her. I think she knows something about Anna's newest results. Of course, my mind is racing and I begin to wonder if the bleeding has become a problem and is not stopped. I pray and wait.

Well, the nurse was right about one thing. Around 5:35 am the thunderous sound of shuffling shoes is headed into intensive care. I hear them coming. A group of five or six doctors and medical students are here. I think. This is a small space, it's dark and I can't see them all, so I'm not sure exactly how many there are. They are looking at charts and talking to each other. I am invisible to them.

Finally, I break in and ask, "What about the CAT scan?"

The doctor looks at me and says, "The bleeding has stopped and she will need therapy."

Then they all turn around and leave. Thank you. The bleeding has stopped. But, what does "she needs therapy" mean, I ask myself? Oh, for Heaven's sake. Couldn't they have taken thirty seconds to explain? We're new at this. Harborview has its reputation because it's the best trauma center around. However, I could use a little warm and fuzzy at this point. I start to get very upset about the doctor's comment. This is nuts. It is 5:45 am I call Deb.

Deb picks up right away and I say, "The doctor said she will need therapy. What does that mean?"

Deb explains, "What he means is she will need physical therapy and perhaps other therapies to regain her abilities. This is normal with a head injury."

I am so thankful that Deb is my friend and that I actually have someone with her knowledge to call. I feel better because I feel informed.

"I'm so sorry I called so early Deb," I blurt out, "but I had no idea what the doctor was talking about and it scared me."

"It's okay. I'm glad to hear from you," she says, "I'll be in a little later."

After I hang up my phone, I realize this situation has become a little too big for me to handle alone.

I call my sister Ann. "Ann, I think you better come up. The situation has just changed. Anna and I won't be home for a while and I need help."

"I will catch the next flight to Seattle," Ann says, "I'll be up there in a few hours."

A few minutes later Ann calls back. Teensie our little sister, is also on her way.

Sisters are great, especially mine.

Our first night at Harborview is almost over. I lie on my cot watching Anna, waiting for the hours to pass. She's still not responsive and not aware what is going on around her. She was fitful all night and seems to be fighting to come back. Her legs would kick out and she would thrash around before settling back down. I would jump up off my cot and say something to her, kiss her, or just look at her to make sure she was okay. It's been a long night. But a good night. Everyone's alive. Thank you.

I see sunlight and want to call Greg. I need to talk to him about the CAT scan, Ann and Teensie coming up, and find out how Max is doing. I wait as long as I can, then call.

"Hi," he says, "How is Anna?"

"She had a fitful night," I tell him, "and according to her doctors she's going to need therapy. I already talked to Deb this morning and she'll be in a little later. How's Max? Oh, and Ann and Teensie are flying in today."

"Oh, okay," he says, "Pam is taking the day off to be with Max, so I will be there once I get him settled. He's okay. I'll tell you more when I get there."

"Okay, see you in a little while. Bye." These are my final comments before we disconnect.

Pam is taking the day off. I am so thankful and can rest knowing Max will be very well taken care of, while Greg and I spend the day with Anna and try to piece her and our lives back together again. Thank you.

It's still very early when our nurse tells me the doctors have decided Anna will be moving out of intensive care today. Anna and I will be moving to the burn floor which, apparently, is the floor that usually takes in the younger patients at Harborview. She is still not responsive or aware of what is going on around her. I am emotionally exhausted. I'm sure all of us are.

When Greg arrives, I fill him in on all the details he's missed and ask him about his evening with Max.

He says, "Max is doing okay and he is very concerned about Anna. He told me that right after the car settled on the light pole, he held Anna's hand. He talked to her and got no response. He thought she was dead. Then he crawled out of the Explorer to go get help. When the firemen and medical people arrived, he kept screaming at them wanting to know if she was breathing. They kept telling him to get away from Baby Blue, but he continued to scream wanting to know if she was breathing. Finally, one of the fireman said, 'Yes, she is breathing.' At that point, Max made his way to the curb and sat down."

"That's a lot of hard information for Max to give you," I respond sadly, "I can't imagine the pain Max must have felt, crawling out of the car and leaving his little sister."

"Yes, it was horrible for him. He had a hard time getting it out," Greg says, "We both slept in our bed last night and said a prayer together before falling asleep."

It sounds like they had a calm rest. For a seventeen-year-old boy to need his dad to be near him while sleeping, certainly suggests signs of pain and anguish. Max needs his dad. Max loves Greg and they have always had a great father-son relationship centered around their love of sports, particularly basketball. Even though Greg was on the golf team in high school and did not play competitive basketball, Greg has always been supportive of Max and loves to be around Max and his friends. He coaches Max on and off the basketball court and Max listens. Even when we think he is not listening, he is.

I call Lisa to bring her up to date. I tell her Anna is going to be moved out of intensive care today and that my sister Ann is flying up this afternoon and Teensie will arrive this evening. Lisa immediately volunteers to pick Ann up at the airport. That's a good friend. It takes the stress off me to find a ride for Ann. Ann will be coming in around noon and Lisa said she would bring Ann straight to the hospital from the airport. Thank you.

Teensie is coming in around 7:00 pm. Perfect. Ann and Teensie will take care of everything and now I don't have to worry about what is going on at home. Teensie is flying in from Alabama and I am not sure who will pick her up. We have had so many people ask how they can help, yet I am not sure how to ask someone for an airport run. Maybe Greg should go get her and bring her to the hospital and then he can take Ann and Teensie home when he goes home for the night. Yeah, that might work.

Greg's cellphone rings and it's a fraternity brother of his, Jeff Hale. Jeff is now a personal pilot, and used to work for Airlift Northwest. They are the ones who airlifted Anna to Harborview. Jeff knows them all and is well acquainted with critical care nursing in flight and has flown all over the Northwest rescuing people in life and death situations. Jeff asks Greg how he can help. Greg tells Jeff about my little sister, Teensie, flying in from Alabama tonight and we could really use an airport run. Jeff works right near the airport and said he would be glad to pick her up and take her to the hospital. Now, I have to say, Jeff is one of Greg's most hilarious fraternity brothers and I have always thought the world of Jeff. He is a guy with no fear, a very quick wit, and always keeps everyone in touch. Jeff and I have always had fun together and he also happens to have a fabulous wife, Mary whom I love. How she puts up with him I will never know!

Greg hands me the phone because I need to let Jeff know my sister's cell number and how he will be able to identify her. I give Jeff the number and say, "Just pick her up outside baggage claim and hold up a sign that says 'Teensie.' There is silence on the other end of the line. Then Jeff says, "I will not go to the airport and hold up a sign that says 'Teenise.' He says, "I will, however, go to the airport and hold up a sign that says 'Huge.'" I thought I was going to fall off my cot laughing. Boy, do we need that bit of comic relief. In the midst of all this, Hale gets me in hysterical laughter. I will never, never forget this conversation and when I tell Greg, we can hardly contain ourselves. This is not exactly the place to be keeling over with laughter. Wait until I tell Teensie. She will love this story. Teensie has a great sense of humor.

As the night nurse finishes her shift and leaves, our day nurse comes in. What a relief. Our day nurse is attentive and kind. She checks Anna and starts talking to her as though Anna is just fine. She gives Anna verbal commands and Anna opens her eyes and, without speaking, is physically responsive. Oh, this is so great. Anna understands and is responsive. The nurse says this is good and normal for a head injury. Then our nurse asks Anna what her name is. We stand there and wait, watching Anna process this information and watching the wheels turning in her brain to try to respond. For the first time, Anna ever so lightly, says, "Aaaaannnaaaa." Her speech is very, very slow and deliberate, but this is music to my ears. Thank you.

The doctors want Anna to spend the day in intensive care. They want her to be able to wake up more often and maybe talk. They will have her moved this afternoon or this evening. No visitors today. So, we just sit quietly and watch her for hours.

Well, maybe no visitors. We hear a little shuffle and in walks Lisa with Ann in tow. Thank goodness. Ann is here. I get up and give Ann a hug. Ann looks over and sees Anna and sits down with us. No one says a word. We are trying to be as still as possible and not disturb Anna. Lisa stays for a little while and then has to go. She has put her own family on the back burner and needs to get home and take care of them. I thank Lisa for picking up Ann, bringing her to the hospital, and for just generally being a great friend. She is so funny. She smiles and whispers, "I'll be back tomorrow and I'll drive Ann and Teensie to and from the hospital whenever they need a ride." Lisa will drop everything to help us. She is a better person than I am and I know that.

Anna is sleeping right now. She wakes up about every thirty minutes and looks around a little bit. At 2:30 pm she wakes up and is able to drink a little water through a straw. Our nurse says this is a great sign. Anna has been on a little bit of medication, not much, because the doctors need to assess what is going on. When she wakes up, she is in pain so she is given some pain medication. This really puts her back to sleep. Her little fifteen-year-old body has never seen these kinds of drugs before. At least we know she is coming back. We are watching her breathe, wake up, and go back to sleep. Greg, Ann, and I are just sitting with her, waiting.

It's about 7:00 pm. The doctors have decided Anna can be moved out of intensive care. I don't want to move her. We are getting such great help here and the mom in me says, "Can't we just recover here?" Apparently, that is a no.

Okay, here they are--the movers. Anna is carefully loaded up on a gurney and off we go. Waiting outside the intensive care unit is Taylor Mishalanie and his mom Rhonda. We have known the Mishalanie family since Taylor was little and played T-ball with Max on Greg's T-Ball team. Taylor is from our neighborhood, a friend of Max's, as well as Anna's date last weekend to Homecoming. Great kid. Great family. They walk with us as we begin our room change.

The medical staff is so gentle with Anna and they have no idea how much I appreciate their tender touch. We arrive at the burn unit and enter our room. There are two beds in each room, one on the window side and the other closer to the door. Anna gets the bed closest to the door. Darn it. I wanted to be tucked back in a cozy corner so we had less traffic and more time to be calm and quiet. I also want Anna to have more privacy. Once again, a curtain separates the two beds. When we enter our new room, we see that Anna has a roommate. She looks to be about Anna's age and I think the man sitting with her must be her dad. Not sure. All of a sudden, this girl starts swearing and screaming at this man who I think is her dad and the language and tone is way out of control. Oh, my gosh, how is this going to work? Anna cannot speak and is struggling to regain her speech and awareness. I cannot let Anna hear angry and inappropriate words. This girl is out of control and my instincts perk up to tell me this is not a good situation for Anna. Understandably so, Rhonda and Taylor decide to leave. They do not want to interfere and just came by to be with Anna. I quickly say goodbye and I dart to the nurses' desk. They are so kind. I tell the nurse at the desk that Anna is Christian. She is also trying to regain her speech and mind and she can't be subjected to that language or the volatility that is in that room. The nurse tells me they put Anna in there because the girls are so close in age. Apparently, that is the only thing they have in common. Anna is reassigned immediately. We move one room over, into a room with a window side, with a very kind older woman as a roommate. She is a very large black woman and gives us a big smile and hello as we enter the room. She wants to know what is wrong with Anna. She is so sweet to us. We talk for a moment and then she gives us privacy. We are grateful to have her as Anna's roommate. Thank you.

Anna has been wearing a very rigid neck brace since the accident. Even though she can't tell us, we can see it's very uncomfortable for her and she can't relax. I can only imagine what it feels like; unable to move or speak normally. She's trapped, in a sense. When our nurse tells us that the doctor has approved a new neck brace we are relieved. Anna can have the rigid collar exchanged for a soft collar. This is great news and as soon as the switch is made, we see Anna is more comfortable. She is beginning to stay awake a bit longer each time she does wake up. My baby girl is beginning to recover.

Around 8:00 pm, Aunt Teensie walks into our hospital room. It is so good to see Teensie. I don't see Teensie very much and since there is a two-hour difference in our time zones, even talking to her on the phone can be a challenge. I am so glad she is here and give her a hug. Teensie will be a huge help. Jeff Hale dropped her off to be with us and I have got to remember to call and thank him for all of his help.

By this time, it is getting late and our nurse thinks it's time to let Anna go to sleep. She gives her some medication to manage the pain and shortly thereafter, out she goes. Hopefully tonight will be a better night of sleep for both Anna and me. I must say though, I don't feel tired. I think when something happens that threatens the lives of those you love, you get this amazing energy and strength to carry on.

Greg is ready to go home. He is taking Ann, Teensie, and their luggage back to the house so they can take care of Max and all of our animals. It's been a long day for Ann and Teensie. They must be tired.

"Alright, I'll see all of you tomorrow," I say thankfully and watch them roll their luggage out of the room. I can hear the wheels rolling down the hall towards the elevator. Finally, silence. They're on their way home while I prepare myself for my second night at Harborview.

I put my hair in a ponytail on top of my head and get the old sleeper chair pulled out and ready for my night's sleep. Thank goodness my cotton cream turtleneck and cotton jeans are comfortable. Some clothes are itchy to me and I would go nuts if that were the case here. Greg is going to bring me a bag of my sundries and clothes tomorrow. I haven't even brushed my teeth or looked in the mirror. Don't care.

My made-up bed is right next to Anna and not only can I see her sleeping, I can hear her breathing. Her hospital bed is a little lower than the one in intensive care and I like that. It gives me a better view of her. My sleeper chair is also next to the window. It is a little cold and bright with the outside lights of the hospital shining in, so I close the blinds to help keep the cold air at bay and to keep the light out. We did get a great view though. I can see the lights of Seattle and during the day, I see Mount

Rainier off in the distance. I will see the sun rise. I love morning light and I think it will be good for Anna to have sunshine in the room. All in all, it is a beautiful view. A beautiful view on both sides of my sleeper chair. However, these are old windows and not the best insulation from the cold, so I just pile on the blankets. In a few short hours, the doctors will be coming through with their thunderous clapping of feet hitting the ground, and I must be ready. I will not let them leave again if I am upset or have unanswered questions.

Chapter Four

"You're in a good place: God's hands"
— The Angells

"Good morning," whispers the nurse at about 5:00 am on Thursday.

"Good morning," I reply. The nurses have just changed shifts and she is here to check on Anna's IV and make sure the needle is still placed correctly in her arm. I need to get out of my sleeper chair and move to the other side of the bed, because Anna's left arm is the one with the IV and I'm in the nurse's way. I gladly walk across to the other side of the bed. It is still dark outside and the nurse has turned on a soft light above Anna's bed, so she can see Anna's arm. I stand over Anna and watch both her and the nurse. She very softly turns Anna's arm, elbow side down, and fiddles with the IV needle. Anna wrestles around and then Anna very slowly and quietly murmurs, "Ouuuuuuch. Ouuuuuuch." The nurse asks her, very kindly, "What hurts?" Anna replies slowly, "Myyyyyy Arrrm-mm." The nurse asks Anna, "Does your head hurt?" Again, very slowly and drawn out, Anna answers, "Myyyyyyy Sellllllllfff." Oh my gosh, we have a conversation going on here! She is fighting hard to come back and she is winning! Then the nurse asks her, "Who is that?" and points to me. Anna slowly turns her head towards me and says, "Aaaaaaann." Okay, minor setback, but hey, I'm happy she's talking and I do look like my sister Ann. At 5:15 am we call Greg. I tell him someone wants to talk to him. I am holding the phone up to Anna's ear and she says, "Hiiiiiiiiiiiii Daaaaaaaddddeeeee." Greg and I are thrilled. It's slow, but it's working. Anna can talk. Thank you.

The nurse thought Anna might like some juice. She asked Anna if she wants water or juice. Anna replied, "Juuuuuuuuice. Aaaaaaaaple Juuuuuuice." I start to laugh. By now, I think the nurse is enjoying this as much as I am. It has got to be rewarding to help a patient come alive. The nurse asks Anna her birthday. Anna says, "Deeeeeeccceeeemmmbeeeeeeer Fourrr-rrrteeeeeennnnth." Anna is doing really well on these questions and she remembers things. This is so good. Our nurse has one more question for Anna. "Anna," she says, "Do you know what happened and why you are here?" Anna slowly looks at our nurse and says, "Caaaaaaaar Acciiiiiiiiiideeeeeennnnt." Okay. She knows.

The nurse continues to check Anna's arm and make sure she is comfortable. She adjusts Anna's blankets. When she adjusts Anna's pillows, Anna says, "Moooooove iiiiiiiit. Moooooove iiiiiiiit," and finally irritably she says louder and firmer, "MOOOOVE IIIIIIIT!" Her attitude surprises me. Anna has always been a very direct person, but not usually one to bark at adults. The nurse and I are trying to figure out what is uncomfortable for her and what she wants moved. The back of her neck is swollen and we think this is the direct source of pain. The swelling is coming from the vicinity of her spinal fracture. Apparently, she is talking about the position her pillow is in. We guess the pillow is making her uncomfortable and she wants it moved to another position! The nurse reaches over and readjusts the pillows under Anna's head and shoulders. Now she appears to be more comfortable.

As I move towards the end of the bed, looking at Anna, she holds out both of her arms towards me and says, "IIIIIIII Loooooove Youuuuuu." A wonderful feeling comes over me as I rush to her side for a hug and tell her I love her. She will never know how much I love her until she becomes a mom and has her own children. The love a mom feels for her children is a special love. It is an undying love of redemption and worth. It is a remarkable love and an honor to experience it. As we release our loving hug, the nurse takes Anna's left arm and taps the IV needle. Anna says, "Stooooooooop taaaaaaaapiiiiiiing meeeeeee theeeeeeere. Iiiiiiiiiit huuurrrrtttttsssss." Then Anna smiles. I recognize that smile. She's being a stinker and that is her stinker smile!

Anna and I have a great relationship, or so I think. You never know what perception your teenager has about your relationship with them. I prefer to believe that our relationship is great. I know that over the course of her lifetime, we will both see it as a great relationship, but as a teenager, her perception fluctuates like the wind. It isn't always easy to raise a strong-willed child, but that is one characteristic I love about Anna. I think that when she is a woman, it will serve her well in the future! Greg and I maintain that we are the parents and Max and Anna are the kids. The older they get the more compromising and discussing we do, but Greg and I have the final say. Max and Anna will tell you that I always try to throw in a life lesson or some catchy phrase during our family discussions, to help them along with their decisions. This sits just fine with Max. Well, I think it does. Sometimes I think Max listens and then does what he wants anyway. He is very quiet and respectful. Boys are different than girls. In the case of Max, he just wants to do well in school, play basketball, hang out with his friends, and avoid drama. Anna, however, will go down in a blaze before giving up. Once when she was little, just a few years ago actually, she was in a time out on the love seat in the family room. She was arguing up a storm about how she did not deserve to be in this time out. Finally, she got herself so worked up she screamed, "You're just old and nuts!"

I looked at her and said, "That will cost you a privilege. You cannot talk to me like that." I then made my way to the toy room and burst out laughing! Whenever Anna was in a time out, I had to leave the room because she would stay in her time out, but she would talk continually about how she did not deserve to be in a time out. It was comical. Now, Anna wants total freedom, just like every other fifteen-year old girl. However, in our house, she must abide by our family rules. She really doesn't like that!

I hear the doctors coming. In walk the troops. Each patient is assigned to a specialty team and we are assigned to the surgical team. For a while in the beginning, they did not know if Anna would need any surgery or not. Maybe that's why we are with the surgery team.

"She has Traumatic Brain Injury," says the head of the team.

I have no idea what this means. I've never heard those words before. The doctors aren't quite sure what Anna's outcome will be. They never smile. However, I'm thrilled with her progress and I know, in my heart, that my baby girl is going to be just fine.

Anna and I rest on and off all morning. She is in pain and she is still taking pain medications that put her back into a pretty deep sleep. This is great for all of us because Anna needs rest to heal her body and her mind. I need rest, too. No visitors allowed yet, except of course, family.

Greg is taking Max to his general practitioner this morning and Max's doctor is going to check the stitches in his hand and give Max a checkup. This is what Harborview had asked us to do before they released Max and we are more than happy to have Max checked one more time just to make sure no problems have developed over the last two days.

Anna wakes up for a few minutes and is hungry. I help her eat some yogurt, drink a little juice, and sip some water before she starts to doze off. Because of the medications, she falls asleep on a moment's notice. I just want to make sure she is done drinking and eating before she starts to slide back into her slumber. The nurse assures me she will not choke on yogurt, water or juice and that she will complete her swallowing before dozing off. I worry about everything right now.

I pick up my phone and call Greg and Max.

"Hello. We just finished with the doctor," Greg laughs, "Max asked the doctor if he could play in his basketball game this next Monday night. The doctor told him he did not think it was a good idea to play with stitches in his hand." Greg finds this humorous. It is funny. I think Max feels responsible for the team. He wants them to win and he wants to be part of that win. They have a good chance of going to state this season and he wants to do his best to get them there. He would not want to let them down just because he has stitches in his hand. Max is going to go back to school on Monday. That will be a big day for him and the beginning of getting his life back to normal.

"I'm going to take Max home to rest and pick up Ann and Teensie. Then we will come to the hospital. Okay?" asks Greg.

"Okay, sounds good. How's Max?" I hear a, "Fine," in the background. I must be on speaker. "Okay. See you in a little while. Bye."

Max is not ready to see Anna. Even though he knows she is speaking and eating, he just can't do it yet. That's okay. I have two kids to take care of and for now, Max is not ready to see his little sister in her altered state. I can see how upsetting that would be. We need to give him a little time to heal. Anna is going to live, so he has time to work through this.

When Greg, Ann and Teensie get to the hospital, we quietly watch Anna sleep. I am so thankful my sisters are here. Growing up, the two of them were thick as thieves. They both rode and showed American Quarter horses. I was the outsider. But, as we have moved through our lives, the bond of sisterhood has greatly strengthened. The mere fact that they dropped everything and flew to my side, is a testament to the relationship of three sisters. I would do the same for them in a heartbeat.

Greg is so thoughtful. He has brought one of Anna's lambys from home. When Anna and Max were little, Max had a real lambskin cloth he loved to sleep on. He named it Lamby. When Anna was born, we bought one for her, but she didn't quite like it. What she truly loved were the thermal blankets with satin trim on the edges. She was so little and a bit confused about what exactly Max was calling lamby. She thought it was one of his blankets and wanted a lamby of her own. So, she started calling her thermal blanket lamby. From that point on, both kids had there lambys and we carted both the lambskin cloth and the thermal blanket with us everywhere we went. To this day, Anna still sleeps with her lambys and she now has not one, but three lambys. Just this last Christmas, I bought her a brand new white thermal lamby with satin trim. She loved that present. It was a fun shopping experience for me to return to the infant department for her blanket and made me wonder how many more lambys I will buy in the future. Greg gently lays lamby over Anna's shoulders and up around her face. She loves to feel the lamby's warmth around her head, neck and face. This is tough to do with a neck brace on, but when she wakes up, she will have something comforting and familiar from home that can help keep her happy. I am so glad Greg thought to bring it for Anna.

Ann and Teensie watch as Greg places lamby on Anna. It brings up a conversation that Ann had with Mom years ago. It was about Ann's son, Dane.

"When Dane was little he loved his pacifier, and didn't want to give it up. I finally took it away from him because the dentist said it was ruining his mouth. Dane was upset and I called Mom and didn't know what to do. Mom said, 'It's easier to fix his teeth than it is to fix his mind. Give him back his pacifier.' So," Ann says, "I gave the pacifier back to Dane and all was well." We all laugh. Good advice.

Dane is in college now, very happy, and gave his pacifier up years ago. Looking at Anna, I'm not sure if she will give up lamby or keep lamby and pass lamby on to her own children. But, I do know that gifts of comfort are important and she can keep her lamby as long as she wants and needs her lamby. Right now, we all need lamby.

Whispering, Ann and Teensie tell me they had a great time at the house last night and this morning. First, they ask me about the vegetables that were dropped off by my neighbor, Joy. She and I belong to a Community Supported Agriculture (CSA) farm called the Root Connection. Every week we take turns driving out to the Root Connection in Woodinville to pick up our share of organic vegetables. We pick flowers, basil, herbs, and greens as well as load up our readied share of seasonal harvest into bags and bring them home. Then we divide the spoils and deliver the bounty to each other. Ann and Teensie have never seen some of these vegetables before and want to know what they are and how to prepare them. They discover rutabaga, leeks, and Japanese turnips just to name a few. It's hilarious as we talk about our vegetables and how much fun they had packing them up in containers. The kohlrabi is the funniest story. Ann describes it as "a green octopus with long skinny tentacles" and cannot for the life of her figure out what it is or what to do with it. Cut the tentacles off or eat them? My sisters had a blast with the veggies.

I can just see them in the kitchen trying to decide what to cut, what not to cut and how to pack it all. Too funny.

"Oh, and you have dinners being delivered," Ann says smiling.

A wonderful parent from Cedar Park, Julie Olsen, has organized a dinner train. Julie has a daughter in Max's class and the whole family is incredibly kind. Julie has arranged a meal to be delivered by a different person every other night around 5:00 pm or so starting tonight, Thursday. I can't get over how generous people are and something like this is so very helpful. Julie has even printed out a list, by date, of who will be bringing food, what they are bringing for dinner, and their phone numbers. This is such a godsend. What a wonderful gift. My sisters are excited. And thankful.

Ann and Teensie are only going to stay at the hospital for a few hours. Lisa is coming for a visit and has offered to take them back to our house. They want to take care of Max, the animals, the house, and to be there to receive the much-anticipated Autumn Pork Roast, salad, and cookies that are being delivered tonight for dinner. That sounds so good, it is making me hungry!

"You have to eat something," Greg says, realizing I haven't eaten since we arrived here.

"I can't leave Anna," That's my response. It's true. I won't leave Anna.

"I'll go to the cafeteria for you," he offers. I must admit, now that Anna is responsive, I am getting my appetite back a little bit. Even though I may enjoy a flat stomach for the first time in my life, food is beginning to sound good.

"Okay," I agree. So, off he goes to find a meal for me. About thirty minutes later, he returns with a hamburger and fries.

"This is a pretty big meal for not having eaten for two days," I say digging into the burger immediately. I don't know if it's because I am overjoyed about Anna's progress or what, but this is one on the best hamburgers I have ever eaten. The fries are fabulous. How funny to think of all the popular hamburger places there are to go, and Harborview has the best burger I have eaten in years. I will be having another one of these very soon.

As I am devouring my delicious feast, my dear friend Nancy walks in with a smile and a hug. She says hi to everyone and looks at Anna sleeping soundly.

Before we get involved in any conversation, the hospital's occupational therapist comes in. She wants Anna to get out of bed and walk to the bathroom. The bathroom is in the room and shared by both patients. It is maybe five feet from the end of the bed. Anna has been in bed for two days and the therapist says it's time to get her moving. She gently taps Anna on the chest to wake her up. Anna wakes up to her soft lamby. She's a little groggy and holds her lamby while the therapist helps her sit up. The therapist puts a big, wide belt around Anna's waist. The belt reminds me of the wide cotton web belts we wore in the 80s, only Anna's belt is striped in pastel colors. Its purpose is for someone to hold on to her when she walks so she doesn't fall. She has no balance and will have to learn how to walk again. As she gets out of bed for the first time, she stands and teeters back and forth. She heads towards the bathroom with Greg holding firmly onto the belt. Her legs are working, one foot in front of the other, but she is definitely listing to the left and losing her balance. Greg pulls up the belt and grabs Anna to steady her. As only Anna would do, she stops briefly in front of the mirror above the sink and takes a quick look at her hair. She makes a small adjustment to the hair on her forehead, then continues on into the bathroom with Greg holding the belt. We start laughing. Here she is with all of her injuries and she wants to get a look at herself. She is such a girl. However, she doesn't notice that there is still blood in her hair. She doesn't say a word. That's telling to me. The therapist goes in with her to help and give her a little privacy from the family.

When they are finished in the bathroom the therapist asks Anna to stop by the sink and wash her hands. Anna pauses and looks at the sink and the faucet. She isn't sure what to do. The therapist tells her to turn the faucet on with her hand. Anna waits, staring at the faucet. Then she reaches towards the faucet, wraps her hand around the handle and turns it on. Out pours water as Anna bends carefully to wash her hands. When she is finished, Anna stands back up and looks at the running water. The therapist says, "Anna, turn off the faucet." I look at everyone in the room. We are all waiting. I look at Nancy. Nancy is staring intently at Anna. Nancy is silently mouthing the words, "Anna, turn off the faucet." Twenty seconds go by and it seems like a lifetime. Slowly Anna reaches for the handle and turns off the running water. We all breathe a sigh of relief. The therapist helps Anna weave her way back to the bed. She takes the belt off while helping Anna slide into the hospital bed. Anna lies back and gets comfortable. Getting up and walking after all the trauma she has been through is a huge effort and she is very tired. Out she goes with lamby gently nestled against her ear and cheek.

That was a moment. Amidst our previous humor and optimism, we are confronted with reality. A little bit of fear coupled with silence creeps into the room.

Relaxing back into our seats, we keep the curtain drawn between Anna and her roommate. The rooms are small and with all of us in this tiny space we try to respect the privacy of both patients. Truth be told, it also allows me to focus all of my energy on Anna; praying and willing her to recover.

We no sooner settle in, when another therapist, the physical therapist enters our room. He wants to check Anna first, and then have her walk to a gurney he has brought and left out in the hallway. He's going to take her down to x-ray to have a second x-ray of her neck taken because of the fracture. He has to wake her up from her deep sleep. It's hard to wake her and keep her awake because she is taking such strong medications. He calls out her name, while tapping her chest, calling out louder and louder until she responds. When she opens her eyes and looks at him, he touches her knee and asks, "Anna, can you tell me what I am touching?"

Anna replies, "Patella tendon."

He looks up and turns his head to us and says, "Did she say patella?" We all laugh. At least we know she is paying attention in class.

He belts Anna's waist, stands her up and guides her to the gurney. With his help, she sits and then lies down on the gurney. He straps her down for safety and then wheels her down to x-ray. We wait. Within an hour, we hear the wheels of a gurney stop rolling just outside the room. In she walks with her belt and her therapist by her side. He helps her back into her bed. As he is leaving the room, Ann and Teensie point out to Anna that "He was very a handsome young man." Anna does a quick double take with her wide, white foam neck collar on. She smiles and we laugh. All of this tells me she understands everything that is going on around her. But, the interesting thing is she can't remember anything from minute to minute. When I ask her about the physical therapist and her x-ray, she doesn't remember the physical therapist was even there and that she was taken to get an x-ray. She begins to doze off.

This must be the day for therapists. In walks a gentleman dressed in a suit who introduces himself as the head of Rehabilitation Therapy at Seattle Children's Hospital. He is here to evaluate Anna and see if she is a good candidate for the rehab program at Children's. He talks to her for a little while and asks her a few questions. She does very well in answering and responding. He doesn't stay long and seems sensitive to the fact that this is a situation no parent ever expects to be in. He thinks she is a perfect candidate for their program and suggests she will probably be transferred to Seattle Children's Hospital next week.

With a brain injury, it is difficult to tell what damage is temporary and what damage is permanent. We are not sure what is happening in Anna's brain. It is a time will tell injury. But, for me, the good news is she is walking, talking and has her sense of humor. I pray we are on the road to a full recovery.

It is early afternoon. Lisa arrives with a smile and sits with all of us to visit and catch up on Anna's progress. She laughs as we tell her about everything Anna has been doing and saying today. Anna sleeps. Lisa can't stay too long because she still has kids at home that need after school snacks, homework help, and dinner. We talk for a bit and then Lisa, Ann, and Teensie say their goodbyes and head back home. They want to get home to take care of Max, receive the dinner by 5:00 pm and feed the animals.

Around 2:30 pm, Candice and Debbie Whipple quietly walk into the room to visit Anna. Candice is leaving in a few hours for a volleyball tournament but wants to see Anna before she leaves. Debbie sits down and Candice walks over to Anna's side. I tell them about Anna's progress today and I can see relief on Candice's face. I ask Debbie how she and Candice found out about the accident.

Debbie widens her eyes and says, "Well, the whole family was home that morning because we were getting ready to go to our great uncle's funeral. Candice got a call from Riley. He told her Anna and Max had been in a car accident. Max was okay but Anna was airlifted to Harborview. Our whole family went into hysterics. So, Carly drove Candice to the hospital. Roy and I went to the funeral. I was sobbing uncontrollably at the funeral. Everyone assumed it was due to the death of our great uncle. I couldn't say anything."

Candice is watching Anna as she begins to wake from her nap. Anna looks up at Candice and says, "Hi Mizbot." Mizbot is a name Anna affectionately uses to refer to her friend Amie. Candice laughs and tells Anna, "It's not Mizbot, I'm Candice." Anna laughs and calls her Mizbot again. Candice just laughs and tells Anna she is leaving for a volleyball tournament in Yakima and will be back on Sunday. Anna promises to call her every day to see how they are doing. These girls are so funny. Candice wants to style Anna's hair in a French braid. Anna is very excited about this and pulls herself up just enough for Candice to be able to reach around and do her braiding. I am thrilled Candice is willing to do this. Anna's hair is still dirty and bloody. But, like a true friend, this is not an obstacle for Candice. She just wants Anna to look better and be more presentable. She wants to make Anna feel better. She wants Anna to be her normal self.

Anna can barely stay awake during the braiding session. Candice is very gentle, making sure not to pull or tug on Anna's head. She struggles to finish before Anna falls into her nap. Finally, French braids in, Anna's sound asleep. Perfect!

"Candice, we need to get going. You need to get to the bus," Debbie says. Candice looks at her sleeping friend, happy to have seen her, praying she recovers. This is hard on Candice and I know she and Debbie will be helping to pray us through this.

Greg and I are tired. The road ahead is unknown. We have each other, our kids, our families, our friends, and our faith. That's enough. We are in good shape. Greg likes to be busy and it's a good thing. He has created a blog and spends part of his time at the hospital updating everyone. It's helpful for him to occupy himself with his techie side and communicate to everyone about Anna's progress. He can report all the new and unusual things she is doing and saying to large groups of people. There are so many people that want to see her. This is a great way to update them and let them know when she will be able to receive visitors. The comments he receives back have been incredibly supportive and kind. He is such a great dad and good person. He loves all of us so much and it seems like the older he gets, the better he gets.

Anna wakes up about 5:30 pm and is hungry. She asks for, "Maaaaaaac aaaaaaand Cheeeeeeese." and she receives some mashed potatoes with gravy, a bit of broccoli hidden in the potatoes, Jell-o and warm applesauce. She eats a little bit of everything. Her throat is a little sensitive and raw because of the intubation tube. She doesn't remember the tube, but she does know her throat hurts.

Anna doesn't remember anything about today either. Not even what she has eaten or who came into her room. She has no idea the occupational and physical therapists have been here or that she went for an x-ray. Her lack of memory is concerning me.

After dinner Anna has another visitor. Her friend Kayla and Kayla's mom Barbie come into the room. Kayla and Barbie drove to the accident scene the morning of the accident. After Max and Anna had been taken to the hospital, a group including parents, kids, and employees from Cedar

Park went to the accident scene and prayed. It is quite remarkable to me that they did that. Very powerful. It was one more cry to God to please take care of Max and Anna in this crisis. The group encountered a woman sitting on the curb with her head down. Scott Angell, the husband of Debbie Angell from school, approached her. She told Scott she had come to the accident scene and for some reason, she couldn't leave. She did not know why. She did not know our family, but was drawn to the accident scene and couldn't leave. Scott invited her to pray with them. They all joined hands and circled the taped off area. They prayed. Then they prayed some more. I am so thankful for all of them. Prayer is huge.

Kayla takes one look at Anna and puts a brave smile on her face. It isn't because her friend looks beat up, but because she is hooked up to an IV, has blood in her hair and is simply not herself. This is a scary thing for a fifteen-year-old to see. They think they are invincible. But, Kayla is always upbeat and happy. Tonight, is no exception. She gives her friend a hug and Barbie sits down. Anna can't talk a lot and Kayla takes a moment to text a friend to tell him how Anna is doing. Anna notices that she is texting someone and blurts out, "Who are you texting?" We laugh at this because it is a quick burst of uncontrollable emotions. She also said it fairly rapidly considering her other words have been so drawn out. Kayla tells Anna who she was texting then puts her phone away.

Barbie and Kayla stay and visit for a while, but it's getting late and time for Kayla to get home. Even though she has school tomorrow, Barbie says, "Kayla really wanted to see Anna." It was good for Anna and I am so glad they came. Everyone hugged. Within the hour, Anna has forgotten Kayla and Barbie had been there. I didn't forget.

Chapter Five

"The Browns are holding up remarkably well.
They have an extremely strong faith"
— Mark Gauger

Friday morning. Early. Still dark. We had a great sleep last night. Anna slept soundly without a lot of fidgeting and interruptions. The medications certainly help that, but because she is improving it gives her a calmer more relaxed sleep. I hear them coming. The herd of doctors charge in around 6:00 am and talk to each other while standing next to Anna's bedside. They look at their charts, chat and leave. Anna sleeps through the whole thing. I, however, pop up out of bed like a piece of toast every time they come into the room. I stand by Anna's bedside while they talk about her condition and I try to glean information from their conversation. It's a sight. Anna in her bed with blood in her hair, hooked up to an IV and knocked out. And then there's me with a ponytail on top of my head in the same turtleneck and jeans. No makeup, same clothes, no changes. Who cares? I don't.

Our shift nurse comes in and says, as per doctor's orders, "Today we change the medications so she won't be so sleepy and will be able to stay awake for longer periods of time." The doctors have decided to let her wake up a little more to see how she feels. I am thrilled about this because I get to communicate more with my baby girl. Today Anna can have visitors and will see friends that have been waiting to come for a visit since the moment we got here. Anna's friends love her and have a need to see her. They have all been praying and crying for her. With new medications, maybe she can stay awake long enough to visit with them. We should have a fun day.

Ah. Dad's here. Greg comes in with a smile and a kiss for both of us. He grabs a chair and takes a seat. Anna is awake and she is able to spend some time talking to us. Greg notices how well she is verbalizing and all the progress she has made in the last twenty-four hours. He has updated the blog to let everyone know she is accepting visitors, but that she does have scheduled therapy appointments throughout the day so please call first. She has a little breakfast and is still awake. Deb Fly comes in. Bless her. Deb has been here every day to check on us. I will never be able to thank Deb enough for all of her help. I think she knows everyone in the hospital and we are certainly being very well taken care of.

This morning Anna is having her eyes checked. She will take a wheelchair ride downstairs to the eye clinic. When the attendant comes in to escort Anna to her appointment, we put the belt around her waist, she grabs lamby and we walk to the wheelchair in the hallway right outside the room. She does a great job, still needing both the waist belt and our guidance. A little wobbly, but she walks to the wheelchair and sits down, covering her shoulders and lap with her lamby. The attendant straps her in and off we go. Today, I'm going with her because the attendant says he is leaving the two of us to wait for the eye doctor. I get to go into the appointment with Anna. Good.

The elevator doors open. There is a family standing in the elevator. The mom, the dad, and two kids are pushing themselves into the corner to make room for us. They look at Anna in her wheelchair. As the attendant is wheeling Anna in, she looks at the family and says, "Hola!" The family looks at Anna with big smiles and expressions of surprise and says, "Hola!" Anna smiles a slow, sly smile. When we get out of the elevator, I laugh and ask Anna why she is speaking Spanish? She says, "They were Mexican and I was saying hi." She is quite pleased with herself and this tickles me.

We arrive at the eye clinic and the attendant leaves us there for our appointment. I check us in and sit with my baby girl all bundled up in her wheelchair with her sweats on and a lamby wrapped around her body. She is getting tired and says she has a headache. This is one of the few times Anna has complained of a headache and I'm concerned. I walk up to the desk and ask how much longer we have to wait. Anna is tired and is in pain. The receptionist says it will be just a few more minutes. Well, thirty minutes later we are entering an examination room. This whole process is so slow and Anna is beginning to ache all over. Finally, the eye doctor comes in. This is a public hospital and he sees all kinds of activity here and judging from the waiting room, he is a very busy man. He is a bit abrupt and wants to know what is going on with Anna. I explain about the car wreck and the eye check is to make sure there is no debris in her eyes. The doctor dilates her beautiful hazel eyes, tests her vision, and examines for glass fragments and debris that she may have received from the accident. He says her eyes are fine and I breathe a sigh of relief. Even though we did not think we had any eye issues, it is good to get them checked off the list of possible problems. We go back to the front desk and call the attendant. He appears almost instantly and up we go, back to Anna's hospital room. There were no people in the elevator for her to talk to, so it is a quiet trip. This was a big outing for Anna and she's exhausted.

The sun is glowing through the hospital room window. I can see Mount Rainier. I can see part of the Seattle skyline. It is a beautiful day in so many more ways than one. I look around our tiny room. Greg and Deb are here and Anna is settling into her bed and starting to doze off. She will have visitors and appointments in this room today. She will be able to talk to Max from this room. Doctors, nurses, and therapists will take care of her and help her on the road to recovery in this room. Greg and I have had our lives changed in this hospital and in this room. Anna and I live in this room. God is also in this room. Our tiny little curtained-off room is full of hope, love, and change; not only for our family, but for friends and all those that know about the accident.

Deb gets up to leave when Anna's lunch is carried in. We gently wake Anna up by tapping softly on her chest. She needed her rest. Anna said not only did her head hurt, but her neck and herself hurt. We will have to pace the visits as best we can. The nursing staff is terrific about this. They know when visiting gets to be too much. Our nurse tells me she will monitor the visitors. Anna needs rest to heal and her healing is first and foremost on everyone's mind.

Today for lunch, Anna enjoys chicken, mashed potatoes, and beans. She is eating every bite and Greg comments, "She must be hungry because she would have complained endlessly about this meal at home." Funny how meals taste better, especially to a teenager, when they are served anyplace else but home! I, however, am having a hamburger from the cafeteria. Yes, with fries. Fabulous. As soon as Anna is done eating, the nurse gives her some strong pain medications for her neck and head. She falls asleep as I am finishing my hamburger.

It is about 1:30 pm and the occupational therapist comes into the room to talk with Anna. It is taking him a few minutes to wake her up because of her drug induced sleep from the pain medications. He taps her chest carefully and her eyes open and she wakes. She looks at him and says, "Hola!" He laughs and asks, "What day is it?" She says, "Viernes!" He turns to us and says, "Is she speaking Spanish?" Greg answers, "Yes,

Spanish is her favorite class." Greg and I can hardly contain ourselves. First this morning, speaking Spanish to the family in the elevator, and now this! What a riot. And how her brain is working is very curious. We're having a Spanish Day!

Within minutes after the occupational therapist has left, a new therapist comes in and introduces herself as the cognitive therapist. She wants Anna to perform a few verbal and mental tasks. She explains to Anna that the first test she is going to do will be to ask Anna to name as many words as possible, beginning with a letter from the alphabet that she will give Anna. This will be a timed, one-minute test. She sits down with her note pad and Anna gets comfortable and mentally ready. Anna is very competitive and even though she is not fully herself, she focuses on the therapist with a look of steely resolve. The therapist gives Anna the letter P and says, "Okay, go." The first word out of Anna's mouth is, "penis." She looks at us, smiles, and continues to rattle off a series of more appropriate words beginning with P. Greg and I look at each other and look away. Where is she getting this? Goofball. Then the therapist asks her to list as many words as she can think of starting with the letter S. Without hesitation, Anna belts out, "shit." She looks at us again and starts laughing. Then she finishes her minute with a long line of words beginning with S. What a nut! The therapist looks at us with a big smile on her face and says, "She blew me away. I was not expecting this. She did incredibly well." This is also the moment Greg and I learn a new word. Disinhibited.

In the front part of the brain, there is a filter. This filter literally filters your words and actions. It keeps us in check. It stops us from doing and saying the inappropriate things that we may be thinking. Anna's filter has been damaged because of her head injury. She is disinhibited. She has lost her inhibitions. She has few controls telling her what is appropriate and what is not appropriate. We don't know if this is temporary or permanent. We need to talk to the doctor. Anna thinks she is hilarious, a real comedian! We are worried.

Around 2:30 pm, Ann and Teensie arrive, courtesy of Lisa. My sisters spent the morning taking care of the animals and the house. They had fed Max and made sure he was comfortable. Since Ann was a teacher and Teensie had also taught and currently tutors for the SAT and ACT tests, they checked with Max to make sure he was up to date on his school work. Max is a very conscientious student and I am sure he is getting all of his assignments and homework done. But, an Aunt check never hurts! I talked to Max and we decided that since Teensie is here, maybe she could tutor him on the math portion of the SAT. He had done well, but is getting ready to take the SAT again in a few weeks. He wants to increase his score, particularly his math score. This is Teensie's specialty. Teensie is very excited about this. She is going to start reviewing with him as soon as she gets back home today. This is perfect. We have house sitters, animal sitters, food deliverers, and tutors. I can concentrate on Anna and Max and not worry about all the little stuff, the stuff that adds up to be the big stuff, in my mind anyway.

Ann and Teensie cannot believe the number of people that have called and come by. They find food and gifts on the doorstep. They tell me the dining room table is full of food for the family, presents for the kids, and flowers for the house. Women from the book club I belong to and women from my prayer group, Faithful Hearts, have called, sent letters and cards, come over with food, gifts, and wine. Neighbors and friends of old and new are reaching out to us. Strangers. The dinner train families. Our grocery store at the top of the hill, QFC, let my sisters know they will bring groceries to our house if we need anything. Everyone is amazing. It is also a beautiful thing to witness, first hand, the way people bless one another. I love that my sisters get to experience all of this. I love my sisters and I love my friends and family. Unbelievable. Good. Good. Good. Thank you, God.

Ann and Teensie are still having a great time with the food and being at our home. They loved the Autumn Pork Roast meal. They are still having a blast with the vegetables. Tonight, they will receive a pasta dish with a salad delivered to their doorstep. They can hardly wait.

Ann gives me an update on what is going on at home. "Max is quiet but good," she says, "and the animals are fat and happy." I remind her Max is a man of few words. Ann thinks Max should have been her son. "But, I'm going to keep him," I tell her.

Three cats, one dog. Ann says she and Teensie are worried about Anna's petite ten-year-old calico kitty Belle. Belle loves Anna and comes running the minute she hears Anna's voice. Belle misses Anna. Belle always talks to Anna through a short series of garbled meows. She is a bit neurotic and my sisters think that she is being picked on by our rescue cat, Moses. He is four-years-old, black with white paws and a little patch of white on his left upper lip. Moses is a bigger kitty than Belle and he is a stinker. Moses loves me and me alone. His fears dictate his mood and he can be quite a pill. When we hold him, we have to have a gentle but firm hold on his front legs or he will suddenly become fearful and grab our heads with his claws. We all love Moses, but he is a challenge. Ann and Teensie are working on keeping Belle and Moses apart and on comforting Belle. Jazz, Max's cat, is Belle's brother and loves everyone, especially Max. Jazz is an incredible cat. He's a big kitty and sports a beautiful black and white tuxedo with long, soft fur. He is convinced he is a human being. Jazz is the most loving, communicative cat imaginable. Not a day goes by that Jazz is not picked up and held by everyone who enters our house. He is also Moses' mentor. Moses follows Jazz everywhere. The very first day Moses came to live with us, Jazz took Moses under his wing. Moses shadows Jazz, he would be a mess without him. Then we have Sammy dog. He's a Labrador retriever/border collie mix with a touch of white at the end of his tail. It looks like he dipped his tail in white paint. He is too smart for his own good and loves our family. He is an uncontrollable licker and uses his tongue to express himself. He loves all of us and sneaks into Max's room to jump up on the bed and keep Max company. He is not allowed on the bed, but once Max pets him, he decides it's okay and stays. I am sure Sammy and Jazz are loving Max, and helping Ann and Teensie take care of him. However, Ann and Teensie have decided Sammy needs some training. He goes a little crazy when the doorbell rings. Barking and carrying on. Yes, it is a bothersome behavior, but I have not been able to convince him we are not under siege every time someone is at the front door. But now, how lucky are we? We also have dog trainers in our house!

Anna is looking around the room and listening to the conversation. She is watching her aunts as they describe what is going on at home and I can tell she misses Belle, her own bed, and her own home. She turns to Lisa and smiles as she says, "How do you say 'Hasta Luego' in Spanish?" Lisa starts laughing and says, "I think that would be 'Hasta Luego.'" Anna bursts out laughing. Then she says to Lisa, "You are funny." Anna is surely rediscovering her wit and humor today!

Now that she has an audience in her room, she is really starting to talk. And, she laughs at everything. The medications are keeping the pain at bay and allowing her to stay awake for longer periods of time. However, we aren't sure what will come out of her mouth next. That part is a little worrisome.

Anna abruptly says, "I need to pee." Then she laughs and looks at me. She remembers. She knows I don't like the word pee. I prefer tinkle. But, she wants to push it. So, we strap her up with her belt and I hold her belt and arm as we teeter towards the bathroom. We reach the bathroom and out of the clear blue, she looks at me and says, "Fuckin – A." Okay, that's enough. I say, "Anna, that's inappropriate and we do not talk like that." She bursts out laughing and thinks she is hilarious. She just swore at her mom. How great is that? And she can blame it on the head injury! We haven't mentioned the word disinhibited to her. Not yet anyway.

As we are finishing in the bathroom, she looks up at me and says, "How do you say 'I'm done' in Spanish?" I chuckle and tell her I have no idea, but we can certainly ask her Spanish teacher. She thinks this is a great idea. I do know that under normal circumstances, Anna would never have me in the bathroom with her while she in tinkling. It all reminds me that these are not normal circumstances, but I am very glad we have any circumstances at all. Life is good and I thank God that I am able to escort my fifteen-year-old daughter to the bathroom.

Anna slides back into bed and I carefully unhook her belt and take it from around her waist. She lost a little weight because she did not eat for a few days and she has a little bit of a restricted diet here. The funny thing is though, Greg noticed she was very protective of her lunch today. He thinks she is territorial about her food. I laugh and hope she can eat a little more tomorrow. Food is strength and fuel for recovery.

"Well, look who's here," says Greg as we all look towards the door. He always gets a big kick out of Anna and Max's friends. In walk Lisa's daughter Katy, and Amie. Amie and Katy know each other through Anna. Anna met Katy when they were both three-years-old. They have never gone to the same school but are in the youth group at church together and went to daycare together at Lisa's. Katy is a good girl and loves Anna. Amie and Anna were born three days apart at Swedish Hospital. Amie's dad is a fraternity brother of Greg's and is our financial advisor. Mark is a good man and is married to a wonderful woman, Julie. Julie brought the girls today. Amie and Anna have been thick as thieves since they were babies. One time, the three of us went to Target and I bought them matching dresses. They loved that and I have the picture to prove it. They may go a period of time without seeing each other, but they are connected in a special way.

We are so glad they are here. Both girls are uplifting and kind to Anna. Anna is not her usual self and it is hard not to notice the change. For the girls, I can see it is a little scary. From the viewpoint of a fifteen-year-old, you have this friend and she has this accident. She can't remember things from minute to minute, she has blood in her hair, she is hooked up to an IV, and she says inappropriate things. Yet, there are glimpses of your friend in her conversation and mannerisms. It is hard for the girls. They aren't sure what to do. So, they laugh. Laughter is the best medicine.

Thankfully, the nurse comes in and announces it is time to give Anna a shower and wash her hair. Yeah! This is Anna's first shower since the accident and I am glad she will get the dirt and blood washed out of her hair. I think she will feel better. I will. Our nurse puts on Anna's waist belt and walks her into the bathroom and closes the door.

Amie and Katy are very excited. They devise a plan and say, "We are going to brush her hair, and ask her if she wants us to braid it. Where's the brush? Where are her hair things? How long will she be?" Greg, Lisa, the aunts and I scamper around the room looking for supplies. It's not like we have a lot of hair things from home, but we will find something! We search our purses and find a few items. Katy and Amie decide to go to the nursing station for rubber bands and dash out of the room to collect them and anything else that might be available from the nurses. Anna is going to love this. We all look on in amusement as they return with rubber bands and assorted hair adornments.

Just in the nick of time. Here comes Anna all wet and clean. She can't put a towel around her wet hair because the weight of her hair and the towel would place stress on her spinal fracture. So, her long hair hangs straight down, dripping wet, ready for her friends' attention. The nurse sits her on the bed, leaving the belt on. She explains to the girls about the belt and about Anna's neck injury and shows them where the swelling is on the back of her neck. Although Anna continues to wear her white neck brace, the nurse says, "Girls, you must be very careful when you comb her hair. There can be no pulling or yanking or movement of Anna's neck." The girls nod in understanding. They are so gentle with Anna. They comb cautiously and carefully, not allowing for any unnecessary head movement. They are laughing and moving at a snail's pace. Unusual for fifteen-year-olds.

Finally, the combing is done. Amie says, "Do you want braids?"

Anna says enthusiastically, "YES!" So, here they are, Katy and Amie, braiding their friend's hair. A beautiful picture. These girls have good hearts and kind spirits. They are good friends to Anna and are probably wondering what her future holds. Yet they reveal nothing except their kindness and wild laughter as they make their good friend look more like her old self. I think to myself, "Thank you girls." Thank you, God, for these girls.

As the laughter continues, Lisa and Julie tell the girls it is about time to get home. They will all be driving home in rush hour traffic and need to get a start because they have a good forty-minute drive ahead. Ann and Teensie are leaving with Lisa and she will drop them off at our house. This has been a good visit. Hugs for everyone and the girls hug Anna twice before leaving. Anna loves her friends and they love her. A little while later, she doesn't remember they were there. I'll never forget it.

Greg and I can tell that Anna is getting hungry. She says her neck hurts. I check the hallway to find our nurse and tell her the back of Anna's neck is hurting. She comes in and gives Anna a little pain medication. The nurses at Harborview are so wonderful. They are taking such great care of Anna and are doing a tremendous job of monitoring her pain and medications. The back of her neck is very swollen and the neck brace, while necessary, is uncomfortable. After her shower, she had put on a fresh neck brace. The other one is drying by the heater in our room. She laughs and thinks it's funny that she now has two neck braces.

The rattling of the trays and the squeak of the dinner cart gives us notice that dinner has arrived. Anna sits up, ready to eat. Greg's observation is correct. She is getting territorial about her food. She starts eating the moment the tray is set down in front of her. Wow! She is hungry. No conversation, just eating. Watching her eat makes me hungry. Greg offers to go to the cafeteria to pick out some food for us. I would like another hamburger, but two in one day is a bit much. Comfort food certainly has its purpose. Greg goes to the cafeteria and quickly returns with salads and sandwiches for our dinner. We are all fed and happy as Anna dozes off and we carefully adjust lamby to cover her shoulders and rest against her face. She looks content.

Greg starts working on the blog. He likes to update it every day, and is excited to let everyone know Anna had visitors today and how everything went. He talks about her eye appointment and her improvements. He also thanks every one for their prayers and support. It amazes me how many people have responded to the blog and are appreciative of the information. I didn't even know what a blog was before the accident! What a great tool to communicate with.

While Greg is blogging, in walks Mark Pavlovic. Pav, as we affectionately call him, was in our wedding, is married, and has three kids. He is a great guy and has a quick wit. He also has a son, Anthony, who is one year older than Anna. Anna thinks she is going to marry him and has had a crush on him for years. The first time Anna was old enough to notice Anthony, we were at a Christmas party at the Pavlovic's house. They have a huge, old, beautiful home on Capitol Hill in Seattle. Old wood millwork beautifully stained in deep mahogany tones, a fabulously wide staircase, oversized rooms, tall ceilings, and a sprawling floor plan. There were lots of friends and neighbors at the party. The food was delicious, the house looked beautiful, and the atmosphere festive. There was a small group of musicians playing in the corner of the living room. All the kids were running through the living room, past the musicians, and down the stairs. At the bottom of those stairs was a fun room filled with a piano, a pool table, pizza, pop, video games and television. A kid's dream. All of this made a lasting impression on Anna. When we got home that night and I was putting Anna to bed, she asked, "Can we have a band live in our living room to play music for us?" I wanted to fall over laughing, but I did not want to laugh at her misunderstanding. So, I explained, "They were hired to play music for the party. They don't actually live at the Pavlovic's house. They were just there for the party."

"Oh," she says. Then she talked about Anthony. For years, we have talked about Anthony.

Pav looks at Anna sleeping and quietly say, "Hi, how are you?" to both Greg and me.

Before we have a moment to respond, Anna's eyes pop open and she says, "Where's Anthony?" We are all so surprised because we thought she was asleep and because she didn't even say hi to Pav.

Immediately, being the quick wit that he is, Pav replies, "Well, aren't you even going to say hi to me first?" Anna starts laughing. Looking at Pav she says, "Hi, where's Anthony?" Pav tells Anna he is at home but will visit her soon. She rests in the knowledge that Anthony will visit her soon.

Pav stays for a while before needing to get back home. We begin to wind the day down and prepare for the night ahead. My phone rings. It is Wendy Legat, Lindsay's mom. Wendy is great. She loves Anna and is checking to see how Anna is doing. I fill her in on the day. Then Wendy says, "Good. Lindsay is having a hard time. I need some good news for her." Lindsay, having been to the hospital the night of the accident when Anna was in ICU, is struggling with her friend being so badly injured. Wendy explains, "Lindsay rarely cries. Yesterday I heard a noise coming from Lindsay's room and found her sprawled on her bed sobbing uncontrollably. She is so sad and so afraid for Anna." Lindsay loves Anna.

This tells me Anna's and Max's friends are suffering with the unknown outcome of the accident. They know Anna is improving, but they also know she is not herself. For the first time in most of their lives, they recognize their own mortality. They are seeing firsthand what can happen in a moment that can change your life forever. It's frightening.

We are certain Anna will have more visitors tomorrow. I may go home for a few hours in the morning to see Max and take a shower. It will be four days since the accident and I would like to have a full shower and wash my hair. Not just a bath with water and a washcloth. Greg is going to come back in the morning and stay with Anna. Maybe I can drive the car back home and return later with the aunts and Max, if he is ready. We will be moving to Children's Hospital on Monday and I'm not sure when I will have another opportunity to get home and clean up. So, tomorrow looks like the best time to go home.

Greg is finishing with the blog and we think it is time Anna calls Max. She has been talking about him today and wants to see him. She can't figure out why he hasn't been to visit her. She doesn't understand that he is afraid to see her. Seeing her makes everything real. The accident, the hospital bed, the neck brace, the walking belt, the forgetting, and the disinhibition, will all become our new normal. But, her voice sounds fairly strong and she can carry on a conversation with him. We think it will be good for them to hear each other's voices. Kind of a signal that everything is getting better, our family is healing and they can reconnect.

Greg asks Anna if she wants to call Max. She says, "Yes!" We dial the phone for her and she holds it up to her ear. Max answers. Good. Anna is unable to tell Max about her day because she can't remember her day. But, she says, "I love you, Max."

Max replies, "I love you too and I am coming to visit you tomorrow." Anna is thrilled and so are we. Tomorrow Max gets to see Anna for the first time since they were both in the emergency room. This will be good therapy for both of them.

Chapter Six

"Our love and prayers"
— The Johnsons

Saturday morning. Here they come. I hear their shoes pounding against the floor. I am used to their schedule now. There are lots of them today. I don't have any new questions for them because I have had numerous conversations with the nurses about Anna's progress. Both the doctors and the nurses have told me that the reality is, this is a wait and see situation. Will her memory be fully regained? Will she be the same girl she was before the accident? Will she be in and out of hospitals? Will her disinhibited brain filter repair itself? What do we have to do for her to help her? Are her spleen, kidney, artery, brain, and spinal fracture healing themselves? Every day I see huge progress. I pray every night and day that the progress continues and that every test has good results. I talk to God and ask Him to heal her. I thank Him again for saving Max and Anna and tell Him I know my children are another one of His miracles.

I believe in miracles. When my mom was dying, she flew up to see me with Ann as her escort. I was eight months pregnant with Anna. Mom came up to Seattle on my request to see a doctor here that had helped the mother of a friend with her cancer. I had made an appointment with him and it was worth a try to save Mom. When they came down the ramp and into the airport terminal, Mom was in a wheelchair with Ann carefully maneuvering her through the crowd of passengers exiting the plane. She looked pretty darn good. I saw a cross hanging around her neck. This was new. We were not raised going to church and at that time in our lives, Greg and I weren't going to church either. I believed in God and that He had a son, Jesus, but that was it. I knew nothing about the Bible. So, to see the cross was a good thing because it was a statement about eternity. But, I didn't fully understand until a few years later. The following day, Ann and I took Mom to her doctor appointment. He told us he believed in miracles. He told my mom he believed in miracles. But, he also told her to get her life in order. He then told Ann and me what we could expect, barring any miracles. That doctor was right on. To the day, he told us how Mom would do, when she would need to have oxygen, and when hospice should come in. Looking back at that sad and difficult time, I see that the miracle was not in healing Mom, it was in saving Mom. She had accepted Christ and chosen God just weeks before her death. As I sit in this hospital room right now, that knowledge makes me a happier and fuller person. It also gives me renewed strength knowing she is here, somewhere, in this hospital holding the hands of her daughter and granddaughter.

As thoughts of my mom linger, Anna begins to make noises and slowly wakes up for breakfast. She had a great night's sleep and her physical pain is becoming less demanding. She's well rested and alert, looking forward to today. "Some of the girls from the team are coming today," she says with a huge smile on her face. Her basketball team. Word travels fast and apparently, there will be lots of visitors today. She is very excited. At this age, your friends are your buoy. Actually, at any age a true friend is your buoy. And, a gift.

She is eating her cold eggs when her daddy walks in. She sure loves him. "Hi Dad," she says with eggs slopping around her face. I must say, she is not the most coordinated eater these days. Greg takes one look at her and the eggs and laughs. She has no idea why he is laughing, but she laughs along with him. Too funny. She says, "My eggs are cold," as she slaps her whole meal down and guzzles her drink. We discuss her upcoming day and I tell her I am planning to go home, shower, get myself organized and come back in a few hours. She is completely fine with this plan. I get a goodbye hug and a kiss from Greg and Anna before I turn and walk out of our little room.

Driving home feels odd. It is the first time I have driven since the accident. The first time I have been in the car since my life has changed. Every road, every turn, every place is familiar, but I am seeing everything through different eyes. As I get ready to turn down Holmes Point, as I have done hundreds of times before, I realize where I am. I am here at the scene of the accident. Not much time to think. I turn right and drive down the winding road to home. Everything looks the same. Everything is the same, except me. Change comes unexpectedly sometimes. Because of this change, I am thankful for the adjustment God has given me. He has given me a new perspective on the important things in life. Family. Be they blood or acquired, family is the bottom line. My dad calls my generation the bottom line kids, only he is referring to my generation's love of money. Unfortunately, the bottom line is often at the expense of peoples' lives. Money can be replaced, people cannot. As I pull into the driveway and press the button on the garage door opener, I relax. I am home and in a place where love lives.

I am greeted by my licky-dog. He loves me. You would think I had been gone for years. Maybe, to him, I have. I give him lovies, avoiding his tongue, and try to walk into the house through the garage door without tripping over his gyrating body. His tail is slapping the wall and his hindquarters can barely contain themselves. "Okay, Sammy," I say, "I love you, too." Finally, we are both safely in the house.

Ann and Teensie are in the kitchen. Eating. What a fabulous spread of food. Teensie says proudly "I've sampled everything. It's all delicious." I wish Mom was here. She would love to see the three of us bound together and here for each other. I miss her so much. Moms are the glue of the family.

"Where's Maxie?" I ask looking around the kitchen. He loves to eat, so I am surprised he is not in the kitchen, with his aunts, pigging out. This smorgasbord of food on the kitchen counter is his kind of eating! What a variety. Max loves food. He has never, ever been a picky eater. He is a healthy eater because we have emphasized healthy choices his whole life. Max will choose healthy any time over junk food. Most importantly, he is driven by the fact that he is an athlete and the better the food, the better the game. Ultimately, for Max, it's about the game.

"He's still sleeping," Aunt Ann says. Well, he is a slug. Max sleeps more than anyone I know, and loves every second of it. When I want to wake him up, I find Jazz and let Jazz into his room to kindly wake him from his slumber. Today is no different. Max doesn't know I am home and I can't wait to surprise him. Sometimes Max has a touch of the teenage boy testiness if I wake him up, so Jazz is the perfect guy to do the job.

I find Jazz and carry him upstairs like a baby. He loves that, rolled over on his back purring. I slowly open Max's door to let Jazz creep in to wake him. Jazz does his usual routine. I watch as he slowly enters Max's room and looks around. I really and truly think Jazz is listening for breathing noises, indicating life, and senses his boy sleeping soundly, waiting for him. Jazz slowly walks across the room in a silent, cat-like way and jumps up onto the bed. He nuzzles his way under Max's arm and Max carefully pulls Jazz towards his body and hugs him. They are both in heaven. This is my cue. I gently say, "Hi, Bug, I came home for a little while to visit you and take a shower." He nods. I look at my once-little boy and suggest, "Why don't you shower and come down stairs for some food and see me before I go back to the hospital." Max grunts, his teen-age angst showing, and indicates he will be down shortly. Well, shortly can mean ten minutes to one hour. I add, "I am going to take a shower and I will see you downstairs."

Within an hour, we are all downstairs eating and loving the fact that we are together and Anna is alive and safe with her daddy at the hospital. As I predicted, Max loves all the food. He smiles when he talks about how good everything tastes and tells me everything about what he has eaten since he got home. Max looks good; relaxed and at peace. Today is the day he will visit Anna. I think he is looking forward to it, yet is a bit ner-vous about seeing her in her unusual mental state. Max doesn't verbalize this, but I can tell from his attitude he's ready to see her. He knows she's improving and she's not blaming him for anything.

I look at Max and remind myself of all the time that has passed from pregnancy to the teenage years. I have loved our kids from the moment I knew I was pregnant. I have kissed and hugged them so much and so often that they are used to and comfortable with affection. Today when Max sees Anna, I know they will hug and express their love for each oth-er. It's natural to them. It's what they know.

There is a knock on the door. Sammy runs to the door barking. As usual, I grab Sammy's collar and hold him with my left hand as my right hand opens the door to see who's here. It's Lamont Franklin, Max's bas-ketball coach. What a wonderful, supportive surprise for Max. I release Sammy and he excitedly darts for Lamont; the poor, unsuspecting man. He has not had the pleasure of meeting Sammy before. As soon as I peel Sammy off him, I guide Lamont into the family room to sit and visit with Max. After a little conversation about how everyone is doing, I excuse myself to go upstairs to get some clothes and sundries together for the hospital. It is good for Max to have some time to talk to Lamont. I don't hear, but I am sure the entire conversation is about basketball. What a surprise! Actually, I hope it is about basketball. Max is comfortable in that conversation. He can contribute, and be proud of himself.

Just as I come down the stairs, I see Lamont and Max at the front door. Lamont is getting ready to leave. The three of us stand at the front door. "Thank you for coming," Max and I chime in together. Lamont nods. Sammy also thanks him by sniffing and shoving his nose at Lamont. Hopefully, Lamont is not offended. In our house, if you don't love an-imals, you have entered the wrong place. I hug Lamont and then grab

Sammy's collar to hold him away from Lamont so he can get out the door. As I close the door behind him, I am so thankful Lamont came by. It was good for Max and me.

Max and I talk about our plan today. "Okay," I inform him, "you're aunts and I are going to the hospital in just a few minutes. Are you coming with us?"

"Mom, I want to wait until Dad gets back home this morning and I will go to the hospital with him this afternoon. Okay?"

"Okay, Bug. That will work," I reply, "Dad will be back once I give him the car. He's going to work from home for a few hours. When he's done, you two can come to the hospital." Perfect.

I turn to Ann and Teensie, "Greg will bring the three of you back here late this afternoon. Is that okay with you guys?" They both nod yes. Good plan.

Ann, Teensie, and I load into the car with my luggage and our purses. Ann has a purse big enough to carry anything and everything a person may need at any given moment. Her purse weighs a ton. She totes an assortment of items that most people would leave at home. I ask her what in the world she has in that purse. Teensie and I start laughing when she reveals her stash. She has the usual wallet, glasses, and Kleenex, but also lists perfume, a bag of earrings, makeup, lotion, mirror, tweezers, scissors, dental floss, gum, Vaseline, notepad, pens, bracelets, and hair ties. I do not know why she is not in physical pain from lugging all that stuff around. She is a walking drugstore.

Everyone wants a latte. Starbucks. QFC at the top of the hill has a Starbucks inside. For me, this is such a treat. It begins to feel like my regular life again. I'm a true believer that every woman should do something kind for herself every day. It doesn't have to be a big thing, just something to make you enjoy yourself and give you a moment to pause in a busy schedule. For me, a soy latte with a little whip cream on top is a gift to myself. It is not a daily ritual, maybe twice a week, but I love it and it is something I look forward to. Today is my first day out of the hospital and I am going to have a soy latte with my sisters. We are all excited. Teensie loves coffee and she loves Starbucks. She drinks more coffee than anyone I know. Teensie goes for the exotic drinks too. Not your basic latte. She has flavors and combinations and all sorts of fun with her coffee. It is really something else to hear her order. Her drinks always look fabulous and taste delicious. This is a treat she gives herself, and I think Teensie deserves a special treat today for all of her help.

We are standing in line, the three of us, talking quietly about the hospital, the situation, the accident and about life. There is only one lady in front of us and she is giving her order. Teensie says something and I tear up. Then Teensie tears up thinking she has said something to make me cry. She didn't. We are just all a bit raw and tears are important releases. Maybe it's God's way of clearing out the sadness so we can let in the goodness. The woman in front of us keeps turning around and looking at us. Finally, she turns around and says, "Are you Anna Brown's mom?"

I say, "Yes." She introduces herself as Jan Carroll.

"How's Anna doing?" she asks me. "I have to tell you what happened with my kids the day of the accident." Jan pays for her coffee and we order. As we wait for our coffee, Jan tells us her story.

"The morning of the accident, I was in my car with my two children. On our way to school, we drove by the accident. Once we passed the accident scene, we had to pull over. My young daughter pulled out her rosary and began her Hail Marys. This is highly unusual for her. My daughter does not do this on a regular basis. The three of us prayed. Then we continued on to school and I dropped my kids off. That afternoon when I picked up my kids, they told me that their school, St Brendan Parish School, had heard about the accident, and was saying prayers for your kids."

"Thank you for the story," I respond. Once again, I think, prayer saved my kids. Heaven surely was lit up Tuesday morning. When Jan mentioned the name of the school, I understood. Anna knows some kids there. Between texting and phoning, word had traveled quickly. I am so glad to hear this story. For me, this is yet another example of the power of praying and how prayer impacts so many lives. Jan is a very nice woman and I am so glad she told us her story. So glad the accident brought her daughter to pray and so glad she shared all of this with us at Starbucks. I guess you never know where you will be when something unexpected happens that brightens your life. This story certainly made me feel good and I think it was good for Ann and Teensie, as well.

We got our lattes and drank in not only the coffee, but the story we had just been told. How interesting that Jan was at Starbucks at that very moment we had stopped to get a treat. My first time out of the hospital in days and to run into her in those few minutes was amazing. No accident there. And people say they can never see God at work--pshaw.

As we load back into the car, I call Greg to tell him we are on our way. Anna is expecting visitors soon and both she and I are looking forward to seeing the girls. It will be different for them to see their teammate in her current mental state, but hopefully this will be a great experience for all of them. I'm a little worried about how they will receive Anna. After all, she is not herself and we are so uncertain about her complete outcome. I want to protect her. I want to shield her from being talked about. It's hard.

By the time we get to the hospital, park the car, and find our way up to Anna's room, she has visitors. The room is full of kids, laughing and talking. Anna is totally in her element and very excited to see everyone. I think it makes her feel normal. Anna is a people person and she loves a good laugh. Mr. Ian, a teacher from Cedar Park is here, too. Mr. Ian has taught math to both Anna and Max and is an excellent teacher. The kids have a great deal of respect for Mr. Ian and I am thrilled that he is here. So is Anna.

"I said the F word to my mom," she announces to the entire crowd. She is laughing uncontrollably because she finds this hilarious and then adds "I didn't even get in trouble!"

Mr. Ian looks at Anna and says, "Well, Anna, your mom may have something to say to you later!" She thinks this is incredibly funny. At least she is having fun. Mr. Ian looks and me and says, "She is disinhibited."

I look at him and say, "Yes, I know." Mr. Ian talks to me for a minute or so about a previous experience he had had with a student that was disinhibited. He is a good source of information and I am glad to hear a little bit about this condition. We don't know much because everything is so new. Every day is new.

Anna is acting quite loopy. She tells everyone she falls asleep often and quickly because she is on medications. She turns to Greg, "What am I on Dad? Viagra?" Everyone bursts out laughing.

Greg looks at her and says, "No, Anna. Vicodin." I think this comment has just made everyone's day. Even though she is starting to get tired, she is so happy to have her friends there. She rallies to stay awake. They are sitting everywhere. There are kids on her bed, on my chair bed, against the window sill, in metal chairs. There is standing room only. All of the adults are standing. The kids are carefully crawling all over Anna.

Three of her teammates have brought her a paper bag filled with funny surprises. Two of the funniest treasures are the black plastic glasses and the diamond-like studded tiara. Anna puts the tiara on and then plants the huge, black oversized glasses on her face. This is really comical. The glasses keep falling off, so the girls keep putting them back on. When all is said and done, the tiara and the glasses are on, not straight, but they are on. She looks like she has had quite the night. Her braids are loose and disheveled, she has a bandage on her eyebrow, a huge white foam neck brace, a crooked tiara, huge crooked black plastic eyeglass frames, and finally, hospital clothes. She is a sight. To me, a wonderful sight, but nonetheless a sight.

Staring at her with much amusement, the physical therapist comes in with a walker. "Okay Anna. It is time for you to get out of bed and take a stroll around the floor," he says. I know she will need assistance. Her balance is still off. Immediately her teammates jump up and prepare themselves to help her walk the floor. I am not so sure about this. It worries me to have her toddle around without professional assistance. I look at the therapist. He sees my concern and explains to the girls how to support her and keep her safe. We strap her up and give her the walker. She does pretty well, but sways to her left side. Her teammates quickly realize her limitations and move in close to flank her and keep her from falling. This experience silently lets them know Anna will not be playing basketball anytime soon, if ever again. While they are still laughing at the sight of this tiara-wearing girl cruising around in a walker, I imagine there is sadness and confusion in their hearts right now.

They disappear around the corner and are temporarily out of sight. I'm on alert, listening for their voices. Then I hear them laughing as they make their way up the far side of the floor and back towards the room. This is a lot of work for Anna and now she will give back the walker, take the strap off and get cozy in her bed. She is so happy her friends are here. I am so happy her friends are here, too.

As Anna begins to fade, everyone says their goodbyes. It has been a great day for Anna. Friends are so, so important in life. They hold us up, they guide us, and they keep us sane. Anna is lucky to have so many friends. Before she falls asleep completely, she perks up and wants to call Candice. Candice is in Yakima at a volleyball tournament and Anna wants to wish her good luck and hear her voice. Candice is a good gal. Anna calls Candice and leaves a message. She is sure Candice is in the middle of a game.

Greg leaves for home. Ann, Teensie and I relax in the room and watch Anna sleep. Lisa comes by to sit with us. Deb Fly comes in to check on Anna and on me. We look at tonight's dinner menu. They will be having leftovers tonight, as well as other foods that have arrived from people not on the dinner train. Plenty of food. My sisters also want to do some cleaning. Okay by me! And some more dog training. Yes!

The latter part of the afternoon is calmer, yet still busy. I look up and see Jeff Hale sneaking in for a visit. He has a large plastic container of red licorice tucked under his left arm, a treat for Anna.

"Hi," whispers Jeff, which is not easy because Jeff's voice is very boisterous and fun, "I contacted the flight crew at Airlift Northwest that had transported Anna. I know the nurses. They're the same nurses I used to fly with when I worked there. They wanted to know how Anna was doing. I gave them an update and told them I would be visiting Anna today." What a great guy. I ask Jeff for their address and promise him I will send them an update when we get our lives pulled back together. Jeff says, "They would love that. They don't always know what happens to their rescued patients and knowing they were part of a positive outcome is always welcome and appreciated." I talk to him about his Huge airport run and thank him again as we all break out in laughter. Jeff starts laughing. He's so funny. "Well," he says, "I gotta go. Tell Anna hi when she wakes up and tell Greg I'll talk to him later." Jeff walks out of the room leaving us staring at this gigantic container of red licorice.

Anna is exhausted from all the activity and is weaving in and out of sleep. She is starting to get more calls and drop-in visitors. Greg had written on yesterday's blog that she is ready for visitors, can't wait to get home, and she is very excited to get back to school. This signals everyone, both kids and adults alike that she is improving and it is a good time to visit. Lots of people have been waiting to come to the hospital and love on her. It is healing for Anna and our family to see people. Every mom that walks in, delivering their child to Anna, has the same gut wrenching picture. Andy Bang's dad said it best. He said "This is every parent's worst nightmare." He is right, but it is also every parent's biggest thanks to God. Max and Anna lived.

Anna perks up as soon as he walks in. Max. He's here. This is the first time he has seen her since the emergency room. He smiles. She smiles. They hug. He sits next to her on the bed and they start chatting about random things. Has she heard from Candice and how is the tournament going? Who has come in to see her? What else does she know? All of these conversations are similar to their conversations at home, at least the ones I am privy to. Max is at ease and I see in his eyes he is relieved and glad to see she is improving. It is obvious to see she is not her old self, but compared to what he saw at the accident, this is prayers answered and hope on the horizon.

It is dinner time and everyone is hungry. Greg, Max, Lisa, and the aunts are gearing up to go home. Before they leave, Anna's dinner arrives. It is meatloaf. As she is devouring her dinner, she says "I don't like meatloaf." Of course, her plate is practically licked clean by the time she is done. It is so funny to see her eat. She has no manners to speak of and eats everything put in front of her. It sure would be nice if she would eat everything when we get home. We are not sure when that will be. All we know is that we are still leaving for Anna's rehabilitation at Children's Hospital in two days. The transport ambulance is set and we will be leaving at 10:00 am Monday morning. I am looking forward to this for Anna and the beginning of her rehabilitation. She will have her own room with her own bathroom. I have also heard that the beds are bigger and more comfortable for us extras. Yay!

Everyone gives hugs and kisses, then leaves. It has been our best day yet and we are all excited. Anna and I settle in for a great night's sleep after a terrific day of friends and family. We should sleep well tonight. Every night gets easier for Anna. She's used to wearing her neck brace and finds a comfortable position to rest. She falls asleep so quickly. I just stare at her, thanking God she's alive and here with me.

Sunday. Early. They are coming. I hear the loud rhythm of their shoes clapping against the floor. I pop out of bed. They are satisfied with her progress. They leave. I get back in bed. There's a little more sleep to be had.

The sun rises as we slowly awake. Our Sunday begins with a visit from the nurse. She checks Anna's IV and talks to Anna about how she feels and if she is comfortable. We briefly discuss Anna leaving for Children's Hospital tomorrow. The nurses are going to miss Anna. Harborview is a public hospital and heals people from all walks of life. Anna is a happy teenager with a bright future. The nursing staff has enjoyed Anna. She is constantly surrounded by happy people and laughter. She brightens everyone's day. The nurses have been great to Anna and our family.

This morning Anna is getting another shower. Our nurse comes in and puts Anna's belt around her waist and gently guides her towards the bathroom for a good body scrub and hair wash. For a brief moment, I feel no responsibility. Looking around the room, I see the mess. The room is easily cluttered because it is so small. While the shower is running, I put chairs away, fold up my bed and pick up Anna's belongings. Not much different from home! I sit down to gather my thoughts. Today will be another fun day for Anna with lots of friends and family coming by. Sunday is a good day to visit because most people have a little free time. It will be great to see all the visitors and watch Anna heal in their company.

One visitor we will not have today is Max. Greg just called to remind us that Cedar Park is playing in their high school fall league games this weekend and Max is going to the game today. He will sit on the bench, be part of the team and support Coach Franklin. He can't play because of the stitches in his hand and I'm sure this will drive him crazy. But, Max is excited because the Cedar Park boys won two games yesterday, beating two 4A teams. This is quite an accomplishment for our 1A team. Greg says Max is thrilled. Our boys are really good this year and it would be a great ending to Max's high school career if we made it to State. How fun!

Basketball season in our family is always something to look forward to. I'm the team mom for both kids' teams. We have a group of volunteer moms that prepare pre-game dinners, bus-snacks for away games and take shifts selling tickets to the games. We also scream a lot in support of the teams during their games. It's fun and it consumes hours of time every day for months. The only one who doesn't particularly like it is Sammy. He rides in the car and sleeps in the car for hours on end. The single thing he is happy about is that he is with his family, although he would much rather be playing ball at home. Basketball season is not his favorite time of the school year. Oh well.

Greg arrives without my sisters. They have stayed at home. Ann and Teensie are going to clean the house, train Sammy on his front door greeting manners, and organize the newest arrivals of food and gifts. This afternoon they will receive Pesto Pasta Casserole and salad. They are doing what they do best. They are taking care of a family, my family. Neither one of them can believe what so many people have done. They are still surprised by the constant stream of generosity. The goodness continues.

"Hamburger" is going through my mind when the physical therapist casually strolls into the room to take Anna on a walk around the floor with her walker. He looks at her, smiles, says, "Let's get you belted up and go for a walk. Two laps today." This ought to be funny. One lap was a big deal yesterday.

So, all belted up, she wobbles her way to the walker. One thing I will say about Anna is that she has always been a hard worker. If she takes responsibility for a job, I know she will work hard and give it 100% of her effort. Her recovery is no exception. I can see in her eyes, she is only accepting one outcome: complete recovery. She grabs the walker with determination and with the help of her physical therapist Anna takes charge of the floor. She veers a bit coming out of the shoot and she is a little slow, but like the race horse Seabiscuit, she knows who her competition is (in this case, herself) and she is determined to win. The wheels of her walker squeak as they roll across the linoleum, slowly passing the doorways to patient rooms and storage areas, skirting the outside of the nurses' station at the end of the hall and rounding the outside corner to head down the home stretch. Here she comes, smiling and laughing as she struggles to keep her stride and balance. As she pulls up to her door, she looks up, says hi and heads down the hall for lap number two. With her therapist at her side, she continues to stay upright and fights to gain control of her body. She finishes lap number two and glides into her room, tired but happy to have been out and about. Anna falls into bed. She is exhausted. Success.

Greg and I oversee her nap and talk about lunch. Hamburger for me. Greg thinks this is funny as he leaves for the cafeteria. Anna wakes up from her brief nap when her lunch arrives. While she is inhaling her food, the friends start pouring in. Since only a few of these kids can drive, we get to see their parents, too. I love this because, as a parent, I know they are worried for Anna and for their own child. It is a good opportunity for them to see Anna. I think both kids and parents must come in here, take one look at Anna and wonder if she will ever be the same. It's scary. It is also a great opportunity to explain to the parents what is really going on with Anna and her injuries and, in turn, they can reassure their own kids. The more accurate the information, the better off it will be for Anna when she returns to school. Everyone feels better and has the correct information. I need to protect Anna from rumors. I am her mom.

Greg comes back with my hamburger and I have to guard it from hungry eyes. Kids everywhere. I keep telling them to go to the cafeteria and get their own. They just laugh as more kids flow into the room, excited to see Anna. The party continues with visits from relatives, our friends, Anna's friends, and teachers. Amazing as it is, Anna continues to stay awake as people come in to see her and call to talk to her. She is getting stronger while her friends are praying for her, and entertaining her through her recovery. She loves every minute of this.

As the afternoon winds down, and the room clears out, we are tired. Anna has had a wonderful day and is exhausted. Greg is leaving for home and has a fleeting opportunity to hug her and tell her he loves her, before she slips into a deep sleep. He says he will write on the blog tonight that "this has been a great day for Anna."

It's late afternoon and while Anna is sleeping, I think I will look at one of my magazines. I love magazines. They give me ideas for my home and my life. I have about seven subscriptions, all concerning home and gardening and they are a respite for me. Like comfort food. I love to see them lying around the house. I love the smell of the pages, the sound of the paper as each page is turned and most importantly, how they make me feel. I keep them organized at home and often refer to back issues. I actually pull out past issues during the holidays and set them around for people to enjoy. To read one of my magazines from home is comforting and reminds me that when all the hospital stays are finished, we have a great house to go home to and a great life to rejoin. Just seeing my magazines stirs up feelings of relaxation and happiness, both good things, particularly now. I sit back and flip open the cover.

Anna sleeps soundly. I look up and see Candice and Debbie Whipple tip toe into the room. Candice is back from the volleyball tournament. We talk softly and wait for Anna to wake up. Her dinner will be here in a little while and she will certainly wake up for that. Candice is very tired but wanted to see Anna again. I tell Candice the next time she sees Anna it will be at Children's Hospital and that she is being moved there tomorrow morning. Candice and Debbie nod. Debbie is so great. She just sits and relaxes in a chair in the room. No hurry, no pressure. We are all slowing down and letting the pace of the past few days melt away while we watch Anna sleep.

Within minutes we hear the dinner cart rattling towards the room. Anna begins to stir. She wakes, blinks and lets her eyes adjust as she peers at Candice. Big smile. Anna pulls herself up and says, "Hi, Candice." She knows who Candice is and starts telling Candice who came to visit today. She remembers. Not everyone, but she remembers. This is a milestone. This is great. I can't wait to tell Greg. This is the first sign her memory is coming back. This is big. I can't wait; I call Greg. We are both elated.

With Candice by her side, Anna gobbles down her dinner. Debbie and I sit comfortably and talk about the tournament, school, and the girls. I haven't spent much time with Debbie and am glad to have the opportunity to visit with her. She is calming and giving. Debbie makes me feel very relaxed. We watch the girls. They're so funny sitting there talking about their lives. It's almost as though nothing has happened. I think Candice can see the improvement in Anna since her last visit when Anna had her confused with Amie. This must make Candice feel better. Anna is improving.

Candice has got to be tired. In the last several days, there has been a death in her family, her dear friend Anna has been in a serious car accident and she has played in a volleyball tournament across the state. That's exhausting. As relaxing as it seems while we sit and visit, this has been a very big week for all of us. Each of us is tired.

Candice glances at Debbie and tells her mom, "I need to get home to do homework and get ready for school tomorrow." Before they leave, Candice throws lamby over Anna. I hug Candice and see the smile on her face that tells me she's not so afraid anymore. She sees Anna is improving.

Anna falls asleep immediately. She's out for the night. I read my magazine for a short while, before finally turning out my light. I say a prayer and thank God for His help. Today was just the beginning of the rest of our journey and I am glad to have seen so much hope. Tomorrow we go to Children's Hospital. Rehabilitation here we come!

Chapter Seven

"May God continue to bless your family with His care and His love"
— Pastor Mark and Dee Lieske

I beat them. I'm up and waiting for them as they march through the door and gather around Anna's hospital bed. Every day they have come in with commotion, charts, and stares. Today, they come in with huge smiles and very happy faces. The lead doctor is smiling so broadly that I am amazed at his beautiful white teeth and how different he looks when he smiles. I can see that they are pleased with Anna's progress and really happy about her graduation to Children's Hospital. For the first time, they offer conversation and make sure I understand that Anna is on the road to recovery, telling me, "We have done all we can do for her." Seriously, they are delighted. Of course, this delights me. Anna is sound asleep as they look at her, say their goodbyes and leave the room, still smiling. It must feel good for these dedicated doctors, with all the broken bodies they see, to be able to smile and deliver good news. I am thankful for them.

The sun is peeking through the blinds and I open them, ever so slightly, to let in a little light. Anna is beginning to stir. Today is going to be a big day for all of us and I would like to get a head start on preparing her for the transfer to Children's. Our shift nurse walks quietly into our room. Anna's head pops up and she studies the nurse for a moment and then says, "Hi." Our nurses have been fabulous. They love Anna and have always been available for her. They have seen how Anna is surrounded by family and friends who love her. I imagine these nurses take excellent care of anyone that is put in their care, but to see the constant stream of family and friends tells them Anna is a great kid who is loved by many people. Love is a powerful tool. Love speaks without uttering one audible sound.

Our nurse looks at Anna, "Hi Anna, is there anything you want before you leave today?" Oh boy, I can see the wheels turning as she thinks for a minute.

"Well," Anna says, "is there anybody who can do French braids?" I laugh at this request. Anna's hair has been bloodied, braided, washed, braided and washed again.

"Yes," says our nurse, "as a matter of fact, there is someone who is quite good at French braids, and she knows all about basketball. Let me go see if she is available." Out walks our nurse as Anna's eyes light up with interest. We decide to pack up while we wait for Anna's mystery person to come to the room and braid her hair. Even though we have only been at Harborview for six days, we have clothes and personal belongings strewn all over the room.

I am just about done scrounging around the room and the bathroom when in walks this tall, beautiful black woman. She has a broad, wonderful smile. I immediately like her. Her presence fills the room with a quiet sense of strength and confidence. She introduces herself to both of us and tells us she is a nurse from the burn unit as well as a varsity girls basketball coach for one of Seattle's public high schools. She carefully sits down on Anna's bed and says, "I understand there is someone in here that wants French braids."

Anna's eyes are dancing as she smiles and says, "I do."

"Okay," says the nurse. She wants to know exactly how Anna wants her hair braided and then sits Anna carefully on the end of the hospital bed, minding the neck brace, and begins braiding. They talk about basketball and being a nurse in the burn unit as she braids Anna's hair. What a moment. This is really exciting for Anna and I am sure she is going to want to call her dad about the lady who braided her hair. Greg is always up for a little basketball talk.

She's doing a beautiful job on Anna's hair. Anna looks in the hand-held mirror and says thank you to her new friend. "I have to go back to work now," the nurse declares. As she bids us goodbye, she wishes Anna well and walks out the door.

Anna looks so young in her new braids. She wants to be such a grown up, yet she still looks like a little girl. I realize the time will come when I will look at her as a young woman, but for today, I see her as my baby girl. Anna sets the mirror down and declares she is very happy with her new do. It makes her feel good about herself at this time of confusion and change. She decides she should put on a little makeup today. Never know who you might run into on the way to the hospital! She will be lookin' good in the ambulance.

At 10:00 am sharp, two men knock on our open door and cruise in with a gurney. "Okay," I say to Anna, "Here we go!" The two guys are smiling and relaxed as they load Anna up and walk out the door. I grab our luggage and turn around for one last look at our room. A lot has happened here in a short period of time. Good things. Anna's roommate is sleeping. I whisper goodbye and close the door.

The ride is uneventful. Thank you. I sit in the front cab with the driver and Anna rides on the gurney in the back with the second attendant. I wonder if she will remember any of this. She has remembered some of her visitors, but not all parts of her days. It is certainly interesting to watch how her brain is healing and working.

Arriving at Children's, the ambulance pulls into a garage to unload us. This garage is for the use of ambulances and special arrivals only. You would never even notice this garage if you didn't have to come here. There is a special entrance for patients in their transport vehicles. While the attendants unload Anna, I grab our belongings. It occurs to me that we are now part of a group of people who have seen these special entrances and back halls reserved for patients. As amazing as these hospitals are, I pray we never arrive this way again.

Everything is so organized. Greg is waiting for us and we are going to the Train Wing. I have been in Children's before, but today I'm looking at it through different eyes. I notice all the fun colors on the walls and the beautiful artwork. There are colored lines on walls and floors to lead you to your destination. Sections are broken out by colors and objects. Children's Hospital is beautiful. For everything that goes on here, the building maintains a feeling of warmth and comfort.

We arrive at room #3143. There's a sign on the door that says Anna Brown. She likes that. It reminds her of her own room at home. When she and Max were little, I had their names hand painted on their bedroom doors. Anna's name looks like it is written with a pink ribbon. There are flowers and vines weaving around the first A and the last a of her name. It's fabulous. On Max's door, we went for the lodge look. In keeping with the same idea, the first and last letters in Max's name are flanked by perfectly detailed pinecones. There are antlered moose heads on top of each point in the letter M. Even though we've had to repaint the doors, the area surrounding their names remains untouched. Seeing Anna's name on her door at Children's feels one step closer to being home.

"Oh my gosh! This room is huge," I blurt out. The head of Anna's bed is up against the right wall in the middle of the room surrounded by all sorts of electrical outlets, wire metal baskets, lights, and assorted hospital details. The sink is also on the right as you walk into the room. The bathroom is on the left, with a sink, toilet, and shower inside. Just past the bathroom is a closet unit connected to a counter top with cabinets above and below. Lots of storage space. My twin size pull-out chair bed is on the far-right end of the room in a little nook area surrounded by large windows. There is a rocking chair next to my chair bed. These rooms are set up for one patient per room and one pull-out bed for a family member staying with the patient. Children's has done a great job of making their patients feel comfortable in these rooms. I can see that the room is prepared for any medical emergency, but the overall feel is calm and inviting and I am looking forward to staying here with my baby girl.

Anna is placed in her bed. She snuggles down with lamby and falls asleep. Greg and I hang up her clothes and put the rest of her things in the drawers. She has a collection of wonderful cards from friends, family, and our church. We set them up on the counter for her to see when she wakes up. There are also two envelopes full of well wishes and drawings. One from the Sunday School kids at our church and one from the youth group at our neighbor's church. Anna has not seen them yet. She will love them. They are all so fun, drawn and colored with lots of bright colors, stick figures and misspelled words. They're perfect.

Greg and I have just finished moving in when we hear a light knock on the door. "Hi, I'm Dr. Crew. I'm the resident that will be working with Anna," he says. Anna is sleeping when he taps her on the chest to wake her. She isn't very happy about this and Dr. Crew gets an immediate dose of her displeasure. He is young, handsome, and unfazed by her crankiness. Good. "Hi Anna, I'm Dr. Crew." He gets no reply, just a cranky stare from our darling daughter. Dr. Crew immediately launches into Anna's schedule, "Today at noon, Anna will meet her therapists. She will have an occupational, physical, and speech therapist as well as an educational liaison and hospital representative. Oh, and she will also have a psychologist, nutritionist, and recreational therapist watching over her." Wow. He looks at Anna and says, "You can rest for a bit longer, but you must be ready to start meeting with your therapists at noon." Anna, obviously not thrilled, says okay, as she cuddles up with lamby and drifts back to sleep.

At twelve o'clock sharp, the back to back meetings begin. Her first therapist explains to us that every day the occupational, speech, and physical therapists will come to the room to pick Anna up and take her to her therapy sessions. When they are done, they will bring her back to the room where she will wait for her next therapist. She will meet the others involved in her case at various times throughout her stay at Children's. Anna will be given a schedule of her appointments so she will know every day what time each of her therapies are. Today, each of the therapists will introduce themselves and explain to us what their individual therapies will do. Then they'll take Anna for a short therapy session. Greg and I nod in understanding. They have this down to a science.

To get Anna ready for her first session, the therapist sits Anna up and places the guide belt around her waist. They toddle off to begin her journey on the road to rehabilitation. Greg and I continue to put her personal things away and set up her room while she is gone. We are so glad she is in safe hands because it gives us a moment to take a breath. It is another moment without fear, knowing she is safe and working towards regaining her life back. It feels good. I actually feel a little relaxed and very comfortable.

Within thirty minutes, Anna is returned to the room and placed in bed, with her guide belt on, to wait for her next therapist to arrive. She snuggles down into her bed and falls asleep immediately. I am sure she can only rest a moment or two, but she is exhausted and is asleep before her head touches the pillow. I've never seen anything like it. When the next therapist comes in to get Anna, she explains to us what the therapy does as she taps Anna on the chest to wake her up. Anna gets up slowly and again, toddles off with her therapist. When they return, Anna is placed in her bed and falls asleep instantly, only to be tapped on the chest for the last time, to wake her for her final session. By the end of the third session, Anna is so exhausted from today's activities, the therapist puts her in bed and out she goes. All of the therapists are women and all of them are incredibly kind and supportive. The third therapist shows us the rehabilitation journal that was given to Anna. It has her name on it, pictures and names of all her therapists and support personnel, as well as a schedule of tomorrow's appointments. Every day Anna will write down the following day's therapy times in her journal and the therapists will make notes about her progress. Part of her therapy is to keep the journal updated with the appointment times and type of therapy. As I look at tomorrow's schedule, I see she is going to be one busy girl. I hope this journal will help her to focus and force her to use her memory.

With all of her sessions finished for the day, we get good news! Every one of her therapists reports that she did a great job and they anticipate she will only need to be in rehabilitation at Children's for maybe a week. But, we won't know for sure until this Thursday. That's when we have a meeting with all of the therapists and doctors to hear what their decisions and recommendations are for Anna, based on her progress and their evaluations over the next few days. None the less, this is exciting and positive news. Looking over at my sleeping baby girl, I am proud of her. She has always been feisty and determined to do what she wants. Anna possesses the perfect trait for this situation. She is going to have to work hard and stay focused. Who says God doesn't have a plan?

After an hour or so, Anna starts to emerge from her deep sleep. She's hungry. I should have known. The hospital representative had told us earlier about everything available to us in the hospital, including a kitchen with healthy snacks across from Anna's room. It is for the patients and parents in the rehabilitation unit. I walk over and am amazed by what I find. The refrigerator is fully stocked with individual milks, yogurts, cheese, fruits, and snacks. The cupboards have cereals, breads, protein bars, peanut butter, jelly, eating utensils, and an assortment of yummy treats. How fun! I pick out some yogurt and cheese for Anna and cross back to our room. It is so quiet on this floor. I have not seen any other parents or patients. I have heard noises coming from other rooms, but not actually seen a person. Perhaps we should take a little stroll around the unit after Anna is done with her snack.

As I give her the yogurt and cheese snack, I tell her about everything in the kitchen. She is very excited, particularly because it is right across the hall and this girl loves her snacks! I can see the wheels turning--midnight food!

While I watch her eat her snack, I notice she looks better after her nap. She was pretty wiped out from the ambulance ride and the therapies. When I ask her about the ambulance ride from Harborview to Children's, she doesn't remember it. She doesn't remember the ambulance ride at all.

Before I have a moment to be discouraged, her room phone rings. Anna picks up. It is the security officer at the entrance to the rehabilitation unit. Some of Anna's friends are here for a visit. They must have come straight from school. The officer names each person specifically and wants to know if it is okay for them to come to the room. "Of course!" she says, thrilled to have visitors. Immediately her energy level has increased and she is ready to party. Friends are great.

A group of girls from school come into the room smiling and laughing. Their arms are loaded with gifts, get well signs and assorted treats for Anna. After a few minutes of high-pitched shrieking, hugging, laughing and joking, they settle onto Anna's bed to discuss the latest school gossip and fill Anna in on all the important news she may need. They forget that Greg and I are in the room and talk wildly about what is going on at school and who is dating who. Honestly, these girls are a riot. They are all talking at the same time, interrupting each other, drawing in shallow breaths of surprise, and laughing. Now this is entertainment.

Finally realizing they have got to find places for all the assorted stuff they brought, the girls patrol the room searching for spaces to display the candy, signs, and stuffed animals. The signs go up on the wall where Anna can see them every morning when she wakes up. The stuffed animals are carefully placed in a wire basket hanging from the wall next to the head of Anna's bed and the candy is strategically placed in a dish on the middle of the countertop for all to share. When they have put their finishing touches on the room and they think it looks perfect, we decide this would be a great time for Anna to go for her first stroll around the floor.

I gather Anna's guide belt, wrap it around her waist and tighten it. A couple of the girls haven't seen the belt yet and don't fully understand why Anna is wearing it or what it is for. So, I explain the purpose of the belt and show them how we hold onto the belt to help Anna stay balanced and to catch her if she veers off to one side. This is hard for all of them, even the ones who saw Anna at Harborview. When the girls arrived today, they came into the room and saw their friend sitting on her bed. At that moment, she appeared to be her normal self. They laughed together and talked about familiar things. While preparing Anna for her stroll, they see she is unable to walk without assistance and that she struggles to maintain her balance. The reality of the car accident and the severity of Anna's injuries have just become part of their world. Fear. They are scared.

Greg goes on the walk with the girls and I stay behind in the room. As they walk out through the door in a cluster, I see that everyone is walking closely together, supporting Anna both physically and mentally. We are so blessed to have Anna's friends in our lives. They are making a difference in her recovery. They have volunteered themselves by helping another person and taken a step away from self-concerns. They don't realize what a positive impact they are having on our whole family.

The walk around the floor is not long. When they get back, they are laughing about something Anna did. This is not surprising. The girls can't wait to tell me, and I'm sure a few other people, about their adventure. Greg looks quite amused. "So," I ask, "what happened?" Apparently, they witnessed a little bit of the disinhibited behavior from Anna. Nothing major, they say, but nonetheless, funny. When they left our room, they wobbled by the reception desk in the rehab area, making sure to have a conversation with the receptionist of course, then continued on past many of the patient rooms, past the wall with the white board listing each patient's daily therapy schedules, and finally heading down the home stretch, past the snack room and into Anna's room. At some point, which is unclear, they walked by the security guard. At this particular moment, Anna asks the girls, "Where are all the boys?" The security guard overhears this and obviously thinks Anna's comment is quite funny. Here is this teenage girl with a guide belt on, surrounded by her dad and her girlfriends, out for a stroll and she wants to know where the boys are. With his quick wit, he replies, "They're coming." All the girls, including Anna, laugh because they know Anna likes boys! While they are telling me this story, they burst out laughing all over again when they get to the part about the security guard.

What a day. As the sun begins to disappear, the girls are getting ready to leave and we are tired. They have school tomorrow and for us, a lot has happened today with Anna, and we want to call Max. Today was his first day back to school since the accident. I'm sure he was a little nervous. Max doesn't like to call attention to himself. And I bet he didn't want to answer any questions. I look over at Anna. Her friends are walking out the door and her eyes are closing as she snuggles up with her lamby.

Before we call home, we look at Anna's rehabilitation journal and see that tomorrow she will be busy with therapy from 9:30 am until after 2:00 pm. One of the fun things we see on the list, is pool time, and the pool is 93 degrees. Anna enjoys swimming and the pool is part of her physical therapy treatment. She is going to love that! We also realize Greg will have to bring her bathing suit in the morning. Otherwise, she will have nothing to swim in. Details. Better start a list.

Greg says, "Let's call Maxie." He picks up his cellphone and dials our home number.

One of the aunts answers and tells Greg, "Max is resting, but, hang on a minute and I'll go get him."

We wait a minute and then we hear a groggy "Hello,"

Greg says, "How was school today?" Max starts by saying that school went pretty well. As the story unfolds, we find that not only did he have a great experience at school today, but he is talking freely and comfortably about his day. This is a lot of information for Max to give us. It beats the heck out of "Fine, everything was fine." Apparently, the high school kids had made a giant Welcome Back sign and most all of them had signed it. The school's video production class made a videotape of well wishes from the students, for Max and Anna and gave Max a copy to keep.

He said, "No one really asked me any questions about the accident." We gather that both teachers and students just loved on him all day. I suspect Brad and Josh protected him throughout the day. Probably wouldn't let many people talk to him. I can just see them flanking him as they walked through the halls from class to class. Three good friends. Two making sure one was safe.

Max is also very excited about a last-minute trip he's been invited to go on with the Allens. Normally, Max goes nowhere during basketball season, concentrating on games and practices. But, since he can't play or practice yet, and we have some pretty unusual circumstances, it might be a good idea for him to take a long weekend and go. He says he has Coach's blessing and wants to know if we will let him go. We don't have much time to decide and we know the Allens will take good care of him. He needs a little healing and relaxation. "Yes." we tell him. There's no better place to lift his spirits than to spend the weekend with Brad at Disney World in Orlando. The happiest place on earth. Right? Right.

Max isn't leaving until late Wednesday night, so he wants us to tell Anna he will come by tomorrow after school to see her. She will be thrilled. Max sounds good. I am so happy and relieved. One down.

No sooner do we say our goodbyes and our I love yous to Max, when the room phone rings. It is the security guard again. He says there are a bunch of Anna's friends and their parents here for a visit. "Send 'em back!" we tell the guard. Greg taps Anna on the chest and tells her she has a bunch of people here to see her. She promptly sits herself up, neck brace and all, and readies herself for her friends.

Friends are important to Anna. She is one of the most social beings I know. Of course, she comes by this trait naturally. My dad has always been very social. Dad is fun. He has lots of friends and business acquaintances. At one point, I think he knew everyone in Las Vegas. Really. I've never heard of anyone who didn't like my dad. When we were growing up he was very involved with a local charity and the Rotary Club. He had actually been the president of his Rotary Club. He's very outgoing and has a very big personality. While his ability to go out socially has changed because of the Alzheimer's, he is still one of the most likeable people I know. Just like Anna.

When I look up, there are kids and parents streaming through the door. As the last body is finally in the room, I count fourteen people. They are filling every space available. They are all over the room. On her bed, leaning against the countertop, sitting in chairs, propped up against walls. Most of the kids are from her soccer team and a few more from school. Everyone is mingling and chatting. The parents are so excited to see Anna. They didn't see her when she was in Harborview and this is the first opportunity they have had to visit her. It gives everyone a chance to witness her recovery. It's like a party. Our room is a loud, joyful place.

Before we know it, it's dinnertime and Anna's meal comes rolling through the door on the white cart. Immediately everyone's hungry. The group begins to disperse, all of them going home for their own dinner and family time. How wonderful this has been for Anna, the kids, and all of us parents. Greg and I thank them all for coming to visit and they assure us they will be back. We hope so, because visitors make a big difference in a patient's attitude. They feel loved.

Greg and I are pooped. We sit back to relax for a second before Greg updates the blog. Anna is happy. Greg tells her Max is coming by tomorrow to visit her before he leaves for Disney World. She smiles. She can't wait to see him. I think she misses him bugging her and I know Max misses her. She is starting to get tired again and melts back into her bed and her lamby. She's had a great day.

While Greg blogs, I pull out my twin hide a bed and get all my stuff organized. Books, magazines, cellphone, clothes, makeup, towels, and my journal. I wrap the sheets around the bed and Greg finishes his blog and leaves for home. Anna falls asleep and here I sit with my calendar trying to figure out tomorrow. I am beginning to need an outing or I may lose my mind. Ann and Teensie are going home on Wednesday. I call Lisa and ask her if she can come over tomorrow around lunch time and bring my sisters. While Anna spends the day in therapy sessions, I would like to take them out to lunch as a thank you for all of their help. Lisa has left the day open, no surprise there, and will be over around noon. We will go to University Village for lunch. I know the perfect restaurant. Italian. Yum. Perfect. I pick up my magazine and nod off. This has been another big day. Thank you.

Chapter Eight

"As you know, prayers work!!!!"
— Bev and Alden Harris

"Go to Hell." These words hang in the air as my smile fades and worry works its way into my heart and head. I know. Disinhibited. I know. But when your fifteen-year-old daughter, who knows better, tells you to go to Hell, it's alarming.

It's only our second day here. Tuesday morning. We are standing in the bathroom and I'm helping Anna get ready for her day of therapy appointments. She is still wobbly and needs help with her balance. If she falls in here and hits her head, that could cause more trauma and possibly permanent damage. All she really wants is her privacy and her life back. Instead, she gets her mom in the bathroom with her. I can understand how she must feel. However, I do have to tell her that she cannot talk to me like that and that her language is completely inappropriate. She doesn't really care right now and we both just want to get through this, so we continue on and get all our business done in the bathroom as quickly as possible. When we step out of the bathroom, Dr. Theresa Massagli is standing in the room, patiently waiting for us. Dr. Massagli is Anna's primary care physician in rehab. Anna walks right past her, wet hair and all, sits down on the bed and begins combing her hair. Nice.

We had briefly met Dr. Massagli yesterday after Anna's physical therapy sessions. She had come in to introduce herself to us and tell us a little bit about Anna's brain injury and rehabilitation. I look at Dr. Massagli, "Anna just told me to go to Hell!"

She smiles and says, "This is the part of her brain that has been damaged and is disinhibited. This is not unusual and Anna will say things that may be completely inappropriate and out of character."

Dr. Massagli's timing is perfect. I need reassurance and Anna needs to hear what is going on with her brain. Even though she is disinhibited, she recognizes she is not right, she is not herself. I also realize that I am starting to take this personally, as though my parenting has not been up to par. It embarrasses me a little bit. When your child says inappropriate things, it's hard to hear. You think you have failed as their navigational beacon. Dr. Massagli assures me that, in Anna's case, it is her traumatic brain injury speaking and both time and rehab will help her. Whew!

9:30 am: Anna's occupational therapist comes in to pick her up for her appointment. Belt on, ready to go. The post therapy report is a good one: vision good; visual perception: age appropriate; visual motor integration and fine motor coordination: more difficult. Anna has some work in front of her. She has always been a hard worker. Thank you.

10:00 am: Speech therapy. Working on cognitive communication and she stuck with it. Nice job. Thank you.

11:00 am: Physical therapy in the pool. Greg arrives with her swimsuit just in the nick of time! After therapy, in walks a wet Anna with her physical therapist. Swimming was hard work for her, but she did well. Thank you.

Into the bathroom she goes, with a little help from her therapist, to dry off and change her clothes. She is starving and ready for lunch. Greg is going to stay with her for lunch and work from the hospital while she is in the rest of her therapy sessions. She should be done around 2:30 pm. Today's the day I get a little break.

It's just about noon when I hear Lisa, Ann and Teensie coming down the hall for our lunch date. I am taking them to Piatti's Italian restaurant at University Village. I love this restaurant and am excited to have lunch with my sisters and Lisa--my first outing! Knowing that Greg is here and Anna is in good hands is the only reason I can leave her and feel good about it. Ann and Teensie are going home tomorrow and this is my last chance to see them and thank them and Lisa for all of their hard work and patience in supporting our family.

Before we leave, everyone sits for a few minutes to catch up on Anna's therapies. They see her wet hair. "Anna. I hear you went swimming," Aunt Teensie says laughing.

Anna looks at her and says, "It was hard and I don't like it! I had a real hard time balancing and that will affect my basketball game."

I don't think she realizes basketball is not an option at this point, but we will wait and see what the doctors have to say on Thursday. I am so glad my sisters have been able to see progress while they've been here. It is really important for them to go home knowing we are going to be okay and that things are moving forward in a positive way. We have all survived and they have played a huge part in making sure everything ran smoothly at home for Greg and Max, while I was concentrating on Anna.

It is a beautiful, sunny fall day and it feels so good to be outside. The restaurant staff is waiting for us as we walk through the doors and are seated at a round table in the middle of the main dining area.

"If you guys want to have a glass of wine, go ahead. I can't right now," I offer. Even though it sounds delicious, I am not ready to be that relaxed and carefree yet. I know we have a road ahead that requires my full attention and I want to be completely available at all times, both mentally and physically.

We all pass on the wine, but certainly not on the bread. Lunch is absolutely delicious. Everyone loves their food. I think we also love the fact that this is an occasion we are overjoyed to be able to celebrate.

Our conversation is lively and fun. Ann and Teensie are anticipating tonight's dinner of chicken parmesan with rice, followed by dessert. It sounds like we have more food at our house than we know what to do with. But, they assure me that it is all being eaten by our family and all of us know that this gift of meals is much appreciated. Teensie is still in heaven over the taste of it all. She reiterates that she is sampling everything to make sure it is alright. Lisa and I laugh at this. We can imagine the trays of food being passed around, with Teensie insisting she try it all first! It's hard for me to believe she could get her hands on any food before Max. There must be a race to the door every time the doorbell rings. And if Teensie and Max are running to the door, I am sure Sammy is wagging his tail right beside them.

We are full. Sitting at the table, filled up by bread and Italian food, we sit back and rest for a bit to digest and relax. We have time to spend together before I need to be back to the hospital and I have one more adventure in mind. There is something I really want Ann and Teensie to see. Lisa and I had already perused most of the local stores in September, including Pottery Barn for their exciting, new fall creations. Ann and Teensie don't live near a Pottery Barn and I know they will really enjoy the merchandise and displays. The store is always warm, inviting and comfortable. Merchandising at its creative best.

We load up, with jackets and purses in tow, and waddle down to Pottery Barn. It is truly a feast for the eyes. Everyone is mesmerized by the look and feel of the store. It calms us and comforts us as we look at pumpkins, pick up treasures, and smell the scents of fall. Just being in the store makes us smile. We stay for as long as we can, but eventually find ourselves winding our way back to Lisa's car, passing by a number of other interesting stores. Before we reach the car, Ann suddenly says, "Wait, I want to go back and buy something I saw. I'll be right back. Teensie come with me."

Off they go leaving Lisa and me standing in the middle of the walkway with me yelling out, "We'll meet you at the car!" They are so funny. I will miss my sisters.

It has been a wonderful afternoon as we stroll back through the halls of Children's, finding our way to Anna's room. She is just returning from her final therapy appointment and she can barely keep her eyelids open. We help her crawl into her bed and tuck her into her blankets and her lamby. Ann and Teensie say their goodbyes and give her big hugs. She smiles, says goodbye and drifts off into a deep sleep.

Greg stands up and quietly whispers, "I have to go home and get some work done there. I will take your sisters home and come back later with Max."

"Okay. That sounds good," I concur. Max leaves on the red-eye tomorrow for Disney World with Brad and his family, and wants to see Anna today and tomorrow before he leaves. This also gives my sisters time to pack and have a little downtime before dinner arrives. Maybe they can have that glass of wine then!

I hug my two sisters and thank them again for everything they have done. They will never know how helpful and secure it has made me feel by having them here. They have taken care of my life while I stay with Anna. They have been amazing. And of course, my friend Lisa has been a godsend. I know we would never have transitioned our lives so smoothly if not for these three women.

"Well, I think I'll stay for a while," Lisa says as she settles comfortably into the little rocking chair and looks at Anna. Good.

"Thank you, Lisa," is all I can say. She has been driving back and forth to the hospitals for a week and we really haven't had time to talk. I thank her for everything she has done. She is tireless. She has her own family to tend to, yet, continues to take care of my family and make sure everything runs smoothly for me. We talk about our kids. We talk about our husbands and laugh at our stories. We talk about our animals. Then we just sit, both of us thanking God for the many miracles He has performed in the last week for my family. Only the closest of friends can be open, comfortable, and silent all at the same time. Lucky.

Too soon the time comes for Lisa to return home. Anna wakes up as

Lisa pulls out her keys and readies herself to go. Lisa silently nods and hugs both Anna and her lamby, which engulfs Anna like a warm cloud. She then gives me a big hug, turns, and walks out the door.

"I'm hungry," flies off of Anna's lips. It's not quite dinner time yet, so I run across the hall to the snack kitchen and get some tasty morsels for her. She gobbles down her snacks and answers her hospital phone. Friends want to come over later and she excitedly says, "YES!" I tell her that Dad and Max are coming soon and Dad is bringing his swimsuit. We haven't told Anna yet, but the therapist thought it would be good for Anna to get in the pool again this afternoon and Greg has volunteered his services. This is fine with me, after our filling Italian lunch, the last thing I want to do is get into a swimsuit!

Anna starts laughing about Dad and his swimsuit. I tell her they are going for a swim and apparently, this is quite amusing to her. "Why?" she wants to know. So, I explain how it helps her motor skills and coordination and she can have fun, too. Well, Anna is always up for fun, and since she will be swimming with her dad, she is ready to go.

When the boys arrive, Max gives Anna a hug and they chat for a while. Then off we all go to watch Anna and Greg swim. The pool is nice and warm as they play a game of Horse. Anna wins. Greg swears he did not let her win. I am not really surprised by this, as Anna is one of the most competitive people I know and she has beaten both of the boys playing Horse in our driveway at home. Playing basketball in the pool is really good for her. She can't fall over, yet she can do what she does best -- shoot. Sounds of laughter and triumphant screams echo off the walls in the enclosed pool room!

By the time we get back to the room, Anna is, once again, exhausted. I help her dry off and she puts on her favorite sweat pants and a tee shirt. She slowly crawls into bed and wraps her lamby around her body. She likes to make sure lamby is touching her face, so she pulls lamby up around her chin and snuggles down in comfort. She looks so peaceful. We are used to seeing the thick white brace around her neck, yet when lamby is pulled up to her face, the neck brace disappears and she looks as though nothing has happened and she has not a care in the world.

The three of us watch her sleep as we quietly chat. This is a great opportunity to check in on Max and see how everything is going for him. He is very happy. His sister is looking good and making great progress, school work and basketball are falling into place, he is being fed amazing foods, his aunts are taking good care of him and, of course, he is going to

Disney World with his best friend. What a life! We are all very blessed.

Next week is Max's birthday. He will be eighteen years old. We have reservations for Max and a group of his friends to go to dinner at Maggianno's Italian-style restaurant. We have really been looking forward to this surprise party for him. He has been completely unaware of the plan because he doesn't like to call any attention to himself or, Heaven forbid, plan ahead! But, Greg and I think we are going to have to cancel the party and I have decided to tell him about it. I want him to know that not only now, but before the accident, we were thinking about his 18th birthday and what that signifies. He is such a great kid and his birthday is now overshadowed by the accident and by our hospital stay. So, I tell him and his reaction is so Max. He smiles and says, "That's okay, I don't really care." I am not sure if I believe him, but sometimes things like this seem to be more important to me than to anyone else. I just want to create fun, loving memories for the kids.

Anna wakes up hungry. She wants to show Max the snack room. Although it is just about dinner time, I am sure Anna will eat all of her dinner and I know Max really wants to see the snack room. Max would probably not go in there by himself. He knows it is primarily for the patients and Max, like me, is a rule follower. We come by this trait naturally. We get it from my dad. Right is right and wrong is wrong. But to be invited to the snack room by a patient makes it perfectly fine to explore the cabinets. He smiles. Out they go and we can hear them talking about the food options as Anna opens and closes cupboards to show Max the selection. Greg and I look at each other and smile. It is great to have them together. Thank you.

They're not quite done with their snacks when dinner arrives. Max gobbles up the rest of his treats and Anna readies herself for her feast. This, of course, makes Greg and Max hungry, so they are ready to drive home for the chicken parmesan and rice dish that awaits them.

Max hugs Anna and tells her, "I'll be back tomorrow after school to see you before I leave for Disney World." Anna wants to go with Max. She loves all things Disney. Both the kids love Disney. I love Disney. Disney movies, Disneyland, Mickey and Minnie, all of it. When they were younger we took them on the Disney Cruise to the Caribbean with three days at Disney World. We all had a blast both on and off the ship. Anna had her whole head braided and loved it. Max won this huge stuffed shark that we had to carry all over the place. The blue and white shark was so big it would not fit in our luggage. Thank goodness, we were able to carry it onto the plane coming home. That shark is still roaming around Max's bedroom with the stuffing falling out and the seams splitting open. But, to this day we still think that was the best vacation we have ever been on. So many great memories. Thank you.

Anna is throwing food into her mouth as the boys walk out the door. I watch her and recap the last week in my mind. We have made a lot of progress and have seen a lot of changes in Anna since we stood in the emergency room with nothing but hope and prayer. She is in a mental and physical battle for her life. The behaviors of being disinhibited creep through my thoughts. Anna has always been very upfront and straightforward. If she thinks it, you are going to hear about it. Being disinhibited, for Anna, takes her conversation to a whole new level. It scares me. I am also worried about the memory loss. Her short-term memory seems to come and go. She can't quite get a hold of it. These fears, along with thanks for the progress we have made, will be in my prayers tonight.

Ahhhh...she is pushing her empty tray away. I smile at her and ask, "How was it?"

Anna looks at me with a big grin and says, "It was okay." Well, it must have been more than okay because she practically licked the plate clean. She slowly slides back down into her bed, pulls lamby up to her face and falls asleep. With all the company she has had, she is surrounded by stuffed animals. She has grabbed one large furry, brown ball of an animal and has curled her body around the softness of her new friend. Sleep, baby girl, and let your body repair itself.

As in all the days before this, I watch her breathe while reading my magazines and making lists of things I need to do and people I need to thank. The list gets longer every day, but I am happy to be here and happy I need to thank people for everything they have done. Both kids are alive. Prayers are being answered and everyone we know, including people we don't know, have been instrumental in the outcome of this accident. Both thankfulness and fear reside in me.

Ring. Ring. Ring. Anna moves around and I jump up to answer the hospital phone. It's the security guard outside the Train floor entrance. Anna has guests and he wants to make sure they can come back. Anna opens her eyes and looks at me just as I tell the guard, "That would be great, send them back." Anna sits up and we fluff her pillows to keep her comfortable and not put too much strain on her neck. It is a nice surprise to see that she is not overly concerned about her appearance.

She is a fifteen-year-old girl after all. Since the first moment she has had visitors, she has not once tried to primp before she saw them. I like that. Anna is a surprise. Sometimes she can't spend enough time in front of the mirror and other times she could care less. Goofy girl.

Anna is all smiles. We can hear them coming through the hallway with their giggles, high-pitched conversation, and lots of shuffling feet. They burst through the door, every one trying to get in at the same time, looking at Anna and maneuvering around her bed for the best seat. Seated or standing, we are thrilled to see each other, passing out hugs and hope. Friends are remedies. Their presence is uplifting for Anna and they bolster her inner strength. Her friends come from different groups in her life. Since we have made her go to church and attend a private Christian school from the 3rd grade on, she now has church friends, public school friends, private school friends, soccer friends, basketball friends, and friends of those friends! It is a huge network of kids and each group is a blessing to see as they come through these hospital doors.

This group happens to be a combination of friends. They all know each other through Anna, and watching them talk, you would think they'd known each other forever. As the conversation's lively beat continues, in walks Mr. Ian from Cedar Park. All the kids love Mr. Ian. He's a great teacher, a strong Christian man and has helped all of them make it through high school math at many different levels. Mr. Ian smiles and gives a quick nod to Anna when he walks in. All the Cedar Park kids say, "Hi Mr. Ian," and are, of course, happy to see him. Mr. Ian leans against the wall and watches the kids. I smile and walk across the room to chat with him. He watches Anna and notices she is better.

He says, "The kids at school have been worried she wasn't going to come back." I am not sure if he means physically or mentally, but I know they have been worried about both of these possibilities. I am really glad Mr. Ian is here. He is the perfect one to calm everyone's nerves and clearly explain to the school how Anna is recovering, thus avoiding misinformation and confusion with her classmates.

Listening to their conversation, I can hear the kids getting a dose of Anna's disinhibited brain. She says slightly inappropriate things to her friends and they think she is hilarious. She actually is pretty funny right now, but this is not something I would want to continue. A job and a career would be very difficult without some sort of filter to stop every thought from entering her conversation. Though I must say, some of today's teen idols appear to have no brain or brain filter at all!

I hear one of her friends ask her how long she will be in the hospital and when will she be able to go home and get back to school. She says, "I don't know." Then loudly, as though I am in another room, she yells, "Mom, how much longer will I be in here?" This is the perfect opportunity for me to let them know we don't have an answer to these questions yet. I tell the kids that we have a meeting on Thursday with Anna's doctors and therapists to figure out what we do next. I also tell them how incredibly well Anna is doing in therapy and how her therapists say they have never met such a motivated patient. This doesn't surprise any of them. They know her well.

The clock ticks on and both the kids and Mr. Ian need to get back home. It sounds like everyone has homework to do and Anna is getting tired. I am tired too, but want to talk to Greg and make sure all is well at home. The kids hug and promise to come back another day as we readjust Anna's pillows and she gently lays her head down. She pulls lamby up around her and I wrap her sheet and blanket round lamby. By the time their footsteps can no longer be heard in the hallway, Anna is asleep. I turn back to look at her and I think to myself, I sure love this girl.

Quietly, I phone Greg to check in and let him know about tonight's visitors and what went on after he and Max left. He is glad to hear that Anna had a great evening with friends and that Mr. Ian stopped by. He is getting ready to write his nightly blog and wants to add tonight's activities to his update. I talk to Max for a few minutes and he sounds good. He is really looking forward to having lots of fun with Brad at Disney World. This will take him away for a few days and allow him to enjoy life and not worry about us, even though I know he is still very worried about Anna.

When Greg comes back on the line, he says, "I want to spend the night with Anna tomorrow night." My heart races. This means I will go home for the night, away from Anna. I haven't been away from her since the accident. Momentary panic sets in. I pause. Then, I come to realize this is also a great opportunity for me to spend time with Max before he leaves for Florida. I can help him get packed, chat with him after school, have dinner with him, and see him off on his Disney vacation. I haven't had a moment alone with Maxie since the accident. I love that boy. Okay, this will work. Plus, I also have to remember that Greg has not spent one night with Anna because he has been taking care Max and everything at home, as well as, working from his home office in the evening. Good plan.

"Okay," I say.

We say goodbye and I love you and plan to talk in the morning. As it stands, Anna's therapies start at 9:30 am and end at 2:30 pm tomorrow. Greg and Max will come by after school to visit, and then I will drive home with Max. Stacey McAllister has volunteered to take the Ann and Teensie to the airport in the morning. What a great help. She's a wonderful person. Many of our neighbors have helped out or volunteered to help us in one way or another. We have a very unique and special neighborhood. Thank you.

As I finish looking at magazines and checking my list, my body tells me I am exhausted. Cellphone off. Lights out. Sleep.

Chapter Nine

"I will be on my knees today praying for Anna and Max"
— Michelle Dufenhorst

It's Wednesday. My mind wakes up before my body is ready. I try to be stealthy as I look at my phone to check the time. It's so early and Anna doesn't need to be up for hours. I don't want to get up and roam the halls because I want to be in the room in case she wakes early. I don't want her to be alone. So, I lie here, contemplating a move to the bathroom or pulling out my mini flashlight that will allow me to peruse my magazines. I decide the bathroom is my best option. I quietly slip out of my little chair bed and tip toe across the room. Anna is oblivious to me as I close the bathroom door and turn on the light. It's cold in here so I hurry. When I get back to bed, the mini flashlight comes out, along with my calendar and notepad that are so neatly stored in my canvas tote. It's not easy to be quiet with paper rustling about, but I am actually doing fairly well. I look at Anna. She is so peaceful and in such a deep sleep. The chances of her waking up are slim, considering she is still taking medication for the pain and swelling. But, nonetheless, I'm as quiet as a church mouse.

Today is the day Ann and Teensie go back home to their own families. Tonight, Max leaves for Disney World and Greg spends the night with Anna. This is also the night I go home to sleep in my own bed for the first time in over a week. I am sure the animals will be thrilled because no one, but no one gives them more attention than I do. I also get to spend some time with Max in the comfort of our own home. That will be nice. There are a lot of new changes happening today which represent forward progress for us. Thank you.

Anna's feet and legs are moving around a tiny bit. She is waking up. The clanging of metal dish pans and rolling wheels can be heard outside our room in the hallway. As the noise gets louder, Anna stirs and opens her eyes. Here comes her breakfast tray. Anna is irritated to have to wake up, but excited about the food. She slowly pushes lamby to the side of the bed and sits up, getting ready for her morning meal. Dr. Crew comes in to check on Anna and review today's therapy schedule. He is very nice to Anna, even though she continues to be a bit testy with him. Therapy starts at 9:30 this morning and ends around 2:30 this afternoon with a little rest and lunch in between. She has a full schedule and a full day.

Anna loves her food and cleans the plate. She drinks her milk, gulps her juice, and licks her lips. That must have been one awesome breakfast. I'm not sure what was on that plate, but whatever it was, it's gone now.

Anna starts to climb out of bed to get dressed and I run over to her with the belt. I quickly cinch her up and help her balance as we head for the bathroom. She hates that she needs help from her mom to get into the bathroom, so I sit her down and give her some privacy. When she's done, I rush back in to steady her. We walk out of the bathroom and get her dressed for the day. She places one leg at a time into her sweatpants and I hold tight to the belt. She is unsteady; but standing. She's doing a great job with her balance and coordination. These tasks are things she has done, and we all do, every day in our lives and think nothing of it. Right here, right now, this is a big deal. I have to sit Anna on her bed, because the belt needs to come off so we can put on a new shirt. Finally, mission accomplished and she is ready for her first therapy session. That will be occupational therapy, then speech therapy and finally, physical therapy. Then she breaks for lunch and at 1:00 pm she starts all over again. Anna will be tired.

While she is gone, I make phone calls to school, home, and friends who want to know how Anna is doing. I am sort of communication central, even though Greg's blog has been a great tool for everyone to follow Anna's daily activities and progress. I still cannot read a book, which has always been a sign that my mind is far too preoccupied with current events, thus unable to relax and focus. It is comforting to talk to friends and family on the phone. Their support has kept me afloat in what I would describe as an endless sea of uncertainty.

The days seem to be moving by at a fast pace. Tomorrow is our meeting with all of the doctors and therapists. We are really looking forward to this because it will be our compass and our guide to Anna's immediate future. Thus far, her therapy reports have been very encouraging and tomorrow is the summation of her progress. Tomorrow we will determine where we go from here. Tomorrow is a very big meeting.

I am sitting in my chair with my pen and paper, trying to prepare questions for the team meeting tomorrow, when the security guard calls. I have a guest. In flies a good family friend, Jan Rood. Jan is married to Marty and they have a set of twin girls that will graduate from high school the same year as Anna. Greg has known Marty since he was a little boy. They have golfed together for decades and have been friends forever. Jan is very upset. She has tears in her eyes as she rushes toward me explaining she just received a call from Marty and knew nothing of the accident. I feel so bad for Jan. She is devastated. I just hug her and tell her about Anna's past week and assure her we are improving every day. I understand how she feels. When you are a parent and you hear about children involved in any accident, you are heartbroken for the family. And when they are children you know, it can be overwhelming. Jan is so worried that she is interfering and says she had to stop by but will not stay because she doesn't want to get in the way of anything. I assure her it's perfectly fine that she's here and explain to her that Anna is in therapy right now. Jan can't even sit down. She wants to know if there is anything she can do, she hugs me and dashes out as quickly as she dashed in. I pick up my pen and paper and make a note to call Jan later and see if she is okay.

My cellphone rings. It is Ann and she is just checking in, letting me know that both she and Teensie are at the airport getting ready to catch their flights home. I thank them again. Ann says, "You're welcome." I make a note to send gifts to my sisters and a thank you note to Stacey for taking them to the airport. My thank you list is getting very long. I smile. I'm grateful there is a need to send so many thank you notes.

Anna comes in from her physical therapy session and plops down on her bed. She is pooped. A little rest until lunch time will help her make it through her therapies this afternoon. She grabs lamby, closes her eyes and out she goes. I just sit in my chair and watch her in between making notes and looking at a magazine. She's my baby girl.

The familiar sound of the lunch cart reaches my ears and I look at my watch to check the time. Anna hears the lunch cart as it approaches her room. She slowly pulls herself up to a sitting position, wanting to make sure she is ready for her meal. I have to laugh to myself about Anna and her newfound affinity for food. I have never seen her love her food so much. Ever since she was a baby, she has been a bit of a finicky eater. Max however, will eat just about anything, and if you tell him how good it is for him, he will eat twice as much. Anna, on the other hand, is only concerned about the taste, regardless of the content. Meals will surely be interesting when we get home. I wonder if we will ever again hear, in her most horrified voice, "What is that?"

Anna finishes her lunch and pushes the cart aside. We have a few minutes to talk, but her eyes are heavy and she looks very tired. I sense she would love to get a little more sleep before her final round of therapies. "If you want to take a quick nap, I will wake you up at 12:45 so you can be ready for your 1:00 occupational therapy," I suggest. She doesn't even answer. Lamby up. Anna out.

When she wakes up there is no arguing about getting dressed and being ready to go. She knows she has to work hard if she is going to get better. We have not discussed basketball, soccer, school or anything about her immediate future. It will be up to the doctors to give us direction for Anna. I personally would like to put her in a bubble, but I do realize that is no way for a person to live their life. It's the mommy in me that wants to protect her from harm.

Her therapist comes to pick her up. On goes the belt and off goes Anna. She told me she was going swimming today and she's not very excited about it. Since physical therapy is her last therapy of the day, I hope when she gets back there are smiles. Her brain is continuing to heal and improve but we still see a lack of filter in her conversation, particularly when she gets frustrated or angry. And who better to take it out on than her mommy?

I decide to walk down to the swimming pool and watch Anna during physical therapy. Purposefully, I have not gone to any of her therapy appointments. I haven't even asked to go. She and her therapists need to work together without me looking anxiously over anyone's shoulder. Anna needs to do this hard work for herself, without worrying about me. I eventually find the pool and quietly sit down on a bench alongside the pool. The room is warm, moist, and typical of an indoor pool. The smell of chlorine is hanging in the air, and noises are bouncing off of the walls. I observe her. When the therapist asks her to do something, she does exactly what they ask her to do and works hard to force her body towards recovery. I can see the determination on her face. I am amazed at her strength and stamina. She looks so strong and alert. She is one tough baby girl.

When the swimming session is over, we walk back to our room with her therapist holding her belt to balance her. We talk on the way up the stairs and her physical therapist says Anna practiced walking on a line, balancing on one foot, dribbling a basketball, maneuvering the soccer ball, and shooting baskets before her swim session today. During which by the way, she swam sixteen laps. She smiles and says, "Anna is doing great." This is so wonderful to hear. Anna laughs.

When we are back in our room I look at today's therapy journal entries. All of the little things that happen to Anna in her sessions are neatly written in the therapy journal Anna keeps. Her memory and body may be trying to reconnect, but her handwriting has been consistently neat throughout her journal. Certainly, the brain is a complex organ. Today's entries also tell me that during occupational therapy Anna counted money, counted change, and calculated change on paper. Anna is in the advanced math class at school and yet, for now she is relearning how to count. Her therapist says she had a nice effort. I'll take that to start.

Her speech therapy is where her memory issues surface. They worked on directions, a deductive reasoning puzzle, comparing and contrasting words, alphabetizing words, definitions for words, and they played the board game Taboo. Her speech therapist said "Anna needed help remembering what we had done today and telling me all of our activities at the end of class." So, there we have it. Retention. But, I thank God that she is alive and I pray she will be completely healed. God is good and I'm certain He is not only with us, but He has never left us.

Anna is starving. Swimming is hard work. Anna turns to me and says, for the first time, "I want to go home." Then she adds, "because it's too much work to stay here." This statement is coming from someone who can accomplish almost anything if she sets her mind to it. I surmise she is fighting her best fight to get better. Anna is not and has never been a quitter. She is assessing the situation and steeling herself for hard work. I am proud of her. I look at my little fighter and let out a little laugh, knowing we are both in this for the long haul.

We go to the snack room for a treat before the boys get here. Anna picks out some yogurt and string cheese. She loves string cheese. And of course, she must have a few crackers to go along with the string cheese. There are also small containers of fruit. Anna picks up one of these and we gather the necessities, a spoon and napkin, and walk back across the hall to Anna's room. She sets her food down on top of the bedside cart and I help her into bed. I roll the cart close to her so she doesn't have to twist and turn to eat her snack and sip her water. It's always great to see her relaxed and awake without too much pain. The pain seems to be getting better and I notice she doesn't want to take too much pain medication. The pills really knock her out. She wants to be more alert and awake. She wants her normal life back.

As soon as she has finished her snack, she wants to rest. Swimming took all of her strength and she curls up with her lamby, once again burying her head into a large stuffed animal. Her eyes close gently and she begins her afternoon nap.

While Anna naps, I start to pack the things I need to take home tonight. I have a few toiletries, clothes, and magazines to take with me, but most everything will stay here. It's only one night, I tell myself. Looking around the room, I see we have become quite comfortable. Shoes, clothes, makeup, purses, magazines. Everything we need for a hospital stay. But it's not home and after Anna's comment, I think both Anna and I are beginning to want to go home. I would live in this room forever if I had to, but thanks to God, that won't be necessary. I think about our meeting with the doctors tomorrow. It will be exciting to hear what they have diagnosed for Anna and for our family. We still have lots of time to pray and I will certainly be doing that.

Here come the boys, softly entering the room. They look at Anna and see this curled up ball with a neck brace, encircled by lamby and a large stuffed animal. Max is quiet, but smiles and gives me a hug. Greg gives me a hug. This has certainly been an interesting time for our marriage. We have both embraced individual roles. I see Greg as the caretaker at home and the one responsible for anything outside of the hospital room that pertains to the well-being of the family. We haven't talked about it, but I am sure he sees me as the one responsible for overseeing Anna and all that pertains to that. Many of the things that may have been important to us two weeks ago, have absolutely no significance today. Our personal schedules, laundry, sports practices, and daily responsibilities have taken a back seat to the well-being of our family. We have been given the ultimate opportunity to see our lives from a different perspective. We have reduced everything in our lives to the things that are most important. Those things are our kids and people. Relationships, family, and living a good life are the most important things we can be involved in. Be positive, be uplifting. Be thankful.

A visiting friend suggested Greg and I may need counseling after this. She said couples have a tendency to drift apart, blame or be angry with each other. The beauty of our situation is that it was so well crafted by God, that there's no reason for us to point a finger at each other. The day of the accident I was pretty much dressed and ready to go when Max called me. Greg was in position in downtown Seattle, near Harborview, when I called him. We tag teamed it. I saw them off at the scene of the accident, and Greg received them when they arrived at Harborview. They were driving my dad's gift to them, their Ford Explorer, a heavy SUV. Because Greg usually worked from home on Tuesdays, they would often drive his Acura to school for easier parking and they frequently gave Brad a ride to school on Tuesdays. That would have put three people in a small car getting hit by a large full-size truck. Someone, if not all of them would have been killed or permanently disabled either mentally or physically. Everyone involved, both parents and kids, would have been unable to recover. Lives and years of friendships would have been destroyed by blame and guilt. Our neighborhood would have become divided. But instead, God created an environment where everyone worked together to help one another. There was no place for blame, only room to pray for the miracle of healing. It was His perfect plan.

A little movement from Anna's bed catches our eyes. Max walks over to the side of the bed and waits patiently for her to wake up. She opens one eye at a time and looks around, seeing Greg first, then me, and finally Max. She smiles and rolls onto her back. Max says, "Scoot over, I'm coming in." Anna gets an approving, little, corner-of-the-mouth smile on her face and moves her body to the edge of the bed, making room for her big brother. Thank goodness there's a guard rail. Why do I worry so much?

Max plops down beside her and they both fold their arms over their chests. It's not good body language, but there is no room for arms when you have two teenagers in a hospital bed. Greg takes a picture of them together in the bed. Anna's expression reads, "Whatever Dad," and Max dons a fake smile. Moment captured. Max lies in bed with Anna and watches TV. They share a little conversation and laughter here and there, but just laying side by side and being next to each other is the best way they know how to comfort themselves. We just hang out as a family until I insist Max and I get going. Max still has to pack and be ready for the airport by 9:00 pm tonight. I check the dinner schedule and discover that this particular night is for leftovers. Max and I decide to pick up freshly made burgers and fries on the way home. Anna is jealous.

Max pops out of bed and gives Anna a big hug. His face tells me he has mixed feelings about leaving her, but it will be great for him to get away. This is a rare opportunity and it certainly came at the perfect time. Thank you.

I hug Greg and Anna and kiss them both goodbye. Again, because this is the first time I have left Anna for an entire night, it's hard to leave her.

I feel very anxious about it and a little nervous, I guess. But, it's exciting to have a few hours of alone time with Max. Every time I've seen him since the accident, there have been other people around. Spending a few hours alone with him, will give me a chance to get a read on him and see how he is doing. This is not always easy with Max. He holds his emotions inside. When he was little, I made up a story about a man with an exploding brain. Max wanted to know if the man's head really blew up. I explained that this particular man was different. He kept everything he felt, from sorrow to joy, in his head. He never told anyone how he felt or if he was upset. When the man got older, he had so many feelings stuffed into his brain that his brain exploded. We couldn't see the explosion, but the man had to go to a doctor to find out how to fix his brain. The man had to let all of those emotions fall out of his brain before he could get healthy again and be better. I repeated the exploding brain story many times throughout the years, often tailoring it to a specific situation. However, Max is hardwired to keep things to himself. So, trying to figure out how he is really doing is not going to be easy. This is why spending the weekend with Brad is a godsend. They talk to each other.

Crossing the bridge to the parking garage is a quiet time. Max and I are hungry and tired. It's dark, it's raining, and it's cold outside. So, we zip up our coats, hold our heads down and make our way to the car as quickly as possible. Once inside the car, we crank up the heat and head home. Max is in good spirits as we cruise towards Kidd Valley, one of our favorite hamburger stands. There is just something about comfort food that gives it the name it rightly deserves--comfort!

Max runs in and gets the burgers while I wait in the car. It is rush hour traffic and once we get the burgers, we make our way back into the bumper to bumper string of car lights and head towards home. This will be great. Home. Of course, Sammy is waiting, along with Belle, Jazz, and Moses. Sammy's tail is flailing from side to side and his body is being led by his tail. We can barely get past him and through the door, when Jazz darts into the house before the door closes. Good heavens.

I feed Sammy, remembering the rule my mom taught me. "Always feed your animals first, as they cannot feed themselves," she would say. By the time we sit down, our hamburgers are lukewarm, but we enjoy every bite. Local burgers, nothing better. Max finishes his dinner and runs upstairs to get packed. He doesn't really need me to help him. As a matter of fact, he would probably shun any help. He needs his space and I certainly don't need to bother him. If he feels like I am asking too many questions, he clams up. Having a relaxed couple of hours at home will be good for both of us. Just being in the house together gives me a sense of normalcy. I clean up our little mess and notice a Pottery Barn bag on the counter. I open the bag, only to discover a rectangular Peacock tray I had admired, along with a note from Ann and Teensie. They left me a gift. That something they had to run back to buy after our lunch date, was a present for me. I love it. I make a mental note to call them later. What a nice surprise. Thank you.

Grabbing my luggage, I start up the stairs to our bedroom. Within a short period of time, Max comes in and we watch a little TV. Not too much is said, but I can see he is relaxed and happy to be going on a little mini vacation. This lets me know he is okay, or at least he is beginning to be okay.

The phone rings. It's Pam. "Hi," she says, "we will be leaving for the airport in about fifteen minutes."

"Okay, Bug," I say, "that was Pam and you need to be ready to go in fifteen minutes." Max gets up off our bed and goes to get his luggage and take care of any last-minute details.

He comes back to my room with a smile on his face and says, "I need money." Typical teenager. Why not wait until the very last minute to check the details? I give Max all of the money I have. When Pam and Brian pull into our driveway, I tell Pam Max has only $50.00 to his name. Pam completely understands and tells me if he needs more money, they will give him some. "Thanks Pam, that would be great," I reply, "We will pay you back whatever we owe you when you guys return."

Pam says, "No problem." The Allens are neighbors everyone would love to have. They are generous and caring people. We are so lucky. Our neighborhood is so lucky.

As I watch the Allens drive off with Max, I stand on the porch in the pouring down rain. I am alone. Well, except for three cats and a dog, two of which stare at me when I come back through the front door. Both Sammy and Jazz look at me as though wanting to know, "Now what?" while Belle and Moses are just glad to know someone is available in case they need anything. God places many things in our lives for a reason. I now know why we have a sweet licky dog that begs for attention and a fabulous cat, Jazz, that needs human contact every moment of every day. I'm not yet sure about Belle and Moses. But, I know all four of them love us. We need them.

It's about 9:10 pm, I call Greg to check in. He says, "Anna is getting ready to go to bed and I am blogging. We are just hanging out watching Anna's favorite TV shows and laughing." Anna loves her daddy and I realize the importance of Greg staying with her tonight. I have the privilege of being in the middle of Anna and Max's lives every day. Sometimes it's overwhelming and Greg comes in for comic relief. With teenagers, it can be exhausting to be the constant anchor at home, yet it's equally hard to let go of that job. I wait for a glimmer of fun. I am fun and sometimes no one seems to know that, except me of course. So, when Greg always gets to be the fun guy, it's a good thing, but it makes me a little jealous. Greg is watching television shows with Anna that I am horrified by. The values, the language, the lifestyles. I want to make comments throughout the whole show, leave a lesson. However, my message is usually lost on the frustration of my children's response to my comments. Being a mom is not easy.

Saying good night is quick and sweet. We are all tired and ready for a good night's sleep. Sam and I fumble around at home for a while, doing laundry and putting things back in order. I talk to him and he looks at me with his all-knowing eyes and his head cocked to one side. He truly is a smart dog and I am sure I would value his opinion if he could communicate it to me. Really.

Finally, it is late enough to get into bed. I do all of the usual things that I have been unable to do, or do comfortably, before I actually get into bed. I take one long, hot shower, scrub my face, brush my teeth, take my vitamins, and finally, snuggle into my warm flannel pajamas. Routine is good. The television goes on. I am trying to divert my attention to a good TV show. I crawl into bed and try to focus on the TV. This is not going to work. I turn the TV and lights off. Lying in bed, I run myself through a relaxation routine. Starting at my toes, I concentrate to relax, while working my way up to my head, waiting as each part of my body relaxes. By the time I get to my head, my toes are tense again, my mind is racing and my eyes will not close. This is going to be a long night. I say a prayer and ask God to help me find some sleep. By the time morning arrives, I realize, I did get a few hours of rest and am thankful for that.

I jump out of bed early and get ready to go back to the hospital. Shower, teeth, hair, necessities, and out the door, but not before feeding the animals and giving Sammy and Jazz some lovies. It feels good to be going back to Anna. At this point, it is best for me to be with her than away from her. Hopefully, the next time I am sleeping at home, she will be in her own bed, at home with the family.

Chapter Ten

"We are thrilled that Anna is progressing well."
— Grace and Eric Brod

Rounding the corner into Anna's room, I let out a sigh of relief. There they are.

"Hi," I blurt out. "Hi," is the short but sweet response. Anna is getting ready to go to therapy and Greg, looking both tired and happy, is helping her pull on her sweat pants and carefully put on her favorite white tee shirt. Her white foam neck collar is temporarily off as the tee shirt slips over her head. He is very careful with her and as soon as the tee shirt is on, Greg immediately puts the neck collar back in place. It looks like she is wearing a short sleeve white turtleneck. She is ready to go.

Doctor Massagli and Anna's occupational therapist walk into the room together. The therapist is here to pick Anna up for her first session. The doctor says, "Anna, I want you to make a list of what you think are your strengths and weaknesses, as well as your goals for your future. You can make your list while you are with your therapist this morning." Dr. Massagli also hands Greg and I a questionnaire to fill out about Anna and what we think are the most important things that the Children's rehab team needs to accomplish while she is here. We will be reviewing all of this information at our meeting this afternoon at 3:00 pm.

As Anna heads out to therapy, Greg and I sit down to fill out our questionnaire. The first question asks if there is anything we want to share that may help them in working with her. We immediately start to list her wonderful character qualities. She is funny, fun, quick witted, competitive, determined, a hard worker, task oriented, stubborn, independent, very social, a good student, and has a great sense of humor. We also write down that she is a Christian, plays basketball and soccer, likes boys and has three cats, one of which is Belle, her cat, and a dog named Sammy.

The answer to the second question -- What are your recovery expectations? -- comes quickly. We expect a 100% recovery. This includes reentry to school as soon as possible, the ability for her to safely function at home (shower, stairs, walking) and to function independently. We want her to leave Children's ready to assume her former life and to be safe in the school and home environment both physically and mentally. These are our goals. We don't think they are too lofty. We have faith.

As we finish our last sentence, Anna comes back from therapy with her occupational therapist and has her questionnaire filled out. She hands us her paper and heads off to therapy with her speech therapist. We look at her list. Under strengths (and things that have gotten easier), she writes eating, taking showers by herself, walking straight, remembering things, pain is better, and she can control her language. Under weaknesses (and things that are still hard), Anna lists balance with fast motions, getting dressed, staying awake, feels weak, and is mean to people. She then listed her final notes as her goals. Anna wrote, "Be normal again, back to school – easy to pay attention, and go on vacation."

As we read through her list, some of it makes me laugh and some of it breaks my heart. I am so thankful she is alive and I will forever be grateful for that. As her mom and someone who loves her more than she can understand right now, I see her struggles as so foreign to most people. The one weakness about being mean to people, I will assume is referring to me, tells me she knows her behavior towards me is, at times, rude. This acknowledgement is good. I am glad she is aware of and remembers her behaviors. Good sign. Having been with her, for the most part, non-stop since the accident, I know the only person she has been mean to is me. Well, maybe Dr. Crew got a little taste of that, too! Overall, we find her list revealing and are glad to know how she feels about her current progress. And, apparently, she wants to go on vacation. Too funny.

Anna won't be back from speech therapy until 11:00 am. Greg looks at his watch and then at me. I know he has work to do and would like to go home for a few hours. We take a moment to call Max and make sure he has arrived safely in Florida and see what he is doing. He sounds great. There's fun in his voice and laughter in his conversation. The flight was good, he slept, and they are at Disney World this very moment and having a blast. Good. All is well with our whole family and everyone is safe at this very second. I welcome this unguarded moment. We are so thankful and happy. Greg and I say our goodbyes to Max and tell him we will talk to him later. He knows about the meeting today, but we have not made a big deal out of it to him. He is too much of a worry wart when it comes to Anna. We hang up and relax for a minute.

"Okay," Greg says, "I have to go home and work, but I will be back at 2:45 or so." Off he goes, leaving quietly before Anna returns.

Sitting down in my chair bed, I look out our windows to see it is pouring rain outside. It's very dark and windy. This is not a great combination in the Pacific Northwest. Together, wind and rain can cause huge trees to fall, power to go out, and forest debris to scatter about the streets and driveways. I say a prayer for Greg to get safely home and back to the hospital this afternoon. The weather for tonight calls for high winds and rain. Yuck. Even though I love living here and love the romance of the rain, coupled with the wind, it is a little scary at times.

I hear my baby girl laughing. She must be done with speech therapy and on her way here to meet her physical therapist. This time, she doesn't even have a moment to rest. Her speech therapist walks her into the room as her physical therapist comes in to pick her up. Anna sighs, realizing there will be no rest until after her third therapy session. She will be back in time for lunch, probably have a small nap and then she will start her therapies all over again at 1:00 pm. Off she goes with her belt and neck brace, both neatly wrapped around her fragile little body.

I peek at the dinner list and see that Greg has a mystery dish coming tonight. A dinner commitment but no dish specified. He will just love that he doesn't have to cook! I am interested to know what the dish will be. All of the food has been enthusiastically welcomed into our home, as well as being fabulous. This is a great break for our family. It's like living in a variety of restaurants. Every night the menu changes, as well as the cook and their style of cooking. This is certainly a welcome treat for all of us. Truth be told, I am not known for my cooking. I have always been more concerned about our food's content rather than producing a gourmet taste. I cook simple, fresh, mostly organic meals. I am not big on smothering anything in fatty sauces or cooking anything with batter. However, baking is another story. Baking is something I love to do. Baking is relaxing and rewarding to me. It is my comfort food. Butter. Flour. Eggs. The only problem is if I bake it, I eat it. I eat most of it. Except for my chocolate chip cookies. The kids and their friends devour those, leaving little for the rest of us. This is a good thing. It makes me feel good.

While I wait for Anna to come back, there is something I have to do before the meeting. I pick up my phone, dial Cedar Park and ask for Lise Smith. I talk to the ladies in the front office for a few minutes and update them on Anna's progress. They are so wonderful. The whole school is still praying for Max and Anna and they are thankful for Anna's progress. Great school. Great people.

The front desk transfers me to Lise's room. Lise is Anna's math teacher. She is also acting as liaison between all of Anna's teachers and our family. Lise picks up her room phone and I identify myself. She immediately wants to know how Anna is doing. I give her a brief update and begin talking to her about Anna and her future at Cedar Park. Even though our meeting with Anna's doctors is this afternoon, I want to know how far behind she is and what we need to do to get her up to speed in her classes. Lise says our goal rides on November 1st. That is the end of the first quarter and if we can catch her up, she will have grades and not incompletes. If Anna has incompletes in her classes, that could mean summer school or not graduating with her class. Knowing Anna, summer school would be okay, but not graduating with her class would not only be unacceptable, it would deeply crush her. Lise tells me she will contact all of Anna's teachers and find out what each one requires from Anna in order for Anna to get a grade and complete 1st quarter. We leave it at that and decide to talk again in a few days, both after today's meeting and after Lise gets the information we need from the teachers. I tell Lise thank you and we part knowing this will not be easy. It is October 18th, nine days after the accident. Although Anna's memory is improving, she still cannot remember most things from hour to hour. Nor can she walk on her own without her belt. For school, the biggest problem is memory. She will not be able to complete her work if she can't retain what she learns. I pray for healing. She is one determined girl, but even Anna can't control all of her body's healing processes.

Oh, good timing. The minute I hang up the phone and am done praying, Anna returns from physical therapy. I can't wait to tell her I talked to Lise Smith and we are formulating a plan. She will be excited. I think it will make her feel like she is on the road to, in her words, normal. She looks tired as she, once again, plops down on her bed while her therapist removes the stabilizing belt. She grabs lamby and out she goes. I guess I will have to tell her the exciting news later. Her therapist and I look at each other smiling and silently nod.

Unfortunately for Anna, her nap is a short one. In rolls the lunch cart. Anna's little body slowly responds to the noise of the lunch cart and she rolls on her back to sit up. She presses the up button on her hospital bed and pushes lamby to the side. Up she comes and sits herself straight up to eat. She is quiet. I know she is tired. After lunch, the therapies will repeat themselves. At 3:00 pm we will break for the meeting. After that she will finish her therapies. This is going to be an exhausting day for both her body and her brain. But, every day is a good day when you can see your family and tell them you love them.

When Anna eats her last morsel, she relaxes back into her bed and lowers her body. She looks over at me with heavy eyes and I tell her about my conversation with Lise. Her reaction tells me this is exciting news for her. Her eyes widen and a broad smile grows on her face. She wants to get back to school. She wants to get back to her life. Anna is fighting every day to improve both physically and mentally. She is a fighter. There is no doubt about that.

At 1:00 pm, her occupational therapist enters the room with a smile and encouragement. "Okay Anna, let's get that belt on and get going," she tells Anna.

"Okay," Anna says.

Greg arrives about 2:45 pm, followed by Anna and her speech therapist. We are all a little anxious for the meeting. I pull out a notepad and pencil, wanting to make sure I write down anything and everything the doctors and therapists have to say that will help us maneuver through the rest of Anna's life.

It's time. We make sure Anna still has her strap on as the three of us make our way out the door and down the hall to the conference room. Okay, big breath. Here we go!

When we walk through the doors to the conference room, we can see that it is full of people. There are doctors, therapists and counselors. This is quite a team of professionals, ready to give us their assessment of Anna. At the end of the long conference table, there are three empty chairs. We walk towards them and take our seats. This is it. This is a big deal. We may not be given complete answers, but we will be given a comprehensive professional opinion of what is going on with Anna and what we can expect for her future. I am both excited and worried at the same time.

Dr. Massagli starts the meeting by making sure we know who everyone is. We have met all of them and everyone nods in agreement. She has a tall pile of paperwork in front of her as she begins passing around the assessment forms for all of us to see. Everything looks great at a glance, but I notice that question #6 is not checked off. This is the question about returning to school. As I continue down the list, I read that overall, they are all in agreement that Anna is progressing beautifully. They can't believe how motivated and determined she is. They note her progress improves daily. Thank you.

Dr. Massagli is doing most of the talking and we are listening and taking notes. When all is said and done, we are pleased and encouraged for Anna. The plan is for Anna to stay at Children's until next Wednesday, the 24th, and continue to have her therapies each day. They will be testing next week for improvement in complex information. She still needs assistance at this. Someone needs to be with her at all times to assist her with self-care skills. As for her medications, the plan is to decrease her pain medications as the pain lessens. This is really great news because the pain meds make Anna so tired. It's hard for her to concentrate when she is so tired all the time. She can do school work, but the decision to return to school will be made next week. In the meantime, Anna is being given a weekend furlough to go home. We are thrilled! I look at her face and see a beaming smile with excitement in her eyes. We get to take her home after 12:00 pm on Saturday and we have to be back at Children's on Sunday by 8:00 pm. This is so exciting. Naturally, there are rules. She has to wear her belt, her neck brace has to be on at all times except when showering, she must be accompanied while climbing the stairs and moving around the house, she needs to have a bench to sit on in the shower and we have to leave the lights on at the top of the stairs in case she gets up at night. As for being disinhibited, everyone agrees this will hopefully come to an end, for the most part, at some point. It is very difficult to predict, but as her brain heals, the unfiltered behavior will dissipate. Let's hope it dissipates completely. Only time will tell. Then, most importantly, her memory is discussed. This is tough. Children tend to recover faster and more fully than adults do with traumatic brain injury. Anna is improving daily as is evident in her speech and occupational therapies. But, the brain is a complex area to predict. This is truly an unknown. They expect her to recover significantly if not completely, but we will not know until it happens. This is a huge prayer and we know hundreds of people in various parts of the world are praying for Anna's full recovery. Greg and I will move forward, counting on and praying for a full recovery.

And finally, the sports issue. She can have absolutely no contact sports for one year. At the end of that year, she will be reevaluated to determine if contact sports are possible. Dr. Massagli gives us a list of what is considered a contact sport and what sports are considered safe for her. All of the sports she plays are prohibited. Anna is obviously upset and asks if she can play basketball this season. She isn't grasping this conversation. The answer is a resounding no. Her basketball career has come to an abrupt halt. She can no longer follow in her older brother's footsteps. As I look at this little fifteen-year-old girl who has just had her dreams taken from her, I realize she still doesn't get it. She may never play basketball again in her whole life. She doesn't realize she is just lucky to be alive.

The doctor continues, telling us that after Anna goes home from the hospital permanently, she will continue on with her therapies at Overlake hospital in Bellevue. Twice a week she will go to the hospital for occupational, speech, and physical therapies. How long this will continue will be decided as she progresses in each therapy. In six to eight weeks Anna will be seen by her primary physician and evaluated to make sure she is physically healthy and there are no signs of any other problems.

Greg and I leave the room thrilled. She's alive and on the road to recovery. Anna leaves the room trying to process this new information and come to terms with her limitations.

Our meeting ran a bit longer than expected. Little did they know they were talking to the Queen of Questions. In college, a friend of mine called me Why. I want to know everything. I am a detail person. In this case, particularly, it's a good thing.

Time has slipped by and Anna is late for her afternoon physical therapy session. Since her physical therapist was in the meeting with us, it's no big deal, but it is time for Anna to go. Perfect timing. Exercise will take her mind off of the basketball conversation and give her some time to process the information she just heard.

The sports conversation, of course, was not a surprise to Greg or me. We are happy to have her safely removed from any danger and know she needs time to heal. We are just going to have to figure out how to keep her involved with her team and keep her attitude positive and undefeated. She has a new basketball coach this year and they don't know each other very well. Even though Anna had gone to open gym this summer and met both the coach and her husband, they don't really know Anna. They only know the team is counting on her this year to help them get to state. This will be challenging news for the new coach. We've heard she's wonderful and hope she will work with us through this difficult and challenging time.

Greg and I are so excited Anna can go home for the weekend and go home permanently next week. We laugh that she is coming home on the 24th. The day before, October 23rd is Max's 18th birthday. I guess he will be celebrating his birthday at Children's Hospital. Dinner and cake. We will invite Gramma and Grandpa, too. That will be fun. Wait till we tell him. Maybe Gramma can bring the cake. I don't thing I can bake here!

Greg and I are waiting for Anna to come back to the room before he leaves for home. I am in my chair bed and Greg is sitting in the rocking chair next to Anna's bed. It is really dark and stormy outside, but he wants to say goodbye to her and make sure she is okay. This is a little quiet time for us to let the message of the meeting sink in. We are both relieved to hear good news. We sit in silence with our own thoughts of what the next few weeks will bring and how our lives will continue to change.

The laugh. We hear the laugh. Anna has a boisterous laugher. It's part of her fun personality and something that separates her from many of her more introverted friends. She walks into the room with confidence. She hands us her journal, wanting us to read today's entries. We flip the pages to October 18th. The first entry is from this afternoon's occupational therapy session. She has written, "I looked up a recipe for tacos so that I can cook it on Monday." I read it out loud as all of us burst into laughter. Anna cooking. Now that will be something to see. The second entry is from speech therapy. The therapist wrote, "Anna worked on defining same/different aspects of words and words with multiple meanings. We played Whiz Kids as well." But the third entry is what was so exciting to Anna. In Physical therapy, Anna "worked on her basketball skills. She dribbled, shot, and attempted a slow pivot. It made her dizzy, but she was proud of the accomplishment." We congratulated her and she was beaming. Greg gives her a hug and we let her bask in the knowledge of a task well done.

Greg is ready to go home so we decide not to bring up the meeting. Anna doesn't keep her feelings to herself, so if she has something to say about today, it will come out once she has processed it. Greg puts his coat on, Anna says, "Bye Dad." and I tell him to drive carefully. The wind and rain look even worse and it is now the beginning of rush hour. He is going to have a long and interesting drive home.

As always, I say to him "Call me when you get home to let me know everything is okay." He promises to call, but always forgets. So, I give him what I consider enough time to arrive at his destination, wait a while and then call. He always apologizes and says that he forgot. It is a ritual.

By the time I call, Greg says the drive and the weather was unbelievable. The wind is strong and the rain is pouring down. He's glad to be home. There was dinner waiting for him on the doorstep and he is safe and sound, being carefully eyed by three cats and Sammy dog. He's going to feed all of them, eat his dinner and call later. "Sounds good to me, I'll talk to you later. Love you. Bye," are my parting words.

I'm hungry. Anna's dinner should be here anytime and I think I will run down to the cafeteria and get some food before her cart arrives. Then we can eat together. She likes that plan. She's tired and wants to take a quick nap anyway. I make sure the guard rails are up and she is sleeping as I slip out to get my dinner. I make it quick though, because this is the first time I have left her in the room alone and it makes me very nervous.

The cafeteria has excellent soups and salads. I grab a little of both and head back to the room. She is still sleeping when I return, and the sound of the squeaky meal cart wheels can be heard coming around the corner heading our way. She has had a long day. Six therapy sessions and one meeting. Anna is sound asleep. I think I'll wait until the cart comes in to see if she will wake up. My little, baby girl.

I watch her. Such a blessing. Max and Anna are the best things to ever happen in our lives. We thought about not having kids. I was really into my career and Greg was on the fence about kids. We didn't go to church on any regular basis and really had no God connection. I always believed, but never practiced. Always prayed, but never gave thanks. When we got married, we bought a house in Ballard. Actually, Greg had owned it with three of his fraternity brothers and we bought them out. After one dog, Greg's MBA degree and a little remodeling, we wanted to move. We wanted to live in Seattle, so we looked all up and down the Seattle corridor. When we couldn't find what we wanted, we actually looked on Bainbridge Island. I think Greg was humoring me, because after two houses, he said no, he did not want to deal with a ferry to get to work. I did what most people do. I thought about who I knew and contacted a friend of mine. She was one of my previous bosses, who had become a real estate agent. The only problem was that she represented houses on the east side of Seattle, across the lake. We had emphatically decided not to move to the Eastside. It was too far from Seattle. But, she said, "Hey, I have this house, blueprints, but not built yet, not on the market, great lot and in Kirkland." It was a Monday afternoon. I was leaving Tuesday morning for LA on a buying trip and we decided to go look. My friend met us in Kirkland, drove us along Lake Washington and past a beautiful park up to a lovely lot on a dead-end road with a greenbelt behind it. Tall evergreens were surrounding the area with a little view of the lake. Hmm. She always was a good salesperson. We went home, talked about it, and made an offer that night. The plans had an open two-story entry, kitchen, dining room, living room, family room, and four bedrooms.

Our fate was sealed. Apparently, we would be having a family at some point. We were in the suburbs with four bedrooms and 1/3 of an acre. I thank God for that decision. We moved in on our 2nd anniversary and are still here. We now have an addition, a large toy room for the kids. We built the toy room in 1990, a year after Max was born. Lots of great memories here.

Looking at Anna reminds me of all the wonderful years we have had together. Nothing is ever perfect, but I know parenting is a road I am glad we did not miss. As Anna begins to waken, I am thankful for our lives.

She's awake. She hears the cart and slowly raises the bed to get ready for dinner. She is groggy and hungry. But, she is happy and smiles. I give her the Max update in Disney World and she says, "I wanna go." We both laugh. We both would love to go.

In comes the dinner cart. Before it is locked in place, Anna has her fork in hand and is barreling down on her food. No doubt we will be going to the snack room later. Tonight, she wants to watch a little TV and just relax. I doubt she will have any visitors because of the storm, but there will be texting and calling for sure.

It is really howling outside and very, very dark. Anna and I decide to call Greg, check in and say good night before we get involved in a TV show. "Hi Dad," she says, "Really? Wow!" Then she looks at me and says, "Mom, the power is out!" When she finishes talking with her daddy, she hands me the phone.

"Hi honey, the power is out?" I ask.

"Yes," Greg says in a relaxed voice. "And," he says, "all the cats are in the garage, Sam is right here with me and everything else is fine." He knows me so well. If the animals aren't in at night, then all is not well in my world. It's routine. I must have all three cats in bed, Sammy pottied and upstairs, the alarm on, and all doors and windows locked.

Greg isn't sure how long the power will be off because he hasn't called the power company for an update. But, we both assume it is a downed tree and that may take a while. Most likely the storm has caused power outages in a number of places and emergencies will take priority. Greg and I are both glad it happened tonight rather than last night when I was home alone. He is a bit calmer about these things than I am. God knows what he is doing and thankfully I was spared a lightless night.

Greg says he got a phone call tonight. Greg starts laughing when he tells me Mark Pavlovic called and they want to bring an Italian dinner over tomorrow night to the hospital. Mark told Greg both he and Kari will be there along with their youngest daughter and their son Anthony.

He said, "Make sure and tell Anna that Anthony is coming." This is, of course, in response to Mark's visit last week to Harborview when Anna asked where Anthony was before she even said hello to Mark. We both find this so funny. Anna will love it. Anthony. Her future husband, she thinks.

We end the conversation with, "Love you," and, "See you tomorrow," and, "I hope the power comes on shortly." Greg will get cold without heat. Thank goodness it's not freezing outside.

Our connection is barely broken when I tell Anna that the Pavlovics, including Anthony, are bringing us an Italian dinner tomorrow night. She is thrilled. Anthony is a great kid, and completely unsuspecting of Anna's designs. This will truly be an evening to watch. Too bad Max isn't going to be here, he would get a big kick out of watching Anna tomorrow night.

When Anna stops smiling, texting, and talking, we decide to watch TV before we go to bed. The hard part is agreeing on what to watch. I want calm and uplifting, she wants real life drama. We finally agree on a show, well sort of, and then lights out. Actually, Anna gets some pain medication and it is immediate lights out for her. I stay up a little longer and read my magazines and recap the day in my notebook, keeping track of Anna's progress. Writing in my notebook helps me stay organized and feel like I have some control over my life. Seeing progress is like seeing God's work on paper. Anna is doing better and the prognosis is positive. Perhaps while she is gone to therapy tomorrow, I just might hop on the bus and take a break tomorrow. University Village is so close and I need some fresh air. A little retail therapy would feel good. It will give me back a piece of my normal life and bolster me for what is ahead. Moments of pleasure are always uplifting, important and necessary. Tomorrow I will also get a grande soy latte with a little whipped cream at the Village Starbucks. No one makes a better soy latte than Starbucks. Anna starts therapy at 8:30 am, has a lunch break and is done at 2:30 pm. University Village opens around 10:00 am. I will check the bus schedule in the morning and plan my get away! Sweet.

Chapter Eleven

"Gone but ever present"
— Rachel Staudacher

It's Friday. Anna and I both had a great night's sleep, even though the wind continued to howl until the wee hours of the morning. It's a little early to call Greg and we're not sure if he had such a great night's sleep with no power or heat. We hope the power went back on in the middle of the night so he could wake up to a warm house, have a hearty breakfast, and get a little work done.

Anna is enjoying her hot breakfast and I am starving. As soon as she is done and we get her off to her 8:30 am occupational therapy appointment, I am going to shower and go get some food in the cafeteria. Let's see, she'll be back at lunch and then afternoon therapies. Maybe I will wait until her afternoon therapies to go to University Village. Then Greg and I can be with her during lunch. Greg can be with her this afternoon while I cruise through University Village. Hmmm, that might work.

Breakfast must have been great. I look over at her tray and her breakfast plate is completely empty. She looks up at me and pushes the meal cart out of her way. She smiles and I walk over to the side of the bed and help her get out and stand up. We don't put the belt on quite yet because she needs to get her clothes on. Anna holds me for balance while she places each leg in her sweat pants. Now for the tee shirt. This is becoming an obsession. It has to be a white tee and it has to have short sleeves. I laughingly tell Anna it's a good thing we don't live in the South because white after Labor Day is a no-no. Thankfully, we have a clean, white tee shirt that meets all of the necessary requirements. I help her pull it down over her head before we place her neck brace back on and wrap the belt around her waist. Just as she finishes with her socks and tennis shoes, in walks Anna's therapist to pick her up for her first session. As they walk out the door, I watch them toddle out together with the therapist holding Anna's belt. For the first time, I notice Anna has lost quite a bit of weight since the accident. She looks thin. I think to myself how thankful we are to have both of the kids alive and functioning. Thin we can fix. So many other things I cannot fix. But, I know God can and I know He is still holding onto all of us this very moment.

Pulling myself up out of my chair, I look up and see my friend Tracy standing in the doorway. What a surprise. Tracy and I are in the same book club and I find her hilarious and lots of fun. I really enjoy her company. Tracy had brought some incredible treats to the house last week. My sisters had told me that this beautiful blond woman from book club had brought over a plate of pastries or cookies or something out of this world. I knew it had to be Tracy because she makes the most incredible food. She's an excellent baker and cook. Teensie raved about these treats for days, and may have single handedly eaten most of them all by herself.

Tracy works and it seems like an unusual time for her to be here. I invite her in and ask her what's going on and she explains that she has just checked her youngest daughter, Ellie, into Children's. Ellie is scheduled to have surgery today. It all happened so fast. The doctors need to remove a growth on her leg. I am shocked and ask Tracy if everything is okay and what do the doctors think the lump is? Tracy is very calm and says, "Everything will be okay. They just need to remove a benign bone tumor that's making it hard for Ellie to walk. It's not cancer or any life-threatening disease, it's just a weird growth that's causing all sorts of pain and problems." She has to get back to Ellie and just wanted me to know they are in the hospital staying in the next unit over. Ellie's room is just down the hall. While Tracy is walking back to Ellie's room, I say a prayer for them.

By the time I have showered and eaten, Greg arrives. Anna isn't back yet, so his timing is perfect for us to talk a little bit about the rest of the day and bringing her home tomorrow for the weekend. We are excited to see the Pavlovic family tonight and can't wait to share a big Italian meal with them. It's so nice of them to bring us dinner. This will be lots of fun and very healing for us. This accident has scared every parent we know, and I'm sure parents we don't know. When you are on the inside and living the struggle, it is easy to see the daily accomplishments and progress. We need to continue to let everyone know their prayers are working and Anna is improving. Greg and I continue to talk to people and he blogs about what is going on. Hopefully, hearing about all of the positive strides forward will take some of the fear away from our friends. We all internalize. It's natural. I know many of our friends are thinking,

"This could happen to anyone. What if it was our kids?" These thoughts can be terrifying. But, Greg and I feel fortunate. We have faith and we are getting both physical and spiritual support. Nothing beats that.

It's just about noon and in walks our tired little girl. Although she's starving, she wants to lie down and take a nap before lunch arrives. We know it will be a short one because her schedule says she starts her work all over again in one hour. I hear the cart.

Greg is staying the rest of the afternoon and through dinner. He's very tired, but the power did go back on in the middle of the night and he was able to get a little sleep, breakfast, and some work done. He also says he will work while Anna is at therapy this afternoon. Perfect.

Anna eats. She is improving in that task and is becoming more co-ordinated daily. I check the bus schedule from Children's to University Village and leave just about the same time Anna is leaving for therapy. I give her a big hug and a kiss and tell her, "I will be back later. I'm going over to University Village. Dad will be here."

Of course, her immediate response is, "Would you like to buy some-thing for me?" What a surprise.

I step outside into the cold fresh air. Last night's storm blew all the clouds away and what we have left is a beautiful, sunny fall day with a few scattered branches strewn about the ground. The air smells so pure and I just want to stand and breathe in deeply, taking in the beauty and richness of the Pacific Northwest. If I close my eyes, I know I will smell pine mixed with wet ground and I will feel the depths of this clean air all the way down to my toes. I love living here. I love the rain, the trees, the cold winter nights, and most of all, the beauty of the seasons.

Standing at the bus stop prompts me to remember I have driven by this bus stop hundreds of times and never noticed it. The kids' pediatrician is just down the street across from Children's Hospital. We purposely chose a great pediatrician that was near Children's, but I never actually thought we would be staying here. It was just in case. We wanted to have a doctor with access to Children's Hospital. I think about all the trips down here for colds, strep throat, fever, and the numerous other reasons we take our babies to the doctor. Now, here I stand, ready to catch a bus to go shopping. Sounds fun, seems trivial. I have to force myself to get on the bus.

University Village is an open-air shopping experience. The stores range from Pottery Barn to cute, privately owned boutiques. It really is fun. Feel-ing more receptive to shopping, I step off the bus and immediately see the

Gap. That seems like a great place to start. I can probably find something for Anna and Max there, as well as myself. Good idea. I love to buy the kids little presents. It doesn't have to be an expensive gift, just fun. By the time I get out of the Gap, I have four thermal tees, two scarves and a pair of socks. They were having a buy-one-get-one-half-off sale. Anna gets two of the thermal tees for layering pieces, Max gets the fun socks and I get the rest. I'm planning on sharing the scarves with Anna. They have little sparkles in them. It's their Christmas collection. Very fun.

I wind my way through the village and start to feel a little anxious about being away from the hospital. I call Greg to check in and make sure everything is okay. "Everything here is fine," he says, "You don't need to come back yet. Enjoy yourself." He obviously hears a little stress in my voice. While I appreciate his kindness, I think he wants time to do some work that he wouldn't be able to do if I was sitting there talking to him. That's okay. I understand. As long as everything is okay, I will look around a little more and head back to the hospital after I have checked out a few more stores. I walk slowly through Pottery Barn even though I was here a few days ago with my sisters and Lisa. So much to see and it all looks so great. Then I make my way around the village and end up at Eddie Bauer. By the time I have walked through the village and seen much of the new fall merchandise, I am ready to go back to the hospital. I check the bus schedule. I have to do a little walking this time, as the bus pickup is on the street side opposite the Village. I hurry. I make it just as my bus is coming around the corner. Thank you.

It's about 3:30 pm and Anna is back. She's sleeping with her lamby cuddled up around her face. Greg says she was really wiped out when she got back to the room. He shows me her journal. Today she worked on describing words, naming categories, playing Whiz Kids, and focusing on attention tasks. In physical therapy, she worked really hard on jumping, stepping, and rhythm drills. Little things that were once daily occurrences are, at this point, daily struggles. All of these newly accomplished tasks are milestones for her. We are once again reminded that there is a road ahead to get her back to herself. She wants so desperately to get back to her normal life. I am amazed at her determination and strength. Her therapists are very encouraging and daily write in her journal that she has worked hard and done a great job. They are working so hard to help Anna recover. Anna is working so hard to help Anna recover.

When Anna wakes from her nap, we remind her that the Pavlovics are bringing dinner to us tonight and will be coming over about 6:30 pm.

She looks at the clock and figures she has about two hours to get ready for her company. But first, she's hungry. Greg offers to step across the hall and get her a snack to hold her over until dinner. She's all for that as she starts to climb out of bed asking where her makeup is. Greg and I immediately bolt towards her and I grab her belt from the drawer. She is completely clueless that she is still unstable. Her mind is fixed on finding the perfect clothes and putting her makeup on. For the most part, Anna has been sporting the natural look, which, by the way, is great on her. As her mom, no makeup is good with me. She really doesn't need it. She has long brown hair with red and gold natural highlights, big hazel eyes, long dark brown eyelashes and perfectly shaped dark eyebrows. Fortunately, she inherited beautiful full lips from someone. We're not sure who, though.

So, we are off to the races. Anyone who has a teenage daughter knows that when they are trying to find the perfect outfit to wear, it is best if you leave the area unless your opinion or input is solicited. This is a much better job for dads. On that note, I decide to take a little stroll around the hospital and stop by to see Tracy and Ellie. I knock lightly and Tracy gets up and comes over to open the partially closed door. It was a long surgery and Ellie is asleep. I quietly enter the room and we sit down on Tracy's bed, which in this room doubles as a couch. We talk softly about the surgery and their plans for the next few days. It looks like they will be here for a very short time, depending however, on Ellie's abilities when she wakes up. She will be seen by her doctors tomorrow. Ellie was in a lot of pain after the surgery and Tracy is trying to get her through this part of recovery. The nurse walks in to refresh Ellie's pain pills. I say, "I have to go. I'll see you tomorrow. You're welcome to come for a visit any time or I will stroll down before we leave to take Anna home for the weekend." Tracy nods. She needs to talk to the nurse. As I'm walking out the door, Ellie begins to stir. I think to myself, "What are the chances that one of my friends would be at Children's at the same time we are here?" Especially someone I am so comfortable with. Hmmm.

By the time 6:30 rolls around, Anna is in jeans, a white tee shirt, and a hooded sweatshirt. She has made a loose braid with her hair, and is sitting comfortably on her hospital bed. We are all hungry and excited to see the Pavlovic family.

The room phone rings and Greg tells security to send them back. We can almost smell the Italian spices before we see anyone. We look toward the door, and there stand the Pavlovics. It's funny how everyone pauses to look at the room number on the outside wall, to make sure they're in the right place. I would do the same thing. No one wants to walk into the wrong room in a hospital and interrupt another patient. Greg says, "Come on in." Mark and Kari are carrying bags of food, accompanied by their youngest daughter and, of course, their older son, Anthony. Everyone hugs and says Hi. Anna is thrilled and the smile on her face says so.

The smell of the food is delicious. We have lasagna, salad, bread, and a bottle of red wine. They know me well and have forgotten nothing. They even brought plates, napkins, cups, and silverware. This is fabulous. I imagine this is what it has been like at home for Max and Greg, when the dinners and treats have arrived ready to eat. Heavenly.

Mark is the only one who had seen Anna at Harborview last week and can see the improvements she has made since then. Everyone is smiling, eating, and I am sure, thankful. It's a great celebration and we will never forget this dinner and the time the Pavlovics have taken out of their lives for our family. It's such a blessing to have friends.

We carefully clean up and try to get any red sauce we may have spilled off of Anna's bed. We made a big dent in a very large plate of lasagna and the rest of the food is gone. Even the red wine is gone. I sense this is one of Anna's favorite meals since she has been in the hospital and we all continue to tell the Pavlovics thank you. As they gather their coats, I think about what a treat this has been. They are good people.

Anna has put her best self forward and she is excited and tired. Greg gives her a hug and a kiss as she gets up, belt and neck collar on, heading into the bathroom to wash her face and brush her teeth. He says his goodbyes to both of us. I stand waiting for Anna to come out of the bathroom so I can help her take off her belt, get into her pajamas and crawl into bed. She has had a big evening.

When she's all ready for bed, she lies down, takes her pills, pulls lamby up around her face and closes her eyes. I give her a little hug and gently kiss her forehead. Dimming the lights, I get myself ready for bed, too. It's a little early for me, so I read my magazines and go over my notes. In a little while, I will call and make sure Greg got home safely and make sure all is well at home. It's been a good day. Thank you.

Chapter Twelve

"Our thoughts and prayers are with you"
— Todd and Candis Brink

Yay! It's Saturday morning and today is the day my baby girl gets a weekend furlough for home. But first, she has morning therapies. We are trying to get in as many therapy sessions as possible before Anna leaves next Wednesday to go home permanently. This will only benefit her and we are all for it.

Well, Greg and I are all for it. Anna is another issue. She is so excited to go home today and see her kitty Belle, hug the rest of the animal crew, have friends over and sleep in her own bed. She doesn't really want to do morning therapies.

"It's not a choice," we explain to her, "Let's get up, put on the belt and get going." She is testy. When her therapist comes to pick her up, we are relieved to hand her over to capable hands. The immediate transformation in attitude is remarkable. Greg and I know we get the brunt of her emotions, but to see her immediately morph into a happy, smiling girl with her therapist standing by her side makes us laugh out loud to each other. Teenagers. Love them.

Greg pulls out Anna's weekend duffel bag when my cellphone rings. It's Anna's math teacher, Lise Smith. "I have great news." she says. "All of Anna's teachers are going to adjust her schedule a little bit and work with her to catch up on important material. They will help her regain her footing in each class and be available to tutor her during their free periods, before and after school. They are all committed to get her through this semester. We will have her drop yearbook because of the amount of work, time and organizational skills involved. Instead, she will be given a study hall for 4th period with Bill Bettinger. Then, I will work with her 5th period for honors math. I want her to leave her math book at home and use another book during class, plus I have additional materials available in the classroom. In English, Anna will have to read Beowulf and take some vocabulary tests. Biology and world history will pick up where she left off."

I interrupt Lise, "I'm concerned about Spanish. Spanish requires a lot of memorization and that's not Anna's strength right now."

"Ok," Lise says, "Let's let Spanish go. I spoke to Amy Bettinger. Anna can be a teacher's aide to Amy. Anna will be allowed to rest if she gets tired and will get as much help as she needs." I can't thank Cedar Park and her teachers enough. They are truly a godsend. Thank you.

Lise wants to touch base again on Monday. Next week we will fill out the necessary forms to get Anna's changes made and signed. Lise has done a wonderful job in setting Anna up for success when she gets back to school, which, miraculously looks like it may be Monday the 29th of October. We will have to see how she does at home, but it is amazing to imagine Anna back in school just twenty days after the accident. Prayer works. Thank you.

Anna comes back from her final therapy, physical therapy, and we receive wonderful news. The therapist thinks Anna's is becoming increasingly steady on her feet and may not need a lot of outpatient physical therapy. She still needs to wear her belt this weekend and there will be two more days of therapies before we go home next week. We know that after she is released from Children's, she will begin with outpatient therapy in occupational, speech, and physical therapy. We just don't know how long she will have to continue with each of the outpatient treatments at the hospital closest to our home. Only time will tell. Anna is thrilled to hear this news. So are we. More progress a little at a time.

I know what she is thinking. She is thinking basketball. Greg also knows, because he turns to Anna and says, "This would be a good time for you to work on your golf game." Anna laughs. We don't even know if she likes golf! But, she gets a gentle reminder that contact sports are out of the question for at least one year. We're not sure if she is retaining that information or trying to ignore it.

Anna packs up her weekend bag and we walk out of Children's into the brisk fall day, excited to be going home. It is only the second time she has been outside since the accident. The first time was the ambulance ride from Harborview to Children's. The air feels good to her. Cold, but good. And, the sun's out. Perfect.

On the ride home, I talk to Anna about her weekend, "Okay, honey, we will be home tonight and tomorrow, but back to Children's tomorrow night by 8 pm. You heard your therapist say you have to wear your belt when you are out of bed. And, you need to have lots of rest. Dad has bought a stool for you to sit on in your shower, just like the one you use at Children's."

"That's weird, Mom," she says, but she understands.

"As for your medications," I continue, "We are in the process of cutting back on the pain killers and continuing lightly with the pills that reduce the swelling on the back of your neck. You have to wear your collar the entire time you are home."

"Okay, Mom," she says in a bored and slightly irritated voice.

Anna has friends and relatives coming over to visit her tonight and tomorrow. We want her to enjoy this, but not overdo it. No setbacks. Her brain needs an unusual amount of rest in order for her to continue improving and healing. She understands all of this, but she is such a social girl, that I'm not sure she will know when to relax and rest. We'll just have to watch her.

We pull into the driveway and take her into the house. Sammy is so excited and I hold Anna as I guide her to the couch to sit. Sammy needs to say hello with his tongue before we attempt to go upstairs. He is beside himself. His girl is home. Anna loves this and spends a few minutes giving Sammy his lovies. Then Jazz, the most affectionate cat in the house and maybe the world, sees Anna and saunters over for attention. Anna loves Jazz and picks him up for a kiss and conversation. Everyone is in heaven. This is its own kind of therapy.

When we get her up the stairs and into her room, she snuggles down into her bed. Her own bed. Originally, my mom and dad bought it for Greg and I as a housewarming gift. It's a beautiful bed. It is made out of a whitewashed pine and has a partial wooden canopy that extends over the top end of the bed, held in place by a solid pine headboard. It has two curlicue corbels for the canopy, pine side boards and a tall footboard. The story was that the bed was made by monks or priests in Oregon. I can't remember, but it does have an interesting origin. It is handmade and a little top heavy, but sturdy and very safe for sleeping. For years, Anna begged for another bed, even offering to sleep on her mattress on the floor. She wanted a new bed. I could never figure out what the issue was since this bed is so different. Then I realized that was issue. It is different. Needless to say, I will never get rid of this bed because of the sentimental value and it's a fabulous bed. Eventually, we moved past the I want a new bed discussion. However, it then became the I want a new mattress discussion. Help!

I hand her a soft, clean lamby. She pulls lamby up to her chin and wants to know where Belle is. She knows the kitties come when I call them and I tell her I will go call Belle and bring her in the minute she gets home. Anna closes her eyes and falls asleep. Finally, at home. Finally, in her own bed. She looks so happy.

I open our bedroom window and call Belle's name. She comes running across the roof top and up to the window. I scoop her up and tell her I have a big surprise for her. We walk down the hall to Anna's room and I place her on Anna's bed. Belle sees a lump in the bed and realizes Anna is home. She loudly cries out to her mama. Anna opens her eyes and says, "Come here Belle," as she holds open the sheets. Belle trots across the bed and disappears under the covers. She snuggles her head around Anna's neck brace and the two of them fall asleep. Animals are so great.

It's quiet in the house. All the animals are napping and Greg is watching TV. Everything is in order. I take one look in the mirror and call my hairdresser, Vicky to see if she can squeeze me in for a cut and color. I'm overdue. Vicky is such a good person. She says, "Come on over around three, how's Anna?" Vicky talks fast and we cover a lot of ground whenever I see her. I can't wait to chat with her today and get refreshed. She's lots of fun.

Anna is still sleeping when I leave. Greg is glad I am taking the opportunity to get out and he promises to hold down the fort and keep Anna in check. It feels good to be home and doing something that is part of my regular routine. I think about stopping for a soy latte. Good idea.

Vicky is hilarious. She wants to know how Anna is doing, when she's coming home for good, when she's going back to school, and finally, she wants to know everything. I fill her in on the details as best I can and thank her for sending her brother to the emergency room at Harborview the day of the accident. Vicky says he was really reluctant to visit because of the privacy laws and he did not want to get fired for checking on us. But, Vicky convinced him to go and I let her know how appreciative we are that he came to check on Anna. I also ask Vicky to tell her brother that is was okay with us and we are thankful that he popped his head in.

Driving back home is relaxing. Winding down Holmes Point and nearing our home is different than it has been the last couple of times. I can breathe. I can rest in the knowledge that we are mending physically and mentally. It feels good. I feel good.

Ah. As I pull up our drive, there are cars parked alongside our picket fence. Anna's friends have arrived. She must be awake and in full swing by now. How fun for her. I hear the laughter the minute I open the door.

Sammy is beside himself with excitement and the girls are upstairs on Anna's bed. Greg is downstairs snacking and fixing some snacks for the girls. He says the screaming and high-pitched laughter has been non-stop, but not to worry, Anna is fine. The girls know about her neck and her neck brace, as well as, the belt she wears to stabilize herself when they walk with her.

I venture upstairs, trying to get ahead of Sammy who is so thrilled we are home, he can't relax. It makes me laugh walking down the hall and hearing all the giggling. When I enter the room, the girls turn and look at me with big smiles on their faces. Anna looks at me and says, "Hi." I will only stay a minute because I know they don't need a mom here to chat with. They have come to see Anna. Greg yells that the snacks are ready and the girls all jump off of the bed. I grab Anna's belt and cinch it around her waist to help her down the stairs. She does remarkably well and I plop her down in the toy room to eat, talk, and watch TV with her friends. They are all smiles and having fun.

After a movie and lots of treats, Anna's friends leave, knowing she needs her rest. She fell asleep during the movie and is a little groggy. Candice stays with Anna a little longer while we move her upstairs to her bed and give her lamby to wrap herself around. Before Candice leaves for home, the girls want one last picture of the two of them. With Anna in her dark blue Cedar Park sweatshirt and white neck brace, we snap a picture of two best friends leaning into each other. Candice gives a shy smile while Anna's eyes are closed and she flashes a fake grin. Funny photo, good memory.

Candice bids us all goodbye and drives off happy, I detect, that her friend is getting better.

Before Anna has a chance to nod off, the doorbell rings, Sammy goes crazy, and dinner is delivered. Tonight, our chef is Anna's yearbook teacher, Ms. Yeazell. We all know that Anna is not able to continue in yearbook, even though she has been dying to be in this class for years. It is so kind of Ms. Yeazell to bring dinner to us, yet alone Anna's favorite of orange chicken. We put the belt on Anna and walk her down the stairs to see her teacher. It's the first time she has seen Anna and her reaction is so positive. Smiles and hugs. Anna is very happy. She really likes Ms. Yeazell. She is a tough teacher and doesn't allow any nonsense in the classroom. Yet, she's big-hearted and clearly loves her students.

Ms. Yeazell hands us the hot dishes of mashed potatoes and broccoli along with the orange chicken. We thank her for the wonderful food and for the home delivery. She doesn't stay long, just a moment or two to catch up on Anna and see how she is doing. Aside from Mr. Ian, she is the only teacher to see Anna recently and we are glad she will be able to relate Anna's progress to the rest of the staff. The minute Ms. Yeazell is out the door, Anna is poking at the food as we carry it to the kitchen. Hungry again.

After dinner, Greg sits down to update the blog. He had forgotten to give an update yesterday and wants to make sure he keeps everyone informed of Anna's whereabouts and healing. Anna is very tired and I walk her upstairs and help her wash up for bed. She is understandably slow and by the time she lies down, she is half asleep. It is amazing to me how the body handles pain, healing, and stress. It sleeps to recover. I know when I get emotionally upset, I sleep. Coming home for the weekend is a big deal and her brain and body have had lots of activity today. She needs her sleep.

Our bedroom is just down the hall from the kids' rooms. We love it this way. The kids have to pass by our room to get to their rooms. There have been many times Greg and I have been hanging out in our room and the kids stop by on their way down the hall. They usually throw themselves down on our bed and conversation begins. Sometimes it's light conversation and sometimes it develops into deeper conversations. We are always available and they know that. Having everyone's rooms in close proximity to each other is a great thing when you are raising kids.

It's time for me to sit and relax. There's an old chair and ottoman I bought at a thrift store that sits in a corner of our bedroom. I have covered it to hide the bright yellow faux velvet fabric that has been clinging to this chair since it was made, probably in the 1950s. I have thrown a creamy off-white blanket over it and the ottoman is also covered in an off-white throw. The rest of our bedroom furniture is painted a creamy vanilla and our duvet cover is made of a creamy off-white matelassé fabric. Our floor to ceiling curtains are also off white, as well as the paint on our bedroom walls. This is our choice. When we are in our bedroom, it is calm and serene.

Sitting in my chair with my feet propped up on the ottoman, I call Deb Fly. I haven't seen or talked to Deb since we've been at Children's. I want to fill her in on what is going on with Anna and what the doctors said at our meeting this last Thursday. It is great to talk to Deb. She is calming, humorous, and always fills in the blanks for me. She is such a terrific friend. I have truly been blessed and feel honored to have so many supportive and incredible women in my life. Girlfriends are gifts that need to be cherished.

Greg finishes the blog and comes upstairs. The house is locked up, Sammy has gone potty, the kitties are in the garage and we are tired. Max's flight is scheduled to land at 11:57 am tomorrow and he should be home around 1:30 pm or so. We don't have to have Anna back to the hospital until 8 pm tomorrow night, so Max and Anna will have a chance to hang out and talk about Disney World. We think Greg's brother Doug and his family might be coming over tomorrow, too. Doug's wife Becky is one of the nicest people you would ever want to meet. They have a set of twins that love Anna and Max not only because they are their cousins, but because they are older and the little cousins think Anna and Max are cool. Anna and Max get a big kick out of this and enjoy hanging out with them. Tomorrow will be a full day and we are looking forward to it.

We wake up Sunday morning well rested. A good night of sleep was had by all. Thankfully even Sammy slept through the night without waking us up. He usually makes a lot of noises when he sleeps. Sighs, breathes rapidly, runs in place. It's like having a newborn in the house. It's very hard to sleep through this, but Greg manages while I lie there with my eyes wide open.

Greg is downstairs cooking breakfast and it smells delicious. Eggs, bacon, toast, coffee, and orange juice. Yum. Once Anna gets a whiff of this, she will fly downstairs. I need to watch for her and make sure she has her belt on and gets assistance on the stairs. I pull myself out of bed when I hear her coming. Downstairs we go to a huge spread of breakfast foods. Greg has outdone himself. Everything looks terrific.

During breakfast, Doug calls and says they'll be over this afternoon for a visit. We don't normally answer the phone during meals, but this is an unusual time in our lives. His timing sounds perfect. They will be here after Max gets home and just in time to see both Max and Anna before we have to go back to the hospital. The four cousins will be able to see each other and hang out together. The twins are a little young to fully understand what has gone on, but they do understand there was a car accident and Anna and Max are lucky to be alive. It will be good for Doug and Becky to see Anna's progress after having seen her at Harborview in the emergency room and a few days after the accident.

Max and Anna are the first grandchildren on Greg's side of the family. This is the first time there has ever been a crisis like this in Greg's family. It has been very scary for Greg's parents, brothers and their wives. Greg's brothers both have kids seven years younger than Anna and nine years younger than Max. As parents, our goal is to keep our kids alive and safe. That is easier to do when they are little because we have control over their lives. Our accident is a snapshot into every parent's future, something we all pray never happens to us. Our accident has made all of us painfully aware of the lack of control we have not only when our kids get older, but also in life. This is why faith is our stronghold and prayer continues to be our conversation. That day, angels held our kids tight and protected them from harm. Thank you.

After breakfast, Anna climbs up the stairs and back into bed. Even though she holds tight to the banister, I guide her up the stairs to her room and into bed. She does really well. Her balance is improving and her coordination is smooth. This is a relief. When she comes home on Wednesday it is good to know she can walk up the stairs, shower, and maneuver throughout the house. She is also beginning to remember some of what goes on from hour to hour, day to day. Thank you. These little steps and signs of recovery are encouraging for her and an answer to prayers for us.

Anna rests, I clean and do laundry, Greg reads the paper and then goes outside to work in the yard. I hear voices. Male voices. Oh good, Maxie must be home. I run outside to see him unloading his luggage from the Allens' car. He looks great. This trip was a good idea. I walk over to him, wanting to run of course, and give him a big hug. He hugs me back in a way that tells me he is glad to be home. His first words are, "Where's Anna?"

He quietly pushes her door open and creeps into her room. He looks at her laying there with her lamby up around her face and her white neck brace wrapped around her neck for protection. She slowly smiles and opens one eye. Tease. They both smile and Max carefully crawls up on the bed. Goofy kids. I half way close the door and walk away listening to Max answering Anna's questions about Disney World.

"The twins are here!" I yell up the stairs, "They just pulled in the driveway. Do you want them to come up or do you guys want to come down?"

"We're coming down," yells Max.

I hear them getting out of Anna's bed and Max is asking about the belt. Down the stairs they come with Max holding onto the belt around Anna's waist. This is a first. He has seen the belt but not been part of the guide process. He walks her down cautiously and is very careful not to get in her way. They make their way to the toy room at the same time the twins are entering the house through the laundry room door. Lots of people talking, both kids and adults, as we all end up with Anna and Max in the toy room. Anna sits down on a little chair by the computer and Emily sits on her lap. Anna wraps her arms around Emily's waist and gives her a little squeeze. Andrew sits in front of the computer and wants Max to show him how to play a game. The kids are happy.

Greg and Doug decide to watch some sporting event on TV. Becky and I have a chance to break off and go into the kitchen to talk. I bring her up to date on Anna and I can see the relief in her eyes. Still scared, but so happy to hear about Anna's progress and what our plans are in the near future. Neither one of us can believe she will most likely be back to school next Monday. It is amazing.

I can't believe how fast this day is disappearing. In a few hours, we have to go back to the hospital. The cousins are still playing in the toy room when I hear Anna say she is tired. It's time for her to rest before we eat and leave for Children's. She is taking the responsibility of saying she has to go lie down. Good. Max, Andrew, and Emily take Anna upstairs to bed as Doug and Becky gather coats and shoes. This has been a good visit for everyone and we really appreciate Doug and Becky coming over and bringing the twins. After they pull out of the driveway, I run upstairs to check on Anna. She's asleep.

Oh good. This allows me a little time to visit with Max. I say visit, but he would say question. If only he would volunteer information. I just want to know how things went on his little vacation. It must be that my high school journalism class ruined me. I just want to know the six basics: who, what, when, where, why and how. This is not unusual for a mom. Why is this always such a surprise to my children? After looking at so many child-rearing books, it must be that I do my own thing regardless. Maybe I should listen more. That's what Greg says. Listen to what? Everyone tells me things except my own children. Hmmm.

"Okay, Bug," I suggest, "Tell me about your trip. Give me one paragraph of information, with no less than three sentences."

Max opens up a little, "I had a great time. I am very thankful I could go. The rides were fun, the weather was okay and I am glad I went with Brad." That's about as much information as I can get. Not many specifics, but an overall view of his weekend. I'll just have to live with this information until I can talk to Pam and hear more about the fun trip they had.

Greg is humored by my conversation with Max. The three of us are in the kitchen and Greg is preparing leftovers. This is not an unusual situation. Greg and I often have resorted to asking Max for a paragraph or two of information. We even specify that it must be something we don't already know. I often ask myself if this is normal. According to the parents of Max's friends, he is not only hilarious, but talks all the time at their houses. I wish he would talk more at home, but I am always relieved to hear he is talkative and engaged with other people. I just love that boy.

Dinner is ready. Max volunteers go upstairs and bring Anna down to eat. He knows that after dinner, we will pack our bags for our final three days at Children's. It's comforting to think about coming home permanently with Anna. Even though the physical healing began hours after the collision, being in our home together will be an emotional hurdle we have overcome. We didn't overcome it by ourselves. We have overcome it through prayer and faith. Thank you, God.

The shuffling of two sets of slippers is a welcome sound. Down the stairs and into the dining room they come. Max has a hold of Anna's belt and guides her to her chair. Anna feels perfectly capable of accomplishing this herself and lets us all know it. Actually, her balance and coordination are improving so quickly, there's little doubt she could have walked herself downstairs and to the chair without incident. However, our instructions were to belt and guide her and we are not willing to take any chances with her healing body.

We always eat in the dining room. Our dining room table belonged to my dad's parents, my grandparents. My grandfather died before I was born and I barely knew my grandmother. Family issues. It seems sad now that my sisters and I didn't really know our grandmother. We have all inherited her beautiful earthly possessions and each one of us treasures the opportunity to take care of them. The dining room table, along with many of her personal belongings, is beautiful. The table is heavy, dark wood with a plank top and heavy, carved, pedestal legs that resemble large musical instruments. It extends to nine feet for our family gatherings and any other occasions, including opening up our home for end of season sports parties. The chairs are full of character and expression. I love owning family history and having my kids sit at their great grandparents table to pray, eat, laugh, and enjoy life. One day these treasures will be taken care of by my kids, then their kids and so on down the line. I love that. It makes me feel good.

Our dinner is hot, filling, delicious, and almost gone. Thank goodness for all of our meals. There is another one coming tomorrow night and Wednesday night, the night we get home. These meals are truly a blessing, allowing us to focus on the needs of our family. We appreciate them so much. I check the list with the meal plan and see that meals are scheduled through November 8th. I feel a little guilty because we will be home on October 24th, but have been told by Julie, the coordinator that everyone insists on feeding us and that this is their way of helping. Well, they are helping more than they know. It is humbling to see so many kind people, taking time in their daily lives to prepare a meal for our family. Thank you.

Max walks Anna back upstairs after dinner. I follow them up and collect my overnight bag and a few new magazines for our hospital stay. Anna gathers her belongings and Max takes her bag downstairs. We are ready to go back. Max runs back upstairs and brings Anna back with him. It's time.

Anna kisses Sammy, Belle, and Jazz goodbye, telling Belle she will be back in a few days. I think Belle understands her, but I can't be positive about that. Moses is in the garage and cranky I'm sure, so she just yells out, "Bye Mosey." while Greg loads our bags into the car. The kids hug goodbye and we strap Anna snuggly into her seat belt in the back seat. Off we go, with Max waving and pets watching us as we make our way slowly back to the hospital.

Children's Hospital has such a convenient entry and exit to the parking garage. Greg pulls up to the drop off area to unload the bags and let us out to wait while he finds a parking spot. It is a little cold outside, so Anna and I move inside the doors. Greg isn't gone long, and grabs our bags on his way into the building. Up to the Train floor we go and into the room we left behind yesterday. Everything is as we left it, nothing moved, nothing changed. Greg slips Anna into her bed and she raises the back of the bed up to watch TV. Greg unloads Anna's things into her drawers and I set my bag and my tote of magazines off to the side. We are all settled in.

Greg pulls his keys out of his pocket and wants to get back home to be with Max and to catch up on some work. It must be difficult to know you have a responsibility to get your work done while your baby girl is in the hospital recovering from a car accident. I don't know how he does it. I couldn't concentrate. I am amazed by his ability to focus.

He hugs Anna and gives her a little kiss on the forehead. She loves her daddy. We hug and kiss good- bye and I tell Greg I will call him later. Off he goes as I settle into my chair and watch TV with Anna. This was a good weekend and a great relief to know that Anna is able to function independently at home. She will need a watchful eye, but she is ready to move forward. I suppose weekend furloughs are a test. If they are, I think we passed with flying colors.

Chapter Thirteen

"I saw her as a leader. An inspirational leader"
—Sherri Staudacher

Monday morning. We both wake up refreshed and energized, having had a glimpse of home. This week will bring a close to our hospital stays, answers about returning to school, outpatient therapy appointments, and any remaining needs we may have at Children's. It's exciting and we are looking forward to the next chapter in our lives.

Anna is ready. She bounces out of bed and gets dressed. She's belted, of course, with me standing right next to her. She eats breakfast, brushes her teeth, and waits for her first therapist. This is the first time she has been ready to go and waiting. It's a great sign of her determination and sheer will power. Her occupational therapist comes in, looks her in the eye and says, "Anna, today we are doing some new things. Are you ready?"

"Yes," Anna replies, "Let's go." Anna wants her life back and she wants it back now. You can see it on her face and in her eyes. They leave the room with Anna belted, ready to take on the world. Thank you.

Lise Smith wants me to call her today, so I quickly shower and get ready for the day ahead. My notes are near my chair, and I sit down to pull out Lise's number and see what else is on my calendar. My calendar reminds me that Max has an appointment with a sports medicine doctor. This is related to his lower back and muscle strain due to basketball, having nothing to do with the car accident. It is a reoccurring soreness and Greg thinks Max should be checked out before he starts his season. We were in the process of arranging this appointment before the car accident. I know Max is glad he's going today because basketball is his passion and he wants to be completely ready and in top physical condition when the season starts.

Glancing at my calendar is a reminder of a full week. I am glad to resume my life and get back into our regular family schedule. I may miss the quiet of the hospital, but I am much happier having the bustle of my life as a wife, mom, volunteer, maid, and overseer of the cottage. Tomorrow is Max's 18th birthday. I just can't believe it. It seems like just yesterday we got up at 5:30 am to go to the hospital to free him from my body. He was ten days late and I am certain he was not interested in entering this world. No doubt he was trying to stay in his warm, comfortable surroundings as long as possible. After being induced, watching my contractions on a monitor, pushing for hours, trying to pull him out with forceps and then watching his heart rate decline, the emergency Caesarian section produced a 9lb 3oz, 22 inch, black haired baby boy. It was almost five in the afternoon and everyone was thrilled.

My mom was here to help us with our first baby, waiting with Greg's parents in the waiting room. Moms are intuitive. She told me later that she knew something was wrong. She was getting very concerned and was relieved once Max was delivered. Just before I was wheeled into the recovery room, the doctor had told the nurse to lower my head because my blood pressure had dropped so quickly once Max was born. However, once in the recovery room, the nurse forgot to lift my head back up and I was beginning to feel like my head was going to explode. Mom emphatically told the nurse to raise my head. She realized I was in danger of having some sort of medical emergency if I stayed in that position any longer. As I look back on that moment, I know she was right. A mom's job is never done and I am so thankful she was there. It's just so hard to believe so much time has passed since that day in the hospital. Tomorrow will be a rewarding celebration as well as a memorable one and I'm sure my mom will be celebrating his life right along with the rest of us. Who would have guessed Max's 18th birthday party would be held in a hospital? Now this is one Greg and I will never forget.

I reach for my cellphone and give Lise Smith a call. This afternoon I will call Garron Smith, the high school Principal, and let him know when we think Anna will be back in school. That will be a fun phone call to make. Lise answers. She is in class and will call me a little later. "But," she quickly adds, "A woman phoned Garron, saying she is the education coordinator at Children's, and wanted to know if Cedar Park was equipped to handle Anna's special educational needs." Lise went on to say this woman told Garron, "You're not getting the same Anna Brown you had."

Stunned, I say, "WHAT! Lise, she doesn't have any special educational needs."

"Well" Lise replies, "I didn't think there were any problems based on our previous conversations, but the education coordinator has created some confusion about what Anna may require. Garron has talked to the special education teacher from the grade school and asked for his help, if need be."

I know that Cedar Park is not equipped for special education in high school. Lise gathers that I am fuming. She says, "But, let me tell you what Garron told her. He said, 'We will take Anna Brown back any way we can get her.'" This comment from Garron speaks volumes about Cedar Park and about Garron. He's no pushover by any stretch, but he does have the best interest of his students in mind and I have always been convinced he will do whatever needs to be done to help a child succeed. Besides that, he gets a kick out of Anna and she thinks he's the greatest. Because of Anna's humor in her antics, I do believe she has been given a lot of grace at Cedar Park. And she just received more. I will never forget what Garron said to this woman. It's true, words are important.

Lise finishes with, "I will call you after school and we can set up a meeting with Anna's teachers this week."

"Okay, thanks Lise. I'll talk to you later." When I hang up, I am heartened by Garron's reply, but furious with this woman. I know exactly who she is. She has come in a few times to talk to me about Anna because the education coordinator we were assigned to was out of the office for a few days and she was filling in for him. But he's back, and will actually be meeting with Anna this afternoon to evaluate her. I am supposed to meet with him tomorrow and discuss reentry into school and her class schedule. He is certainly going to get an earful from me. I call Greg.

Greg is very calm. We talk through the situation and Greg's response is, "Wait and see what you hear from Tom," our education coordinator, "then call Garron tomorrow with the evaluation results." Of course, this is the best thing to do, but I am still angry. Here is my child fighting to get her life back and doing remarkably well and this woman is feeding misinformation to her school. It is infuriating and unprofessional. For the second time since the accident I have run into someone I want to slap.

Fortunately, there is time to calm down before Anna gets back. This is probably a good thing. I allow myself to think about going home. It's exciting and I am thankful to be getting back into our rhythm of life as a family. I haven't thought too much about being home because my priority has been to take care of, and be with, Anna. But now we have school, Max's basketball season, Anna's rehabilitation, and the holidays to look forward to. I can return to the nest and huddle around my family. Thank you.

Anna walks in tall and confident. She doesn't even look tired. Very proud of herself, she hands me her journal and says, "Read this Mom." I look through her morning activities and see that she has been a busy, busy girl today. Anna has done some important activities today that give us insight as to how she will function at home. She has made scrambled eggs with a little help from her therapist in operating the stove. To me, this indicates she can be in the kitchen, supervised, and has a little understanding of how appliances work. At home, we have a gas stovetop, which has an open flame, and it is important to keep all of us out of harm's way while Anna relearns how to live her daily life. Anna also found two locations in the hospital by using a map and asking for directions. The therapist notes that Anna did a great job, and only asked once in a confusing way. She also found a car in the parking lot while safely navigating the traffic flowing in and out. This is wonderful news. It suggests she is aware of her surroundings and is making decisions to keep herself safe while walking in public areas. These are unconscious decisions we all make every day as we move through life, but for Anna, she is learning to be independent and trying to take back the life she once had. I tell her I am so proud of her.

The therapist is also very proud of Anna's accomplishments. She knows how hard Anna is working to heal her body and she is continually impressed by Anna's determination to move forward. As the therapist sits Anna on the bed and takes the belt off from around Anna's waist, she says, "Let's make something with boiling water tomorrow!" Anna lets out a little laugh and says this activity sounds like lots of fun. A simple thing like boiling water has become a marker for us to make sure she's ready to come home. I know she will be successful.

Anna snuggles down in her hospital bed, waiting for lunch. For the first time, she isn't curling up with lamby and falling asleep. She is alert and awake. Our weekend furlough has given her a glimpse of her normal life that she so desperately wants back. She is not going to let anything get in her way. Anna is taking on her injuries with incredible determination. I know her. She will conquer.

Today is the first time that Anna and I have an opportunity to sit quietly and talk to each other. While we have been alone most of the time during our hospital stays, there have not been many times when we have been alone together that she has been awake or without visitors or both. This is a new opportunity. We have about an hour before her next therapy and I see she is relaxed and happy. We talk easily about her afternoon therapies and I remind her about her appointment with Tom, the education coordinator. She wants to know what he is going to do.

"Well, he is going to give you a few tests to determine how to integrate you back into your classes and homework. It will be a map for us and for Cedar Park, to ensure you are successful. It will give us a little heads up in areas you may struggle with. For example, Cedar Park needs to know what to do with you if you get tired or are having comprehension problems. The tests may tell your teachers what to watch for. It is just a few tests to give us a glimpse of your strengths and possible areas of weakness. It's no big deal."

"Oh, okay," she smiles and understands. Of course, I don't mention the conversation I had earlier with Lise. The odd thing about that whole incident is that this woman who called Garron never even talked to Anna. She came and saw me a few times, but never tested or spent time with Anna. Weird. Maddening.

Lunch arrives and Anna sits up in her bed to eat. She really loves being waited on and at this point she will eat almost anything put in front of her. Having your meals delivered on a tray and rolled right up under your nose is very convenient. Wait until she gets home. Back to reality we go. No meals will be delivered on trays, just the ring of the dinner bell will be enough to signal dinner is on the table and every one will have to come to the dining room table to eat it! I can't wait to see the response. Such a novel concept.

We spend the rest of her lunch hour talking about Max, school, the hospital, and going home. We are both excited about home and I can see a sparkle in her eye when it's mentioned. She's a little concerned about her next few weeks with outpatient physical therapy and her return to school, but she says she is ready. I tell her it's time to move forward. She agrees.

Anna's therapists have decided to meet her at her therapy appointments rather than back in the room. I will not see her again until she's done with her final therapy session this afternoon. The first therapist arrives just as we finish our conversation. Perfect timing. She wraps the belt around Anna's waist and off they go. Anna is looking more balanced every hour and walks out the door without much guidance. The belt continues to be our insurance policy just in case she gets dizzy. The dizziness seems to be mostly related to quick movements of her head, like when she is in physical therapy and practicing some of her basketball moves. The dizziness is scary. I pray it's not permanent. She is still healing inside. We have to be patient.

I call Greg to check in and Max picks up Greg's cellphone.

"Hi," I hear.

"Hi Bug. What's going on?"

"Uh, Dad and I are on our way to my doctor appointment."

"Oh good. Call me when you are done and let me know what the doctor said. Okay?"

"Okay." Of course, I know I will end up calling them to find out the results. I am impatient and they forget. Drives me nuts.

I mention to Max that dinner tonight will be veggie pasta salad and garlic bread. "Ummm, sounds good," he says.

"Yes, you will love it, Bug," I tell him, knowing he loves pasta. "Okay," I remind him, "call me later and let me know about your appointment." I hear a half-hearted acknowledgement and a little irritation of a second reminder as we say good-bye and I set my cellphone down.

Sitting back in my chair, I look around the room. Amidst Anna's stuffed animals, clothes, posters, cards and flowers, there are wire baskets attached to the wall, tubes intermittently popping out from connections to a larger piece of something, medical equipment suspended from the ceiling hanging over the bed, emergency buttons, a dozen electrical outlets behind Anna's bed with color coding in red, blue and tan, as well as a horizontal sliding clamp type apparatus reaching from side to side behind the hospital bed headboard. This room is equipped to handle things I will never be able to imagine. We have looked at this room as our home for the past week. The look and feel of the room is so warm and inviting that the reason for the equipment is never truly realized unless you need it. It becomes invisible. I think to myself, after all, this is a hospital room and it is ready for a variety of needs for kids in rehabilitation. I wonder about all the families that have come before us and stayed in this room. I pray they have been as successful as we have been thus far, and that they are home having a good life. I am so impressed by both Children's Hospital and Harborview. We are very fortunate to live in a city that supports both top-notch healthcare and emergency response. I thank God for all of this and for the people that have been given the gift of medical interest. It is a sacrifice in their lives and I know it. I want them to know they are appreciated and thanked for their time and life changing dedication. From the person who volunteers to push a treat cart around, to the receptionist, hospital guard, nurses, doctors and staff, they all make a difference. They have made a difference in my family's life and I will forever sing praises and thanks for each and every one of them.

The room phone rings and I answer, only to hear the guard tell me we have visitors. I say send them back and moments later Patty and Josh Orrico appear at the door. Josh is Max's good friend and teammate. Josh is one of the boys I snuck into the emergency room at Harborview to see Max. Patty is Josh's mom and a very calming influence over me at the boys' basketball games. Patty sits and watches the games while I talk, jump up and down, and eventually get up and pace back and forth at the top of the bleachers. She is a good person and very kind.

It's so great to see them. They have been praying for our family and are thrilled to hear how well Anna is doing. Josh has received a few reports from Max, but they have been spotty and not much information. I am sure it was along the lines of she's doing fine, which, of course, explains it all and nothing. Patty has been following the blog, but nothing new has been posted since Saturday. So, I fill them in on Anna's weekend at home and tell them how excited we are to have her coming home permanently on Wednesday. It feels so good to say we are going home. Thank you.

Josh smiles as we look up and see Anna come through the door. She loves Josh. We all do. He spends lots of time at our house, and if this season is anything like last season, I'll be wiped out of my freezer full of homemade pesto by the end of January. Josh eats more than any kid, or person, I have ever seen. Patty has even offered to buy us groceries. Dinner is a snack for Josh. The first thing Josh does when he comes into the house is look for food. I love that. I love that he is so comfortable at our home that he walks in, opens the cupboards, and the refrigerator door to find something to eat. The other boys give him a hard time, joking with him about his food intake, but they all love him. He is a great kid. Always smiling.

Anna and the therapist walk towards Josh and Anna hugs both Josh and Patty. The therapist takes off the belt, says goodbye and tells Anna she will see her tomorrow. Anna says goodbye and sits down on the bed to talk with Josh. They're so funny. Josh is very protective of Anna. Even though he has three sisters of his own, I think he assumes a little responsibility for Anna not only because he is Max's friend, but because he genuinely likes Anna and Anna genuinely likes him. He thinks of her as his own little sister. They're funny as they sit on the bed and catch up. Patty and I laugh at them and then have a moment to be thankful for them and the friendships that have been created around all these kids.

As usual when Anna has guests, the visit passes quickly. It's just about time for Anna to be tested by Children's education coordinator, Tom.

Josh and Patty say their goodbyes and give hugs and promises of prayer. I walk out the door with them and across the hall to get a snack for Anna. She is hungry and should have something to eat before her testing begins. I know both my kids well and they are much more alert and easier to be around if they have eaten. I pick up yogurt, a hardboiled egg and a little salt packet, a nutrition bar, string cheese, an apple, and water. I'm not sure exactly what she wants, but this protein will be good for her and she needs to have her fruit.

She is propped up in her bed when I dump all this food on her tray and roll it around until it is just under her chin. She pulls herself up further and begins eating. "Thanks Mom," I hear in between bites of apple and yogurt. "You're welcome, Poo," I reply.

She looks up from her food and says, "Don't call me that."

I laugh inside. I've been calling her Poo for as long as I can remember. Sometimes she likes it and sometimes she doesn't. It doesn't really matter to me. She is my Poo and I love her. She'll just have to get over it. She needs to eat. Food promotes an attitude adjustment.

When she's finished eating, Tom comes in and I get her ready to go. Belt on. Off they go. I pray she does well. I am still angry about that other woman. I can't wait for Anna's test results tomorrow.

Naturally, I have not heard from the boys about Max's doctor's appointment. I also want to speak to Lise Smith about Anna while Anna's not in the room. I think I will call Greg and Max first to get the results and then give Lise a try. Better make this snappy and get things going here.

Greg answers the phone with, "Oh, we forgot to call you."

"Oh really," I say, "I'm so surprised." He half way laughs, sensing a tad bit of sarcasm in my voice. But, I ask him to tell Max that Patty and Josh were here to visit Anna and that we had a great time together. Max will like that.

The doctor wants Max to go to physical therapy and confirms that this recurring soreness is due to repeated use of the same muscles. Max is a point guard nine months out of the year, if not more. He has a regular season, plays in recreational leagues and then he plays basketball with his friends. It's nonstop and it's hard on his body. The conditioning is great, but it's not cross training. It's the same use of the same muscles over and over again. That's hard on a body. Physical therapy starts immediately because basketball workouts start in three weeks and Max needs to be ready and pretty much pain free. We are all glad to get this underway and Greg says Max is looking forward to doing whatever the physical therapist prescribes to alleviate the soreness. Good.

Greg thinks he and Max will probably stay home tonight unless I think either he or they need to come. "It's okay," I say, "I need to call Lise Smith. Anna is with the education coordinator and you guys have dinner coming in and hour or so. Don't worry about it. We're fine. Anna hasn't napped today and she will probably be really tired." Greg is okay with that and actually, I am looking forward to some quiet time with Anna. Tomorrow night is Max's birthday celebration and the following day we go home. I do ask Greg to call and verify with his mom that they will be at the hospital tomorrow night at 6:00 pm and that they are bringing the celebration cake. He will take care of it, no problem. We confirm that we will talk later tonight.

I reach for my bag as my cellphone begins to play music. It's Lise Smith. Oh good.

I pick up, "Hello, I was just getting ready to call you." Lise says she's had a very busy day, but has some new ideas for Anna's return, depending on her needs.

"I've spoken with Anna's teachers again and everyone is willing to be flexible and do whatever they need to do to accommodate Anna's return. I spoke to Amy Bettinger, and she has a few ideas. Anna can have a late arrival and drop first period if she needs to. Or, she can use first period as a prep period and either help in the English Department or do her own work to stay on top of things. This scenario may require some kind of summer program, but it is an option to transition Anna back into school now and have her graduate on time with her class. I can also tutor Anna for her 5th period class." Lise emphasizes that this is all based on Anna's needs. Lise and I agree we won't know what her needs are until she actually gets back to school, but it is good to have some ideas in mind before we get there.

"Okay Lise. That's great. Anna's in testing with her education coordinator as we speak. So, after the test results come in tomorrow, I will call you and Garron."

"Good," Lisa says, "I am going to schedule a meeting with you, Anna, Garron, Amy, and Anna's teachers for this Thursday at 3:00 pm."

"Perfect," I confirm. At least we have a plan started and if we need to change everything later we will, but for now, we are planning on getting Anna back to school next Monday with some sort of schedule, allowing for rest and help. Thank you.

It is late afternoon, almost dinner time when Tom and Anna come back into the room. Tom says everything went very well, Anna did a great job and he will have the final test results tomorrow morning. Tom wants to meet with me at 11:30 am. Anna can join us as soon as she is done with her morning therapies. He wants to make sure Anna hears the results as well, and can ask questions if she needs to. After all, they are her results and his recommendations affect her reentry to high school and the rest of her sophomore year. Anna is visibly pleased with her performance and is absolutely thrilled it's over. No more testing. She has just a few more days of hospital therapy and then home at last.

We call Greg. With good news, I think. Anna wants to talk to her daddy and I hand her my cellphone. They have a few minutes to catch up on today's activities before we hear the cart wheels rolling towards our room. In comes Anna's dinner. She looks at the tray, lifts the lid and says goodbye to Greg as she hands me the phone and begins eating. I let Greg know we will call him later. Anna's already attacking her plate and I am going to run to the cafeteria in a few minutes and grab something to bring back to the room. I am starving, too. It's difficult for me to leave Anna, so I have lost a little weight due to lack of food, as well as the emotional stress which leaves me without an appetite. I wait for Anna to finish her dinner and then leave for the cafeteria. She turns on the TV the minute my feet pass over the threshold. Goofy girl. I hope we can agree on a show.

She eyeballs me the minute I walk in her room. "What did you get?" she asks.

I must be honest, as she is straining her eyes to get a look at my plate. "Hamburger and fries," I say, "do you want a treat from the kitchen?"

She thinks for a second and says, "Sure."

I set my plate down and go get her some yogurt and fruit. This ought to satisfy her sweet tooth and silently persuade her to leave my tray alone. There's no point in both of us eating poorly. Thank goodness my yearly physical was in July. My cholesterol was 191. Since we usually eat lots of vegetables, fruits, chicken and fish, these fatty meals on a regular basis will destroy my plan to control my cholesterol through food. My doctor would not be happy.

Anna sucks up the yogurt and munches down on apple slices. She's full. Thank goodness.

I remind Anna that tomorrow is Max's birthday and Gramma and Grandpa are coming to the hospital with a cake to celebrate. I let her know we will probably order pizza, just to make it easy, and all of us will venture down the hall to the recreation room for the party. Both of us think this idea sounds like fun and are looking forward to a party on our last night here.

While Anna flips through channels on the TV, I call Greg to check in one last time. He and Max are fine and have just finished their dinner. It was delicious, according to Max, and Greg agrees. With the knowledge that all is well with our family, we say good night. I promise to call Greg after my meeting with Tom tomorrow morning.

Sitting back in my chair, I see Anna's eyes are getting heavy. She has had lots of therapy today and tomorrow holds the same full schedule. When she lowers her bed, snuggles with lamby and closes her eyes, I slip the remote control from her grasp and turn off the TV. Once again, she's fast asleep. I turn out her light, get ready for bed and thank God for a great day. Amen.

Chapter Fourteen

"We thank and praise God with you"
— Pastor Craig Patterson

"Happy Birthday to you, happy birthday to you. Happy birthday dear Maxie, happy birthday to you." Anna and I belt out the song at 7:30 am, over the phone, knowing Max will be leaving for school by 7:45 am.

He's happy. He says thanks when we finish our rendition of the birthday song, which has a few new notes and a unique harmony added to the mix. Anna and I want Max to know we are thinking about him today and that we love him.

"Have a great day and we will see you tonight for your big birthday celebration," I add.

"Okay," he quickly responds, obviously wanting to finish his morning routine. We send him our hugs and hang up the phone.

Anna and I look at each other and smile. She really loves Max. Anna has never blamed him for the car accident. I find it interesting, even though we know it was an accident, that she has never pointed a finger or tried to put blame on anyone for her situation. This is a testament to her character. She focuses on her recovery and works as hard as she can to regain her life. What happened that day is not nearly as important to her as what is happening today or what will happen tomorrow. Thank you.

We hear the cart rolling down the hall. Breakfast is on its way. Anna pulls her lamby up around her shoulders and gets herself ready for her meal. While we wait for the cart to roll in, Anna and I review today's schedule and talk about tonight. She won't be done with her therapies until 4:00 pm this afternoon. I remind her again, that Gramma and Grandpa are coming for Max's birthday celebration. "Oh, that will be fun," she replies. She has forgotten that they will be celebrating with us. However, she does remember that this is her last full day at Children's. I tell myself one step at a time and say a silent prayer for her memory and her healing.

Anna is very nice to all the people that work at Children's. Well, except for her testiness with Dr. Crew. Not sure what that's about. Maybe it's because he taps her on the chest to wake her up if he needs to talk to her when she is sleeping or maybe it's because he is very direct and didn't take any attitude from her that very first day. I do know that she can't stand that chest tapping business. It annoys her beyond belief. I suppose I don't blame her. It would be very uncomfortable to have someone tapping you on the chest while you were resting and exhausted. But, it is a very safe way to wake someone up. Every doctor and therapist from both Harborview and Children's have used this technique to wake Anna up and it certainly works. Maybe I should try this at home. Hmmm, that would push the kids over the edge. I think our mornings would go downhill fast.

Anna smiles as the cart rolls in. She says thank you to the attendant as she removes the lid from the tray. Yum. Smells good and looks good. Anna gobbles down her breakfast and enjoys every bite. When she has finished, she pushes the tray aside and swings her legs over the edge of the bed and plants her feet firmly on the ground. I quickly go to her side to steady her. Into the bathroom she goes. Actually, she's walking somewhat normally today. While we are in the hospital, she must always wear her belt to stay safe. So, I grab the belt and have it ready for her when she comes out. She manages to get herself dressed and ready to go. Everything except her tennis shoes. She waits until it's time to go before she puts on her shoes, just so she can climb back into bed and rest. Putting her shoes on has been one of her most difficult tasks. She has to pull her knee up, tilt her head down and manipulate the shoe laces. Initially, we put her shoes on for her. The head movement and balancing of her body made her a little unstable. I put the belt on Anna and we wait.

This morning she has a little change of pace. She will be working with Tom, her education coordinator, before she starts into her regular therapies. She will be in school for an hour, with Tom, to help him finish his overall evaluation and make sure she is ready to go back to school next Monday. Anna knows the actual testing is over, but doesn't realize this morning is important in determining how we should integrate her back into her daily school routine. I am not going to say anything about her meeting this morning. She sees this as just another therapy. That's best. No pressure. I want her to relax and do her best without being anxious about her performance.

Tom comes in and Anna reaches for her tennis shoes. She sits carefully on the bed and slips her shoes on one at a time. She ties the laces and stands up. She's not dizzy. She manages her task like a pro. No problems. They walk out the door and Anna walks without hesitation or imbalance. Tom holds the belt for safety, but Anna is mastering her balance without help from anyone or anything. Deep breaths. Thank you.

The next few hours of the day are mine. Greg and Max won't be coming until later this afternoon after Max gets out of school. I look at my calendar. All I really have is a meeting with Tom and then phone calls to Lise and Garron at Cedar Park. My cellphone is full of messages and Greg has given me a list of people that have called the house. Food, gifts, and well wishes continue to pour in. Today is the perfect day to return phone calls and update my thank you list.

I leisurely work my way through the morning routine. Shower, make-up, hair, and clothes. By the time I am done, Tom has returned Anna to the room and she is waiting for her occupational therapist. I lift my eyebrows and give him a questioning look. He responds, "Anna did a great job. Let's meet right around the corner in the little common area around 11:30 am to review Anna's results." He looks at Anna and says, "Anna, you can join us out there after your speech therapy session." Anna says okay and sits down on her bed. Tom says goodbye and passes Anna's speech therapist on the way out the door. Anna rises and greets her therapist with a smile and determination. Once again, she leaves and won't be back until lunch time. I sit down comfortably in my chair bed and begin returning phone calls.

Before I know it, the clock reads 11:25 am and it's time for me to meet with Tom. I pack up my glasses, pen and notebook and walk out to the common area, just a few feet from Anna's room. I take a seat to wait for Tom. He's on time and smiles as he sits down on the couch. I have learned to read people's faces these past few weeks. If news is promising, I see smiles and a hopeful glint in the eyes. If news is unknown or troubling, there are no smiles and the eyes are serious. This may sound like easy things to detect, but they aren't. The eyes are the messengers. The smile is the bonus. In Harborview, the eyes were serious until the confirmation that she was being discharged to Children's for rehab. Then the eyes danced. They were followed by huge smiles of success. They were right though. She was alive, talking, and moving. That was successful enough for all of us for the time being. Tom's eyes tell me we are in an interesting place with Anna.

Tom reviews the results with me and tells me there are gaps in her performance. My heart skips a beat. But, he says, "None of these gaps are unusual for a patient with traumatic brain injury." Anna's brain is still healing. He thinks it is in Anna's best interest to return to school next Monday, but he has a few suggestions for us to follow for Anna to be successful. He suggests:

- Tutorial help should be available in all subjects.
- Organizational skills need to be watched. Make sure she has access to outlines and notes for each class.
- Weekly feedback on her progress from her teachers so she does not become overwhelmed by school work.
- Everyday/week she is heading towards full recovery. One year of growth is a significant marker.
- She is disinhibited, (I know that) and the teachers should be aware of this.
- Watch her attention span. She needs to sit at the front of the class.
- Our house rules and school rules stay the same. Keep a schedule and keep her on task. She may exhibit more defiance than usual, but no excuses for her.
- Treat her as normally as possible so she feels normal.
- She should stay involved with her basketball team. No running until her collar is off.
- She should have an escort from class to class so she doesn't become overwhelmed. She can't carry her own backpack and will need help with books or heavy items.

Tom sums up his evaluation with additional test results. He reviews Anna's actual test scores with me. Some of the scores and percentiles look good and others frighten me. I want to know how she did, but I am hesitating. Do I really want to know or do I want to continue to faithfully believe she will be her old self again? I am her mom. I love her. I am filled with peace knowing she will be healed. I am going to go with what I know. She will be healed. Peace.

Tom continues to explain that Anna is in great shape given she has suffered a traumatic brain injury. Her overall performance tells us she is ready for school and will be fine if we can tweak her academic schedule a little bit and follow through with his list of suggestions. The areas she has the most trouble with are memory, processing, and expression. It's all about memory and processing. I know that. But to see it in black and white attached to a score and percentile is heart wrenching. Anna doesn't need to see some of these scores right now. I don't want her to be discouraged. I don't want her to see these. I will never show her these. Now I know why Tom and I are reviewing these scores without Anna here. Fear begins to creep in.

Tom can see my fear. He looks at me and says "She can go back to school on Monday. I will forward the test scores to Cedar Park today. She can go back to school. She's okay. She doesn't need any special assistance or require any special help, aside from what suggestions I am giving you."

My mind is reeling. I am remembering the academic Anna, the smart Anna, the quick-witted Anna, the competitive Anna. I am remembering my Presidential Award for Outstanding Academic Achievement Anna. At this moment, in my minute of panic, God taps me on the shoulder and lets me know she's going to be fine. She has some work to do. Look at the progress we've made in the last two weeks. She's going to be fine. She's healing. Trust me.

I calm down, look at Tom and listen to his words of encouragement, "This is normal. Most of her scores are within normal limits. Her brain is healing. She can go back to school and she will be fine." I relax back into the couch and continue looking at her test results. I will stay positive and remember that she is alive and she is healing. She is my baby girl. The most important words I have heard up to this moment are this is normal. That's what Anna wants and that's what all of us want. We want Anna to be her normal self.

We are waiting for Anna when Tom asks me if I have any other questions or concerns. I open my notepad and look at my notes to review the list of questions I had prepared for our meeting. Ahhhh. That woman. The other educational coordinator. I explain to Tom how she interfered in his absence and I relay to him the conversation she had with Garron Smith. I continue by explaining that this woman has created confusion and given misinformation to Garron, thus making it appear that Anna needs a special education teacher and other special assistance at Cedar Park. I convey my irritation with her and with the perception she has fabricated about Anna's condition. Tom sits calmly, listening to my story. When I am done, he smiles. Tom is very professional. He says Anna's test results speak for themselves and he will forward those to Cedar Park as well as his own recommendations as her educational coordinator. Enough said.

Here she is. Anna Brown. She sits down on the couch right next to me. Her therapist smiles and waves goodbye as Anna turns her head and looks at Tom. "Well," he says, "you can go back to school on Monday." The smile on her face speaks volumes. She's thrilled, relieved and anxious all at the same time. Tom doesn't go over every detail of the test results with Anna. He just gives her the big picture, including areas she will need to work on and things that may be difficult for her. He explains to Anna that she might get tired and need a break. She might not make it through a full day of school at first. She may find remembering things difficult. He lets her know that all of this is normal. Tom makes Anna feel normal. This is what she needs. He shows Anna the list of suggestions he and I have already gone over. She looks at them and understands. While she is nodding yes with her head, I know that what she really hears is back to school on Monday. Those are the most important results to her and that is all she cares about. Good. Good for her.

Tom is done and Anna is ready for lunch. Tom reminds us he is available if we have any more questions as he gives me his card. I thank him for helping us and for listening to me rant about his coworker. He smiles. I really like Tom.

Lunch is waiting for Anna when we reach the room. It's sitting on her rolling tray, pushed into position over her bed, waiting for her. Her afternoon of therapies starts in a few minutes, so I remind her to eat up because she will be leaving shortly. She pushes the rolling tray aside, climbs into bed and pulls the tray up to her lap. Let the eating begin. I'm hungry, too. I guess I will go down to the cafeteria while she is in therapy.

Anna has physical therapy as her first appointment this afternoon. She likes this particular therapist. This lady gets Anna. When she comes in the door to pick her up, Anna smiles, knowing they will have work, fun, and lots of laughter today. The therapist incorporates Anna's love of basketball into some of her physical therapy exercises. It is a hard work for Anna, but she loves it. This lady is the one who said to me, "I have never seen anyone as determined and motivated as Anna." By allowing Anna to practice some of her basketball plays in therapy, she has given Anna additional confidence and desire to improve her physical well-being. This is one of the reasons Children's Hospital is so great. Thank you.

I grab my wallet and walk out the door with them. They make their way towards the stairs while I begin winding my way to the elevators and down to the cafeteria. I think about all the blessings that have been heaped on our family. People have been amazing. People are amazing. We all get caught up in our everyday lives and our everyday routines. But when others are in crisis, the true spirit of mankind emerges and we flock to each other in support. It's a beautiful thing to be part of. It's a beautiful thing to witness. People are good. People are important.

I must be cautious about my lunch choice today as I cruise around the cafeteria trying to make a decision. We are having pizza and cake for dinner. Oh, the saturated fat. I think a salad would be good for now, considering I sit most of the time during the day. My body will be in shock next week when I get back into my workout routine and my daily life. It's not often that I sit down at home. I am on the go from the moment I get up in the morning until the moment I crawl into bed at night. Monday, Wednesday and Friday I am up early in the morning with the family. Greg leaves for work, the kids leave for school, and I leave for the gym. Tuesday and Thursday, the kids leave for school, I leave shortly thereafter for my teaching job and Greg works from his office at home. Of course, in the midst of all of this, there are breakfasts to be served, lunches to be made, dishes to be cleaned, and four animals to be fed, watered, petted, and loved on. Since I won't leave the house until our bed is made, the kitchen is spotless, and the house is picked up, life is fast and furious. No time to sit down! Oh, and did I mention laundry? One of Max's sweatshirts is a load on its own. "Why do they make them so heavy," I ask myself, "why?"

With my wallet tucked under my left arm and the food tray loaded up with a large plate of salad and a tall glass of iced tea, I carefully make my way back to the room. Sometimes, but not today, I stay and eat in this little area just outside the cafeteria. One day there was a lady selling jewelry, scarves, and other interesting little items right here in the hospital by the cafeteria. I didn't buy anything, but it was really fun to look. However, today I will eat in our room. Life is about to change again and I really want to make my calls and take a look at my calendar. There are appointments to cancel and appointments to make for Anna and Max, as well as decisions Greg and I need to make concerning our family. Staying organized helps me feel as though I have some control. If I have some control, then I feel like I have a purpose and it helps me stay focused. By staying focused, I can stay strong. Strength is crucial right now. I am going to do what I do best. Organize our lives.

After the final crunch of lettuce is heard, I dial Lise Smith to give her the update on Anna. She answers her cellphone and I review some of the information Tom gave me this morning, emphasizing Anna can go back to school on Monday and doesn't require any special education allowances. She will need to be watched, rest if necessary, and we will see how it goes. Anna may have a few glitches, but her test results, overall, were normal given the circumstances and Tom feels she will be fine. Lise is so kind and very anxious to help Anna reenter into Cedar Park. She reiterates that the teachers are ready to help in any way and she reminds me about our meeting at 3:00 pm on Thursday.

"Tom has a list of suggestions," I tell Lise, "so, I will bring those with me to the meeting and make sure everyone has the information on the list. He is also sending Anna's evaluations and test results to Cedar Park." "Good." replies Lise. We both understand that this is, at least, a starting point. I make sure to tell Lise I am going to call Garron next and let him know he can ignore what the other education coordinator had told him. I will also tell Garron the final evaluation and test results are on their way and Anna will be back to school on Monday Three weeks after the car accident. We both agree this is a miracle.

I am excited to talk to Garron. He is so supportive of Anna. He is fully aware of the changes made in Anna's schedule and wants me to know that, just in case, he has talked to the elementary special education teacher and this teacher is available if we need him. I thank Garron, assure him and reassure myself, that those services will not be necessary. It's done. I was finally able to clear the air on Anna's behalf. Thank you.

With the test results in, discussed, and on their way to Cedar Park, I sit back. I feel like a weight has been lifted from my shoulders. Relief. Anna is going back to school. Anna is leaving the hospital. Max is in school and preparing for his basketball season. Our family is coming back together. Our lives have been changed forever. Were we complacent? Were we moving through life and not taking time to appreciate the importance of family? Probably. I think that's natural. In one fell swoop, God took our family, put us in a cup, shook us up and threw us back into the world. He changed us. He told me everything was going to be okay. I believe Him.

My calendar is loaded with plans scheduled before the accident. Some I call and cancel, others I call and confirm. We still have doctor appointments to schedule and outpatient therapy appointments to review. Lots of things planned. But, one thing I do know, life continues on all around us and while we are reentering the race, the most important thing is the people. Not the activity, the people.

Here she comes. Oh, she's tired. She thrusts her journal into my hand and then plops herself down on the bed. Her therapist barely gets the belt off. Anna scoops up lamby. She's out. Again.

These are her last journal entries. The journal tells me she had lots of brain exercises today. She had to use her memory, listening to stories and then answering questions about those stories. That must have been hard for her. She also played word games and solved brain bogglers. She boiled water in occupational therapy and worked her body hard in physical therapy. She's exhausted. Determined, but exhausted. I close the hospital door and sit in my chair to watch her. So quiet, so peaceful. I think to myself, "Get your rest Poo, your next adventure begins soon." I smile, she sleeps.

I wish my mom was here. I mean physically here. She would have been terrified initially, but then she would have put her game face on and charged forward with support and found a way to lace a little humor into the situation. I think she would have called Teensie, grabbed Ann, and flown up here within hours, even though I would have told her to wait until we knew what was going on. Moms that participate in their children's lives are the glue of the family. They have an intuition that no other human being on the face of the earth can possess. I wholeheartedly believe the saying Mom knows best is 100% true. A mom knows her children better than anyone else and has the uncanny ability to steer her child in the right direction. However, along with this gift goes the title of dumping ground. They go hand in hand. Like salt and pepper. A child has to have someone to blame for something at some time. That would be the mom. Heaven knows I dumped on my mom, particularly in high school. I never told her I was sorry for my selfishness. She knew me better than anyone and let me be myself. I am sure it was hard for her at times, but she let me stride confidently forward and conquer my life without one word of criticism. She was a great mom and I know she would have thoroughly enjoyed Anna, as her grandchild. If she could have spent one day with Anna, no doubt the word karma would have been fresh on her mind. I would love to hear her say it. I wish my mom was here. Physically.

Max calls. They're almost here. He's happy and excited to see his baby sister and celebrate his 18th birthday with the family. I guess I'd better pick up a few things and tidy up the room for the party tonight. Greg's blog and Anna's phone skills have put the word out that tonight is a family celebration and not the best time for visitors. Everyone knows tomorrow is the big day. Anna is going home. Her friends have already told her they will be visiting the minute school gets out. Thank goodness we will have dinner delivered tomorrow night. What a treat.

Anna is still sleeping soundly when I hear the familiar patter of Max and his Nikes approaching the room. I call all of his shoes basketball shoes, even though he would debate they're not all basketball shoes. He actually has a shoe obsession, I am sure of it. And, they're all Nikes. Greg also wears Nikes only his walk is softer. Anna even wears Nikes. I am a New Balance girl, myself. I think about our shoes. I'll have to make sure they're all contained when I get home. I trip on them daily in the garage. Everyone, except me of course, leaves their shoes wherever they happen to walk out of them. I'll need to police that for Anna. No tripping and losing your balance allowed. Greg's and Max's shoes are the size of small watercraft compared to Anna's and mine. I'd better talk to the boys about putting their shoes away. It will only be the millionth time. Maybe this time they'll pay closer attention.

In they come, quietly, noticing that Anna is sound asleep. I lip sing Happy Birthday to Max and give him a hug. He just looks at me and smiles. Then I remind Greg, before I forget, that we have a meeting in the morning to review the therapist's final evaluations. They will update us on Anna's current progress and give us ideas and strategies to help her be successful at home. The final decisions about outpatient therapy will be made and given to us in writing so we will know where to go and how to proceed. We also have to complete the paperwork for check out and fill out a survey concerning our stay at Children's and the care we received. That will be easy. How many times can I say excellent. Greg says he'll be here around 9:00 am anyway to help us pack up and get ready to leave. Good. We should be on our way home as soon as the meetings are done and the last of the paperwork is filled out. Hopefully, that will be right around lunchtime. In roughly twenty-four hours we will be home. All four of us. Home. Thank you.

Oh. We see movement in the bed. Her legs are stretching out towards the foot rail, her arms loosening up around lamby and we watch the slow but sure opening of her eyes. She just lays there for a moment, motionless, with eyes fully open, watching. I wonder if she's really awake as we all look at her and get no reaction. Her eyes move across the room and settle on Max. She smiles. Yes, she's awake. What a goofball. She's so dramatic.

Max starts laughing at her. She just looks around the room with a big grin. I guess the party has begun. Max tells her to scoot over and positions himself next to her on the bed. He turns on the TV. They watch TV, but all the while Anna is grilling Max on the latest news from Cedar Park. She can't possibly go back to school without being in the know! Honestly.

Gramma and Grandpa arrive with cake and gifts. They have a bonus. Salad. Where's the wine? Aha, they have thought of everything. We order the pizza and get ready to go down to the party room. Since we can't reserve the room, it is first come, first serve. Even though I have rarely seen anyone down there, (please not tonight), we would love to have Max's celebration outside of Anna's hospital room. Anxiously, I run down to the party room to take possession of the table and chairs. Sure enough, just in time. Visiting kids follow me into the party room to play games and goof around while their parents visit with patients. Fortunately, I have commandeered a table and six chairs. We are ready for Max's birthday celebration.

I lay out a few birthday decorations. This is not what I had planned for Max's 18th birthday. But, I count our blessings and I am thrilled we are here together and everyone is alive. The funny thing is that Max could care less where or how we celebrate. Since he hates to call attention to himself, this celebration is just perfect for him. He has food and his whole family. These are the most important pieces in his life right now. This is good. Thank you.

The visiting kids run out as quickly as they ran in. The room is empty once again. I hear the voices of my family coming down the hall towards our little party. Greg has the pizza in hand, Gramma has the cake and Grandpa is carrying both the salad and the presents. They set everything down on the decorated table as Max walks in with Anna. "Happy Birthday," I scream, as though it's a big surprise party! He smiles. Max sits Anna in the chair next to him, both of them eyeballing the pizza. "Time to eat," Greg announces opening up the pizza box. I am glad Gramma brought salad because this pizza is going to disappear quickly. Greg dishes up the salad with a piece of pizza on each plate and I give everyone a fork, napkin and a drink. Grandpa opens the wine and pours a glass for Gramma, Greg and me. Very fun.

When the last piece of pizza is eaten, Gramma brings the cake to the center of the table. Greg lights the candles and we sing the Happy Birthday song to Max. We sing loudly. He smiles. He's tired. We gobble up the cake in seconds. It's not every day we have chocolate cake around here or at home. Cake is usually a birthday thing for us. We are more of the chocolate chip cookie eating crowd. This is a special treat. Our celebration is not only a milestone because it's Max's 18th birthday, it's a miracle that we are all together and intact both mentally and physically. Thank you.

Max begins to open his gifts. He doesn't have too many, but he really doesn't care. He always opens presents, says thank you, and sets them off to the side in a pile. He's done this since he was little. It's not the gift so much that excites him, as it is the opening and the surprise of the present. We have never been a family that knows what their birthday or Christmas gifts will be in advance. We do wish lists and then we wait and see. It's the anticipation of the gift that is so exciting. Max loves that part. We all do. So, once again, next to Max sits a small pile of gifts. He's done. He's thankful. He's thankful for lots of things this year and we are thankful for him.

We clean up our mess in the party room, making sure to leave it as we found it, ready for the next group to celebrate their milestones and miracles. Back to the room we go, with packages and family in tow.

We are able to hang out for a little while, but Gramma and Grandpa want to get back home. They don't live too far from the hospital, but it is dark and raining outside and they are ready to go. Anna and Max give them big hugs and say goodbye. That leaves the four of us, our little family, all bundled together in celebration of Max. It's wonderful. I watch Max. He's a happy boy. He's strong inside. I'm proud of him. I love him.

Naturally, our conversation becomes a discussion about basketball. Max has been cleared by his doctor and is ready to play. His stitches are out and his hand is healed. Coach Franklin has his point guard back and Max is looking forward to the challenge. This is the year. This is the best team Cedar Park has had in years and we have a great shot at going to state. Max is excited to be part of this team and all of us, including Anna, are thrilled for him. Going to state would be the perfect way to end his senior year and his final days as a varsity basketball player. After everything that has happened this last few weeks, a successful season would be one more blessing.

Anna handles this whole conversation beautifully. She loves Max and his basketball buddies. She wants only success for them. In the midst of discussing our chances of going to state, the conversation switches to the varsity girls team. We wish the same success for their team. Most of them are seniors this year and have taken Anna under their wing from the minute she joined the varsity team last year as a freshman. She was their one and only baby on the team last year and they loved her. It was remarkable how they included her in everything they did. Half way through the season, Anna became a starter. It was awesome and they were proud of their baby. They were excited about Anna this up-coming season. She is their best legacy and they adore her. Everything has changed now. But, those girls have visited Anna consistently at both Harborview and Children's hospitals. They've made her laugh and she has made them laugh. They are great girls and have been unbelievably supportive of Anna. Anna has no memory of how many times they have come to see her, but I remember and I appreciate every visit, every laugh.

"Well," Max sighs, "I better get home and do some homework. Thanks for the party, Mom."

"Happy 18th birthday, Max," I whisper and give him a hug. He hugs me back. He walks over to Anna smiling and hugs her in her bed. Greg gives Anna and me a kiss and the two boys in our lives walk out the door, Greg in a heavy coat and Max in a heavy, hooded sweatshirt. It's raining and cold outside. Once again, I will call home before I go to bed and make sure they arrive home safely. Then I can relax.

Anna and I are tired. Anna gets up to wash her face and brush her teeth. Within minutes, she is curled up in bed with lamby wrapped around her shoulders and face. I say, "Goodnight, Poo." as her eyes close and she drifts into a deep slumber.

No magazines tonight, just a quick call home and sleep. They're home and everyone is safe. "Goodnight my family," I say to myself as I close my eyes and think about going home tomorrow. I feel good. Thank you.

Chapter Fifteen

"In a brief moment, the kids realized life can be fragile"
— Judy Raynor

As I lie awake in my special little chair bed, knowing this morning is going to be busy, I dwell on the importance of home. When I was growing up, we lived in a four-bedroom ranch style home in the desert of Las Vegas. At that time, we were considered to be way out in the desert. And I do mean way out. There were three streets in the middle of nowhere, surrounded by desert creatures and tumbleweeds, grouped together with a series of individually built homes. It was a mismatched group of people that wanted to live out in the open and raise their kids away from the dangers of big cities.

We had moved from Southern California to Las Vegas where my dad bought a General Tire franchise. He wanted to keep us out of trouble. I'm sure most people thought my parents were crazy, particularly our extended family members. But, in California, we were surrounded by kids getting into unhealthy situations and an environment not conducive to enjoying the positive benefits of nature. It was a turbulent time. It was the 60s and the Beatles had just come to America, as well as, free love, free sex, free drugs, and hippies. Although he grew up in Southern California, and graduated from USC, Dad's conservative upbringing and service in WWll led him to believe that raising his family in Southern California was not a good idea. I probably would have done something very similar to what my parents did. Move.

Yes, Las Vegas was an interesting choice. But that is where the business opportunity came up, plus we were so physically removed from what Sin City was all about, that we were never exposed to the dealings of the real Las Vegas until much later in life. We were allowed to be kids. Thus, after a few months of apartment living, my parents bought a house. We grew up in this house that became our home. We had a much-loved German Shepherd named Heidi and later, another German Shepherd, Dresden.

She was a little crazy. Over the years, we raised a few horses, cats, a donkey named Sweet Pea, a chihuahua my mom referred to as Poopsie and at one point, chickens, and a pig. The lot next door eventually became ours and my parents built an arena for the horses. Ann and Teensie both loved horses. Me, not so much. I loved dolls, clothes, human friends, and eventually, boys.

When I left Las Vegas to go to college at Oregon State, I never truly moved back home. The Pacific Northwest was, and is, my kind of place. No tarantulas sauntering across the street in the baking heat, no vinegaroons peeking out of their holes in the ground, no black widow spiders building a nest in the middle of the night in your hallway, and no scorpions to be found running around the yard. Oh, and no flying beetles that shed their skins and left them sitting, intact mind you, on the branch of a tree. I hated those beetles. Yet, Las Vegas was my home growing up. My mom was a stay-at-home mom and my dad made sure we were well taken care of. Life wasn't always perfect, but it was our life and we had a place we called home. People make memories in homes. I think home is a warm word. And today, my family is going home. Our home. More memories to be made.

It's early, but I call Greg. He's excited. His plan is to get Max off to school, take care of the animals, shower and come to the hospital. This sounds good to me. We will start getting Anna packed and then go to our final meeting with the doctors and therapists. We will finish packing up after the meeting and then we will take our baby girl home.

Quietly, I slide out of bed and gather my clothes. I take a quick shower and get ready for the day. Anna is still asleep, but the sound of the food cart will be waking her up shortly. Looking around the room, it is obvious we have a lot of things to pack up. Not just what we came in with, but all the gifts, cards, posters, stuffed animals, candy, and assorted other items that have made their way into our lives these past two weeks. I hope Greg brings the larger of our two cars.

My thoughts are interrupted by the familiar sound of the breakfast cart. We both hear it. Anna's eyes pop open and she does a little stretch to wake up. She smiles. She knows today is the day. Home at last. She pulls lamby up around her shoulders and sits up. Anna's meal on wheels with direct delivery to her bedside has arrived. By the look on her face, I can see there will be a few things she is going to miss.

I laugh at her and she knows why. She is hunched over her plate scooping up her eggs as though this will be her last meal. The lid was barely off the plate when she began eating. She looks at me and smiles. Then she moves on to the fruit and the roll. I just smile back and shake my head. She is a funny one.

While she finishes attacking her breakfast, I begin to pack up my belongings. Not too much for me, just clothes, magazines, and my purse. Easy. The chair bed folds back into itself after I remove the sheets and blanket, making sure to set the linens and pillows in a neat stack in the corner. I am the person who makes her hotel bed and puts all the towels, washcloths and other wash in a pile in the bathroom. Greg doesn't understand this. I know from experience it is easier to clean if you don't have to spend time picking everything up first. It sure would be helpful for me if I got that kind of assistance at home. Just trying to make it a little easier for housekeeping!

Anna is ready for her shower and I suspect Greg is on his way. Anna swings her legs around to the side of the bed and stands up. I walk with her into the bathroom, but she showers alone and comes out partially dressed. She still is not supposed to put a towel on her head because of her neck injury, so she blots her hair with the towel as best she can to get the excess water off. I help her get her clothes ready to put on. Her choice is not a surprise. It's the same thing she has been putting on every day. I ask her if she would like to change things up a bit today, but no, a white tee shirt and sweatpants continue to be her best look. Thank goodness for washing machines. She picks out a pair of white socks to match and crawls back into bed.

In comes her daddy. We have about an hour before our meeting with the hospital staff and Greg sits down to chat with his baby girl. I ask him to look around our room and make note of all that we need to take home with us. We both laugh. The girl has friends, no doubt about it. "Yes," he says, "I brought the Pilot. There's plenty of room for all of her stuff." At this comment, Anna looks around the room and starts to laugh. She had never noticed how much had accumulated these last two and a half weeks. "Where are you going to put all of this?" Greg asks.

Anna just looks him straight in the eye and says, "My room."

This of course makes me laugh. Anna's room is already packed to the ceiling with teenage stuff. Every nook and cranny is crammed with pictures, hats, jewelry, and anything else she can possibly collect. This will be another deposit of memories she will one day filter through and hopefully remember the love that was poured out to her by so many people. We put a few things in a pile and load them into a paper bag. Soon enough it's time for our meeting. Off we go.

This meeting is much less scary, for us, than last week's. We are more relaxed after having a week of feedback about her progress and watching her grow back into her normal self. We all sit down and look over the review of Anna. The packet of information labeled discharge summary begins with the day of the car accident and ends with today. Each therapist has written a comprehensive evaluation of Anna's results and suggestions for us to help her continue on with her daily life. As Greg and I take a moment to read the at-home exercises, we can detect the gaps in Anna's abilities based on what they want us to do. There are things like the memory tray, a game that is usually played with toddlers or at a wedding shower. We are to place ten to fifteen items on a tray, let Anna look at it for one minute and then she has to close her eyes. We take a few items off the tray and Anna is supposed to tell us what is missing. There are letter games, word games, number games, comprehension games, auditory and expressive language games, and a battery of additional memory exercises. Anna has trouble recalling words, numbers, events, and general information. As the doctors note, this is all part of having traumatic brain injury. My prayer, and Greg's, is that, while her progress has been fabulous thus far, she continues to regain her memory and abilities to bring her full circle back to her normal self. She is definitely up to the job and we will do whatever we need to do to help her.

All of Anna's test scores are listed. We review her outpatient therapy schedule and her dos and don'ts for the next year. Anna will come back to Children's on December 19th and meet with her therapists and Dr. Massagli for testing and her final follow-up at Children's. After that, all follow-up will be done by her primary physician. She does have one more scan scheduled at Harborview before the end of the year. This will be a check on her neck to make sure everything is healing correctly. Once again, Dr. Massagli reiterates the no contact sports for one year and gives us another copy of the list which classifies every sport by noncontact, limited contact or contact/collision. Here it is in black and white, no discussion.

Everyone is pleased with Anna's progress and very hopeful about her future. There are suggestions concerning reentering school and how to ease her back into her schedule. We discuss her class schedule changes and the doctor lets Anna know it will be okay to take a nap or rest during the day if she needs to. We tell them that Cedar Park has already made arrangements for her naps if she needs them, as well as, additional help from all of her teachers. Everyone is on the same page and it's all about healing Anna. Her therapists and doctors have truly been amazing and we are so thankful for them. Their help has been invaluable. They probably think they are just doing their job, but to us, they have helped put Anna back together and that is an incredible gift. Thank you.

We leave the meeting grateful and happy. Anna seems to understand her shortcomings and challenges. The interesting thing is that she knows she is not herself. It's as though she can see who she was and who she is now. This gives us lots of hope. If she can see who she was, then she knows the difference between the two and has the capability to relearn all she needs to know in order to regain her former self. It's very confusing because we are still warned that the brain is fickle. We don't know where we will end up when all is said and done. Only time will provide the answer.

I look at my baby girl as we walk back to the room. She's still so confident, still so ready to conquer the world. I am thankful that she has those characteristics. They will see her through this. They will see her through life. I am proud of her and all of the hard work she has done this past two weeks. She's awesome.

Looking around the room, we prepare ourselves for the packing. "Well, let's get started," says Greg. Anna climbs into bed. We look at each other and smile. She wraps lamby around her shoulders and closes her eyes. She's tired. That's okay. Tired is her normal right now. Greg and I begin to pack her things in bags and boxes, leaving her clothes for last. While Anna sleeps, Greg makes a few trips to the car and loads up some of her new possessions. I can't help but continue to wonder how all of this will fit in her room. Oh, well.

In the middle of all the packing, lunch arrives for Anna. She's still very tired and sits up slowly to accept her tray. Greg and I realize we are starving. He says he will make a cafeteria run for us and I am more than happy to sit and be with Anna. While he's gone, Anna eats and we talk a little about going home. She's so ready to be in her own bed with her lambys and her kitty Belle. Needless to say, Belle will be thrilled this afternoon when Anna gets home. This will be one happy reunion. I don't have to remind myself to be thankful that there will even be a reunion. For the rest of my life, I will be thankful for every moment of these last few weeks and every moment of everyday in our future. We got lucky. God gave us grace.

Greg returns with the food. It's comfort food. Anyone who knows my husband knows that comfort food is not high on his food chain. So, for

Greg to have come back with comfort food tells me he just wants everything to return to normal and for everyone to be happy. It makes me laugh to myself. But, I have to remember that he has been home taking care of Max, the house, the animals, and his job. Worrying about Anna has been a thread woven throughout his entire day and all of his activities. I have been with her. I knew minute to minute what was going on. It was easier for me. Now that we are going home, he can relax a bit and maybe some of that worry can disappear. He's a good man.

Anna is finished with her lunch and Greg and I finish ours and return to our packing. Anna lays her head down on her pillow, once again wrapping lamby around her shoulders and face, closing her eyes for her final nap at the hospital. I still find it remarkable how fast she falls asleep. She is completely out, oblivious to the noises surrounding her.

We finally pack up Anna's clothes and Greg takes a few more loads to the car. We are ready to go home. But come to find out, we can't leave until we have reviewed and signed the final discharge papers. Apparently, they won't be ready until around 3:00 pm. So, we wait while Anna sleeps. I sit in my folded-up chair bed and Greg in the rocking chair. Waiting. Thinking. Thankful.

A little before 3:00 pm, the discharge nurse comes in with the papers. To our surprise, she is a past member of our church. What a coincidence. We talk about Anna for a few minutes, sign the papers and wake Anna up. We look around the room, pick up lamby and a few other little items of ours and walk out the door. I turn around for one last look. What a great place. What an incredible hospital. I close the door.

Anna walks out to the car with her belt secured around her waist and her white neck brace comfortably in place. Greg holds the belt, but Anna does not weave. She walks perfectly straight. We find the car and load her into the back seat. We strap her in, which irritates her because she wants to do it herself. But, to look down and fasten the seatbelt is a strain on her neck and we ignore her objections. Safety first. We'll deal with the attitude later. We drive out of Children's Hospital a different way than we came in. We drive out of the parking garage with a healing child, not into the transport receiving garage with a child in need of much medical assistance. What a great day. Thank you.

Driving through familiar territory, Greg wants to know what's for dinner. I pull the list out of my tote which is resting next to my leg in the front seat. Let's see. Tonight, we have a mystery dinner. The list says we do have dinner being delivered. But, I'm just not sure what it is. I tell him it's a surprise and he's good with that. I think he just wants to make sure we don't have to cook. This is a big day and we have to make sure Anna is safe in her environment at home. She is so comfortable there and yet there are so many things she can't do by herself yet. She won't be left alone for a while until we are convinced she is safe.

We arrive at the scene of the accident. Anna looks around. We talk about where Baby Blue was and where the white truck was that hit them. However, the light turns green and we turn right, headed down Holmes Point westward towards our own street. Finally, we pull into the garage. We're home. Max is home. I hear Sammy barking. He's going nuts. I have to get into the house first and get Sam under control so he doesn't knock Anna over. He will be so excited to see her. I wedge my way through the door and Sammy, while Greg unloads Anna. "Calm down, Sam." I say to him while keeping eye contact. I put him in a sit stay. He's sits in place whining and wagging his tale. His entire body is in motion while he tries desperately to stay in his sit. I love this dog. I tell him, "Good boy. Good listening ears."

What a reunion. We bring Anna in and sit her down in the family room on the love seat. I tell Sammy okay and he immediately darts to Anna. Sammy showers Anna with kisses and runs to get a toy to show her. Within seconds he is back in front of Anna with his red rubber toy. Anna laughs and says, "Oh Shammy, oh Shammy." in her little girl dog-voice. He is so proud. Anna rubs his ears and gives him some lovies. He is so happy she's home. We all are.

After her brief stop on the love seat, Greg takes Anna upstairs for a rest. Within minutes, Belle is at our window waiting to come in and get hugs from her mama. How did Belle know? Animals are amazing. Greg finds Max sitting on Anna's bed. He's waiting his turn to spend time with his little sister. Greg takes Anna's belt off, pulls her covers back and helps her into bed. He then goes to get Belle from the window. Finally, she's in her own bed with her kitty and her brother by her side. Oh, and of course Sammy has joined them all, landing in the center of Anna's bed. Perfect spot, within licking distance of his kids. Picture perfect.

Greg and I unload the car and haul Anna's suitcase and gifts up to her room. We find an out of the way spot in the corner to place some of her new belongings. She wants to hang some of the new pictures, make a scrapbook, and arrange her other gifts later, so we make a pile of things to be done and make sure they are out of her walking path. We talk about tonight. Max has his first basketball game. Anna wants to go but knows she can't. She asks anyway. No big surprise there. We gently tell her not tonight, but if all goes well, maybe this Friday we can all go see Max play at Cedar Park. Tomorrow after school, we have a meeting with her teachers, the counselor, and principal Garron Smith. Greg reminds Anna she still needs to get her rest so she can do her best. She nods. She doesn't like having restrictions, but she understands.

We are talking about Max's game when Sammy barks and scares the heck out of everyone. The doorbell rings, Belle hides under the covers clinging to Anna and Greg gets up to answer the door. He is irritated with Sammy. The barking drives Greg nuts. I look at it as our built-in warning system. Sammy can hear the steps of a cat and see a squirrel in the next county. He lets us know something is going on before we hear a thing. The only problem is that he doesn't discern between a butterfly landing on the flowerbox and a stranger coming into the driveway. Minor details to him. An invasion is an invasion, regardless of the perpetrator.

Greg opens the door to let in Candice, the first in a string of Anna's friends. By 4:30 pm. her room is full of friends and noise. Greg looks at me and says, "Music to my ears." I agree. Music indeed. The kids don't stay long, well, except Candice. She won't leave Anna's side, but she's practically a member of the family. We are happy to have her stay and share dinner with us. The rest of the kids know Anna is tired and that this is our first night at home together as a family in weeks. They also have to get to their own homes, eat dinner, do homework, and go to tonight's basketball game. Anna is so thrilled they came. They have uplifted her and it's wonderful.

They leave as quickly as they arrived. There's a string of cars pulling out of the driveway within minutes of each other. Our meal has been delivered and we sit down. It's an early dinner and short lived, but what a treat to have all of us gathered around our dining room table. Max has to get dressed and leave for his basketball game. Greg isn't sure if he should stay with Anna or go to Max's game. We rarely miss the kids' basketball games. Their sports are part of our family life and that's the way we like it. Some times are busy, and some times are crazy, but we just do it and realize this will come to an end sooner than we would like. We decide Greg should go to the game. Candice and I will be here to watch over Anna. Max deserves to have his dad at his game. We're trying to get back to normal. Right?

The boys leave for the game and Anna and Candice sit up on Anna's bed talking and laughing. They're on the phone, they're off the phone.

They're texting, they're talking. Anna's safe, in her bed and I can relax. By relax, of course, I mean clean up dinner, do laundry, and clean the house. Let me not forget that two men have been living in this house for over a week without help. It scares me. I really don't want to look too closely at either the hardwood floor or the carpet. To see too much means more work for me tonight and I'm tired. Maybe I'll look closer tomorrow. Good idea, tomorrow.

I hear the girls winding down, and I know Anna must be exhausted. When I reach the room, I see Anna sleeping and Candice texting. Candice just lets her sleep, knowing that's what she needs to do. Candice is happy just to be near her friend. She saw Anna slip in and out of sleep in the hospital and knows this is not unusual. They are quite the pair.

Candice looks up and says she needs to go. Anna wakes up and the girls say their goodbyes. I walk Candice to the door and thank her. I love Candice. She's hilarious and faithful. A hug and a goodbye, mingled with a see you tomorrow as I watch her get in her car and drive off. By the time I walk back to Anna's room, she has fallen right back to sleep and I suspect she's out for the night. Tonight, we will not worry about washing her face or brushing her teeth. She's home, she's happy and she's asleep. Good enough. And she hasn't even asked for pain medication.

The boys get home late and come into the house quietly. Cedar Park won. The team looked good according to Greg. Really good. Max played well and didn't miss a beat. His hand is fine and it didn't bother him at all. I look at Max. He looks tired and hungry. We usher him to the refrigerator, the shower, and then to bed. He falls into bed and I'm pretty sure is asleep before we turn off his lamp. He's had a big day, too.

Greg and I are happy and tired as we put the kitties in the garage, lock all the doors, turn off the lights, set the alarm, get ready for bed and finally, turn off our lamps. Tomorrow afternoon is another big hurdle. It's time to meet Anna's teachers, the counselor, and high school Principal to discuss her re-entry to school. This will be scary and exciting, but this is one meeting we are glad we are going to. We say thank you and close our eyes.

Chapter Sixteen

"All the best and lots of prayers for you guys"
— The Roods

Greg maneuvers the car through a sea of mingling teenagers in the Cedar Park High School parking lot. Anna is so glad to be out and about, watching the crowd of kids she is so desperate to rejoin. She sits up straight and looks out the window with her bright white neck brace wrapped comfortably around her neck. We did not put the guide belt on today. The doctors said she should be fine, we just have to help her if she needs us, and prevent her from carrying any heavy objects. No backpacks. No books, and careful on the stairs. She can't have any strain on her neck.

She smiles watching the kids. So exciting.

We pull into a vacant parking stall in front of the high school. Anna slowly pulls herself out of the car and stands on the sidewalk. Greg and I join her and the three of us begin to make our way towards the multiple sets of double doors that open into the high school. The first thing I hear is, "There's Anna Brown." A group of girls from Max's senior class are hanging out in front of the school and turn to see Anna. I know these girls. I know most of their parents. They have been praying for us. They smile and say nothing. They are trying to act normal and give Anna some space. We smile back and say hi. They just watch Anna, trying not to stare. Well, I tell myself, she is a walking miracle. Not something we see every day. We're glad to be here.

Cruising through the halls of Cedar Park feels great. We can visibly see that Anna is excited to be here and thrilled to be getting her life back to normal. Some kids are smiling and say hi while others hug her carefully. Most everyone looks very surprised to see her up and walking around. I think this is comforting for the kids. They've been praying for us ever since the accident and now they get to see the results of those prayers.

Entering the classroom, we see Garron Smith, Anna's counselor Amy

Bettinger, and all of Anna's teachers sitting in a circle, waiting for us to arrive. This is the first time any of them have seen Anna since the car accident. Anna says hi with a broad smile on her face. So funny. They are full of smiles as well. What a relief for all of us.

Garron opens the meeting with a prayer. As we pray, I keep thinking how fortunate we are to be at this meeting and have our kids at Cedar Park. I know the teachers have been very worried and have been praying for us. We are so thankful to have them in our lives. As everyone raises their heads, all eyes fall on Anna. She just looks around at them. She's still not herself, but she's getting better. I wonder if they can tell.

We begin with a discussion about Anna's recovery. The easiest way to explain what has happened to Anna's brain was a visual explanation given to us by the director of rehabilitation at Children's Hospital. He said, "Traumatic brain injury is as though all the files have been dumped out and must be put back. Some files end up in the wrong place and must be pulled out and refiled." Greg and I recount Anna's progress and encourage the teachers by letting them know she is getting better every day of every week. This process may take a year to find some of her files, but the prognosis looks great.

"There may be holes," explains Greg. He tells them, "For example, she may be able to figure the square root of numbers, but not be able to do fractions. One way you can help Anna is through watching her organizational skills. Please check her planner, seat her at the front of the class, help her with outlines and review her class notes. She may need tutorial help in all or some classes. Anna is disinhibited. This means she has lost the filter that lives in the front of her brain. She may have inappropriate responses to things in the classroom. Her attention span may vary, and she may become fatigued and need to go to the nurse's office for a rest. Please keep her on a schedule. Routine is good for her and helps keep her organized. She will have an escort to carry her back pack from class to class. We have already arranged this with a classmate. Please give him a little grace if he is late to his classes. He is helping Anna. If she gets upset for any reason, call Amy. Amy will help her to figure out what is going on. She may be tired or overwhelmed. She also has a no contact rule for her athletic career for one year. Then she will be reevaluated to see how her brain and other injuries have healed. We are not sure when her neck brace will come off. When it does, she will be allowed to exercise with the basketball team, as long as she does only drills and no contact. This will help her body remember. And of course, Anna wants her normal life back. She admittedly feels a little foggy at times, but this is not unusual for traumatic brain injuries. Please treat her normally. It is more detrimental to her healing if you treat her as though she were different. And finally, please watch her body language. You will most likely be able to tell if she is overstimulated or needs rest. Anna is assertive, as we all know." Everyone laughs. Greg continues, "She is trying to be her normal self. This may cause her to overdo it a bit, so we just ask that you let Amy know if you think she is doing too much. Forward progress is the key. We will have her in school Monday morning and see how she does throughout the day."

There is silence for a moment while everyone processes the information. Then they smile. Each of them confirms what we already knew. They are willing to do whatever is needed to make Anna successful and help her graduate on time. What a tremendous group of people. Thank you.

Amy reviews Anna's new class schedule. Her Spanish teacher is disappointed that she will no longer be in class, but understands that learning a second language right now may be too difficult given the amount of memorization involved. Yearbook is also out because it requires a tremendous amount of after school time and is a very organizational type of class. Anna will be a teacher's assistant for the rest of the semester to make up for the lost credit. We will review her classes and credits at the end of the semester to figure out where she is and what to do for the remainder of the school year.

As the meeting winds down and we finish with all the questions and answers, Garron says a closing prayer. We stand to leave, and Anna gets all kinds of hugs and good wishes from her teachers. She's excited to come back and they're excited to have her. I think we all are uncertain how this is going to play out, but we are off to a great start. We leave the meeting knowing Anna's best interests are at heart and praying she can make it through the rest of the school year.

The gym is unlocked and we pull the double doors open hoping to find Anna's new basketball coaches. We haven't met them yet and would love the opportunity to talk to them. They're a husband and wife team. The wife is the head coach and her husband will help with practices and games. We've only heard second hand about their plans for Anna and how supportive they've been. We really want to meet them.

The gym is full of boys playing basketball. It's the select team. There's Max. It's great to see him back amongst his teammates and getting ready for tomorrow night's game. He's in his element. We wave. He nods. Typical boy. Greg, Anna and I pass through the main gym to the auxiliary gym. Nope, no girls' coaches there. We'll have to meet them later, maybe wait until high school practice officially starts.

On the way to the car, we see kids still milling around the school. They are aware of her presence but don't want to interfere. Even kids that don't know Anna very well, feel connected to her. Because the entire high school has been praying for Max and Anna, every student is involved and has a personal connection to our kids. It's a beautiful thing. Yes, it is.

Anna's hungry. What a surprise. We are having turkey kielbasa and vegetables tonight for dinner. The dinner train continues and it is still such a wonderful blessing. Even though we're all under one roof, we are still busy watching Anna and adjusting our lives. So many little details of everyday living were dropped from our lives and now need to be taken care of. I tell Anna to be patient, she can have a snack when we get home and we will have dinner when Max gets home from basketball practice. This seems to work. She agrees to the snack.

The minute we walk in the door, Greg gets Anna a snack and takes her up to rest. I sit down with my calendar. Before the accident, Anna was in the middle of taking driving classes. She wanted to drive the day she turned sixteen. That is obviously not going to happen. Driving schools are expensive and I have to check to see if she can finish the classes later. I call the driver's education school. The lady is so nice. She knew about the accident from other kids in the class and has been praying all along for Anna. That's amazing. But apparently, there is a state law about missing classes, rescheduling and the timing on finishing the course. However, she gives me the name of a person from the State Licensing Department to contact to see if we can finish the classes later without having to completely reenroll and pay the full amount. Secretly, I am all for taking the classes over. Anna can't remember or retain information very well right now, so how can she possibly remember anything she learned in driver's education before the accident or retain any new information? She's going to have a fit. Oh well. This will be another moment in teenage paradise. I laugh to myself. Safety is the main concern here, but she's not going to understand that. I make a note to contact the Licensing Department tomorrow. It's always helpful, at this particular time in life, if my decisions are backed up by a higher authority. Then I can't be blamed. I love it when it works this way. Not that I have a problem saying no, as my children would attest to. It's just easier when I don't have to be the iron fist, as my dad used to call it, every time there's an issue. Yay!

While Anna continues to rest, I continue to take care of business and rescheduling. Back to our busy, normal lives we go. While I know this is a good thing, I am fully aware that the most important things are God, family, and friends, not to mention the animals!

Let's see. No more soccer practices. No girls' basketball yet. Put revised boys' basketball schedule in my calendar. Moses needs to go to the vet. I need to pay bills. Book Club is coming up. Read the book. Friday Bible study has resumed. Yearly school pictures to reschedule. Go over the pickup schedule for Root Connection with Joy. When should I resume teaching pre-school? Cancel my spot in the CPR class. Call Michelle about operating the concession stand for basketball games. Start working out again. Reschedule the chimney cleaning. Hand off the Turkey Lunch to Lisa for our church Thanksgiving. Remember Tuesday night's mandatory boys' varsity basketball meeting. Pictures are due for the yearbook. Buy a car for the kids. Put Max's physical therapy appointments in my calendar. Reschedule jury duty. And, make dessert for Saturday night's neighborhood Halloween party at Scott and Kim's.

There, I think that's good for starters. Thank goodness, I hear Anna coming down the stairs. I jump up to make sure she's okay. She will save me from myself. Thank you.

"I heard Max drive up," says Anna. This is code for where's dinner? I have to laugh, knowing Max will be starving after practice and I'd better get cracking! I guess I'll set the table, lay the food out buffet style and stand back.

"Ta-Da. Dinner is served!" I announce minutes later. This is remarkably easy. I like this.

Everything feels normal, sort of. With the four of us at the dining room table, basketball practice over and homework to be done, it looks very much like old times. Of course, no one had a neck brace on before, but for all intents and purposes, we are doing the same thing we have done for years during the week. We are having dinner at our dining room table. Wonderful.

The kids love our turkey kielbasa dinner. Max goes through the list, as best he can remember, of all the delicious food he has eaten since the meals first started on October 11th. He makes sure to include the dinners as well as other treats that have been brought over. Looking straight at Anna, he lists cookies, cakes, pastries and snacks that he thought were fabulous and she never saw. He actually is remembering a lot and Anna can't believe all the food she's missed out on. If she only knew the outpouring of love and kindness that was, and is, being lavished on our family I think it would be humbling to her. Greg and I tell her stories of who came to visit, who called, who sent messages. We even show her some pictures. But, she still isn't retaining the information very well, so we just keep repeating ourselves. It's okay. Maybe one little thing will spark a memory. We're just looking forward and taking one step at a time for now.

When Max's food conversation is finished, they both get up from the table and Max takes the dishes into the kitchen. I don't want Anna to help yet, I just want her to learn to move around the house safely. So far, so good. But, we've barely been home.

Greg says, "Max and I will clean up and while you take Anna upstairs."

Anna immediately responds, "I'm getting a little tired, but I would like dessert first."

What a surprise. This is definitely a trait from my side of the family. My dad loves Oreo cookies. When he comes to visit, I purchase a bag just for him. If it's a special time of year, I'll buy the seasonal Oreos with the colored middle. He loves them. Sometimes I purchase two bags. I know they're not the healthiest choice, but there is something to be said about enjoying life's little pleasures. And my mom? She loved ice cream. Well, she basically loved dessert. Particularly homemade desserts. My mom made the best cream puffs I've ever tasted. Now, those were special. Mom usually made those during the holidays. Absolutely fabulous. Dessert brings back a lot of good memories for me. I love dessert, too.

I scrounge around the pantry for treats while Anna checks out the freezer and refrigerator. It doesn't take long before I hear her say, "Ah, ice cream and brownies. Yum." We look at each other and I pull out two plates. I certainly can't let her eat alone!

After eating a good size portion of warmed brownies topped with ice cream, Anna looks at me and says, "That was good." How can I deny it? It was delicious! She starts to stand up and move towards the stairs. I give Greg a nod, and up Anna and I go.

Since the accident and the hospital stays, she hasn't been able to take very good care of her skin. We need to get back on track with everything. Face, teeth, hair, body and overall hygiene. She's so tired and she wants to skip the nightly routine. It's hard, but I make her wash her face and brush her teeth. She can shower in the morning. We barely get through that part of her routine and she's exhausted. Anna had a big day today and she was great. I watch her crawl carefully into bed and I help her pull her sheet, blanket, and comforter up around her shoulders. Then I help her with her lambys. I tuck the first one around her face, making sure to allow for lots of air flow. The second lamby is laid out on the pillow next to her. I lay the third lamby on top of the comforter. Sometimes I wrap lamby around her sleeping pillow, like a pillow case, but tonight her head is already down and there is no reason to have any more neck movements. Her lambys are her comfort food and also her security blanket. They connect her to her normal life and make her feel safe. She can barely say good night as she slips into a deep slumber. Greg comes in to say goodnight and she is already out. We both smile. This is nothing new. We are two weeks into watching her fall asleep the minute her head nears the pillow.

We quietly pull her door to a close, leaving just a few inches of space open so we can hear her if she needs us. Max is still downstairs rummaging around the house before he goes up to his room to do his homework. I hear him in the toy room. This room houses the games, movies, toys, computer, and TV. He likes to relax a little after basketball and dinner. Usually he turns on the computer and plays for a while. Sometimes I go in and tell him to turn it off, but he usually finishes before I have to say anything.

Tonight, I can see he's tired. I look at him and he says, "I still have a little homework to do." He turns off the computer and gathers up his backpack, stuffing in all the things that have spilled out. On his way upstairs, he turns and asks, "Are you coming to the game tomorrow night?"

I tell him, "Yes."

He says, "Anna, too?"

"Yes, neck brace and all," I answer.

Max nods his head and smiles. He wants us there. He wants Anna there, too.

When the dishes are done and the last counter is wiped down, Greg and I sit for a minute to recap the day. It's been a long day packed with new beginnings, as well as, a return to our familiar lives. We are so thankful. Tomorrow our family will go to the game and begin our first full weekend at home with our kids and neighbors. Saturday night is the neighborhood Halloween party at the Blackburn's. Sunday is my bill paying day and Monday Anna goes back to school. "Here we go," says Greg, "back to our normal life."

Upstairs, Max has his door closed but I see a light underneath the door. I walk softly down the hall, peek in on Anna and then lightly knock on

Max's door. "What?" is his, ever so slightly, moody response. So teenage boyish. I open the door slowly and whisper goodnight. Without looking up, he says, "Goodnight."

I say "Eyeballs." He quickly looks up and I smile. Eye contact is important. I close the door and see Sammy lying down at the end of the hall. The closer I get to him, the louder the thump of his tail becomes, hitting the floor in anticipation of some attention. I say, "Hi, kissy dog." and over he goes. It makes me laugh. I sit down next to him and rub his tummy, giving him some long overdue attention. He is in heaven. His eyes start to close and it actually looks like he is smiling. "You're a good boy Sammy," I tell him. It's been a full day for everyone, both humans and animals alike. "Time for bed good dog."

Chapter Seventeen

"We have heard stories ... about prayers reaching all over the world"
— Greg Brown

It's early. No one is up yet and I am sitting in our kitchen nook with a cup of Earl Grey tea in hand, looking out at our backyard. It's a little overcast this morning. The deciduous trees have lost most of their leaves with just a few stragglers desperately clinging to their branches trying to hang on for winter. This is the time of year when the beautiful evergreens reclaim the attention. Cedars and firs stand tall in the greenbelt providing shelter for our local wildlife. We are home to many entertaining animals, including deer, owls, eagles, squirrels, chipmunks, and many varieties of birds. I love the evergreens. They are so beautiful and proud. They are the face of the Pacific Northwest and such a gorgeous face they are. I love it here. Having a few quiet moments to watch the trees is heaven to me. I know the noises of my family will be heard any second as I take my last sip of tea and wait.

There it is. The swooshing sound of water rushing through the pipes signifies our shower is in use. It's probably Max. I hope so. I trot upstairs to make sure life is progressing as it should be this morning. I knock on the bathroom door and hear a grumpy answer, "What?" It is Max in the shower. Good. That will be one less issue to deal with this morning. Max hates to get out of bed and I get tired of bugging him to get up. Greg is crawling out of bed and Anna is sleeping. Perfect. I trot back downstairs to start making breakfast.

Anna is still sleeping as Max is pulling out of the driveway and Greg is in his office getting his work day started. Perfect time for a shower and clean up. I may even have another moment alone before Anna wakes up. Usually there is a Bible study at my house on Friday mornings. But, we are on an extended hiatus from our study until next Friday when Anna will be back in school. I miss our Bible study. It will be wonderful to start up again. The women are fabulous. I've learned a lot from them over the years. They have older kids and have already walked in my parenting shoes. Very helpful.

As soon as the house and I are in order, I peek at my calendar. Not that there are any scheduled activities, but just checking to see what, if anything, I need to do. Taking care of Anna is my primary job right now. Today I want to live in, walk around in, and light fragrant candles in my house. It makes me feel good and it makes Anna feel comfortable and normal in her home. The pumpkin spice candles have been out since the beginning of October. Usually I am the only one who lights them, so the candles have sat unlit since the day before the accident. I look around the house and smile at our extensive pumpkin arrangement on the dining room table, the white ceramic pumpkins in the kitchen, and the smell of spicy potpourri wafting through our home. Outside, two colorful fall wreaths hang brightly on the front doors alerting the neighborhood that fall has arrived at the Brown house. Yet, best of all, my sign 'The Witch Is In' hangs crookedly on a small hook connected to the trio of white bird-houses perched on a copper pole by the front door. It's great to be home and have a full house.

Anna's making noises. She's not out of bed, but I hear deep sighs and long moans that come from stretching first thing in the morning. I check our bedroom window and open it slowly calling for Belle. She is waiting. She wants to see her mama. Carefully Belle walks down the steep roof from under the guest bedroom eaves, and onto the sharply angled but manageable roof to our window. I reach down through the window and pick her up to carry her into Anna's bedroom. The moment I enter Anna's room, Belle leaps out of my arm onto the bed and flies across the comforter into the arms of her beloved Anna. Anna grabs Belle while lifting the comforter and sweeps her under the puffy cover. The only part of Belle that can be seen is her tiny head protruding from the edge of the comforter, nestled against Anna's white neck collar. Belle is purring. Anna is smiling. Animals are the best. They provide a therapy that can't be copied. In our family, pets are essential. Even though some will argue that they are too much of a responsibility and they constantly tether you to your house, our animals are not only loved by each of us, they are loved by all of us as a group. In a way, they bind us together. They are members of our tribe.

I say, "Hi Poo, how are you doing today?" Before Anna can answer, Sammy runs into the room, tail going 90 miles an hour, and hauls himself onto Anna's bed. We do have rules. No dogs on the bed. And, I am a smidge concerned about him hurting Anna's neck with his excited movement. But, at this moment, I let him sit down and get a little loving from Anna. He needs it and she needs it. He lays his head down and rests near her side. I think he knows he needs to be careful and is very gentle in his body movements. "Okay, now that that is over, are you ready for breakfast?" I ask Anna. We both laugh at the situation and the sight of her and the animals all snug and happy on her bed. She nods yes, but isn't quite sure how to extricate herself from those around her and partially on her. I help her by calling Sammy off the bed, which he leaves reluctantly, and we just leave Belle sitting on her special blanket. Belle sheds so heavily, we put a blanket down for her wherever she goes. Otherwise we go through multiple sheets on the lint brush trying to pick up her fur. Her fur is long and plentiful.

Anna eats breakfast, showers, rests, eats lunch, and sleeps throughout the latter part of the afternoon. I wonder how she's going to make it through a full day of school next week. It's comforting to know she can go to the nurse's office and lie down if she needs to. I thank God, again, for Cedar Park.

There's a light knock at the front door. Sammy barks and races to the door, once again out of control. I grab him and pull him away from the door. With Sammy and his collar in my left hand and the doorknob in my right hand, I open the door as best I can without falling over. We have got to get him door trained! There stands Martha Evatt and her son Jon. We have known the Evatts since Anna was three and Max was five. Martha and I both had our kids at Lisa's daycare while we worked. Jon is Anna's age and has a sister, Leanna, who is one year older than Max. Great kids. They had lots of fun together at daycare and got along beautifully. When we left the public school, and went to Cedar Park, we didn't see the Evatts much at all. I know Jon and Anna were in touch on occasion, but that was about it.

I say, "Hi!"

Martha is smiling and says, "Jon and I have come by to mow your lawn." She explains they want to help us in this way and, "Would that be okay?" Once again, I am amazed at the generosity of people and surprised by their ability to identify ways to help others in crisis. What a wonderful way to help. Greg hadn't had the time or inclination to mow. I don't think he's even thought about it. And this is quite unusual as he is a fanatic about the lawn. I am so appreciative that the Evatts have thought of this.

I say, "Yes."

When Jon is done, I offer to pay him, but he and Martha will not allow it. When they leave, I think to myself, what nice people they are and what a great service they have just rendered. Their actions come from the goodness of their hearts and a kindness towards a neighbor. They are another example of the best of mankind.

The afternoon sun is starting to fade. Max's game is tonight and Anna is still sleeping. She wants to go to the game and get back in the swing of things. The gym will be full of classmates, teachers, parents, and friends. I think it would be good for everyone to see her progress before she goes back to school on Monday. I tread lightly upstairs to her bedroom door. It is slightly ajar and I peek in to see if she is beginning to wake. She hears the familiar creak of her door opening and lifts her eyelids to look at me. Belle is still resting by her side and purring in pleasure.

"Hi Schmoo," I whisper, "do you still want to go to the game tonight?"

"Unh--huh," she answers quietly.

"Okay baby girl, it starts at 7:00, when do you want to be there?"

She shifts around in bed and looks at her clock. "Seven," she says.

"Alright," I tell her, "Dad is helping coach tonight so we can leave around 6:30. Okay?"

"Okay," she mumbles, realizing she should probably get up and get ready. I know she wants to look good in her neck brace. Makeup and cool clothes will be required.

At 6:35 pm we are pulling out of the driveway. She looks beautiful. She always looks beautiful to me, but tonight is exceptional. She is so happy, yet a bit apprehensive, to go back to her school and see her friends. It makes her feel normal and confirms she is on the road to recovery. This is a great idea.

We cruise into the parking lot and Anna slides the mirror down from the sun visor to check her hair and makeup. With her thick white neck brace secured, we walk towards the front doors of the Cedar Park High School building. There are a few kids standing outside the gym that see Anna coming and offer supportive smiles and hellos. She smiles a big smile and says, "Hi." We enter through the large glass doors of the school and veer right towards the gym. I detect a little uncertainty in her walk. I suspect she's not sure what her classmates know or what they are thinking. She knows she's not herself, but she doesn't want anyone else to know. That would crush her. She wants to be thought of as the same person she was before the accident. Once again, she wants to be normal.

I pull open one of the heavy metal doors leading into the gym. It's 6:52 pm and the game starts in eight minutes. We walk through the doors which take us to an entry space always filled with fans and, during regular season play, a table to pay an admittance fee to watch the varsity games. We pause. The court is empty. The teams are off the court and back in their locker rooms getting ready to start their game.

Anna takes a slight left towards the front of the bleachers and begins walking to the student section. The minute she is in front of the very first bleacher, every teacher, every student, every parent, everybody on the Cedar Park side of the gym stands up. They start by clapping. Then someone calls out Anna's name. They whistle. They cheer. They cheer our baby girl the same way they prayed for her, with all their hearts. God has answered the prayers of thousands. Anna Brown is a living miracle and everyone here knows it. They are thrilled to see her and she smiles broadly looking at the crowd as she meets up with her friend Candice and they hug. What a welcome. Anna laughs, I cry. What an unexpected moment. Thank you, God.

Suddenly, the crowd roars to life. The Cedar Park Eagles burst onto the floor and we are ready. All of us. The players, the coaches, the fans. This is going to be a great night. I can feel it.

Max is on fire! The team is unstoppable. This is the best team Cedar Park has had in years. They play well together. They have that chemistry which makes good teams successful. The fans love them. We leave the court as victors. What a great night.

In the twelve minutes it takes us to get home, Anna has gone from exhilarated to exhausted. She pours herself into bed and pulls her lambys up around her face. She's out. I kiss her forehead and tell her goodnight. Then I whisper the words she has heard multiple times during her life, "I love you."

Max is downstairs happy and starving. Things are going so well for him at school and he is thoroughly enjoying his senior year. We are so glad. Max is private and after the accident he held everything in. Still does. He doesn't remember much about that day, doesn't really want to talk about it and is visibly happy Anna is home and healing. Thank God he has lots of friends and is playing on a basketball team with a group of outstanding young men. All is well with Max Brown. Boys are easy, well, at least easier than girls. Maybe it's because they aren't so complicated. Maybe it's because they aren't so emotional.

He came straight home after the game to get a good night sleep. He is taking the ACT in the morning and wants to do his best work. He has already taken the SAT twice and will take it again next Saturday. Teensie coached us on this. She had her own kids take the SATs three times and finds there is great improvement each time. She says that the first time they are nervous and don't know what to expect. The second time, they have seen their results and know what they need to improve on. The third time, the test should be taken in the fall of their senior year. Being a senior brings a whole new maturity to the test. This is their best effort and they know what to expect. So, we follow Teensie's advice and make sure Max is signed up. Teensie tutored him on the math section when she was here. Max says he's ready and wants to get all these tests behind him. Then the college selection process begins.

His final ACT and SAT scores will be available in December. This is when the crunch begins. We have spent many hours and will spend many more, discussing colleges with Max. Greg is taking on this roll more than I am. They have two lists. One list is made up of smaller colleges with basketball teams Max could play on, while the second list is of colleges he would love to attend, but couldn't play on their basketball team. He hasn't quite decided what he wants to do yet. I do know they have listed a variety of small colleges on the basketball list and both Gonzaga and University of Portland are on the no basketball list. I am sure there will be more. At least he doesn't have to decide until after the first of the year. By then, he should have a better feel for what he wants to do with his life. Greg has told him he will need to get a scholarship if he wants to go to an expensive school. Max understands this and I think this is one of the reasons he wants to get high scores on the ACT and SAT. The higher his score, the better his scholarship will be. Every little bit helps.

Finally, Max goes up to bed with a full tummy, the kitties are in the garage, the kitchen is clean, Anna is fast asleep, Sammy is lying in his bed upstairs and the house is completely locked up. We turn on the alarm and put our heads on our pillows, thankful for another day.

Chapter Eighteen

"I know"
— Scott Blackburn

We have the neighborhood Halloween party at the Blackburns tonight. Many of our neighbors have not seen Max and Anna since the car accident and Kim tells me they are really looking forward to seeing the kids. Seeing is proof that they are okay. Most of our neighbors have watched Max and Anna grow up and have known Greg and me since we moved into our house. We were two working, thirty-something yuppies when we built our house. Since then, very few people have moved out of the neighborhood and, for the most part, we've known our neighbors for twenty years. It's a great neighborhood and it's loaded up with good people. What a blessing.

The Halloween party tradition was started by Pam and me. When the kids were little, we came up with ideas to have a front porch decorating contest, turn our garage into a Haunted House and follow that up with a big neighborhood party. Every year for more than a decade my garage was transformed into a scary walk of surprises. We strung clothesline up and pinned black plastic table cloths to the miles of clothesline necessary to make walls for winding hallways. Something creepy was around every turn and in every hallway. The kids to this day talk about the haunted houses we did. It was fun. When they left elementary school, and went into junior high, they thought it was a little embarrassing and stupid. We didn't care. Pam, Stacey (who joined us the minute she moved into the neighborhood) and I kept it alive. By this time, the Blackburns had moved in and we had a crop of younger kids to scare, oh, I mean have fun with. Last year was the final year for our haunted house. All the neighborhood kids came and brought their friends. By now, the older kids found it fun again and enjoyed watching the excitement on the younger kids' faces. But, I must say I was glad it was over. Not only had it become a tremendous amount of work, but last year it was creepy. It felt a little unnatural. When I walked into the garage the day before the party, I was uncomfortable. I got a sense of evil. Even the cats didn't want to go into the garage last year. In previous years, we took the walls down after the party just to get an early start on the cleanup. Last year, I started taking them down the minute the last kid was through. It was a relief to have it all gone. I remember we had it all packed up gone by the following afternoon.

Our meal list says we have beef stroganoff with salad and bread coming this evening. Even though there will be food at the Halloween party, this will provide us with dinner for tomorrow night. Yum. The dinners are still such an incredible blessing. I have learned that being home doesn't necessarily mean we are able to be back to our regular routine. I am so thankful that I don't have to cook. To be able to concentrate on my family and not worry about cooking is a huge gift, not only our family, but to me personally. These meal train women are more helpful than they will ever know. Thank you.

I'm starving. Just looking at the meal list makes me hungry. By now, it's just about time for lunch and I hear noises coming from upstairs. Greg is outside working in the yard and Max should be back from his test in an hour or so. I poke my head outside and ask Greg if he's almost ready for lunch. He is. I run upstairs to check on Anna and find her standing in her bathroom looking in the mirror.

"You okay?" I ask her a little puzzled to see her so still, "You in pain, honey?"

"No," she says, "just tired."

"Oh," I say softly, "Well maybe you need some food. Are you hungry?" She looks at me and pauses. I can see something is wrong. She's either not fully awake or she just doesn't feel good. Anna is a fighter and it is obvious she is trying to be normal, but her body is simply still in the healing process. She needs time. Maybe in our excitement to move forward, we have moved too fast.

"Yeah, I'm hungry," she says.

"Okay, I'll go fix lunch for all of us. Max should be home in a little while."

She looks at me confused and says, "Where is he?"

She forgot. I have a momentary reality check. She forgot. "Remember, honey, he's taking the ACT today."

"Oh," she says. She doesn't remember at all.

"Why don't you put on some clothes and come down stairs," I suggest.

"You can take a shower after lunch. The twins are coming over to see you today with Uncle Doug and Aunt Becky."

She smiles and says, "Oh good, it will be fun to see them."

I look at her reflection in the mirror and say, "Yeah, they miss you and want to see you. But, if you're tired, you need to rest."

This is becoming too much conversation for her. She's getting irritated. "I KNOW, MOM," she fires back.

Walking back downstairs, I am glad she's waiting to take a shower until after lunch. She just doesn't seem to be herself right now and I want her to have good balance and to be mentally engaged when she gets in the shower. She does have her shower stool we bought, as well as a non-slip mat, but slipping in there really worries me. Hopefully lunch will give her some strength and nourishment. Good food helps our brain and body to function at its best. Let's hope this is what she needs.

Max pulls in the driveway just as Anna is coming downstairs. Greg comes in and lunch is ready. Perfect timing. After a little food, Max tells us he thinks the test went well and he will be glad when this whole college process is over. Thankfully, Anna is much more alert and ready for a visit with Andrew and Emily.

"Let's go. The party started fifteen minutes ago!" I yell up the stairs. Anna has been napping after a long, fun visit with her cousins, but I hear shuffling and hope this won't take too long. Ten minutes later we are knocking on the Blackburns' door with my homemade chocolate chip cookies in hand. Okay, here we go.

Kim opens the door and we peek in to a house filled with beautiful Halloween decorations and aromatic fall scents. It's fun to see how others decorate for fall and Halloween. This year I am sticking to the pumpkin and leaf theme because it takes me through the entire fall season, up to the moment I switch the house over to our Christmas décor. The only hint of Halloween is my 'The Witch Is In' sign hanging near the front door. That sign is a staple. I will use that sign for years. It's me.

When we enter Kim's kitchen, we see lots of familiar and friendly faces. Our neighbors are the best. They hug all of us and greet the kids tenderly. Kim wants us to say a little prayer before we eat, which we usually do at our neighborhood functions, and give an update to everyone about our lives. Greg defers to me because, as he explains, "Lynn was the one at the accident scene and the hospital most of the time." We all pause for a moment to thank God for our food, family, and friends before I bring everyone good news from the Brown family.

I thank all of them, from our entire family, for their prayers and gifts. I give them a brief recap of what happened the day of the accident and where we are now. This way, our neighbors get the information from the source, so there can be no confusion or misinformation. When I finish, I look around at the faces of the best neighbors anyone could ask for. We have been lucky. I can't imagine what it would be like to drive into your neighborhood every day and pull into your driveway without kind neighbors that make an effort to get along. We are so fortunate. We have Republicans, Democrats, Christians, Jews, and, most importantly, respectful neighbors that watch out for each other. We borrow sugar, butter, flour, spices, copy machines, fax machines, and many other needs from each other. I have actually run across the street with wineglass in hand to get a glass of Cabernet from the Allens. Kim and Scott have walked down the hill to our house with beer in hand when we have been working in the yard all afternoon. We take care of each other's animals and pick up each other's newspaper and mail if someone is out of town. The list of things we do for our neighborhood is endless. Everyone cares about each other and always has a smile on their beautiful faces when they greet you. It's the best. We're lucky.

The party, as usual, is loads of fun and filled with great food. Most of the food is homemade, but we do get a fabulous bakery cake purchased every year by one of our neighbors. She loves these cakes and so do the rest of us. The party goes on for hours and there are lots of stories, updates, and conversation. We all stay. So much for my idea of thinking the kids might need to go home early.

By the time we say our goodbyes and walk back home, Anna's yawning and we are tired. Max, being a teenage night owl, veers off toward Brad's house and says he'll be home later. Greg asks, "Do you have a key?" Max nods. When Max says he'll be home later, that usually means past our bedtime. Since I am the one that gets out of bed to let him in, I appreciate that Greg thought to ask about the house key.

Tomorrow should be a restful day. I double check my calendar when we get in the house. There's not anything noted except going to church and paying our house taxes. I love days like that. And isn't Sunday supposed to be a day of rest? If Anna is up for it, we will all go to church. If we go, it will be the first time back to church for our family since the car accident. I know the congregation would love to see both Anna and Max. They have been praying for us and have sent emails and notes of support since the day we went to Harborview. I do love our church.

Epiphany Lutheran. The people are kind, the church is Bible-based, and we have a great preschool program. Max and Anna went to preschool there. Because of that preschool, we joined Epiphany when Max was three. It's a wonderful, small church with good-hearted people. I hope we can go tomorrow.

At 5:30 am it's still dark and wet outside. My body is not ready to get up, but I can't fall back to sleep. So, I have this conversation with myself about when I'll get up and what I will do when I get up. The big entice-ment is coffee. Then I offer myself toast with peanut butter smeared on top. And of course, the idea of being alone for a few hours is the ultimate draw. By 6 o'clock, I'm starving and can't wait another minute for a good cup of coffee. The mere thought of the coffee's aroma lures me to the kitchen. I carefully crawl out of bed, as not to wake Greg, and Sammy and I walk quietly downstairs. He immediately curls up into a ball on the floor and falls back to sleep. Apparently, he's not ready to get up. But, he loves me so much, he follows me downstairs anyway. What a great pup. With the coffee loaded into the basket, water up to four cups, and lid on, I plug in the percolator. I know it's a bit old fashioned, but my gramma Mamaw, had a percolator and I love the knowledge of that. The four cups of water really make only two cups of coffee, but that's enough. It makes me think of Mamaw. I push the handle down on the toaster and wait. "We are almost in business," I say to Sammy with a smile. He lifts his head and looks at me before taking a deep sigh and going back to sleep. Within minutes, everything I promised myself comes to fruition. Coffee, peanut butter toast and alone time. Perfect.

It's very exciting to have some time to myself. We are all in our own home, safe and sound. Everyone else is sleeping while I have the chance to read, check my email, and prepare my thoughts for this coming week. Anna goes back to school tomorrow. I pray she will have a great week. Max will be there in case she needs anything. I think he'll be glad to have her back at school. It will be good for both of them. I'm not sure how we are going to handle the car situation in the future, but for the time being, I will be driving them. Since he went back to school, Max has been driv-ing himself in Greg's car. He had no problems getting behind the wheel again, and if he was nervous about it, he never said a word. Greg has been driving my car. That will all change tomorrow. We haven't had time to talk about, let alone think about replacing Baby Blue.

With coffee cup in hand, I hear a little movement coming from up-stairs. It's about 8 o'clock. It must be Greg. Max and Anna can't possibly be awake. Sammy lifts his head and looks toward the hallway leading to the stairs. We hear footsteps. It's Anna.

"Schmoo, what are you doing up?" I ask her, very surprised to see her.

"I couldn't sleep and we left Belle in my room last night," says Anna, "She woke me up."

"Oh, I'm sorry Baby girl, I forgot about Belle."

"It's okay, she slept almost all night."

"So, Schmoo, how do you feel about church today?" Well, the look on her face tells me her answer. Even though she has had a tremendous number of visitors and has seen the cards and gifts, she doesn't remember or fully understand all the support and care that have been shown to our family. I give her a little recap, telling her about the emails, phone calls, notes, packages, food, and prayers. It's important for her to understand, just like last night, people want to see her. It answers their prayers. Our church needs to see her. She nods and agrees to go to church. Thank you.

Getting Max out of bed proves to be the problem. With a promise of going out to breakfast after church, he rallies and we finally get in the car and drive into the parking lot five minutes before the service begins. When we walk in, all heads turn towards Anna and Max. Once again, it's great for the people that have been praying for the lives of our kids, to witness God's miracles. Seeing is believing.

At the end of the late service, Heather, our Director of Christian Education, asks us if we would like to say anything to the congregation. This is generally the time when announcements are made. Greg defers the request to me. Again. Truth be known, I think he doesn't like public speaking. That's okay, we all have different gifts. As I stand before our congregation, I thank everyone from the bottom of our hearts and let them know how much we appreciate their prayers and the prayers of their friends. They can see that Anna and Max are physically okay, yet don't know too much about her brain injury. The fact that she is sitting in the pew listening to the sermon is enough said. I tell them that tomorrow Anna will be going back to school, and of course, Max has been back for two weeks. We are doing well and thank them all again for their prayers and thoughts. As I hand the microphone back to Heather, it occurs to me how lucky we are to be here. All four of us.

After the service, both kids and adults are enjoying a moment to talk to Max and Anna. I love it. Our kids have griped for years about getting up on Sunday, their only day to sleep in, and going to church, yet here they are talking with people that have watched them grow up and they are actually enjoying being at church. I wonder how long this will last? At the very least, another seed has been planted.

We load ourselves into the car and the lively discussion of where to go to breakfast begins.

"I don't like their food."

"I don't want to go there."

"We always go there."

"I get to pick."

Oh for Heaven's sake, I am thinking. Isn't the food almost all the same? We have to make a decision. Turn left or turn right. Greg makes an executive decision and turns left. The conversation comes to an end and we drive down Juanita Drive toward his restaurant choice. Thank goodness that's over. I guess we are truly getting back to normal.

We are eating our breakfasts with gusto. Lots of food. Eggs, bacon, toast, hash browns, and pancakes. Between the four of us, there's a virtual smorgasbord at the table. Yum. Max brings up Baby Blue and our car situation. Of course, Greg says they can take my car to school, in which case I say, "Uh. No." I need my car during the day and suggest maybe they take Dad's car. Everyone looks up and laughs while Greg begins to explain why that won't work either. Men are funny.

Much to my surprise, Greg says, "We should talk about buying a replacement for Baby Blue". I had thought we would share cars for a while. Maybe I am not ready for this conversation. Naturally, everyone has something to say about this. The kids want a car that has a cool factor. Greg wants a car that isn't too expensive and gets good gas mileage. I want them to have a huge, heavy Hummer, or the safest car made by mankind with airbags attached to airbags coming out of every inch of the car's interior. Right now, I don't care about the cost. Well, I do, but safety is my primary concern.

Greg takes in everyone's input and says he'll do some research. He is good at this. I know he will research all makes and models of cars and come up with a list of potential options for us. The kids are excited and I am nervous. Greg loves the hunt, so he's happy.

We pile back in the car and head home to laundry, chores, and animals. Anna needs a nap, Max has homework and Greg is going online to begin a car hunt. I am fairly certain that by the end of the day, he will have some ideas about a car for the kids. We shall see.

Before Anna pulls the third lamby over her chin, I remind her about her first outpatient physical therapy appointment tomorrow at 4:00 pm. This will begin our treks to the hospital for her therapies. We will know more this week about how often and which therapies she needs to continue with.

"Also, one more question, Poo. What do you want to do for your 16th birthday?" I ask.

She drops the lamby down on her chin and says, "Orcas Island. I want to go to the Carroll's cabin on Orcas Island with my friends."

Anna's birthday is December 14th. We keep her celebration separate from our Christmas festivities because we believe she should have her own special day. Both Max and Anna usually have two birthday parties. One of the parties includes their friends and the other is a dinner party at our house with Gramma, Grandpa, aunts, uncles, and cousins. This has been an unusual year, no doubt. Max turned eighteen and had the small family party in the hospital while Anna will turn sixteen and wants to go to Orcas Island. That request is out of the blue.

"Oh, that sounds like fun," I say with surprise.

She just looks at me, smiles and says, "I love Orcas Island."

"Okay, I will call Mrs. Carroll and see when the cabin is available."

She looks at me one last time and closes her eyes. She's out again.

Max is lying on his bed contemplating his homework and overhears the conversation. "She wants to go to Orcas Island?" he says with raised eyebrows.

"Yep, apparently," I tell him.

"That's random," he smiles.

We both look at each other and laugh. Very random.

Dinner is delicious. I am just testing it and it is delicious. Guess I'd better ring the dinner bell and let everyone else have a taste. The salad and bread are terrific side dishes and my family is going to love this. I hear them coming. The kids wind their way downstairs and Greg emerges from his office in the garage. The minute we sit down, Greg says "I have some car news." Max can hardly wait, Anna's main focus is about the cars appearance and I just want to see the safety results.

We give thanks and lift our heads. We all look at Greg and he says one word, "Volvo."

Max says, "Cool."

Anna says, "What's it look like?"

I say, "Safety ratings?"

Greg says, "Yeah, cool. Looks hot. It's the safest car on the road." And, he says, they have just what we are looking for at a dealership in Bellevue. As a matter of fact, he's going to call them tomorrow. Well, apparently, we are thinking about buying another car and it appears as though the kids will be driving the nicest car in the family. As long as they are protected, I'm okay with that!

While Greg cleans up the kitchen and Max does the rest of his homework, Anna gets her wardrobe ready for tomorrow and I finish the laundry. Our one day of rest is coming to a quick close as we find ourselves upstairs and getting ready for bed. This will be a big week. Again. But this time, we're ready. I think.

Chapter Nineteen

"God answered our prayers"
— Jayne Vitulli

Music. The sound coming from our clock radio is barely audible. Greg has it turned down so low that I can hardly hear it from my side of the bed. Sometimes I don't hear it at all. But, this morning I can hear the music. I'm ready. Ready to get out of bed. Ready to feed my family. Ready to take my kids to school. Ready to get our family back on track. Ready to begin again. It's a great feeling.

"Okay, Greg, here's today's schedule," I whisper to him while he's pretending to sleep and trying to ignore me. "I am taking the kids to school and returning the dishes from the meal train to the school's kitchen. Then I am coming home and calling Mrs. Carroll about staying at the Orcas Island cabin and I am going to call about rescheduling Max's senior portraits. I have to call the chimney sweeps to come out and clean our chimneys before we start having fires in them. I will call the school around noon and see how Anna is doing. Max is going to work out after school and then meet with Mr. Ian for some guidance in math. So, I will pick Anna up after school and take her to her physical therapy appointment at 4 o'clock and then come home in enough time to leave for book club at 6:00 pm. You may need to pick Max up from school if he can't get a ride. Or, if we are on our way home from the therapy appointment and Max needs a ride I can swing by Cedar Park and pick him up. Don't forget tomorrow night at 7 o'clock there is a mandatory meeting in the high school gym for boys' basketball. Got it?" No answer, just a grunt. He's got it. Well, maybe. I'm on a roll.

By noon, we have not received a phone call concerning Anna so I call the school. She's doing great. She hasn't wanted a rest on her first day back with a full schedule. Wow. She's working hard to get everything back to normal. It worries me. It's a little early in the day to be overly concerned, but I just can't believe she's not tired. I talk to God. Maybe it's me that needs to let go a little bit. This has been such a traumatic experience, maybe I am affected more than I realize. Max and Anna are separate from me. God, please help me to be a good mom and give them space and help when they need it. A fine line. A balancing act. This is not my gift.

Sammy perks up and starts wagging his tail as he charges the front door. Then I hear a knock. I should have known we'd have visitors. Oh fun. Looking through the little peep hole in our door, I see Janis and Karen, fellow teachers, from the preschool. They had called earlier and wanted to stop by. I haven't forgotten, just got focused on Anna and her first day at school. In they come, being licked and loved by Sammy, carrying a huge woven basket filled to the brim with gifts. We weave our way to the kitchen, maneuvering around the excited gyrations of our crazy dog. Janis sets the basket on the island counter top and explains it is from the preschool. It is loaded with gifts, cards, and a letter from the preschool families and the preschool staff. What an honor to receive such a thoughtful present. I know we have been in the thoughts and prayers of these families. I am so appreciative of their consideration and thankful for their prayers. They will never know how much this means. I tell Janis and Karen thank you and that I will be writing a thank you note to the preschool and parents to be sent home with the kids. They say not to rush, but I just want them to know I am going to do it.

Janis and Karen are two people I love working with. They are both hilarious and we have lots of fun together. Whenever I am in charge of leading the music, Janis comes to my rescue. She knows all the preschool songs by heart. She makes me look good, like I know what I'm doing. It's wonderful. Karen is comic relief. We really do laugh every day at work. It's fun.

I ask the girls what happened at preschool the day of the accident. How did they hear?

Janis says, "Well, I wasn't working that day, but this is what I was told. Louanne (our pre-school director), got a call from Heather telling her about the accident and Louanne immediately told the staff. Not too much later, Cami Pratt came to the preschool to support the staff. Her husband Josh had called her because he was one of the firemen at the scene of the accident and wanted her to know it was Mrs. Brown's family." I tell Janis and Karen that I remember him being there. I had their daughter, Ellie in preschool last year. Great family. Janis continues, "When the staff got the news, they all stood in a circle in front of the preschool with hands clasped together and prayed." I thanked them for that. Prayers have been huge, since the beginning, to heal us and help us through this. They agree.

Of course, we talk about Anna and how she's doing. They're happy to hear we are making good progress and that Anna is back at school today. We all know this is a miracle. It was three weeks ago tomorrow, that Anna was airlifted to Harborview. Right now, she's sitting in her classroom. Wow. As for me, I tell Janis and Karen I am not ready to come back to work yet. Not sure I can for a while. Everything depends on the next few weeks. They certainly understand. They have kids, too. Janis assures me that my spot will be covered by the staff. What a relief. It's hard for preschoolers to have a teacher disappear. Fortunately, my replacement will be a familiar face. When Janis and Karen leave, I feel great, knowing my classroom is in good hands and my family is cared about. Thank you.

While I am sitting in the car waiting to pick up Anna from school, I quickly try to finish our book club read. Just a few chapters left to go. The book Tracy picked was 90 Minutes in Heaven by Don Piper. Considering this book was chosen before the car accident, I find it not to be a coincidence, but a God thing. The message is one of salvation and rebuilding. This is exactly what our family is going through. I love that God stepped into my life through a book and is telling me to keep the faith. Thank you.

Reading the last page and setting the book down on the passenger seat, I think about how lucky we are. Anna will not spend years rebuilding her body. She is not living in a hospital. She is getting stronger and healing a little more each day. However, I wonder how she will be, mentally, going forward. Anna has been very challenging, at times, in the last few years. Because she has so many friends from her first few years in public school, she has been lobbying hard to go to our local public high school. She had been working on us with anger, tears, and sadness, to convince us she should go to school somewhere other than Cedar Park. At one point, she said she would go to any of the three large public high schools surrounding our neighborhood. We were seriously considering it. She was wearing us down with her daily stories of unhappiness. This was very hard to hear. She said she didn't fit in. Anna has always been very positive and outgoing. Greg would always tell her she could walk into a room of strangers and know them all by the time she left. She was constantly tugging at our heartstrings. Teenagers can be very convincing.

Yet, then I would see her at school and she was happy, surrounded by friends and having great interactions with both teachers and staff. They all loved her. I was becoming torn, asking myself if my child was so unhappy she was at risk in some way.

After the accident, I feel the whole question of changing schools has been answered. God said no. The support and willingness of Cedar Park to take care of her is unheard of in most schools. Even her friends from our local public high school told her that if she had been going to school with them the day of the accident, the school would have tried to keep it under wraps so all the students could continue their day unaffected. Imagine that. And here is Cedar Park closing down the high school in prayer, keeping the kids informed and letting both students and staff pray and counsel each other. It's not a tough decision to decide between those two choices. Not a tough decision at all.

I look up at the high school building and see Anna, in her thick white collar wrapped around her neck, looking around for our car. She has a friend carrying her backpack. At least she's following the rules and not trying to carry her own pack. That's a relief. I open the car door and stand on the frame of the car, waving my left arm frantically. She sees me and starts across the drive. She doesn't look both ways. Her friend grabs her arm to slow her down. I can see this is going to be a conversation. She's not thinking safety. I am sure it never even came across her thoughts. She has something new to relearn. How to safely cross a driving path.

She's starving. I make an unusual decision and take her to a fast food drive through to get her a quick treat. She's always happier on a full stomach and probably more likely to tell me how school was today. With a little bag of food, off we go, back on the road and driving towards Overlake hospital. I ask about her first day back. She says everything was good. She gets to sit in the front of each classroom and she understood almost everything she heard today. But, she says she has some catch up homework to do tonight. She's happy and doesn't look exhausted. Good.

It takes us a few minutes to find the right place in the hospital for her physical therapy appointment. We're almost late. We sign in and sit down. About ten minutes later, a therapist comes to the lobby and calls out Anna's name. Off she goes to her first outpatient therapy appointment. It's just Anna and her therapist, leaving me in the lobby. This must be another time when I must learn to let go. I open a magazine and begin reading.

The hour flies by. I'm glad. Anna and her therapist come back to the lobby and want to meet with me. Anna is beaming. Her new therapist says, "Anna doesn't need to come back for any more physical therapy. Today went so well, coupled with her physical therapy at Children's Hospital-- she's done." Wow. Great news. That's fabulous. We thought she would be in therapy for four weeks. Anna has worked hard for this and I am thrilled for her. Yay. Thank you.

On the way home, Anna calls Greg to tell him the news. He's surprised. She's so happy. I can hear it in her voice and see it on her face. Victory. With one down and two therapy appointments to go, tomorrow we will drive back to the hospital at 3 pm for one hour each of occupational and speech therapy. I call out, "Ask Dad if we need to pick Max up at school."

Anna asks, then turns to me and says, "No." "Okay, tell Dad we are on our way home." Anna pauses and then tells me that the meatloaf and mash potatoes had arrived at the house. I know this will be a huge hit with my family. We love meatloaf and mashed potatoes. Perfect.

Max is home when we get there and, naturally he's starving. It's about 5:15 pm and I need to get the food on the table by 5:30 pm so I can leave for book club around 6:00 pm. As I suspected, everyone is excited about the meatloaf. Comfort food is good. Not for a consistent diet, but good for a little healing and feeling good. I ring the bell and the family comes running. We sit, pray, and they eat. I will have dinner at book club. Even though the meatloaf smells incredibly good and I consider having a bite, I wait for book club. I know there will be tons of food. The kids tell me the meatloaf and mashed potatoes are absolutely fabulous. They practically lick their plates clean. Yum.

October book club is always at Tracy's house. She is the Halloween Queen and has incredible decorations. We see spiders, cool serving pieces and lots of pumpkins. Every year it's fun to see how she has decorated. And the food! The girl goes nuts. She makes soups, salads, main courses, hors d'oeuvres and desserts that are out of this world. The work she puts into this evening is amazing. This will be my first time with the girls since the accident. I am looking forward to it.

I'm barking out last minute orders, but my family just looks at me and says bye mom. I realize I am a bit over the top and finally, relinquish the control to Greg. Everyone is relieved. Me too. Anna will be asleep when I get home and Max may be as well. So, I hug them and tell them I love them as I leave for an evening of girls only. Part of me wants to stay home. But, it will be great to see my friends and even though I have spoken to each of them individually, I know they are going to want to hear how the kids are doing and talk about the whole situation. That's okay. Knowledge is better than speculation.

I can smell Tracy's dinner when I get out of my car. It smells wonderful. When Tracy answers the door, she gives me a big hug, followed by hugs from all the other girls. We always hug each other when we get together. Heaven knows we've known each other for years. Most of us are connected through our daughters. Book club started when our daughters went into first grade and a couple of the girls thought we should form a club and read books. It was a great idea. Our first meeting to discuss the plan was held at Starbucks on the morning of our daughters first day of first grade. We are an eclectic group, but this is a group of strong women with a wide variety of beliefs. Some work, some stay home, but all of us have kids and all of us understand family and the fragility of life. We have seen each other through various ups and downs with husbands, death, work, and kids. It's not always pretty, but we make it work.

The girls want to know how the kids are doing. I give them an update of both Max and Anna and fill them in on our most recent events. We start talking about the morning of the accident and what they were doing when they got the news.

As we fill up our plates and sit around Tracy's beautifully decorated table, I begin to hear their stories unfold.

Cathalynn goes first. She had just left her house to run errands and was driving towards QFC when she saw a car turned upside down and smashed against a pole by the gas station. She realized it was a severe accident because of all the fire, police, and aid vehicles at the scene. She had no idea who was involved until later that day when Kathy called her and told her it was Max and Anna. She was devastated and hoped and prayed they would both make a full recovery. Cathalynn also said she was amazed at the support and blessings that were heaped on our family. I agree with her. Everyone has truly been a huge blessing to us.

Kathy said she heard about the accident while she was at work. Kathy works for QFC, but not at the same store we do our grocery shopping. Customers were coming in talking about an accident on Juanita Drive. She didn't realize it was Max and Anna until much later in the day when she got a phone call from a friend. Kathy then called Cathalynn. She also called her daughter Talia, a lifelong friend of Anna's.

Tracy's story was short and sweet. She said, "I was driving home from work. I heard about the accident and called Kathy to see if she knew who was involved since the Finn Hill area is such a small community. That's how I found out."

Nancy was easy. She tells the girls I called her from the car on the way to the hospital and she went straight to Harborview. The waiting room was packed as everyone waited for news about the kids.

Karen G. (we have two Karens in book club) got a phone call from Kathy. They are sisters-in-law and very good friends. Kathy told her what was going on.

Hearing the girls relate their stories takes me back to that morning. That morning was something else, and I'm not sure what I mean by that. The word of the accident spread so quickly. I imagine we had more prayers than I will ever know about, shooting up to Heaven that day. I envision Heaven being lit up with pleas of help and healing. Amazing.

Dessert. It looks fabulous, as usual. And, I am already stuffed. The discussion about the book waits until we have finished dinner and are eating dessert. Everyone loved the book. It was an incredible read. And the timing was perfect. Thank you.

It's late when I get home. Greg always forgets to leave the front porch light on for me when I am out late. It's dark and I can barely see the keyhole to the door. I hear Sammy behind the door whining for me. It's a familiar and welcome sound. The second the door is open, his body begins gyrating, again, and his tail is practically swinging in a full circle. It's nice to be loved.

I double check all the doors downstairs to make sure they're locked. Then Sam and I turn towards the stairs to go to bed. He always gets to the top before me. I try to beat him, but he usually bounds up the stairs ahead of me and runs over to his bed. Goofy dog. Tonight's no different. He gets to the top of the stairs and pushes the door open with his nose. Greg is sitting up in bed reading.

"Hi, how was book club?" he asks.

"Great. The girls told me their stories about what happened with them the day of the accident. Do you want to hear them?"

"Sure," he says.

I sit down on our bed and begin repeating what they told me. By the end of my final story, we are both so thankful for our friends and reminded of the huge part they played in our recovery.

I creep down the hall to get one last look at my babies before I go to bed. They are both breathing and sleeping. I can go to bed now.

Chapter Twenty

"She isn't afraid of anything"
— Glenn Raschick

It's Tuesday morning. Exactly three weeks since the car accident. I take a moment to remember and to be thankful for the outcome. It's okay to remember. I allow myself a little grace. Thank you. Then I move on to today's agenda. Take kids to school. Reschedule jury duty. Pay property taxes. Pick Anna up for her two therapy appointments at 3:00 pm and 4:00 pm. Dinner. Mandatory basketball meeting at 7:00 pm. When I look at my calendar, I see that today is also the costume party at preschool. That is always so fun. The little kids are so excited and come in the most hilarious outfits. The moms decorate the art room and throw a party at the end of preschool. Vegetables, juice and cupcakes. The preschoolers love it. I will miss it. That's okay, I'm not ready to go back yet. But, the thought of it makes me smile.

Max and Anna are up, showered and ready to go. With breakfast eaten and backpacks loaded, we pile into the car and drive to school. I remind Anna that I will pick her up fifteen minutes before school gets out and we will go to the hospital for speech and occupational therapy. She says okay as she climbs out of the car and hands her backpack off to a friend. Good girl. She remembers she's not supposed to carry her backpack. I tell both the kids I love them and they reply with their usual love you too. Three words, ten letters. Probably the most significant combinations of vowels and consonants in the world. I say them every day and I hear them every day. That's very important to me.

At 2:15 pm I leave for Cedar Park to pick up my baby girl. When I get to school I go in to sign Anna out and have a moment to talk to the lady in the attendance office. She has been keeping an eye on Anna and lets me know Anna is doing well, hasn't stopped in for a rest yet, and her friends are taking very good care of her. This school is something. Everyone is caring for our kids. It's quite a blessing for us. We talk for a few more minutes before Anna appears, with friend in tow carrying her backpack. It makes me laugh because not only did Anna get excused to leave early, one of her classmates got to leave class just to carry her backpack. Given that he's a sophomore in high school, I'm sure he thinks this is a pretty good arrangement.

Anna's friend hands me her backpack and off we go. She looks good. I ask her if she's tired and she says, "A little, but I made it all day." I hope she's not overdoing it, but I don't say anything to her. Unless we see a problem, we are letting her figure this out at her own pace.

"I'm hungry," are the next two words out of her mouth.

"Okay, we'll stop and get something for you to eat."

She looks at me with a huge smile.

"What?" I ask her.

"The girls asked me if I want to be manager of the basketball team this year since I can't play. I get to sit on the bench and help coach."

I look back at her and smile, "That's wonderful, Anna."

"Yeah," she says, "I met my new coach today. She's really nice and she thought it would be great for me to be the manager and help motivate the team. I told them I would do it. I have to go to practices, Mom."

"Anna Brown," I say, "that is perfect. You will be great at that job. Before you regained your filter in the hospital, you did tell everyone you would be an athletic supporter." We both start laughing. "But, no practicing with the girls. I mean it."

She gives me a little look with a crooked smile and says, "I know Mom and so does coach."

"Okay," I say, "when do practices start? Let's get that schedule to make sure you put it on your calendar." Anna is as organized as I am. But since her head injury, we have to make sure everything goes into her planner. She looks at that planner every day to help her with her memory. Her teachers are making sure she logs homework, assignments, and test dates. We make sure to log her doctor appointments and social events. Having a planner was part of her therapy at Children's Hospital. Planners are great. They are a tremendous help to Anna. Now if it was Max and I wanted him to use a planner, he would think I was insane, and would be happy to tell me so. He refuses to use a planner of any kind. Just stores everything in his memory. I have no idea how he remembers everything. Next year when he is away at college and on his own we will see if it is his great memory or his insane mother that reminds him about his obligations. That will be interesting.

With snack in hand, we enter the rehab facility at the hospital. Anna is whisked away for her first appointment: speech therapy. I read and wait. At 3:45 pm, Anna and the speech therapist come to the lobby to get me. I follow them back into a smaller room. The therapist is very kind and says, "I am concerned about Anna's short-term memory and want to continue. I think we should schedule four weeks of speech therapy and Anna should come in once a week. Hopefully that will be it."

"Okay." It is okay, I tell myself. We do know her short term memory is not working well. This is a good thing. Back to the lobby I go.

When her second appointment is finished, Anna comes out to get me and says the occupational therapist wants to see me. I collect my belongings and Anna walks us back to the therapist's workroom. She is also very kind. Her news is a little different. She thinks Anna's occupational skills are great and doesn't see any need for further therapy. Anna is very pleased with this diagnosis. "This is good, Poo, you only have to come back for speech therapy. Very good job Anna."

She looks at me, smiles and says, "Don't call me Poo." I laugh. Like that's going to happen. But, I can be more careful about where I call her Poo.

When we get home, Anna finds her dad immediately. "Guess what, Dad?" she says, "I am going to be the manager of my basketball team."

"Really?" Greg says, "That will be great, Schmoo."

"Yeah," she tells Greg, "I get to sit on the bench and help coach the team. Get them motivated." Greg and I look at each other knowingly. This is absolutely perfect for her. She will have no problem yelling out her opinion and cheering on the girls. We still haven't met her new coach, but I love her already.

Anna looks tired. Max is hungry and waiting to go to his final pre-season high school basketball meeting. I wonder how that feels to him. Basketball has been a huge part of his life since he was little. When other kids gave up the game, he forged ahead. He has made basketball his passion for over ten years and this is his final high school season. He has a fabulous coach, tons of support, and is a great success as Cedar Parks point guard. I know in my heart he will always remember his high school basketball career as being fun and uplifting. So will Greg and I.

After we've eaten, I take one look at Anna and decide she and I will stay home. We were all going to go and make it a basketball kind of night. But, she has had two full days of school and appointments and I can tell she's exhausted. In her quest to return to normalcy she may have overdone it a bit. Max understands as he and Greg pile into the car. Max has been on the back burner for the last few weeks and I am aware of that. I hope he understands. If he communicated more, I would know. Guess I'd better do some probing!

We tell the boys we love them and wave from the coziness of our home as they pull out of the driveway. Anna wants to go to bed. I insist that she wash her face and brush her teeth first. She must be on the mend because her attitude reeks of teenage angst.

"Two little jobs," I say, "and then you can get into your comfy bed with your soft lambys." Cranky girl. She quickly accomplishes these two necessities and crawls into bed. Perfect. Bed is a great place for her to be. I hand her lambys to her, give her a kiss and an I love you and turn to leave. I think she's already asleep and I haven't even reached the door yet. Good.

I figure Greg and Max will be gone for an hour or more, so I pick up a few remaining messes and allow myself a moment to relax. This is going to be a busy season for us. Max's senior year and Anna's challenges to recover are a full plate. I can't believe he's a senior in high school. Every parent probably says that. I remember when Mom was dying and she said, "Where did all the time go?" I was too young and too busy with my own kids to fully absorb her words. Now I have those same thoughts. I miss my mom.

Time is flying by alright. We are always so busy and I wonder if this is just the way it is when you have teenagers. If you're not physically exhausted, you're mentally exhausted. It's crazy. I have made a few decisions and excused myself from a number of responsibilities through the end of the year. I simply can't do it all right now. I will not be teaching preschool until after Christmas, I will not be leading the youth sponsored Turkey Lunch this weekend and I will not be overscheduling myself. I will gladly still be the team mom for both Max and Anna's basketball teams, a commitment I made months ago. I will arrange for Anna to have her birthday weekend on Orcas Island with a few of her friends, and I will make sure we are fully decorated for Christmas by the time Thanksgiving arrives. Since the day after Thanksgiving is the start of the Christmas season, I do not wait to decorate. As far as I am concerned, we only have four weeks till Christmas. After Thanksgiving, I want to spend my time enjoying Christmas, not decorating for it.

While I lie on my bed thinking about the next few months, Sammy bolts up and barks. He scares the hello out of me when he does that. The barking is so loud, being the guard dog that he is, that I jump up and race to him to quiet him. I don't want Anna to be awakened. Sammy and I go into the kids' bathroom and look out the window. It's something we do when he barks. I get on my knees and look out the bathroom window with him while his eyes settle on his targeted concern. I follow his trained eye to the source of his defensiveness and we talk about it. This calms both of us. I appreciate his alertness, but sometimes it's just a squirrel or a raccoon foraging in the darkness. But, better to check than not, so here we sit gazing out the window. This time, it's Greg and Max. "Good boy," I say to him, "Good dog Sammy. Let's go greet the boys." Sam's tail sweeps from side to side and bangs the walls as we walk down the hall and downstairs. He's in a big hurry to be at the front door when they come in. Sammy obviously arrives to the door before I do. He can hardly stand it.

"Wow, that was fast," I tell the boys as they step into the foyer. Max nods. Greg says everything went well and that Max's coach Lamont wants me to call him about the plans for meals and about being team mom. Lamont started a very smart tradition. When the boys play at home, we give them dinner after school. It's prepared or heated up in the school's kitchen and the boys come through a buffet line to eat. It's a big dinner for lots of energy during the game. We also try to load them up with carbs and give them a case of water to take to the game. These boys work hard and forget to drink liquids. They get worn out. Our goal is to keep them hydrated and moving. Last year it was helpful. This is a small thing to think about doing, but a huge thing for their energy. When the boys play away, we pack up easy meals and load them on the bus with food and water. No matter if they are home or away, the players have plenty of food and drink. As team mom, I coordinate the meal schedule and handle the communications from the coach to the parents. The parents are always great. They never fail to help. Consequently, they have great kids. Isn't it funny how that works?

Max is hungry again. No surprise there. He and Greg snack while I take Sammy out to potty and begin to lock up the house for the night. When we finally get upstairs, turn out the last light and I pull the covers up to my chin, Greg says, "Let's take the kids to see the Volvo in Bellevue tomorrow." I look at him in the dark. I know this man. This means we're buying a car tomorrow.

Chapter Twenty-One

"School came together...shaping influence on the class"
— Mr. Ian

It's official. We are the proud owners of a black 2004 Volvo S80. The kids have the nicest and safest car in the family. I must say she's a beauty. While we are waiting for the paperwork to be done, I fall in love with the Volvo SUV. Unfortunately, I will not be taking that one home with me. Maybe someday I will get a new car. Perhaps in seven years when everyone is out of college and our bank account can handle another expense. But honestly, Greg knows I am not a car person. The only cars I can accurately identify are the Volkswagen Beetle and the old VW vans from the 60s. That's it. I don't really care about cars. I do like driving an SUV so I can sit up higher on the road. And now, even more so than before, safety is a huge issue with me. But aside from that, I have no other car requirements. As a matter of fact, Greg has chosen our vehicles ever since we've been married. I just drive what we own.

Anna stayed home today and slept. Her head hurt and she was exhausted. I called the school and told them she wouldn't be in today and probably not tomorrow. There's a half day tomorrow. It's okay. I spoke to her math teacher and she is very pleased with Anna's progress. We are gauging Anna's abilities on how she does in math. Math is a lot of memorization and critical thinking. If she does well in math, we feel confident she will be able to handle her other classes. Lise Smith says Anna is doing as well as anyone can after having missed three weeks of math. It's more like she missed learning how to do the math as opposed to not understanding the math. This is fabulous news. Thank you.

By Saturday morning Anna is feeling much better. Rested and headache gone. I think she tried to do too much too fast at the beginning of the week. She just wants her normal life back. I understand that and she is figuring out how much is too much for right now. It's a process.

This morning we are taking Anna to the Jaguars soccer game while

Max takes his final SAT at a local community college. I know he is glad to be finishing his pre-college testing so he can figure out where to go to college. We send him out the door with water, pencils and a calculator. We wish him good luck and he tells Anna to say good luck to the Jaguars. Anna has been a Jaguar ever since I can remember. They are the soccer team she joined when she was just starting out her soccer career. She was a little girl then. None of us have seen the girls play since the accident. Obviously, Anna won't be playing, but Coach Mark called and wanted to know if she could come. Most of the team hasn't seen her and he thinks it would do them a world of good to see their Urlacher at the game. Sporting her thick white neck collar, we head to the game. It just so happens, this game is about forty minutes away, so we leave early enough to swing through Starbucks and get a latte.

It's a beautiful, crisp fall day full of brightly colored leaves and cold air. Gloves and scarves are a necessity. When we arrive at the school and locate the soccer fields, we look around for Anna's teammates. They are practicing on the far field and we walk around another game to reach our side of the field. The girls don't see Anna at first. They are huddled on the field. When we reach our team's sideline Anna stands amongst the team's belongings, wanting so much to be part of the game. As soon as the huddle breaks, one of the girls yells out "There's Anna!" They run to the sideline to see her. It's wonderful. They huddle around her, hug her, and sit her down in one of the team chairs right in between duffel bags and water bottles. She's theirs for the moment. Her face lights up. The parents walk over to say hi and see how everything is. Only a few of the parents have been part of this team as long as we have. Some of them don't know us well because their girls are newer to the team. However, they are all so kind, making sure to tell us they've been praying and thinking about our family. One of the moms I've known for quite a while comes over. Not only did her older son play basketball with Max, her daughter is a good friend of Anna's and has been to our house many times. I give her a hug and we talk about Anna. She's a nurse and is now an administrator at one of the major hospitals in town. I have always liked her, she's funny and lots of fun. I asked her how she found out about the accident. She has a great story that answered a question about one of our experiences at Harborview. She says her daughter called her, crying. The police were anticipating a fatality and the kids were terrified. They knew Anna had been airlifted to Harborview and they knew that meant Anna was in serious trouble. So, this wonderful woman called the ICU at Harborview and identified herself. She also said she understood the privacy laws, but wanted to ask if there was anything that Harborview could tell her that she could tell her daughter. A nurse from Harborview said she would see what she could do. Not much later, she got a call back, telling her that Anna was in ICU and was stable. This was fairly generic information, yet comforting news. She was then able to let her daughter know Anna was alive, in ICU and stable. This explains why we had a few nurses visit us in ICU, as well as the head duty nurse that came in and was so kind. Forget about the privacy laws, I'm glad these people loved Anna enough to stick their necks out and make a call. It's okay with me. Laws may change, but people remain the same. You can't mandate compassion.

As we navigate through the next few days, our activities blend into our daily routine. While the kids are at school, I take care of the little jobs that went by the wayside during our hospital stays. Yearbook pictures are in, senior video pictures are turned in, phoned the spinal doctor at Harborview, got the basketball game and practice schedules for both kids' teams, pulled out the Christmas decorations and got started on our house, picked a book for our Christmas book club meeting at my house and finalized our Orcas Island plans for Anna's 16th birthday. Whew!

Wednesday morning rolls around and I make it to prayer group. This afternoon Anna has a speech therapy appointment and tomorrow afternoon she has an appointment with her primary care physician. On Thursday, Max and Greg are planning a trip to Oregon to look at colleges, and I am trying to go to the poinsettia festival at my favorite garden store, Molbak's, on Friday night. Uh oh, I realize that won't work if the boys are gone. Everything is up in the air. I have no control. Again. But, I have two living, breathing kids and that's enough.

It's Wednesday afternoon and I pick Anna up after school. We grab a fast food snack on our way to the speech therapy appointment. Not my proudest moment in the food department, but I am cutting myself a little slack. At the end of the appointment we receive good news. Anna is doing well and they only want to schedule two more appointments. Then, they think she will be done. She's thrilled. She's worked so hard to get to this point. I am so proud of her. Yay! Success. Thank you.

By the time we get home, our dinner has arrived. This time it was brought to us by Wendy Legat, Lindsay's mom. I don't know how she does it. She has a full house at home, from babies to high school kids, yet she manages to bless us with a meal for four. I've liked Wendy from the moment I met her and think she's a wonderful person. She's always happy, always laughing and always smiling. What a treat to know someone like Wendy.

The boys are hungry, Anna is starving, and all I have to do is pull open the lid and serve. Once again, I am thankful for these meals. They truly allow me time to take care of the needs of my family and not stress out about cooking. We sit down at the dining room table with full plates of hot food. Anna tells Greg and Max that she only has two more speech therapy appointments and then she is done with rehab. Greg tells her, "That's great Schmoo." Max nods in agreement.

Then Max looks at us and says, "I've made a decision. I don't need to go to Oregon. I want to go to Gonzaga. I don't want to play college basketball. I want to enjoy my college life and not spend it in practices or playing in basketball games."

Greg asks, "Are you sure?"

"Yes," says Max.

I wonder if the accident has helped him simplify his decision. Probably. It's a good decision and we are very happy about it. Gonzaga is a Jesuit Catholic University. The campus is gorgeous, Gonzaga is a fabulous school, and this is an excellent academic choice. Secretly, I think Greg is glad he doesn't have to drive to the middle of Oregon and back in a four-day period. Plus, my stress about the boys going on a road trip with the possibility of another car accident has just vanished. Perfect. Oh, and Friday night just opened up. Molbak's here I come! I see more fun on the horizon.

After dinner Anna wants to go upstairs and lie down with her kitty. She scoops up Belle and away they go. Greg escorts her upstairs while I finish in the kitchen. Meanwhile, Max is visibly happy about his decision and I detect a sense of relief that the college search and decision is over. Good. If he's happy, I'm happy. Of course, he did research Gonzaga's intramural basketball program and apparently, it's fabulous. So, he can keep active and pursue his love of basketball through a great recreational program, without the stress of being on a college team. In addition, Gonzaga's men's basketball program is nationally known and widely respected. He can still be in basketball heaven. This is a great choice.

It's getting late and Anna is sound asleep. I pry Belle from the warmth of Anna's bed and place her in her comfy kitty bed in the garage. The house is closing down for the night. All three kitties are in the garage, Sammy is upstairs, Max is in his room and Greg is reading a book stretched out on our bed. The lights are out downstairs and all the doors are locked.

No candles burning and no appliances left on. I put the gate up and set the alarm. This has been another great day.

Before I fall asleep, my mind turns to Max. He is such a responsible kid. And, very funny, too. Max has a great sense of humor. He seems to be doing really well. He has been driving the Volvo to school and back all week. Max loves the Volvo and I think I am ready to let him drive Anna to school. Scared, but ready. He needs to be trusted and it's important for Max to see my trust in him. I will still ask them to call me when they get to school. If they don't call, I will panic. They know I will call the school and track them down. But, I don't want to have to do that. Let's hope they see the importance in calling and letting me know that they have arrived safely to school.

It's Friday morning and I think we will start next week with Max driving Anna to school. I wake her up and look at my little girl wrapped up in white lambys and a neck brace. Today is not the day to stress myself out. Max knows I love him. This is a process for all of us. I would like to take life a little slower today. I will drive Anna to school and go work out afterwards. I breathe a deep sigh of relief, knowing I have a little control for a few more days. Don't we all think we have control? It's a nice myth.

The weekend has been a blur. On Saturday night, our last meal was delivered. It was a delicious meal served to us by a family with a daughter in Anna's class. Once again, I am reminded what a great blessing these meals have been. They have been really important, incredibly helpful, and truly appreciated. Sunday afternoon Greg went golfing. It was his first time since the accident and probably his last time this year. He went with Craig McAllister and had a great game. Greg called after the game to see if I wanted to join them, along with Stacey, for dinner. Another outing. How fun. Since the kids did not have school on Monday and I made sure they had food and were home together, I took a couple of hours off to be with Greg and our friends. It was great.

On Monday morning, I get a call from the head of the video production department at Cedar Park. Even though there are no classes today, Max has two basketball practices and the staff is working. This man wants to know if I would appear in the school video that is shown during an open house for prospective new students. They would like me to tell the story of the car accident and how Cedar Park has been part of our lives during this time. The video is for prospective families to get a look at the school and life at Cedar Park. After what we have been through and how incredible the school has been, how could I say no? They schedule me for Friday morning. I run upstairs to tell Greg and the kids. Naturally, Max thinks this is hilarious and Anna is horrified. Greg thinks it's great. How did I know those would be their responses? It makes me laugh to watch their faces.

This week will be the first week we have no doctor appointments. We will have our first regular week since the accident. We'll be back to our own family schedule and back to cooking. Back to normal. It feels good. But, there will be lots of basketball practices, teacher conferences for Max, and early dismissals for the kids. There is nothing going on this week that is out of the ordinary. I have grown to like ordinary. Thank you.

Anna makes it through the week without missing a class, having a headache or staying home. She is learning to pace herself and get lots of rest. Her studies are going well and she is trying to balance her school life and her social life as best she can. She's looking forward to her birthday and to being the manager of the basketball team. She has attended a number of practices this week and absolutely loves being part of the team. It has given her a look at the game from a new perspective. She sees both mistakes and opportunities for the team. I think this helps her brain. She is actively engaged with the people and things that she loves. She's analyzing. It stimulates her. However, it also makes her tired. At one point, I had to tell her she couldn't go to a practice and needed to rest. It made her a little mad, but we both knew she was tired. Her body and brain still need lots of rest. She still has a fractured neck, healing organs and memory gaps, even though we count our blessings knowing things are considerably better than they could have been. Although we desperately want our lives to be back to normal, we still have the road of healing ahead and nothing but time will lead us to our previous life. Next week is Thanksgiving and we will be surrounded by her aunts, uncles, grandparents, and cousins. It will truly be a dinner of thanks.

Max also makes it through the week with flying colors. His teacher conferences went very well and he has had numerous basketball practices. Max is getting his paperwork to Gonzaga and applying for scholarships. He's enjoying his friends and school and is very much looking forward to basketball season. Max has been driving Anna to school every day and they call me after they have arrived safely. I am beginning to see him getting ready to graduate. Something happens when you are a senior in high school and college looms a short distance ahead. He's preparing himself to let go of high school and plunge into college. I am not so sure I am ready, though.

Saturday night is the school auction. Greg and I usually don't go to this one event, but this year we feel we need to support the school and participate in this wonderful fundraiser. A friend from Faithful Hearts is the chairperson for this huge party and does a beautiful job. Max isn't back from basketball practice by the time we have to leave for the auction and this makes me a little nervous. I don't want to leave Anna home alone. Before I can have a chance to get too worried, there is a knock on the door and Candice stands waiting to come in. Thank goodness. I review the dos and don'ts with Candice as she nods her head in understanding. Greg and I leave for the auction knowing Candice is with Anna, Max will be home shortly, and they have plenty of food in the refrigerator. Hours later, we come home to dishes and food containers sprawling across the kitchen counters. What a mess. Sampson greets us in the kitchen with the back half of his body and tail flailing from side to side and his tongue trying to lick, or should I say kiss me. He finds my leg. I pet him and ask him not to lick me. It takes a minute for him to understand, but finally the tongue goes back in and he lies down to rest comfortably on the carpet. Upstairs, Candice is asleep on Anna's bed with Anna. Downstairs, Max is in the toy room lying on the couch and watching a movie. All is well. Once again, ordinary.

I wake up Sunday morning thinking about Thanksgiving and the upcoming weekend. This is certainly a year to be thankful. Normally by the time Turkey Day rolls around, our home is fully decorated for Christmas and we are ready for the tree, which we get the day after Thanksgiving. It's a tradition. This year will be no exception. Friday morning, we will pile in our car with the Allens leading the way and off we will go to a tree farm. Often times, neighbors, friends, and relatives follow, but always, without exception, we take our dog. It's a party for humans and dogs alike. The owners of the tree farm have two dogs themselves, they hand out candy canes, help cut the trees down, and basically provide a festive atmosphere for all. Some families have a tailgate party there. We always go out for breakfast afterwards to one of the local restaurants. Regardless of the weather, our families have been sharing this event for years. This year, the Blackburns are coming with their dogs and we have rumblings from a few friends that would also like to go.

As for the house, we are mostly decorated. Just the toy room is left. That's where we put the real tree. It's always too big for the room. But that's also a tradition. Maybe I can get the toy room decorated before Thursday. I'll try.

"Oh, my gosh!" I scream out loud to myself. I almost forgot our Christmas poem! This is another one of our Christmas traditions. I write a short poem every year and mail the out-of-state envelopes on Tuesday and the in-state envelopes on Wednesday. To me, Christmas begins the day after Thanksgiving and I try to have that poem in everyone's hand the moment Thanksgiving is over. You have no idea the comments I have had over the years from our friends about our poem. Some have tried to beat me and have sent me their Christmas cards to be received the day before Thanksgiving. I told them that didn't count. Others have sent me their Christmas cards in January for the following December. I told them that didn't count either. However, the funniest Christmas poem story we have is from my friend, Jack Finkelman. Jack is about twenty-five years older than me and I met him in 1978 when I was an assistant buyer living in Portland, Oregon. One year he sent our Christmas poem back to me highlighted with comments and questions. It was hilarious. Jack lives in Florida and I called him with the answers. Jack is the best and I always laugh when I think of that poem coming back in the mail to me.

This year Thanksgiving will be at our house. I'd better get myself pulled together. Our lives are no longer centered on the hospital and the doctors. This is good. Thank you. As I pull myself out of bed, I begin to formulate our poem. Life is moving forward.

Max and Anna are sleeping. Since the accident, we haven't been to church a lot. This is mainly due to the need for Anna to rest and recuperate. Sunday is the only day she doesn't have an activity and the activities are good for her brain. God knows my heart so I am not worried about that. But, I do want our congregation to know we appreciate them and I hope they understand.

As the kids begin to stir, Greg and I sit with our cups of tea and relax on this stormy Sunday. It's great to just sit around for a while and take in the moment. Greg is a terrific dad and the kids migrate to him. That has been a blessing throughout this whole month and a half. The fact that the kids have good relationships with both of us and have not one, but two places to find love and acceptance is a godsend. Thank you.

We maneuver through the day and Thanksgiving week without any problems. Anna is still very tired and has the opportunity to catch up on sleep and friends. Her memory is about the same, yet we are very encouraged by her success in school. Her grades are good. She continues to struggle with retaining new information, but is working diligently to improve. She still does not remember much about 9th grade and her only recollection of this school year is the week prior to the accident. We are not sure if those memories will ever come back and we continue to pray for her healing and health. She has proven to be a very determined young woman. Although this may not surprise anyone who knows Anna, we never know how any person will react to adversity until it is placed before them. She has more than risen to the occasion and we are so very proud of her. Max is doing remarkably well also. He has immersed himself in his basketball team. He continues to heal mentally while watching his sister work her way back to normal. I don't know if he realizes this, but Max needs to see Anna thrive. If she does well, he does well. By the grace of God, we are moving forward and are able to see the progress we have made in the last month and a half. Physically, Max's hand and eyes are fine. However, on Monday he had a doctor appointment. This was a follow-up with the sports medicine physician. The physical therapy sessions have provided relief for Max's lower back. This is crucial to his performance throughout the season, he needs to be in top condition and pain free. Max was glad to get some help and relief. I think he had downplayed his pain because of everything that had been going on. He's a great guy and so quiet, it's hard to help him sometimes. I am glad we got this taken care of for him.

Thanksgiving Day is pretty casual. The kids rest, I cook (and have a cranberry champagne mimosa at 3:00 pm) and everyone eats. This year Uncle Rick and Aunt Debbie are here with Alina. Gramma and Grandpa bring appetizers for all and the Allens stop by for dessert. Uncle Doug, Aunt Becky and the twins were scheduled to go to Becky's family this year, so we miss them but certainly understand the dynamics of sharing yourself with both families. At the end of the evening, Greg packs up the leftovers and cleans up the mess. Gramma wants the turkey carcass for soup, so we send her home with a bag of bones and a few extra treats.

By Sunday night we have a huge, fragrant Christmas tree in the toy room, have been to a basketball jamboree and have gone to Doug and Becky's for dinner. We thought about getting the tree decorated, but everyone is too tired to help. So, we retreat to our rooms early and prepare ourselves for this next week. Regulation basketball season starts. Amen.

Chapter Twenty-Two

"Teenage boys for the first time getting real ...
rocked the student body world"
— Garron Smith

My dad still doesn't know the severity of the accident. Because of the Alzheimer's, I continue to tell him that Baby Blue, the Ford Explorer he gave the kids, saved them when they were hit by a large truck. This makes him feel good and lets him know the kids are fine. I will never tell Dad the whole story. That would be very stressful for him and he may only remember the scary parts. With what he knows now, he makes a joke out of it to Max and laughingly asks Max how he managed to wreck Grandad's car. Max handles this with humor and I try to lighten the conversation. If Dad was healthy, he would have been here in a minute, he would call me every day to check in and make sure the kids are okay. I miss that part of him. I miss Mom, too. I think I'll call him.

With cup of tea in hand, I make myself comfortable and dial the familiar number. He sounds good and is his usual happy self. He's always been a very positive person and that is one of the many things that has made him a popular guy. Throughout his life Dad has had lots of friends and lots of fun. I love that about him. He wants to know how the kids are. He also tells me to remind them how important public speaking and letter writing classes are. This has been a topic of conversation for years. So, I tell him they are taking public speaking, but unfortunately, letter writing is no longer available because of computers. He's disappointed in the letter writing portion of the news, but thrilled they are taking public speaking. Dad swears by public speaking. And to tell you the truth, I think he's right. If you can speak in front of people with confidence and ease, anything is possible. Fortunately, Max and Anna do very well in this field and I'm certain they inherited the skill from Dad. By the end of the conversation, Dad has made me feel uplifted and happy. That, I decide, is perhaps one of the many jobs of parenting. I just learned something new from my Dad. Thank you.

Okay. I freshen up my cup of tea and open my calendar to review our activities this week.

Today, Monday, the chimney sweeps are coming. I have our chimneys checked every year. We have lots of fires in the fireplaces and have had creosote buildup in the past. One year our neighbors called to tell us there were flames coming out of our toy room's chimney. We quickly extinguished the fire in the fireplace and I've had the chimneys checked and cleaned every year since.

Tomorrow, Anna has a rehab appointment in the morning and I have an evening church event. It's an Advent by Candlelight get together, for women only, and I promised I would come. The evening looks clear at this moment, but I am always willing to cancel if Anna is having difficulties or Max needs me. Of course, Max would never admit he needs me, but I do try to stay flexible.

Wednesday, Anna has a 3:00 pm appointment in downtown Seattle with her spine doctor. This is an important appointment. She is still wearing her neck brace and the back of her neck remains swollen and tender. We will find out if her fracture is healing properly and what we need to do about this injury from here on out. I know Anna is going to ask about getting rid of the neck brace. It drives her nuts. Then at 7:30 pm, Max has Cedar Park's first pre-season basketball game. The opposing team isn't in our league, but it's a team that can be very difficult and it's our first real game of the season. It's an away game and I do mean away. It's almost fifty miles away. The plan is to finish with Anna's doctor's appointment and drive straight to Max's game. It will be rush hour and even though the drive should only be an hour, if the weather is bad, this could take twice as long. Anna wants to go, too. I pray we get good news from her spine doctor that she is healing properly, and that we can make it to the game. I think it's important to Max.

Thursday morning, Max has a physical therapy appointment for his lower back. This is perfect timing actually. Physical therapy right after his Wednesday night game may help relieve him from the pain. He will be a little late for school, but this is well worth it. That morning I also will be leaving to go to the funeral for Nancy's dad. He was a wonderful man and had a terrific life. Nancy got her spunk and humor from him. She is going to miss him a lot. His name was Chuck and he was an engineer for the Great Northern Railway in Seattle. When he was working and even after retirement, he was always on the go. Busy. Busy. Busy. Just like his daughter. He will be greatly missed by many people.

Friday night we have a home game, as well as, Blue and Gold night at Cedar Park to kick off the beginning of our league basketball season. This is a rally to get Cedar Park fans excited and involved with the upcoming season. The kids cover themselves in blue and gold attire, as well as, paint. They can be very creative. Anna is already looking for the perfect outfit, even though she will be acting as manager during the girls' basketball game. Thank goodness the weekend is open.

As I predicted, the week flew by. On Saturday morning Greg and I wake up thankful that we made it through the last five days without much difficulty. As it turns out, our week really was crazy. Anna had her spine x-ray done and everything looked good. The doctor said no on physical therapy, no on neck stretches, yes on removing the neck collar and yes, she can practice shooting the basketball. But, absolutely no physical contact can be made. He is concerned about her neck only. His rules only apply to her neck. We reminded Anna that she has a one year no contact rule that will be reevaluated next October and that rule trumps all other rules. She knows, but we had to say it. We did decide to leave for Max's game immediately after Anna's doctor appointment. Good decision. We spent two hours in traffic and rain. The weather was horrible and I thought I would lose my mind. Being a passenger doesn't bring out the best in me, especially if the weather is bad. Cedar Park lost the game. It was a tough game, but the boys didn't let the defeat weigh them down. On Friday, they beat the socks off the team they played for Blue and Gold night. The boys felt redeemed. They played an awesome game. The girls played their Blue and Gold game as well. Anna managed and screamed at her teammates throughout the game, as they also gained their first victory.

Pulling myself out of bed, I creep down the hall to take a peek at my babies. It's so hard to open their doors without making a sound. I slowly turn the knob and carefully open Max's door. Max is out. He doesn't hear me and doesn't make a move as I stare to make sure he's breathing. It's a mom thing. I like to see breathing movements no matter how old they are. I have to hold Sammy back from crashing through Max's door and launching himself onto the bed. His goal in life is to greet and lick his packmates. Fortunately, I have a firm grip on his neck and collar. I have to hang onto his furry neck as well, something he hates. He has a very sensitive gag reflex and if I hold him back by the collar alone, he'd make so many coughing and gagging noises that the whole house would be awake. Maybe even the neighbors. I then close Max's door and look at

Sam. He stares at me, as if asking, "WHAT?" I whisper firmly, "SIT," and, "WAIT." He sits obediently and thinks about the wait. I look at him and repeat, "Sam, you WAIT." I see the look in his eyes. He has acquiesced. He knows he must follow orders. I slowly open Anna's door. It creaks. She's also sound asleep. They're exhausted. I watch for her breathing and see her lambys curled up around her head and neck. No neck collar. She looks good. I start to close the door, when Sam, still sitting and waiting, stretches his neck out as far as it can possibly go, and pushes his nose between the door and the door jam. He just wants a whiff and a look. I look at him and say, "Back away Sam, she's okay." He looks up at me and backs away as we retreat down the hallway. What a goofy dog.

Today is Grandpa's birthday and I remind Greg to call him. Isn't that what wives do? We are the reminders, the family calendar, and the glue that holds everything together. While Greg is on the phone, Max comes downstairs with his duffel bag stuffed with basketball gear and is dressed for practice. He briefly looks up and mumbles hi before I feed him. He's much better after food, so I wait until after he's eaten to ask him what his day looks like. He doesn't know or he's not saying. This is my life as the mother of a high school senior. I get no information. Oh well. I give him a hug and a kiss on the cheek and tell him I love him. Before the door closes, I manage to yell out "Drive safely." He doesn't answer me but I know he heard my words. I really don't need to say that to him, but it makes me feel better. In my mind, these words plant little seeds that may remind him at any given moment to make the safe choice. He is my cautious child and a very safe driver, but I say it anyway. I wonder what he thinks when I say things like that to him. I'm sure he is thinking, "Yeah, whatever Mom," and "Do you really think you need to say that to me?"

"So," I turn to Greg, "Remember this next weekend is Anna's 16th birthday trip to Orcas Island. Just us girls are leaving on Friday and coming back Sunday morning." He nods. This reminds me to call Judy Carroll and go over all the details with her. I need to know about keys, sheets, towels, electricity and heat. I pull out our little peach colored phone book and pick up the phone. Judy is a lovely woman and the mother of one of Greg's best friends, Jud. The Carroll and Brown families have been friends for decades. The Orcas Island cabin has been in Jud's family for generations. Not too long after Greg and I started dating, we were invited up to the cabin along with his parents and Jud's parents. That's when I met Greg's parents for the first time. Greg and I have been many times since and so have our kids. Judy answers the phone and we review the details of staying at the cabin. The deal is set. Friday afternoon Lisa and I will be driving to the San Juan Islands for a weekend with four teenage girls. Fun.

I hear noise coming from upstairs. She's up. Greg and I look at each other and I say, "I'll go." Now that she has the neck brace off, has mastered the stairs, and is very nearly back into her regular routine, you would think I would feel she's completely safe in the house. Well, I don't. I shoot upstairs and knock on the bathroom door.

"Hi Poo, you okay?"

Of course, the response is, "YES MOM!"

Having teenagers in the house is not for the faint of heart. Wouldn't it be nice if someone said, "Thanks for caring Mom!" or, "Love you Mom," even, "I'll be out in a minute, Mom." But, apparently, that's not going to happen. This is when I choose humor over frustration and launch into, "Well good. Are you hungry? Want some breakfast? How about a bird's nest egg?"

Anna softens and says, "Okay. I'll come down." What is it about food that puts everyone in a great frame of mind? I'm not sure, but it works.

Downstairs I go to make a bird's nest egg for my baby girl. My mom made them for us when I was little and my kids love them. They're easy. You butter a piece of bread, covering both sides, take a small glass or cookie cutter and punch a hole out of the middle of the bread (I have been known to freehand a heart and other inventive shapes), heat up the frying pan, put the bread in the pan and crack the egg open over the bread, making sure to drop the egg into the hole. Fry it for a bit and flip the whole thing over to fry the bread and the egg on both sides. Oh, and don't forget to fry the little piece of bread you cut out to make the hole. The kids think this is the best part! When all is said and done, there it is. A bird's nest egg! My kids like them kind of runny so they can dip the little cut out piece of bread into the egg. I can't watch them do that because I like my eggs fully cooked. But, it's a favorite none the less.

Down she comes wrapped in lamby, sporting a high, disheveled and lopsided ponytail, wearing sweatpants and a sweatshirt. She's a vision. Thank you.

"Hi Poo, have a seat."

She looks up and says dryly, "Don't call me Poo." Ah, this requires silence until after the meal. I just smile. Actually, I would like to burst out laughing, but there would be repercussions for the rest of the day. I'll let her eat first. It's better that way.

After her breakfast, I remind her about Orcas Island next week and she remembers. Good. She remembers who will be going and when we are leaving and coming back. Good again. Her memory is getting better. Her brain is healing. Her spine and internal organs are repairing themselves. This is such a tremendous blessing. We continue to move forward and pray her brain completely heals itself so not only her memory comes back, but she is able to retain information permanently. And when I say pray, that is what counts. There are still so many people praying for her. God hears them every day.

Our weekend continues with rest and family time. We decide to drive into Seattle on Sunday and take a ride on the merry-go-round. Every Christmas, the merry-go-round is set up right in the heart of downtown. Very fun. We all love that. Well, most of us. Max thinks it's kind of dumb. But, he has fun in spite of himself. I do make sure to stay close to Anna. She is on a beautifully decorated white horse that bobs up and down to the music. I want to make sure she doesn't get dizzy. Greg helps her on and off of the horse. She takes a few steps. She's good, but her daddy holds on to her, just to be safe. She knows it's for the best, but it reminds her she's not back to normal yet. That does bother her. We make our way home for dinner and a movie. The kids are tired and we head up to bed after the movie, making sure the house is locked up and all the animals are in for the night. Everyone is safe and comfortable. That's the way I like it.

On Monday morning, I review our upcoming commitments. This week is full of graduation meetings, physical therapy for Max, basketball practices for both kids, team photos, Bible study and Greg's office party. Another busy week.

By Friday afternoon, I am ready for the two-hour drive to Orcas Island and for a weekend with Lisa, Anna and her friends. We load up the car with four laughing, soon to be sixteen-year-old girls, and point ourselves towards the Anacortes ferry.

The girls are giddy in the car. They are snapping hundreds of pictures of each other as we cruise up Interstate 5 and cut over to Anacortes. Photos of hugs, crossed eyes, surprised eyes, mouths open, smiles, and anything else they can take a picture of. They are so silly. Thank goodness, we finally get into the ferry line and they can get out of the car. They notice a small strip of beach near the ferry dock and jump out to frolic and take more pictures. All the while they pose, jump, laugh, and swing each other around. The three of them are making sure to be careful with

Anna. Amie, Candice, and Katy have seen Anna through this accident. They have prayed and visited their friend and are continuing to protect her. It scared them. They were forced to grow up a little. But, I can see this weekend is going to be a celebration for them as well, not just for Anna's birthday.

I yell at the top of my voice for them to get back in the car. It's cold, loud, and a little breezy, yet the sun is out and it's a beautiful day. Lisa and I were having so much fun watching the girls play, that we weren't watching the time or the approaching ferry. Fortunately, the girls hear me and run laughing back to the car as we frantically wave our arms to hurry them along. The last person is barely buckled up when I shift the car into drive and we load onto the ferry. Whew.

We are traveling on the Yakima ferry today. The Yakima was built in 1967 and is a Superclass ferry being 382'2' long and having the capacity to carry 2500 people and 160 vehicles. The name comes from the Yakima language meaning to become peopled; black bears; run away; and/or people of the narrow river. I say to Lisa, "Let's hope today it means 'to become peopled' and not 'runaway.'" We laugh. Washington State Ferries are amazing. Anna loves riding them and from the looks of it, so do Amie, Candice, and Katy. It is almost disappointing that the ride is only an hour long. The scenery is absolutely breathtaking. I love living in the Pacific Northwest. The water is a beautiful sea blue and the landscape is so lush with tall evergreens, it's difficult to see the homes that have been built in between these beautiful trees. Occasionally we see a dock or magnificent home hovering over the water's edge. For a moment or two, I dream about living in that home. What a great way to spend an afternoon. It's very calming.

Well, calming until you see four wild girls running around the ferry. They finally plant themselves on the bow of the Yakima, snapping picture after picture. Laugh after laugh. Smile after smile. I should be filming this. But, I think they are taking enough pictures to make it look like a film. Really. I watch Anna. She seems to be holding her own. I must be very careful not to call attention to her limitations. It hurts her and she's working extremely hard to put her life back to normal.

The announcement comes over the loud speaker for everyone to get back in their vehicle. We will be docking at Orcas Island shortly. Lisa and I gather the girls and walk down the stairs to the first floor of the Yakima to where my car is parked. The girls climb into the car, still laughing and we wait to for the ferry to be docked and unloaded. This doesn't take very long, as the ferry workers have this timing down to a science. Within minutes, we're on the road.

After a quick stop in East Sound for groceries, we pull into the driveway of the cabin with the sun setting over the water right in front of us. It's bright and beautiful. The house appears as a dark silhouette next to the water with a small uninhabited island sitting off to the right, not too far from the shore line. Anna has been here before, but this is new to the other girls. They are as awed as any almost sixteen-year-old can be about a place like this. Although they are used to the beauty of the Pacific Northwest, this does take you back for a moment and I do see them each pause and look. Ah, the power of this magnificent creation.

Judy was so thoughtful. She had asked one of the neighbors to come over and turn the heat on, so it would be nice and toasty inside by the time we arrived. Even so, we build a fire in the wood stove to make sure we get the full experience of cabin life. It smells good, it looks pretty, and it makes us feel comfortable and cozy. This is going to be awesome.

As soon as the girls are unpacked, they decide it would be fun to go back into East Sound tonight to have dinner and go shopping. Lisa and I delicately try to talk them out of it with thoughts of games, conversation, and coziness, as well as the assumption that none of the stores are open late in December. We want to keep this weekend positive and with four strong-willed girls, this may be challenging. We promise them dinner out tomorrow night and a full afternoon of shopping in East Sound. After a little grumbling, calling to see if stores were open, and attempts at negotiating, they realize we are staying put tonight and begin exploring their loft bedroom. The room is filled with games, books, puzzles, pictures, and memories of kids sleeping up there. I've stayed up there myself and thoroughly enjoyed it.

Finally, Lisa and I have a glass of wine and relax on the well-loved couches in the family room. The cabin isn't big and makes me feel warm and close to those I hold dear. It's a terrific get away spot. There are two bedrooms on the main floor, as well as the kitchen, shared bathroom, and family room. A big round table with old wooden chairs is set up in one corner of the family room surrounded by a variety of low bookcases full of games, puzzles, movies, and other activities. To keep us warm, an old wood stove sits beside an antique rocking chair, next to a set of stairs leading to the loft bedroom. A wall of windows and one single door, face the water and separate the cabin from a large extended deck. Beyond the deck is a rocky drop to the salty water and a magnificent view of huge trees, long beaches and a little uninhabited island. It's perfect.

The girls are hiding out upstairs in the loft with the door closed, trying to conceal themselves from the likes of Lisa and me. The sun has disappeared beyond the horizon and it's pitch black outside. Through the large, picture windows we can see lights coming from boats moored in Rosario Strait. It's peaceful. Orcas Island, one of the many San Juan Islands, boasts the beautiful Moran State Park and Mount Constitution. If you hike all the way to the top of the mountain, you will be greeted by a stone tower calling you to climb its stairs and gaze at the surrounding islands and waterways. The view is fabulous, yet scary for anyone with height issues, like Greg for example. Thousands of people visit the San Juan Islands every year, making sure to stop at Orcas Island to enjoy the hiking, kayaking, artistic atmosphere, island cuisine, and shopping. That said, and having already told the girls about all the fun things there are to do on Orcas Island, they have informed us they are not interested in any hiking, physical activities or history. Just hanging out and shopping. Slayers of fun, they are.

The loft door bursts open and the four of them hustle down the stairs to be near the wood stove. "We're hungry," says Anna in a very matter-of-fact voice. Well, I think to myself, one moment of relaxation is better than none. Lisa and I pick ourselves up off the couches and move our glasses of wine into the kitchen. We pull out the salad fixings, steak, and bread. This is an easy meal to prepare.

After dinner, the girls check out the games and activities. They find a little TV tucked back in the corner. "Please don't work," I quietly whisper to myself. I don't remember there being a TV here. The girls plug it in and, thank you, no reception. "Must be just for movies," I say. Thank goodness. With that in mind, they pick out a movie, sprawl out on the couches, and cover themselves in blankets. They never make it through the whole movie. Sound asleep. All four of them. They are still half asleep as I herd them up to the loft.

In the morning, the girls are sleeping when I open the blinds on the downstairs windows, and am greeted by a beautiful splash of sunlight cast across the top of the tiny island near our cabin. It's so fun to see an uninhabited island. I wonder if anyone ever goes there by boat. I do know there are sacred Native American spaces that can't be trespassed on, but I'm not sure if this island is one or not. In any case, it's beautiful.

I fill the coffee pot with coffee and water, turn it on and get my cup ready. It's slow. It's old. That's okay. It's also freezing and I need to build a fire. While the coffee drips, I gather paper and wood to start the fire. This wood stove is great. The fire catches quickly and the family room starts to warm up and fill the air with the wonderful scent of burning wood. Ah, a fire and a cup of coffee. I hope the girls sleep really late.

When you relax, and stare out a window into the salt water, it's amazing what you can see. Of course, there will always be the usual sea gulls and assorted birds. But, every once in a while, you will see a soaring eagle, a group of seals swimming, or a whale traveling through the salt water. That's the beauty of all of this. It's an opportunity to enjoy the unexpected.

Lisa comes out of her room wrapped in a fluffy robe and flannel pajamas. She's cold. Lisa doesn't drink coffee, so she makes her way to the teakettle and fills it with water. I wonder if there are any tea bags here. She doesn't seem concerned, as I see her pull her own tea bag from her robe pocket. I should have known she'd bring her own tea. We don't speak loudly, neither one of us wants to wake up the girls. I stare out the window to see whatever I can and Lisa comes over to gaze out the window for herself. Nothing out of the ordinary, but it sure feels comforting. We sit in silence and watch the water.

Since there's only one bathroom, it occurs to me we should get in there before the girls wake up. Once they start their routine, there will be no time, or room for Lisa or me to squeeze into the bathroom. But I'm simply not ready to move yet, so we sit quietly. I think about how the last two months have turned out. Sometimes I have to stop myself from thinking about what could have happened. It's not healthy to think about that. It upsets me. It didn't happen. I always feel sad though, knowing there are moms and dads out there that had a different ending to their story. It's heartbreaking. I say prayers for them.

Uh oh, I hear movement from the loft. I jump up and run to my bedroom. Quickly gathering my stuff, I dart into the bathroom and close the door. Selfish, I think. But, I would like to shower and brush my teeth. Heaven knows, four teenage girls will drain the hot water tank faster than the water can reheat. And then there's the makeup and hair routine. We'd be here all day. I don't want to go into East Sound in my pajamas. Fortunately, it was a false alarm, but I make haste in getting ready. Lisa moves into the bathroom as soon as I am done. Whew. We're done, we made it.

Within a few hours, the girls wake up, eat breakfast, and get themselves dressed and presentable. Before we know it, we're shopping in East Sound. The girls want to shop alone. No surprise there. We check the time and give them about two hours before meeting for a late lunch. When we meet, they want more shopping time. I'm not sure why, East Sound isn't that big. Curious. Then the truth comes out. There's a party at the teen center this evening and they want to go. "Okay," I say to them, "give us the details." Lisa and I decide to let them go after the girls take us over to check out the teen center and look at the evening's agenda. We drag the girls along with us until it's time for the party. This is an adventure on its own. We are in and out of little shops, art galleries, and a book store. They keep finding funny little things to buy and want to spend an unusual amount of time in this one little curio shop. I must admit it is interesting. They have everything from trinkets to expensive gift items.

The afternoon passes quickly and before we know it, the sun has gone down and it's time for the party at the teen center. Housed in an old, two-story building, the teen center is quite big with lots of couches and rooms for a variety of activities. Good news. There's a chaperone at the entrance. The girls don't want us to come in, they just want us to leave them at the door and say goodbye. I look at my watch and tell them to check in every hour, have their phones available, and to make sure they answer if we call. We wave goodbye to four darling girls running up the stairs. The chaperone assures us they will be fine as we linger at the entrance. Okay. We're good. Well, as good as moms can be leaving four teenage girls in a place we've never been before with people we don't know. Lisa and I decide to be available. We had thought about a movie, but we've bagged that idea. Looking around town, our options are the grocery store or sitting in the car. We choose the grocery store.

This proves to be a great idea. It didn't occur to us how eclectic these little town grocery stores can be. They carry all sorts of things because there's nowhere else in town to buy most of this stuff. And, considering it's the Christmas season, they are loaded with things we'd have to go to five stores to find at home. We are having a blast. The one little item we both love is $4.99. It's a nightlight with Santa wrapped around a clear pole coming down the chimney. When you plug it in and turn on the switch the little clear pole full of liquid heats up and the liquid bubbles. We add two of these to the shopping cart.

Lisa picks up some wrapping paper and other Christmas essentials while I find myself in the bakery department looking at cookies. Yum. I look at the smiling girl behind the counter and say, "Just a minute." I track Lisa down and drag her to the bakery to make sure she shares in the calories and the selection. It takes us a while. There are lots of treats to choose from. Finally, we have a bag full of cookies and we sit down at a little table by the bakery to savor our selections. My phone rings. The girls are bored and want us to come pick them up. "Okay, we'll be right there." Lisa and I pack up our cookies, pay for our new treasures and go get the girls.

"That was fast," Lisa says. I am thinking the same thing.

We meet them at the entrance of the teen center. They grab us and chatter, "Come in. We want you to meet our new friends and we'll give you a tour." In we go. It's not a long tour, and our last stop is the room at the top of the stairs, where come to find out, they spent most of their evening. There's a pool table in the room and we all know where there is a pool table, there are boys. Shocking. We meet the new boys. "Okay, fun. Nice to meet everyone. Are you girls ready to go back to the cabin?" I so innocently ask. Well, how silly of me. Anna pulls me aside, within earshot of Lisa. Apparently, Candice has a new love interest and they were wondering if they could get together tomorrow. Am I new at this?

"Well," Lisa and I look at each other, "we are catching an early ferry and I don't think that's going to work." It takes us thirty minutes to drag them out of there. Hormones. Sheesh.

They are still talking about their adventures at the teen center while we wait in the ferry line to float our way back home. It's so early, I'm surprised we are able to get the girls up and out at this hour. I promised them a treat from the restaurant at the historical bed and breakfast by the ferry. Food is a great incentive. We had no choice but to leave early because Lisa is having the church's annual youth group white elephant party at her house tonight. It takes about three hours to get home and going back will probably feel longer than the trip up. At least we can look forward to a beautiful ferry ride. This weekend has been a memorable one. Laughable, yet memorable. I am thankful for the opportunity to be with Anna, the girls, and Lisa. Thank you.

Chapter Twenty-Three

"She wanted to know to what degree she was back to normal"
— Mr. Ian

Christmas is just around the corner. I love Christmas. Our family loves Christmas. We have basketball games, parties, birthdays, Christmas break, and family time. The Christmas season is busy, fulfilling, and stressful. I look around the house and see trees, white lights, swags, angels, nativity sets, Santas, and snowmen. We have special Christmas collectibles and antique bulbs that have been passed down from generation to generation carefully placed in a delicate Christmas bowl. These traditional decorations adorn our house year after year. However, this year I felt differently about decorating the house. I am excited to put everything in its usual place. It makes me feel that life is normal. But, I have experienced a revelation. While Christmas decorations are beautiful, and represent this wonderful time of year, they are possessions. Max and Anna are alive. Our kids are God's Christmas gift to us. Being able to decorate the house is the confirmation that our family is intact. Thank you. Thank you. Thank you.

Anna's actual birthday included two parties and a weekend long celebration of her life. As luck would have it, her birthdate fell on a day with back to back boys' and girls' varsity basketball games. That did not deter us. After the games were over, we trekked back to our house with friends in tow to eat cake and open presents. We gave Anna a huge Vera Bradley tote, full of gifts and heavily stuffed with tissue paper. Lots of tissue paper. It was a big tote. The chocolate cake with chocolate frosting and candles was a huge hit. She had a great time and so did Max and their friends.

Sunday night was the family birthday party with Gramma, Grandpa, aunts, uncles, and cousins. Another celebration we were happy to have. More cake, more gifts, more fun and lots of smiles. Everyone was relieved to see the progress Anna has made. It was a wonderful success and left everyone feeling as though Anna was completely back to normal. Greg and I knew differently. Her memory was a long way from normal. The good news was that no one else could tell.

For the next few weeks, we watch Anna closely and continue with our everyday lives. There are more basketball games, hair appointments, doctor visits, and the neighborhood party. Anna is doing well. She's getting plenty of sleep and enjoying turning sixteen. She's asking about driving. She can't drive. Anna has forgotten all of the information from her driver education classes. She will have to start over. Like most six-teen-year-olds, she wants to get in that car, drive off, and express her new-found independence. But, until she can retain information and heal completely, there will be no driving or driving classes. I am not this blunt with her because she is working so hard to get back to her normal, so I tell her this is something we will look into after the first of the year. She doesn't like it, but she accepts it.

Max is completely immersed in basketball. The team is doing incredibly well. They're winning all their games and are preparing to leave for a tournament in Los Angeles within the next few days. Greg is so excited for Max and the team that he has decided to go with them. I'm glad. It's a nice opportunity for Greg to get away and relax a little. He loves basketball and he loves this team. A group of the dads are flying down to support the boys and the basketball program. Cedar Park has never gone out of state for a tournament or any other basketball related event. This is a first. It's a great idea, even though they will be gone from December 19th until the 23rd. The experience will be invaluable. I remember when Max started playing in the Amateur Athletic Union, most often referred to as AAU. He was little and the team, Eastside Magic, was very inexperienced. I'll never forget one of their first games. We played an inner-city Seattle team on their home court and we got absolutely crushed. I mean slammed. It was a painful experience. The boys and the coaches (Steve and Greg) took the defeat very hard, yet it forced them to step up their game and play smarter. Years later, in the ninth grade, the Magic won the AAU state championship and we went to Tennessee to play in the nationals. It was amazing. There was one game we needed to win to stay in the tournament. We were playing a team from the Texas coast. When we entered the gym, the parents from both teams were scattered on the same side of the court. Everyone was very respectful and kind to each other. While we each wanted our own team to win, I think most of us felt it was an honor just to be there. The game started. The other team didn't really take us seriously. They thought the game was over before it had even begun. One thing, among many great things, I can say about Steve Call as a coach, is that he teaches his boys to keep their heads in their own game. Forget about the other team, play your game. Don't let them get into your head. Well, by the end of the game, the Texas coach and two of his players had been thrown out of the gym and the parents had turned to us and said, "Now, where are you guys from?" It was a huge victory for the Magic. We still talk about that game. The team from Texas fell apart mentally. They tried desperately to get into the heads of the Magic players. It didn't work. That was one of the most important lessons Max has had in his basketball career. I don't know if he sees it, but I do. That game on one sunny day in Tennessee has prepared Max for this year. He's the point guard for the best basketball team Cedar Park has ever had and they have their eye on state. I feel it. They have the momentum. They have the team. They have a chance.

The day to leave for the tournament comes quickly. It's Wednesday, December 19th. The morning is a little crazy. Max and Greg are up before dawn getting ready to meet the team at the airport and fly to Los Angeles. Anna and I are up early as well because today Anna has a very important series of appointments at Children's Hospital. It's her six-hour follow up appointment with all of her therapists and doctors. They are testing to check her progress and evaluate her strengths and weaknesses. We will have her results today and both of us are confident about her improvements. She starts at 9:00 am with physical therapy, followed by 10:00 am occupational therapy, an 11:00 am nurse's appointment in rehab, 11:15 am Dr. Massagli, 1:00 pm speech therapy and at 2:30 pm her psychologist in rehab. It's going to be a busy day.

When we start Anna's appointments, I say a prayer for a safe flight for Greg, Max, and the team. The boys should be in mid-flight by now and I hope they are safe and enjoying themselves. I probably don't have to worry. But, it's part of what I do. No matter how often I give it to God, I keep taking it back. I also say a prayer for Anna and her progress. What I see as her mom, is not necessarily what some professional sees. I can't wait to hear how they think she's doing.

We arrive at Children's a little early. I just want to make sure we aren't late. We walk through the skybridge entrance and pass the cafeteria I had become so well acquainted with. Into the elevator and up we go, knowing exactly where we are and feeling very comfortable with our surroundings. We get off on Whale 6, stop at the security desk and continue on into the rehab wing. Anna walks straight up to the front desk and checks in. I detect she is a little anxious. We sit down in the waiting area and I tell her to have fun. She tilts her head, lifts her eyebrows, smiles and looks at me like I've completely lost my mind. "Fun?" she asks. I guess fun isn't the right word.

"Okay," I say, looking at her expression, "then work hard and do your best. I know you will be awesome." Fortunately, before the conversation can go any further, Anna's favorite physical therapist walks up to us and smiles. Thank goodness. They both laugh and say hi. Anna had a great time with her and it's obvious they are both happy to see one another. Off they go, just like before, leaving me waiting and praying.

While I wait, I reach into my bag of papers and magazines, pulling out the Cedar Park newsletter for December. I had forgotten I had it. It had come in November and I had set it aside to read later. I love that the front of it says "Merry Christmas…. 'but the angel said to them, 'Do not be afraid. I bring good news of great joy that will be for all the people. Today in the town of David a Savior has been born to you; he is Christ the Lord'" Luke 2:10-11. This is perfect timing. It reminds me to say a little prayer and hand today over to God. I continue reading and laugh at the recap of the last few months' activities. One of them was about Homecoming. That was the weekend before the accident. There's a picture of the Homecoming Court, the Royalty as they call it. Max had been nominated and had ridden around in a convertible at one of the football games, waving and laughing with his buddies. Of course, Brad had also been nominated and was riding in the car with Max, which makes for another memory those two will share. That was a fun weekend.

There are also sports scores, branch campus information, and articles about academic honors as well as a letter from the superintendent of the schools. The final article I settle on is one I had known was in the newsletter but hadn't read yet. Maybe I just wasn't ready. It's about Max and Anna. It's titled The Power of Prayer. I read on.

'On October 9, senior Max Brown and his sister, sophomore Anna Brown, were in a serious auto accident on their way to school. The accident sent their vehicle flying into a metal traffic light pole. Anna was airlifted to Harborview and Max was rushed to Harborview by ambulance. The police closed the road and began investigating the accident as a fatality, certain that at least one of them, if not both had died. As soon as the Brown family heard about the accident, Mrs. Brown contacted the school and asked for prayer. CPCS students were informed during their first period class. The shock and concern was overwhelming but immediately the staff and student body turned to the Lord in prayer. The entire secondary student body went to the sanctuary to be lead in prayer by Pastor Joe Fuiten. Pastor Fuiten reminded students of the power of prayer and encouraged them that we are all here to intercede when our brothers and sisters in Christ are in need. Within a few days both Max and Anna were recovering and doing well. Our prayer is now for a full recovery. Not only has this accident had an impact on two CPCS students, it has reminded all of us of the importance of our faith and the power of prayer. Our God is an awesome God! 'Be strong and take heart, all you who hope in the Lord.' Psalm 31:24.'

When I finish reading the article, I am reminded how far we have come in the last two months and ten days. What a miracle it is to have our family intact. Prayer works. The school was amazing. From top to bottom, they buoyed us through prayer. I don't know of many schools that would have taken the entire high school into the sanctuary, prayed and then allowed the students to spend the rest of the day in groups and with the staff praying and counseling each other. It just doesn't get any better than Cedar Park. Thank you.

As Anna comes and goes to her first two appointments, I am able to sit in peace. I don't try to take control. I leave the day with God. When it comes time for our appointment with Dr. Massagli, we're ready. I really like Dr. Massagli. She has been honest and kind-hearted from the first day she walked into Anna's room. We sit down at the conference table and Dr. Massagli hands me the communication sheet. There at the top of the page in bold letters is TBI, traumatic brain injury. I know this is her diagnosis and I know that they are evaluating her because of her brain injury, but those three little letters plunge a dagger of fear into my heart. The fear is almost more powerful now than it was in the beginning. I know too much. I begin to read the results. Her physical therapist reports she's doing great with excellent motor recovery and no significant balance or coordination deficits. Anna has worked hard for this. She pushes herself to regain the strength and balance she needs to play basketball again. The occupational therapist has absolutely no concerns. This is great news. It means Anna's safe in our home. I don't have to worry so much about when she takes a shower or walks up and down the stairs. Dr. Massagli continues on, and reiterates no contact sports for one year. She also recommends we have a follow-up psychological evaluation at the end of twelve months. That's it. One year. Good news.

"Oh," Anna asks as the doctor is leaving the room, "what can I do about the scar on my forehead?" Dr. Massagli recommends we see our dermatologist and use lots of sun block to avoid calling attention to the scar, which won't tan like the rest of her face.

"We can do that!" I blurt out. Funny. With all the things we had to talk about, it comes down to one little scar. Thank you.

Anna and I are excited. She's determined to come back to her normal and this morning has been a testament to her strength. Our meeting with Dr. Massagli is over. Anna's ready. On to speech therapy she goes.

The speech therapist says she's doing great, all areas are within normal limits, except word retrieval speed is slightly decreased. It's her memory again. This is going to be her biggest challenge and the area she has the least control over. I know Anna will do whatever she needs to do to improve her memory, but it's an intangible. Physical improvement she can see. Mental improvement is more difficult. We need prayer.

The psychologist reports Anna is doing great and agrees with Dr. Massagli that Anna should have a psychological reevaluation in one year. One year is sort of a marker. From what we've been told, and it varies in each case, one year is the time in which most of the healing is done. Knowing the strides Anna's made in a little over two months, her progress is remarkable. I like to think of it as a miracle. These are great results. Thank you.

We pack up the few things we brought with us and get ready to go home. Before we leave the hospital, I reach into my purse to check my phone, looking for a message from Greg telling me all is well in California. There it is. Greg had called during our last appointment to tell us everyone had arrived in Los Angeles safely and they are checked into their hotel. The boys had left to practice at a local gym and their first game was in the morning. They're tired but excited to be at the tournament.

Anna and I pour ourselves into the car and leave Children's knowing what she needs to do. Heal. She is exhausted. On the way home in the car, her eyes close as she leans her head on the passenger door and falls asleep. It' only 4:30 pm, but it's already been a long day.

By Friday afternoon, Anna is rested and ready to go out. Amie invited her to see the play "The Christmas Carol" in downtown Seattle and Anna is very excited to be part of one of Amie's family Christmas traditions. Our family hasn't seen this play and I whine to Anna, "I want to go."

She laughs and says, "Moomm, you can't go!" We both chuckle, knowing there's no way I'm going anyway.

Anna carefully picks out multiple outfits and rotates in and out of our bedroom to get a view of each ensemble in the full-length mirror. They all look beautiful, but I think her skirt outfit is too short and I carefully suggest she wear pants. "It's very cold outside and dress pants are completely acceptable," I say very casually. She looks in the mirror, turns slowly in a half circle and retreats to her room. Within minutes she's back with long black pants and a mid-thigh, belted sweater. Darling. Warm. Perfect. She looks in the mirror again, turning from side to side and announces this is the one. I remember being her age and continually choosing fashion over comfort and pain. Since I was in the fashion business, it took me years to fully realize my feet, my body, and my mind were much happier in comfortable, fun outfits. It's something every woman learns at some point in her life. If it hurts, itches or scratches, it's a no. I still wear heels every day, whether it be a shoe or a boot, but if they aren't comfortable the minute I try them on, I don't buy them. No wearing in for me! I measure a shoe's worth by asking myself, "Could I walk around Manhattan in these shoes all day and not have feet screaming in pain?" If the answer is no, back on the shelf they go. Anna hasn't quite figured this out yet. I have, on many occasions, suggested she make sure she's comfortable as she's walking around in shoes that could cripple a person. When she comes home holding her shoes and wearing her slippers, I know the time will come when she will no longer subject herself to this torture. But, for tonight she has made a great choice in her outfit and she looks fabulous. Now let's hope the shoes are a good choice, both for comfort and safety.

There's a knock on the door and Sammy goes nuts, barking and carrying on. I grab hold of his collar while both Anna and I are telling him, "It's okay Sammy, it's just Amie." Amie is laughing. Amie laughs all the time and that is one of many great things about her. Anna gives me a hug and slinks out the door, as Sammy is trying to make a run for it amidst coughing and barking. I yell, "love you!" to Anna, listen for her response and quickly close the door. Sammy sits quietly with his head slightly down. I stand there staring at him until he looks up. "What are you doing?" I ask him.

He just looks at me, once again, with that look asking, "WHAT?" Honestly.

Of course, while I am still staring Sammy down in disapproval, the phone rings. It's Greg. "The boys lost their game this afternoon," he says, "This has not been a good tournament for them from the win side of things, but they have played some great teams and that always improves their game. I know they're disappointed. But, losses show your weak spots. When they get back home and continue playing in our league, they have the advantage of having seen their weaknesses and can work on correcting them. It was a great decision to come to this tournament."

I know Max. He does not like to lose. But, this is a terrific way to improve your game overnight. It will be a bonus for the team during the rest of the season. I just hope when he gets home, he comes through the front door with a smile on his face!

On Sunday night, after Anna's theater outing, lots of sleep and the return of our boys, we have a big, delicious dinner with a dose of excitement. Tomorrow is Christmas Eve. Surprisingly, Anna has basketball practice from 9:00 am to 11:00 am and wants to go to encourage the girls while Max gets a break after the tournament. No practice. The team is exhausted. So, tomorrow I will take Anna to practice and then we will have our usual Christmas Eve day. Sleep. Relax. Church. We are looking forward to this.

"Just one present and I know which one it is. Let me find it," I tell the kids. It's one of our traditions. Every Christmas Eve the kids get to open one present when we get home from church. We usually go to the 7:00 pm service which is full of song and praise and we get home around 8:15 pm. Now that they're older, I drag it out a little bit. I get my tea, talk to the dog, turn on the tree lights, and take my time looking for the hidden Christmas Eve presents. Max and Anna aren't in a big hurry like they were when they were little, but they do love opening their gift. They also know it's going to be the traditional present of pajamas. Maybe I'll shock them some year and change that. No, they'd probably be disappointed. This year, though, the style of pajamas has changed. Anna made it very clear that if she got pajamas, she wanted men's flannel pants, large and baggy. Max made it clear that he doesn't want flannel pants again. They sure are getting picky. From my perspective, it's a gift. That means someone gives you something they chose specifically for you. Simply put, it's not their choice. However, I did listen to their wishes, as it's always nice if they wear the clothes I give them. And I say I because Greg is rarely a part of the shopping when it comes to these items. He's more of the big gift shopper and gets involved when we decide what the one big gift will be. He's very helpful here. It's his one contribution to the whole extravaganza. Well, except for the Christmas tree lights. He does those and the outside lights. He's not happy about it, but he does it. Husbands.

"Okay, are you ready?" I ask while handing them each a box wrapped in Christmas paper and tied with red curling ribbon. They hold their hands out. "One at a time," I blurt out, "Max why don't you go first?" Max pulls the ribbon off and tears through the paper. Inside he finds a pair of 'Max and the Grinch' boxers with a matching tee shirt. How could I resist? His name was on the shorts! He laughs. He likes them. This translates into, he will actually wear them. Good. Anna's next. She pulls the ribbon off and peels the Christmas paper back. She looks at me before going any further. I think she knows I am not buying her large men's pants. She opens the box, and much to her own surprise, she likes what I picked out. In the box lies a pair of large ladies' flannel pants and a strappy, stretch camisole to color coordinate. They both say thank you and I realize I have made it through another Christmas Eve with pajamas they'll wear. Wait until they have kids!

Greg and I don't open a gift. We already have ours. They are sitting right in front of us with their new pajamas. We are thankful. Thank you. "It's bedtime, I call out, "Don't forget Santa has to come."

They make fun of me and head upstairs to their bedrooms. "Okay Mom," which at this age is very similar to, "Yeah, sure Mom."

Traditionally on Christmas Eve, Greg or one of our very agreeable neighbors, ventures out to the side yard and hides outside the kids' bedroom windows, shaking the sleigh bells I have provided for them. We have been doing this for years. I then run into their rooms and ask them, "Did you hear that?" We go to their windows and I throw open the sash while we look out the window and up towards the sky. The bells are ringing feverishly. It's Santa, of course, flying over the house on his way to deliver presents. He will be back later for us, I tell them, after we're asleep.

One year when Anna was little, she asked, "Is that Mr. Riddell over there in the bushes?"

I did what any good parent should do; I denied her reality by asking her, "Why would Mr. Riddell be in the bushes?" Tonight, will be no different, just because it's fun. Greg puts his coat on, muffles the bells and walks out the front door. He's a great dad. I run excitedly into the kids' rooms.

Christmas morning Anna is up early and in our room by 7:00 am. It's funny that she still gets excited for our morning of fun, presents and a big breakfast. Greg and I slowly get up while Anna attempts to wake Max from his deep sleep. He doesn't have the same enthusiasm she does until he is fully awake and both of them are snuggled down under our bed covers watching TV. This is another tradition. They wait while Greg and I go see if Santa came. I make coffee and Greg starts a fire in the toy room fireplace. We feed Sammy, let Jazz in and turn on Christmas music. We're set. Greg goes to get the kids while Sammy, Jazz, and I wait by the fire. Here they come, I can hear them.

This year, for our family gift, Greg and I got tickets for the four of us to go see "Jersey Boys" tomorrow night. Greg and I have seen it and loved the play. The kids will love the music, even though the language in the play is pretty bad. They know the songs because we have heard them numerous times together. Anna has called me into her room when she hears them on a radio station. We love Frankie Valli and the Four Seasons and their songs are perfect for us to sing along. The kids love this gift.

The present opening continues. I love having a bunch of boxes under the tree even if they are simply a pair of socks, underwear, a book or another tradition, their special ornament. We open presents one at a time. It takes longer. It's more fun. We play with our presents as we go along. Eventually we are done. We've had our coffee and I have talked to both of my sisters, my dad, and Greg's family. We are ready to eat. Greg pulls out the frying pans and I get the eggs, bacon, and cinnamon rolls. Yum. Everyone is starving. He cooks, I clean. A little role reversal for Christmas morning. Yes.

Today we get to hang out, watch movies and nap. Normally we host Christmas dinner at our house. This year, Greg's parents are doing the honors. Max is thrilled because he is our resident potato peeler and he is temporarily out of a job. I'm thrilled because, even though I love having Christmas dinner at our house, we have had a very exhausting few months and it is nice to have the day off to just be with our kids and not in the kitchen. Greg, also thrilled, is very happy not to have to clean up this messy meal. And then there's Anna, who doesn't mind one way or the other. Everyone's happy. This is a great way to spend Christmas day. Thank you and happy birthday.

Chapter Twenty-Four

"He showed Himself to be so powerful"
— Cheri Filion

We sprint into January at a dead run. I'm back teaching preschool on Tuesdays and Thursdays. It's so wonderful to be greeted by these sweet little faces. I love it! The preschool parents have been incredible to our family and to have the privilege of teaching their loved ones is a special gift. To watch three year olds in their first year of school is often hilarious. They provide a kindness and humor only a small child can offer. It's so much fun. Who knew after two fulfilling careers as a buyer and then a sales rep, that teaching preschoolers would be part of my life? It's a journey and I thank God for every, okay, almost every day of it.

Basketball season has taken over our entire family. The kids' hours are filled with practices and games, Greg films every one of Max's games for the coaches, and I'm the team mom on both teams. We are all running in different directions and ending up at the same place. Basketball games! It's exciting. Sammy isn't particularly thrilled spending hours in the car while we cheer each team on, but at least he's with us and that is very important to him. He'd rather be waiting in the car than sitting at home wondering where we are and when we are going to be back. I know this because I speak dog. Doesn't every Mom?

In one blink of the eye, it's midseason. The girls' team is struggling. The boys' team is holding their own.

On a Friday night at the end of January, our pivotal game arrives. The boys' varsity basketball team is playing their biggest rival. This will be the turning point. Every year this team has beat us. Every year they go to state and either win or place. Every year it's a mental challenge for our boys to play them. Every year I dread this game. Their coach is a good guy. Their players are good guys. They are also a Christian School. There are no bad feelings about this team, but we desperately want and need to beat them.

We are on our own turf. We're ahead, they're ahead. Cedar Park has never had a team as talented as this. I am fairly certain that I am going to lose my mind. Greg is filming. Anna is cheering on the girls' team. I say a little prayer and ask myself if that's fair. Oh, for crying out loud, this is so stressful. We're in the fourth quarter. We're down to the last minute. The fouls are flying. The score is shifting back and forth. We're down to seconds. The score is even. We have the ball. We score two points. Oh, wait a minute! They fouled us. I am going to scream from the tension. The gym is dead silent as our fouled player stands at the free-throw line. This shot is huge. He bounces the ball. He positions himself. He leans over and bounces the ball once more then pulls himself up with grace and ease as his arms lift the ball over his head and into a slow arc as he releases the ball into the air. The ball seems to float through the air and enter the basket in slow motion. Swoosh. It's good. The crowd goes crazy. The screaming is deafening. Our boys are slapping hands. Back to the free-throw line. The pressure is unbelievable. Silence fills the gym. First bounce. Second bounce. His arms are up. The ball is in the air. It's coming down. It's going to…swoosh! It's good. We're up by four. The crowd is in a frenzy. "Please, just hold 'em," I whisper into my cupped hands, "Come on boys." Our opponent will get possession of the ball. There are eight seconds left. Enough time to change the outcome of this game. Different scenarios run through my mind. I've seen it happen before. My cupped hands are still over my mouth. I whisper again, "Just don't foul them. They're going to be aggressive. They're going to try to get fouled while they go for the basket. They want to go into overtime. They want to win." The referee hands the ball to their player outside the court's boundary line. He looks frantically for an open teammate, wanting to throw the ball in before his time is up. He finds an opening. The ball is in. The clock begins to tick. We guard. We guard smart. They're running out of time. They need to put the ball in the air. They scramble for position. Up it goes. No good. No foul. The buzzer sounds. WE WIN! The floor is immediately covered with Cedar Park fans. I remain standing in the bleachers with my hands flattened over my mouth. I am exhausted. I can't wait to see Max.

The school lives on this victory for weeks. The boys are inching their way to the state playoffs one game at a time. Max is having a blast. This is a great way to wind up your high school basketball career. When Senior Game Night rolls around, it brings tears to my eyes. He's so grown up. I am very proud of him. Just before the game starts, a tunnel is formed on the court by the underclassmen on the team. The seniors sit on the bench waiting, as one by one, their name is announced to the fans. They spring into life and run through the tunnel, slapping hands with their team-mates and bumping chests at the end of the line. Max's name is called. There he is. Jersey number #33, my first baby. And there they are, the eight graduating seniors. They're all wonderful kids. The entire starting line-up and half of the back-up team are graduating. We win the game.

The next day there's a terrific article about the team in the sports section of the Bothell /Kenmore Reporter. It's titled Cedar Park Christian Boys Hoop It Up. The article refers to Cedar Park as being 'led by a trio of three-year starting seniors.' Each of the three get a little press time about their accomplishments. As for Max, they write 'and third, three-year starter Max Brown is the team's starting point guard, leading the team in assists with 7.5 per game and is the player Coach Lamont Franklin calls the 'heartbeat of the team.'' When I read heartbeat of the team, it warms my own heart. Max is a quiet guy and a rule follower. He may not always agree, but he listens to, and does what the coach wants him to do. He's a humble guy and a team player. His friends and their parents tell us he's hilarious. We see glimpses of his humor, but he's mostly quiet at home. He's a good kid. I just love that boy.

Max's good friend and teammate, Riley Bettinger summed it all up in the article, by saying, 'We only have four, five weeks left, and most of us probably won't play on another organized basketball team, yet alone high school. It really doesn't get much better than this.' I think to myself, Max is so blessed to have this experience for his senior year. I can only pray that Anna receives a similar blessing when she reaches her senior year. It's a wonderful way to transition into college, leaving behind good memories of high school.

We roll along with more games, more practices, constant activity, and finally, the end of regulation basketball season. Anna is doing well and continues to heal both her brain and her body. Even though she is back to a regular class schedule, we are very cautious with her physical activities and insist she get lots of rest. She is still not back to her normal self. Anna has been invited to go to Mexico for mid-winter break with a family from Cedar Park that is fully aware of her physical limitations for the next twelve months. When Anna mentions parasailing, I look over and scream "NO!" while simultaneously, picking up the phone and calling the mom she will be travelling with just to check in and make sure we are on the same page. She laughs out loud when I tell her what Anna said and assures me that Anna's most strenuous activity will be raising her arm to put sun tan lotion on. That girl will be the death of me.

This year the varsity girls' team did not fare well and their season ends with no hope of making it to state. Anna had a great time managing the team this year, but is very excited to lace up her basketball shoes and get back on the court. She has chosen to follow in the footsteps of her older brother, and make basketball her life. That terrifies me. I force myself to put that thought on the back burner and deal with it when that time comes. There are so many exciting things happening right now, it's easy for me to quickly dismiss my worries. Boys' basketball and graduation are on the horizon.

The varsity boys successfully played their way through our regular season and the Tri State playoffs. We land a seed for the state tournament in Yakima. It's simply thrilling. The student body and the school are thoroughly enjoying this success. The only fly in the ointment is that the state tournament is at the end of next week, the week of mid-winter break. Anna will be in Mexico and will miss watching Max play at state. Many of the students will be on vacation with their families, and most likely not in Yakima. However, there are a few families that have changed their plans so their kids can follow the team to the tournament. Now, that is dedication.

It's the fourth Saturday in February and the first weekend of winter break. Anna is on her way to Mexico and we are making last minute preparations to leave on Wednesday for the state tournament. Max goes with Greg to watch and film a competitor's game for coach, so Sammy and I are on our own. Mid-afternoon I give my baby girl a call to make sure she arrived safely in Mexico. A quick call, only to find out she's already sitting by the pool slathered in suntan lotion. Good. I can relax, she's safe. I sit down to read. Tuesday night is book club and I'm not quite done with our book. Besides, it's nice to relax in a quiet house. Sammy and I are content. Within a few pages, Sammy is snoring and I can barely keep my eyes open. Jazz jumps up on the love seat and drapes himself across my body. Everybody naps. This is great.

Fortunately, I finish my book just in time for book club. We do have fun at our meetings. There's always too much good food, too many fabulous desserts, a little bit of wine, and lots of chatter. Our conversation is all over the board, yet we manage to sneak in a few minutes of discussion about the book and hear from our next hostess what the title of our new read will be. By the end of the evening we are talked out, but caught up on everyone's lives and families.

Greg and I wake up Wednesday morning ready to go. We throw our luggage in the car, stop by Starbucks for soy lattes and cruise across Interstate 90, bound for Yakima. Oh, and we have an extra passenger. Sampson. Yes, Greg insisted he come with us. I was against it and thought he should stay with his nanny for a few days, but that argument fell on deaf ears. Greg called the hotel and yes, Sammy is more than welcome to join us. Perfect. Pam has agreed to feed, water, and watch the kitties until we get home, so we don't have to worry about them. Thank goodness for Pam.

It doesn't take but a few hours to get there and when we do, the hotel is packed with parents, siblings, players, large duffel bags, and Sampson. Greg registers us and we unload the contents of the car into our room, including cases of water and sports drinks for the boys. We are one floor away from the boys and coaches. Greg picks up the house phone and calls Max, "Hey, Mom and I are here. We want to come see your room." That's code for what Greg really wants, which is to be in the middle of all the excitement. I don't fault him for that. He is sharing the final remnants of high school basketball with his son. Perhaps this next year will be harder on Greg than it is on Max. Fortunately, Greg is very involved with Anna's team and will most likely immerse himself in their filming and the many other needs of the girls' team. That's good.

Max says, "Yeah, come on down." I know these boys well. I can't wait to see the inside of this room. They've only been here for a few hours, but that is plenty of time for four eighteen-year-old boys to cover the floor with clothes, food, and debris. If their uniforms are clean, I'm good. My work is done. The players' rooms dot the hallway. I can see the cheerleaders have been here. They have decorated every one of the Cedar Park players' room doors with bright, round, orange basketballs made from craft paper. Each basketball has one individual player's name written on it. Aside from four of these basketball name plates, they have also decorated the doors with fun party stuff and have created a festive atmosphere in an otherwise bland hallway. It looks great!

Surprise! The room isn't too trashed. Not bad. It's full of testosterone, but not bad. Sammy is in dog heaven with the smells, the boys, and all the activity. Greg keeps him on the leash to contain him. This is nuts. The boys seem to appreciate him, though. Maybe he calms their nerves. Not mine, however.

Tonight's their first game and they're leaving shortly to watch other teams play and get themselves physically and mentally prepared for their own game. It's in a few hours and it's going to be tough. We wish them well with hugs of good luck and say that we will see them after the game. As we close their room door we say to each other, "This is it, after Saturday, it's over."

Wednesday night. We lose by 3.

Thursday. We win by 2.

Friday. We win by 8.

Saturday. We are playing for either 5th or 8th place. We won't be Number 1, but we are further along than any other team in Cedar Park history. The game starts. I can already tell it's going to be an intense game. The best player on the opposing team is a friend of Max's. He played on the Magic with Max for years. At one point, Max is guarding his ex-teammate. Greg and I are watching them and laughing. They must be laughing too. They're tough on each other, but I do see a smile at the end of the series. Funny. Memorable. It's one of those games. Back and forth with the score until we go into overtime. Both teams have had a chance to win this game, yet here we are in overtime. My voice is gone. As the clock ticks down, we are point for point even. When the clock finally runs out, the score is 50-48. We lose. We are 8th in the state and I am proud of the boys. They just made history for Cedar Park.

We greet the boys with cheers and congratulations after the game. They are sullen. But, after a few minutes of hugs and kisses, their mood begins to lighten and smiles begin to emerge. It's not the time to explain to them that it was just a game. Just a part of their young life and that there are plenty more ups and downs to come. It's just a beginning and it's not the most important thing that's ever going to happen to them. We are proud of the team and their accomplishment. What they experienced is a special moment that they will remember for the rest of their lives. Now that's a blessing. Thank you.

The drive back is very relaxing. Sammy is exhausted. I don't think he's ever licked so many people in his life. This is one happy dog. The boys are on the team bus and we pass them waving. It looks like they're having fun. Interstate 90 between Yakima and Seattle is a beautiful drive. With my voice gone, I just peer out the window and stare at the gorgeous towering trees with their snow-capped mountains. Thinking. Tonight, my babies will be back under one roof. Anna's plane comes in around 8:00 pm and I'm sure she'll be very tired. Max will probably go out with his buddies but come home to sleep. He loves his home. He's always in by midnight. We will wake up tomorrow to a full house. Good.

The weeks ahead allow us to get back to a slightly slower pace. Anna has decided to try out for golf, the only non-contact sport she can think of that may be fun. Greg's ecstatic. Golfing is in his blood. He will golf anywhere, any time, and with anyone. Before she can change her mind, Greg takes her out to buy shoes and golfing attire. I'm not sure who's more excited about this new interest, Greg or Anna. She's going to use my mom's old clubs, so Greg cleans them up for her, taking hours to make them shiny and perfect. It's hilarious.

Max has only a few months of high school left. I can't believe it. He's excited. He's ready to go. Our whole family is looking forward to the remaining festivities planned for the senior class. Cedar Park is buzzing with preparations for graduation. They acknowledge their senior students from the beginning of the first month of their senior year in high school and ending on graduation day. It's amazing.

We started with the blessings sign-up. Parents could sign up for any month out of the school year to be on a blessings committee. Each month, the entire senior class is treated to one special blessing from the parent committee. It can be anything from a tasty beverage awaiting them first thing in the morning to a full-blown activity during lunch. Individual committees create their own special blessing, seek approval from the administration and plan their surprise. It's a great idea. I signed up for April with a group of women I've known for years. We don't know what we're doing yet, but we will meet in a few weeks.

All of this is followed by the Senior Tea, the Senior Sneak, the Senior Dinner, graduation rehearsals, and a Senior Lunch. There's so much activity and planning. Naturally, I signed up for everything, wanting to be a part of Max's last year. I look at my calendar realizing I have lots of meetings coming up. Life is getting back to normal and we've been so busy, I didn't even realize it. Thank you.

It's Tuesday March 11th. Tonight, we have the cheer and basketball awards night at school. After the initial prayer and opening speeches, the coaches announce the league awards. Two of Max's teammates made 1st team all-league honors, while Max made 2nd team all-league honors. Riley Bettinger also made all state 2nd team and has been selected to participate in the all-star game this weekend. Good for the boys. The awards ceremony continues, covering outstanding parent volunteers and team grade point averages, informing us that 80% of the student athletes have a 3.0 Grade Point Average or better. That's amazing. Then we have presentations by the individual coaches. From C team boys through varsity girls, we listen to the terrific accomplishments of these award winners and share in the excitement of their parents. When it's time for varsity boys' basketball awards, Coach Franklin steps up to the microphone. He calls his awarded players one by one, making sure to explain how each player contributed to the betterment of the team. The wonderful comments he makes about each of the boys bring tears to my eyes. The final award from the coach is the Coach's Award. This award is not based on points or statistics. It's the award given by the coach to the player he feels contributed the most to the overall success of the team. The gym is quiet. Coach Franklin explains the award and how he chooses its recipient as he looks at his team sitting together on the bleachers.

Coach smiles and says, "This year's recipient is Max Brown!" I cry. Max stands and walks towards his coach smiling. Coach Franklin puts his arm around Max and laughs. He gives Max the award and holds Max to keep him from escaping back to the bleachers. "Let me tell you a story about Max," he says, "At the beginning of the year, Max was involved in the car accident and initially, we didn't know if he would be able to play for us this season. He was to be our starting point guard. Fortunately, he recovered from his injuries and we all know, continued to play as our starting point guard all the way through the state tournament. When we were at the tournament and playing our final game, I was coaching Max from the bench and he wouldn't do everything I was telling him to do. Finally, I called him over and he said 'Coach, just let me play my game.'" Then Coach Franklin said, "At that moment, I made a decision to let Max go and I didn't coach him for the rest of the game." Everyone laughs. I cry.

I haven't cried much about the car accident because God gave me such a sense of peace and much needed strength. But this very moment allows the tears to flow freely. We were given another chance as a family and God has healed Max through Anna's recovery and his success on this team. What a gift. Thank you.

While I'm busy wiping tears from my eyes, the coaches call all the seniors and their parents to come forward for a prayer and final goodbye. There will be pictures. I hope my mascara isn't running down my face. Oh, for Heaven's sake, what timing. Raccoon eyes. Max can't figure out why I'm crying, and Anna thinks I'm crazy. Why is it the dads always smile and look so proud while the moms are teary eyed, red faced, and trying to open our wet eyes and smile? It's not fair.

I get back into the team mom role the following morning, and complete the final details of this coming Saturday's team party for the boys. It's a potluck party at our house. A classmate of Max's is secretly putting together a DVD of pictures and music that will highlight each player and the team's exciting season. This is a special memento for each player and their coaches. Once that is done and gift cards for the coaches are purchased, it will be smooth sailing. However, on Wednesday afternoon we receive some sad, yet not surprising news. Coach Franklin has sent a letter to all of us informing us he is returning to the East Coast. He is leaving at the end of March. His wife is pregnant and had already left to be with her family for the remainder of her pregnancy, so we figured something was going on. He has been good for this team. He came with college experience and pushed them in ways they didn't know they could be pushed. He has coached Cedar Park for three years and the timing was perfect for the school and for the players. He will be missed.

The party is a huge success and both the boys and coaches are surprised by the DVD. It's the perfect gift for everyone. The food is delicious and all of us are enjoying spending time with the boys and their coaches. The party is over in a flash, much like the last eighteen years of these kids' lives. They will go in different directions next year and, most likely, only a few will remain in contact with each other. When we say our last goodbye, lock the front door, turn off the lights and go to bed, we realize it's over. Done. Max is leaving us.

Chapter Twenty-Five

"Hug your kids everyday"
— Jayne Vitulli

Anna continues to heal. Her memory is getting better. She still has a hard time with some things, but school isn't one of them. Candice says Anna can't remember what happens in movies they've watched a dozen times. It's always a new movie to Anna. That worries me, but we have time on our side and months of rest and healing to go. I have noticed Anna is starting to get very lippy. Her attitude is disrespectful. We have always told the kids they can disagree with us, but they cannot be disrespectful. Anna has, apparently, either forgotten this, or is choosing to push the envelope. My vote goes to pushing the envelope. It's time to consult an expert. I call my sister Ann. Her daughter Jordyn is four years older than Anna and they have already been through high school with a daughter playing basketball. Ann basically says, "It gets worse. This is just the beginning." Great. That's not what I want to hear.

For Easter break and for Max's graduation gift, we take Max, two friends, Anna and a friend of hers to Hawaii. We spend one week in the sun with a bunch of good, well mostly, good kids. Let's face it, they are teenagers! Our only scare is when Anna takes on a large wave while body surfing and her head hits the ocean floor. Hard. I freak out. The hit scares her enough to be done for the day and for the trip. No more. I know I'm overprotective, but no more. I need to heal too. One head injury in a lifetime is more than enough.

When we get back home, I keep a special watch on Anna. She's still lippy and I am trying to figure out if this is part of her brain injury and being disinhibited or if it's a teenage girl thing. I don't like it either way. She also wants to get her driver's license. The state won't give it to her without a certificate for driver training. Since she didn't finish the class in the required amount of time, she has to take driver education over again. She's mad about it. I'm glad. I am simply not comfortable with the combination of her driving a car, having an attitude and her loss of memory. Fortunately, she can't start her training classes until the end of June. This is more due to her schedule that the driving school's schedule. Anna is currently playing on the golf team which takes up her afternoons. Plus, starting in May, we have found a wonderful trainer to help her with her basketball skills and her balance. She wants to overcome her dizziness and remaining balance problems so she can be ready for next season. Then in the middle of June we are going to Mexico on a mission trip with our church for nine days. With this schedule, she'd miss way too many driving classes. We have to wait until July. Healing time. Thank you.

We jump into April with unforgettable memories of the past few months. Looking forward to the next eight weeks, we are loaded with activities for the seniors and for special gatherings with the seniors and their parents. Our first event is the Senior Tea. For one special afternoon, it's just Max and me. The Senior Tea is for moms and their graduating babies. Each year, this elegant luncheon is sponsored by the parents of the junior class as a blessing to their upper classmen. Last year, as the mom of a junior, I had the privilege to help with the Senior Tea. It was a wonderful experience. I can only imagine what it will be like this year, as a guest, and attending with Max.

When the day of the Tea arrives, I am greeted in the hallway of the high school by Max. He escorts me to the smaller gym which has been redecorated with white canvas walls, tall greens in elegant urns, beautifully landscaped tabletops, and sparkling lights. Each table is individually decorated with special china and crystal circling a delicious assortment of sandwiches, desserts, and tea hovering around lovely centerpieces. It's just gorgeous and feels very intimate. We sit down at our table with Max's friends and their moms for a beautiful luncheon. Pam and Brad are right next to us, as it should be, the two best buddies enjoying their last few months of high school together. The Tea opens with a prayer. I am starving and I'm sure Max is too. As soon as the prayer is finished, the boys' hands fly towards the sandwiches and I think, "Please leave some for us hungry moms." Of course they do, and we pass the trays of goodies around making sure to try everything. When everyone has their plates full, the program continues with a video production laced with music, featuring pictures of each senior from birth through high school. It's great to see pictures of Max's friends as babies, as well as pictures of the moms from the 1990s. There are a lot of hair comments. Everyone is laughing. Some are crying. There are so many memories for all of us.

When the video is finished and most everything has been eaten, it is time for each senior to stand up and read a personal message to their mom. They have prepared these messages ahead of time and the school has made copies for us to take home. Moms love this and I know I will cherish this message forever. Of course, you never know what your child will say to you, so we sit patiently waiting to see if we want to cry, laugh, or scream when our turn comes.

Max is handed the microphone as he stands up and turns to face me. I look at him curiously. He begins reading his message.

"Dear Mom, first off, I just want to thank you for always being there for me. Whether I need someone to talk to, or I'm hungry for some dinner, I know you'll be able to help me out. I also want to thank you for being so selfless. You have always put the well-being of our family ahead of your own, and you do so much for all of us. I realized exactly how much Anna and I meant to you after the accident. You were with Anna almost every single night throughout her stay in the hospital and therapy and I'm so glad to have a mom who would do that. I am so thankful to have you as my mom and I know it's going to be really hard to head off to college next year, without you cleaning up after me. I know that I don't necessarily show it all the time, but I love you so much and you really do mean a lot to me. Love, Max."

I stand up and hug him. "Thank you," I whisper. I don't think he realizes how much he said to me. The part about not necessarily showing me how much he loves me and that I really do mean a lot to him, is huge to me. He doesn't show it and it's hard to know what someone feels when they don't communicate. As the microphone is passed to the next student, I am still absorbing Max's words. Thank you, Maxie I repeat to myself. Thank You, God.

Two days later it's Senior Sneak Day. In keeping with tradition, the senior class will be pirated off for a day full of surprises, with the destinations only known by the Senior Sneak committee. Yes, I signed up for that committee too. This class is known for their love of Mexican food, coffee with flavored creamer, and bowling. So, the first thing they get is coffee with flavored creamer, bagels with cream cheese, a wide assortment of fruit, various other high carb foods and sparkling cider to get their day started. With plates in hand, they sit on the floor of the auxiliary gym in large groups gobbling down their breakfast treats. When it looks like they are finished eating, we announce it's time to load up, and begin herding them out to the front of the school where buses are waiting to transport them to their next destination. They're so funny. "Where are we going? What are we doing?" is repeated throughout the walk to the buses. I had asked Max if he minded if I helped chaperone the Senior Sneak. He did. Dang. I can't go with them. So, I watch them load up for their secret day of bowling, lunch, and craziness before I have the privilege of returning to the gym to help in the cleanup of their breakfast mess. It's okay. At 10:00 this morning I have to meet a blessings committee mom at Costco and buy food for the April blessing next Monday. Our committee decided to have a Mexican fiesta lunch, including a build your own taco and salad bar. Perfect.

And the party continues. I wish I was a senior at Cedar Park. Of course, being on all these committees has allowed me to include myself in Max's life from a distance. It's working out well and I think he likes seeing me around. He may never admit that, but I'm going to hold onto that thought and keep it close to my heart. Max did tell me the Senior Sneak was lots of fun and his class is certainly livin' the good life.

This morning our blessings committee is at school by 9:00 am to set up for our Mexican fiesta lunch. One mom had prepared her special meat sauce and brought it, marinating, in crock pots. A few other moms had spent their weekend making boxes full of decorations to liven up the student tables and transform the lunch area into a Mexican restaurant. Today everyone has a job. We have been given permission to use the kitchen, so we pull out pots, pans, serving trays, and utensils to prepare our buffet. We load up the serving tables with plates, napkins, forks, knives, and tons of food just before lunch time. We look around at our creation. It looks fabulous. The kids are going to love this.

Within moments after the lunch bell rings, the hall is filled with high school students. The smell of spices, beans, meats, cheese, and chips wafts throughout the building. Passing kids stop to look and want to know who the food is for. "Sorry, it's for the Senior Class Blessing," we repeat to disappointed faces. The seniors line up.

"Wow, this is great."

"Thank you."

"I love Mexican food."

"This is the best blessing ever."

The comments keep coming as they fill and refill their plates with food. Their smiles and words of appreciation are heartwarming. Success. Thank you.

Another week passes. Aside from the fun Max is having, the rest of us continue to be very busy. Anna and I are planning our Mexico mission trip, Greg is traveling on and off for work, preschool is coming to a close for the year and life is moving forward.

Anna has decided she is not in love with golf. She is a fair weather girl, a sit by the fireplace and watch a movie, girl. This whole business of golfing in the rain is not working for her. Greg thinks it's funny, even though I do know he was hoping she would fully embrace the game. She continues to improve both physically and mentally. No setbacks, just forward progress. Thank you.

Max is a lucky boy. Tonight, Greg and I have our final senior celebration with Max. This special event is the Senior Dinner, a semi-formal occasion designed to honor and encourage our children as they prepare for graduation and their future. We arrive with the Allens and manage to locate a table that will seat all six of us. The setting is beautiful. Numerous large round tables are covered in white linen tablecloths with white dinnerware and beautiful floral centerpieces. Tonight, we, as parents of seniors, are given a moment to publicly say a few words about our child. This may be a bit of a long evening, but definitely a memorable one.

As our evening begins with prayer, I remind myself how lucky Greg and I are to spend this evening with Max, and how lucky he is to be here with his friends and people who love him. Cedar Park was an excellent choice for him. He thrived. I'm sure there are numerous things he participated in that I may never know about, but this school has offered him years of positive choices and surrounded him with kids receiving the same offer. That helps.

The food arrives hot and tasty. The room is settling into a comfortable silence while we begin to eat. The low volume of conversation rumbles around until we hear the click and screech of a microphone being turned on. It's time to begin the program. This will not be easy for every parent here tonight. This class has seen its share of sadness and tragedy. It began with our car accident and ended with the deaths of two parents from different families. From what we understand, every senior is here. A parent from every family will speak to their child. As the microphone makes its way around the room, it's fascinating to hear what each parent says to their senior. Some are funny, some are forced, some are serious, some are happy, and some are sad. Yet, all are heartfelt and everyone is proud of their child and excited for the future in front of these soon-to-be graduates. Proud of you is a phrase that is repeated throughout the evening.

There are laughs at hilarious situations parents describe concerning their child, and there are tears as we watch struggling families cope with grief and loss. In the end, there is clapping for all. These kids are graduating from high school and most of them are going on to college. Now that's an accomplishment.

We gather our things, hug other parents and maneuver our way out of the building. Max and Brad walk ahead of us toward the car. Two buddies. Two dressed up buddies. Two loosened ties. Two lives. Two different college choices. One friendship. They're lucky boys.

As soon as we get home, there is a message from my sister Ann. Call me. I pick up the phone immediately. "I need help with Dad," she says, "We had a horrible experience with his doctor's office today. I want you to fly down and help with his rescheduled appointment." Ann has shouldered the responsibility for Dad the last few years and certainly deserves some help. She has also called Teensie to fly in and help. Both Teensie and Ann are much nicer than I am. While I truly love people, and find all of our differences fascinating, I cannot tolerate rude behavior, particularly if that behavior involves my family. If the doctor's office is giving Ann a hard time and Ann needs a backup, I can certainly fly down to Las Vegas and help. Greg makes my airplane reservation.

Before I leave town, there are a number of loose ends to tie up. First, I call my friend Jayne Vitulli to schedule Max's final senior pictures to be taken in our yard. Jayne is our photographer and has been waiting patiently for months for good weather and lighting outside. We were in the process of scheduling the shoot when the kids got in the car accident. Jayne has even offered to take a few shots of Max with our family and our animals. On Sunday afternoon, she will finish the shoot and we will finally be done. I can't wait to see them. Secondly, Anna and I have to start our series of shots and malaria pills for our Mexico mission trip. I am going to see my doctor before I leave town and Anna will see her doctor the week I get back. Perfect. Thirdly, this week Anna starts her personal training sessions to improve her flexibility, dizziness, and motion. Her trainer is a varsity girls' basketball coach from a Seattle team. Greg knows and respects him. Greg spoke with him about Anna's challenges and he has been wonderful enough to open up his schedule for her and has carefully put together a program tailored to her needs and ability. The goal is to strengthen her body and help her regain her balance. People are so good. And lastly, my hair color. I will not be going to Las Vegas with a gray stripe hovering over each side of my part. That's not happening. Such vanity.

By the end of the week everything is taken care of or scheduled. I am comfortable leaving for a few days. Early Friday morning and I mean early, Greg takes me to the airport. He is such a nice man. Thank you.

Dad, Ann, Teensie, and I are ten minutes early for Dad's rescheduled appointment. It might be unnecessary, but I do tell the front desk, "We will not be leaving until we see the doctor this time. Note our arrival time and appointment time." When they finally call us to go to the examination room it is thirty minutes later. On our way to the room, I pause at the front desk to add, "And you do realize we've been waiting thirty minutes for you?" Sometimes my bluntness makes Ann uncomfortable, but she is fine with it today. Teensie and I are reinforcements.

At Dad's last scheduled appointment, Ann and Dad waited so long in the waiting room, the girls at the front desk told her, as they were packing up to go home, "The doctor can't see your dad today." Needless to say, that day was rough on both Dad and Ann. They're lucky my broom and I weren't at that last appointment. Really.

The doctor comes in and he's great with Dad and with us. He's very helpful. He has actually read all of Dad's history and has some wonderful suggestions. He checks Dad out thoroughly. Dad really likes him. I really like my Dad. Here he sits with his three daughters and a doctor discussing his Alzheimer's and the state of his health, and he's laughing and joking. May we all be able to keep our sense of humor as we move into our 80s! By the time we leave, the front desk is closed, lights are off and everyone is gone.

Our dinner reservation isn't until 6 pm so we decide to drive back to Ann's house to relax and visit for a little while before we leave for dinner. Ann makes a quick stop at Starbucks. She and Teensie are addicted. If I drank real coffee this late in the day, I'd still be talking to you at three in the morning. They get their drinks and we're back on the road to Ann's house. Dad is thrilled to have his girls with him. He's a great story teller. And, he's very funny. His Alzheimer's isn't good, but he knows us and is able to live in the moment. He repeats himself every minute or so, but he's happy and he's fun to be with.

The minute we get to Ann's, Dad wants his usual vodka on the rocks. This is our biggest problem with Dad. He can't have alcohol in his assisted living apartment, so when he comes over to Ann's he wants to have a few cocktails. It is hard. One drink would be fine, even two, but he gets cranky if we don't give him more. And tonight, since we're going out for Italian food, we will probably order a little wine with dinner. Dad will want to order more vodka at the restaurant. If we let him drink too much, he will get quite tipsy and can become very testy. Ann has taken to watering down his drinks when she has him over. Tonight, we tell him, "Dad, you can have one at five o'clock, your cocktail hour, because we will be leaving for the restaurant after that. You can have another drink when we get to the restaurant." He can't remember any of this, so the conversation is continually swirling around Dad demanding a drink. This is a problem Ann has been graciously dealing with for a long time. It's frustrating for her. Teensie and I can only imagine.

At 6:00 pm we meet Dad's friend Dotty at the restaurant. We are able to hold him off with one vodka and a glass of iced tea. Whew. Dotty is terrific and very happy. She laughs all the time and, like Dad, has a fabulous sense of humor. They are a pair. Dad orders a vodka on the rocks and the rest of us order a glass of wine. Ann quietly asks the waiter to water the vodka down. He nods his head. Good. Dad is full of stories while we laugh our way through dinner. I am happy to be with my family. Living in three different states and two different time zones is a challenge. I have great sisters. We have wonderful husbands, good kids, and a great dad. Lucky. Thank you.

We load Dad into the car and take him to his home. He's a little tipsy, but happy. Putting Dad in this assisted living facility has been great for him. The place is absolutely beautiful. He was furious at first, even though Ann had brought him here for a few visits. Oh, my gosh, the day we moved him was brutal. But, we explained to him that Dotty couldn't take care of him by herself anymore and he couldn't be on his own because of the Alzheimer's. It took a better part of the day, but eventually he got it. He didn't like it, but he understood it. We moved him into an open concept apartment and within a few days he had new friends. He also found numerous old friends that he had lost track of. It really is a great place. Of course, he keeps telling us, "I haven't lived in an apartment like this since I was in college." That must have been some nice apartment.

Saying goodbye to Dad was sad. Not that I am worried I won't see him on earth again, but as his child, I just remember him before the Alzheimer's. Ann is doing a great job with Dad. It's hard.

Early Monday morning I fly home. The sadness is overwhelming for me. I'm not sure where to turn. All afternoon I try to figure out how to handle this. Then, I remember a phone number I had run across a while back, for families of Alzheimer's patients. I find this little card and I dial the number. The man who answers the phone is so kind. He says

"I started this organization after my dad died from complications due to Alzheimer's. I live in Oregon and devote my time to helping people like you." The moment I start talking about my dad, I begin crying. I am so sad to lose Dad to Alzheimer's. After fifteen minutes of crying and talking, this wonderful man helps me through my grief, making me feel better and stronger. I don't know how Ann does it every day. She needs to talk to this man. But, knowing Ann, she won't.

As soon as I dry my eyes and pull myself together, Anna and I have to leave for her doctor's appointment so Anna can get her typhoid shot and malaria medication. Our mission trip to Mexico is right around the corner. This will be a first for us. I've wanted to take the kids on a mission trip for years, but the opportunity was not available through our church. My hope is that Anna will see a bigger piece of the world and realize how lucky she is to be an American and to be able to help others. We'll see how that goes; she is, after all a teenage girl. But, she's got a big heart and is a kind person. Well, most of the time.

The shot doesn't feel good and Anna winces. She makes me laugh. I tell her, "Here's a girl that's been poked, prodded, bruised, and suffered traumatic brain injury and you're worried about a little shot?" She even laughs.

The next two weeks unfold with Anna's basketball training, mission trip preparation, the last day of preschool and graduation meetings for Max. The most exciting thing to happen is Greg's surprise that he is flying the four of us to Arizona for Memorial Day weekend. He bought the tickets and we are having a vacation. Ever since the car accident, he has certainly wanted to be on the go with the kids. The accident affected each of us in a different way. For Greg, it means we will all be travelling together as often as possible. I mean seriously, we just got back from Hawaii. Now we're going to Arizona? Well, at least it should be hot lying in the sun by the pool. Anna, the sun lover, can hardly wait. I think Max is just happy to be going somewhere. It's a treat.

Arizona is great. No scorpions to be seen, which thrills me to no end. No other scary looking bugs or creatures lurking about the house. The sun is out and we are in the community pool. Even Max, who is not really a water person, is swimming. This was a great idea. We are beginning to realize that once Max leaves for college, we may have limited times for family vacations, long or short. Chances are both he and Anna will have different breaks and they will be working in the summer. So, thank you to Greg.

Good friends of ours live about ten minutes away. It's funny how that works. My dear friend Linda Johnson grew up in Seattle and lived in Kirkland for years with her husband, Alan and their four kids. We went to church together and her son Ryan played on The Magic with Max until they moved to Arizona. He's not only a good kid, he's a tall kid. We had three boys named Ryan on the team, so Alan nicknamed his son, Hoss. The team missed him when he left. Anyway, they are coming over for dinner tonight with three of their kids. I love this family and it's always a treat to see them.

Seeing the Johnsons is like seeing your neighbor every day. Even though we are hundreds of miles apart, from the moment we are reunited, it's like no time has passed. When they walk through the door, both families fall into a rhythm of comfortable friendship and the party begins. Max and Ryan are very quiet. But Shane, the middle son is just like Anna. You jump in with both feet or not at all. Those two get the group going while the others, including daughter Laura, watch as the banter begins. It's going to be a fun night. I pour Linda a glass of White Zinfandel and we sit down on the barstools at the counter to talk. Six hours later, Linda and I have served everyone dinner, discussed our lives in depth and managed to clean up the kitchen. As we say goodbye, Max and Ryan give each other a nod, while Shane, Laura, and Anna hug everyone. Sometimes it's hard to believe how a family can have kids with such diverse personalities. Thank God. If everyone was the same it would be pretty boring.

Monday morning, we hop on a plane home. It was a wonderful weekend and the kids were very easy and relaxed. The flight is smooth while Anna sleeps, Max listens to music, Greg reads, and I look at a magazine. Lisa told me her tension releases the minute she gets on a plane. She said, from that moment on, until we land, we have no control. I am learning to accept that philosophy and hand the day over to God. Well, until I forget and take it back again.

It's the week before graduation. We have pictures, haircuts, appointments, and a stressful, unexpected surprise. Greg has to go to Denver for two days. This is such an important week. I can't believe he's leaving. But, he assures me he will be back on Thursday night just in time to help set up Max's tri-fold pictorial and awards display on Friday.

Cedar Park arranges tables around the interior of the gym, with royal blue tablecloths. Each senior has a designated space with their name displayed above their space. The parents come in on Thursday night or Friday afternoon and decorate their graduating senior's space. After the graduation ceremony, we will retreat to the gym for refreshments and treats while we walk around and see the lives of these kids reflected through pictures and memorabilia in each of their displays. Who ever thought of this is brilliant. While I work feverishly to be original and creative, I get irritated with myself for not having kept eighteen years' worth of pictures organized. What was I thinking? Ah, then it hits me. At the beginning of the year, I wrote a poem on the chalkboard in the downstairs bathroom. It has been up all year and it was written about Max. I will add that to his tri-fold. I run into the bathroom with pen and paper in hand, thanking God I never erased it. I jot down Max's poem, thinking I need to save this.

THE STORY OF MAX
I talked to you before I knew you
I loved you before I saw you
I liked you after I loved you
You loved your toothbrush
You loved my red boots
You loved Anna from birth
Dad loved the bond you two created
Dad loves you
Dad taught you how to be a man
Anna loved you when she saw you
Anna liked you from the beginning
Anna taught you about girls (kind of)
We will cherish you this year
We will miss you when your adventure of life takes you away.
Love,
Dad, Mom & Anna

Reading this reminds me he's leaving. This has been such a whirlwind year. So happy. So sad. So proud.

Finally, it's Friday. Greg's home and we run over to Cedar Park to help with the Senior Lunch and to set up Max's display. The lunch is at noon and we are in charge of bringing fruit. It's not a huge deal, but it is their final honoring from the parents. They are in graduation rehearsal from 9:30 am until 2:45 pm and the Senior Lunch is a nice little break for them to relax, eat, and enjoy their final day at Cedar Park. It's bittersweet for us.

A few hours later, at 6:30 pm, Greg and I file into the sanctuary at Cedar Park. Even the parents have a graduation rehearsal. We are given Max's cap and gown to take home and press, as well as the instructions for tomorrow night's activities. The meeting doesn't take very long, but it certainly makes Max's graduation very real. We ask ourselves again, where did time go. We will be moving him into his dorm at Gonzaga in a few months. Anna will be a junior in high school and we will be nearing the empty nest syndrome. Wow. My life as a stay at home mom will be over. It's been the best job I've ever had.

Anna is getting quite independent and lippy. That girl is adopting a serious attitude problem. But, nonetheless, I still ask God, "What do you want me to do next?" I would love to receive an answer to that question. I have been praying for enlightenment for years. Apparently, my current job is not quite finished. I guess that's His answer.

Graduation Day. We are moving at full tilt before our feet even touch the floor. There are lots of activities happening today. At 11:00 am we attend a brunch for Max's friend Josh and his twin sister. Then it's a 12:00 pm run to the airport to pick up Aunt Ann's son and Max's cousin, Dane. He is flying up for the graduation ceremonies and for the party we are having on Sunday. Dane is coming to represent both Dad and Ann's family and as a special treat for Max. Dane will be seated with Anna, Gramma and Grandpa. Greg and I will sit in a special section which ensures that the parents have the best seats. Cedar Park has an open graduation so lots of family members can come and help celebrate. It's nice they make a special section for parents; otherwise entire families would take up the front pews. This is a thoughtful idea.

It's 4:30 pm. Time for pictures at our house. We take loads of pictures. Pictures with Max and Brad, pictures with Max and Dane, pictures with Max and his buddies, pictures with Max and Anna, pictures with Max, Anna, and all of their friends and finally, pictures with Greg, Max, and me. Everybody's dressed up. Everybody's excited. It's almost time for the big event. The soon to be graduates need to be at school by 5:30 pm, dressed in cap and gown and ready to rumble. Greg and I walk Max out to the Volvo. I hug and kiss him goodbye and tell him to drive safely. The next time I see him he will be a high school graduate. How exciting.

At 6:15 pm we load Anna and Dane into the car and off we go. Gramma and Grandpa will show up closer to 7:00 pm so they don't have to sit so long. Anna and Dane have instructions to save them two seats. We arrive at Cedar Park and drive into a full parking lot. Eventually Greg squeezes us into a parking spot and we stride towards the sanctuary. We take our seats and wait. At 6:50 pm, my eyes search the room to find Dane and Anna. There they are with Gramma and Grandpa firmly planted next to them. Good.

At seven o'clock sharp, graduation opens with a warm welcome from the School Board. We continue with the Processional, Invocation, and a performance by the Revelation Choir. We watch Max as he stands amongst his class, looking around the sanctuary to see where Greg and I are seated. We are trying to catch his eye by doing everything except standing up and yelling, "Over here!" I imagine almost every parent is doing the same thing. To Max it must look like a sea of crazed, smiling parents with low waving hands. Finally, we connect. He smiles. Max's class is the biggest class to ever graduate from Cedar Park and this may be a bit of a long night. The graduation ceremony is a very personal experience for both parents and graduates. Not only does the program list each graduate alphabetically, it includes a paragraph detailing their high school accomplishments and what their future plans are. Every graduate gives a speech. They are given one or two minutes to step up to the podium and speak to their parents in front of hundreds of people. This is the best part of graduation. I love hearing this.

It's Max's turn. He walks to the front of the class and stands behind the podium. He looks at us as we stand up and he starts speaking. He has such an ease about him. My dad would be proud of Max's public speaking ability. I can't wait to tell him. I wish he were here to see his grandson. Max is funny. He's telling a story about Greg. Then he thanks both of us. It's short but it's beautiful to us. He's a great kid. We're lucky. Thank you.

With diplomas in hand and hats in the air, the class of 2008 cheers and marches out of the sanctuary, and over to the high school. We gather our troops, congratulate other parents, and cross the drive to the school gym. Max is already in the gym. He's officially a graduate. He's ready to party.

The gym is loaded with parents, families, graduates, friends, teachers, and administrators congratulating the new graduates and their parents. We circle around the gym looking at the wonderful displays the parents have created to celebrate the life of their child. Wow. There are some very crafty displays here. And what perfect way to get a snapshot of each graduate's life. More memories. Of course, like every other graduate, we find Max in front of his display. They all want to see what their parents have made for their space. It's funny to watch them. Before Max has a chance to run off, we make sure to get a few pictures of all of us with our new graduate. As a matter of fact, there are flashes going off everywhere. There will be lots of pictures and new beginnings tonight.

After an hour or so Max and his friends are ready to go. For me, let it linger. But, I am outvoted and we say our goodbyes. Max is going out with his friends. We have had numerous discussions about tonight and safety with Max. He gets it. All we want is for him to check in and let us know where he's going to be. Max is a responsible kid and he knows after what we've all been through, it's important for us to know he is safe. He hugs me goodbye in his blue gown and promises to call and let us know where he is and if he's coming home to sleep. I remind him to come home by 10:00 am tomorrow, because his graduation party starts at 11:00 am. As he disappears in a crowd of friends and family, I pray not only for his safety, but for the safety for every kid graduating tonight. They're still so young and think they're so old.

Sunday morning Greg takes Sammy to his nanny's house for the day. With Max's party starting soon, he would be in licky dog heaven with all our guests, and I am sure we would be missing a hamburger or two. We decided it would be easier without him this time. Of course, we aren't going to tell him. I'm sure when he gets home he'll smell all the people and food that have been here today. He is too smart. Seriously. Plus, today is for Max. It's just a simple barbeque with neighbors and friends that have watched Max grow up. Three hours. That's all. It's just a brief celebration to congratulate him on his high school graduation and to say goodbye as we send him off to college. When I first mentioned to Max that we would like to have a graduation party for him, he was completely appalled. Then I showed him the poem I'd written to send as the invitation and he was further horrified. We explained to him that this was not just about him. It is a time for our friends and neighbors to see how he has grown and to wish him luck on his new journey. He finally acquiesced (after we told him he might receive a few gifts) and I sent the poem. I was actually quite excited about the poem because it captures the essence of his life. Over the years, I've written my kids many poems. I think they're funny. Max and Anna don't necessarily share my sense of humor at this point, however when they have their own kids, they may change their minds. This is Max's graduation invitation:

ODE TO MAX BROWN
His first word was cheese, as he looked 'cross the room
Pointing up to the counter, the Tillamook did loom ...

Chapter Twenty-Five

He grew taller and funnier, as the years flew right by
From first to twelfth grade, oh so quickly my-my ...
Soon he'll be away, no more lunches in sacks
No more basketball practice, soon no more Max ...
It's off to Gonzaga, he goes as a fan
Our little "bug", is becoming a man ...
To celebrate his journey, an open house we will host
June 8th, 11 - 2, a barbeque ... and toast ...

Well, at least our guests enjoyed it.

By noon, the sun is out and the party is in full swing. We got lucky with the weather. Neighbors and friends are teasing Max and he loves every minute of it. His friends are here, cousin Dane is mingling with our friends and neighbors, Anna is talking with Max's friends and a few of her own, and Greg is at the grill. People are sitting outside in the warm sun just hanging out. It's perfect. Max is making sure to talk to everyone here and to thank them for coming. My training is paying off. He's a nice young man. Thank you.

Chapter Twenty-Six

"A toast. We made it"
— Lisa Brackett

The excitement of Anna's last day of school and Max's graduation is behind us. Anna and I find ourselves at the airport ready to leave for our mission trip to Mexico. It's early, around 5:00 am as I pop the last malaria pill into my mouth and wash it down with three gulps of water. The plane leaves at 7:00 am. This will be Anna's youth group's first mission trip. We are going with Hope Lutheran Church from West Seattle. They have done this same trip for years and have the entire trip perfectly planned. I like that. It makes me feel safe. We're excited. We will fly into San Diego and drive to Ensenada in two vans and a truck, loaded with clothing, quilts made by the ladies of Epiphany and Hope Lutheran, and supplies to build bunk beds for those in need.

Altogether there are twenty-four of us. Lisa and I are two of the six chaperones. Anna, Katy, and Amie are three of the many girls going, along with a handful of boys. One of our male chaperones is AJ, a police officer, which makes me feel much more comfortable and protected. We are only going to Ensenada, with one day trip out to the Camalu Indian Reservation, so I feel safe. If I didn't think this was a good idea, we would not be going. We will be visiting villages to sing and play with the kids, as well as distribute clothing and build beds. Having never done this before, it will be an adventure for us. Hopefully this adventure will broaden Anna's appreciation for her own life as well as soften her emerging and sometimes ungrateful attitude.

When the plane leaves Seattle-Tacoma Airport, it's overcast and cloudy. As we ascend towards the heavens, climbing higher and higher making our way through the cloud cover, we eventually emerge to a bright blue sky and the first light of day. Almost immediately we see Mount Rainier. Its enormous peak jutting up from the clouds and covered with snow, makes a beautiful first impression as we begin our eight-day trip. Fabulous. Before the girls have a chance to fall asleep, I pull out my camera and get a picture of the three of them seated next to each other looking at a magazine and smiling. They're tired. Not too much conversation. With eyes weary from their early morning rise, they close their magazine, settle into their seats, and push the recline buttons. Good night girls. See you in two and a half hours.

Lisa wants to sleep too. I won't let her. This is exciting and we can sleep later. She does not share my sentiments. After much effort to keep her awake, she closes her eyes and slips into a slumber you can only have on a plane. It lasts as long as the quiet persists. Once the carts start rolling, the dream of sleep is over. Needless to say, I am thrilled when the carts arrive. Lisa wakes up and I smile.

When we land in San Diego, we get the vans and meet our mission contacts at Home Depot. They actually live in Mexico and drove their old truck up, to help us get over the border with all of our goods. Both churches have collected donated clothing, and shipped multiple boxes to San Diego to be picked up and repackaged. Apparently, this can cause some issues, because the Mexican government doesn't want clothing brought into their country for resale. Ours is to be given away, but they have to be convinced of that at the border. Interesting. So, we unload our clothes into donated suitcases and boxes given to us through local churches, and stack them into the back of the old truck. We also purchase plywood and two by fours for the bunk beds and load them into the back of the old truck wherever we can squeeze some space. When we are ready to go, the vans and the old truck are packed to the rim with our supplies. Seriously, not an inch of space is unused. Our leader from Hope Lutheran has been doing this for over twenty years. He's got this down to a science.

Off we go towards Mexico. Three of the adult chaperones are approved drivers. Lisa and I are not. We made that choice and, quite frankly, this being our first trip, we don't want that responsibility. We get to ride along with the kids and sit amongst their music, chatting, and laughing. It's fun. Naturally, Anna would rather be in the van I am not in, but the other kids are happy to have me. Lisa and I ride in the same van and put the girls in the van with AJ. We've pretty much decided they need to ride with AJ all the time anyway. Being a policeman, not only do we feel they are incredibly safe with him, he's also the best driver in the group. We figured that out on the drive from the airport to Home Depot and, being the protective moms we are, we already told AJ he has to drive them wherever we go. He just laughed and said, "Okay." I can't even think about Anna getting her head hit in Mexico. She couldn't get the medical care she would require. Am I crazy for doing this? I say a prayer. Lisa thinks I worry too much.

We are arriving at the border. There are armed guards everywhere. Wow. Scary. Our mission contacts are the lead drivers in our caravan. They drive their old truck straight to the parking lot and our vans follow. They have done this many times before and say it is better to stop and declare your intentions than to try to drive through and be pulled out. Guards with rifles approach our vehicles. Each of our drivers carries a walkie-talkie to communicate. Our mission contacts tell the van drivers to stay in their vehicles and they will approach the guards. Everyone sits still. Even the kids are quiet. Anna's in another van. I'm worried. What if we get separated? Lisa's a little alarmed, too, but she never gets as worried as I do. At least one of us stays somewhat calm. After thirty minutes, we are cleared to proceed into Mexico. They did inspect the old truck and wanted to see everyone's passports, but aside from that, we just sat and waited for the go-ahead. We are all released at the same time, so off we go in our caravan. Whew. Our driver picks up the walkie-talkie and calls AJ's van to make sure they are all okay. I think he knows Lisa and I want confirmation. "Yes, we are all okay," AJ replies. Good. Lisa and I can relax now.

This is actually quite interesting. As soon as we pass from the U.S. to Mexico, the highway dramatically changes. There's a huge difference in cleanliness and maintenance. It becomes evident that we are in a different country when we pass by a dead dog pushed up next to the cement barrier. While this could happen anywhere, this dog is on his back with his feet sticking straight up in the air. Obviously, rigor mortis has set in, which signals to me he's been there a while. Hmmm.

Not everyone saw the dog and I don't say anything. It's probably not a good thing to point out on the beginning of a mission trip in a different country. This should be a positive experience for all of us and a dead dog left on the side of the road may cause concern with the kids. We'll just proceed ahead. But, Lisa and I saw it. We can just file that information.

It doesn't take long to arrive in Ensenada. This is a fun little tourist town. Cruise ships stop here for a day of shopping and partying. It's clean, it's busy, it's cute, and it's loaded with restaurants, stores, and street vendors from top to bottom. But, we are staying at a church about five miles outside of Ensenada, so we wave and say adios as we drive through town.

We are no more than a few minutes out of Ensenada when we get a taste of the Mexico we will be visiting. The poverty is silencing. Our residence is a yellow two-story church with a simple white cross attached to the fascia of the second story. The church sits at the end of a long narrow street, lined with homes made of plywood and assorted materials. There are a couple of homes made with bricks and finished roofs, as well as, partially built homes waiting for their owners to be able to afford their finish. Most of the floors are dirt. Our residence has a linoleum floor downstairs and appears to be completed. The downstairs, where the boys will sleep, houses the kitchen, one bathroom with a sink and a toilet, and numerous long tables with attached stools in a large open room for fellowship. We have been instructed to put our used toilet paper in the waste basket next to the toilet, because there's no plumbing system available to support flushing toilet paper. That's a little gross for us Americans, but I suspect it's only the beginning glimpse of a very different lifestyle than we are used to.

The upstairs is accessed by an outdoor staircase off the kitchen and is where the church service takes place. It is also where all of us girls will sleep. There is a raised platform for the pastor and a number of very heavy pews we have to push aside in order to set our sleeping bags and air mattresses down. The floor is carpeted. Lisa and I set our sleeping gear down on the raised platform. Our luggage is sprinkled near the interior walls of the room, both on pews and on the ground. We are supposed to lock our room every time we leave for the mission field, or if no one is upstairs. They have a theft problem. There will even be a house-sitter from the church when we are out of the building. She is supposed to make sure nothing gets stolen while we are gone. There is good and bad everywhere, that is for sure.

As soon as we have set up our beds and luggage, we meet downstairs in the fellowship room. The boys definitely got the short end of the stick. The fellowship room is where the boys sleep, the whole group eats, we have our meetings, we use as a staging area, and it's the only common place for everyone to hang out. Plus, they're right next to the one and only bathroom with a roomful of girls upstairs. This means that every morning they have to get up early, move all of their bedding out of the way, set up the folding tables with stools, use the bathroom, and make the room presentable before the girls come down. Poor guys. That's brutal.

The rest of the day will be broken into three group activities. One group goes to Costco, one group stays to clean the church and guard our belongings, and the final group goes to Home Depot. Yes, there is a Home Depot in Mexico. Lisa and I are surprised. We opt for Costco. Most of the girls, including Anna, Katie and Amie go to Home Depot with AJ and a few of the boys. Good. The rest stay behind and take care of the building.

By late afternoon, we have additional supplies for bunk beds, a beautiful clean church, and cupboards full of food. We also have an endless supply of bottled water. It's a good thing, too. Everyone is thirsty and starving. The kids will be our cooks for the dinner meals and whoever doesn't cook cleans up. Breakfast is mainly cereal and self-serve foods, while lunch will be a make your own sandwich meal. If we are gone for lunch, we will pack a cooler with sandwiches and drinks to have on the road. The good news is that the adults are pretty much out of the line-up for meal prep and clean up. Yay! This is kind of a vacation. Well, no, not really.

The kids do a great job with dinner. Clean-up is pretty easy. Throw the paper and plastic away. Wipe everything else down with sanitizer. That works. But, before we break into music and fun, we discuss a few details, one being the shower situation. Apparently, there are two shower facilities in Ensenada. One is much better than the other. Tomorrow, after our day of visiting and working, we will see which one is open. Showers will be few and far between. Keep your lips closed when you shower and don't let any of the water get into your mouth. Brush your teeth and wash your face with bottled water. And again, no toilet paper in the toilet. Clean your hands with the sanitizer in the bathroom, not the tap water. Another detail, that we all came prepared for, was attire. Girls have to wear long skirts and tops with sleeves. Short sleeves are okay, just nothing sleeveless. We all knew that, so no surprises there. The reason is that it upsets the Mexican women. They don't want their men looking at scantily clad girls. I get that. I would be more worried about the girls though, not the men.

We review the activities for the next eight days and start practicing our songs and the program we will do for our visits to the various churches and villages. We will be singing in Spanish, having a Sunday school type program, playing with little kids and building bunk beds for locals who have no beds for their families. By the time we are done, everyone is exhausted. Sleep can't come fast enough.

We have no window coverings in a room that is wall to wall windows. We have partially covered them with green paper to hide the girls from view when they are changing clothes or are in their pajamas. However, one little detail escaped us. We discovered the next morning, quite early actually, that the already hot sun pours through those windows and the whole room lights up like a Christmas tree. It's hard to sleep through that. It's also hard to sleep through snoring, listening to someone talk in their sleep, and knowing you are surrounded by cockroaches and spiders. But hey, this is an adventure!

The boys ring the bell. Really. They have a little handheld, yet very loud, bell. This is their job and they think it's very funny. The girls have managed to push themselves down into their sleeping bags and cover their faces, bodies, and ears from the light and the noise. But the bell rings loud and clear in the room, meaning time to get up! All Lisa and I hear are groans and slow movements. The first full day of our mission has begun.

Downstairs, the boys have done a wonderful job of transforming their bedroom into the dining hall. The tables are up and the food is scattered across the tabletops within reaching distance of every diner. The girls filter in and out of the bathroom until we are all seated and ready to begin our meal with a prayer. The moment the prayer is finished, cereal boxes are torn open, muffins are grabbed off their plates and fruit is passed around in large bowls. It's a feast with juice, milk, interesting coffee, and of course, bottled water.

Our leader, Jeff, tells us where we're going today and what we will be doing. Firstly, we must introduce ourselves to the locals, because they are very curious about the Americans who visit every summer and bring clothes, quilts, and lumber for bunk beds. The local boys are naturally intrigued by the girls. Jeff warns the girls to stay in groups and be smart about their location.

Secondly, we will deliver quilts and build a bunk bed for a local family that has been chosen by our mission hosts. At the end of our day, we'll go to the shower facility and have our first washing in two days. Sounds good.

As soon as breakfast is cleaned up and the girls are finished upstairs, we lock the door to the upstairs room and open the downstairs doors for visitors. The local boys and girls have been milling around outside for about thirty minutes waiting to come in and meet us. Word travels fast, as does the notice of two large white vans parked on the dirt in the front of the church. There are kids of all ages, including a few moms, that stream in to greet us. How wonderful. Well, we're off to a great start. The kids are having a blast. Our girls are twirling the little kids around, kicking the soccer ball with them, and just simply holding them and carrying them around. So, this is what our mission looks like, I think to myself. This is great.

Just before lunch, Jeff and a few of the boys leave in one of the vans to get the lumber that has been stored at our mission host's house. We couldn't bring it with us to the church because there is a huge theft problem in this neighborhood and the surrounding area. Lumber is an important and expensive commodity. The girls start to set lunch up while the local kids go home to eat, and by the time Jeff gets back with the lumber, lunch is ready. We pray, we eat, we clean up, and we load most of the kids into the vans to begin our journey. Some of the boys and girls will stay behind to police our belongings and play with the local kids for the rest of the afternoon. Of course, Anna, Katy, and Amie want to build bunk beds and are in AJ's van. Lisa and I are in the other van. Anna has made it very clear she wants her independence. Her attitude speaks for itself. She wants to be left alone. She wants to be without her mom. I assure myself this is normal.

Our stop is a few blocks from our church. These bunk beds take quite a while to build. The family invites all of us in to help with the building, allowing us to walk through their small house on our way to the back bedroom. Their daughter and small son have been sharing a blanket on the floor for their entire lives. This is a real treat for them. They will each have their own bed and one of our donated quilts to get comfy with every night. Even though we do not provide mattresses, the little kids are very excited and jump in their new bed as soon as the last nail has been pounded in. One of our kids wraps a quilt around them and we all laugh. Very fun. On the way out of their home, we say goodbye to the mom and her parents as they huddle around an open fire in the middle of the dirt-floored kitchen. There is a pot on a hook over the fire and they are making their dinner, sitting on small wooden stools. Wow.

Outside, AJ corrals the girls into his van. A group of four to five older boys are standing across the street and more are beginning to gather. Not safe. Lisa is very agitated by this, and she has a right to be. The boys are not smiling or engaging each other in a positive way. AJ suspects there may be some drug trade involved. We load quickly and lock our van doors, carefully maneuvering our way out of the neighborhood and back to the church. Scary.

We arrive at the church within a few minutes and unload, though briefly, to collect our shower supplies. Once back in the vans with our whole group, Jeff leads us to the better of the two showering businesses. It's closed. Jeff is visibly disappointed, smiles, and leads us to our second choice. This building isn't as nice as the first, but what do I know? We jump out of the vans and enter into the paying and waiting area for the showers. The waiting area isn't bad. It's not clean, but not too bad. Some of the showers are available and some are not, the cashier informs us, so she asks us to knock first to see which ones are not being used. Okay. We girls decide to go in pairs. When it's time for Lisa and me to go, we put our flip flops on and walk through this dark indoor courtyard towards a recently vacated showering room. We stop dead in our tracks. Nothing could have prepared us for this. Oh…my…gosh.

There are two tiny rooms. The first room is the changing area and the second room is the shower stall. The two rooms together are maybe five feet by three feet. Looking down at the cement floor, there's standing water in both rooms. Yuk. We enter the first room trying not to touch anything, and close the door with one finger. There are two hooks, a seat, and one shelf. Thank the Lord we are such good friends or this would be a complete nightmare. Lisa decides to go first. Since there's standing water on the floor, we leave our flip-flops on, wishing we had brought rubber boots from home. I hold her up and she takes her skirt off, trying not to let it touch the ground or the walls. We see a cockroach run across the tile wall. Needless to say, I hold all of Lisa's clothes, our towels and all of our belongings while she takes the first shower. As our eyes adjust to the darkness, we notice there are small cockroaches darting in and out of crevices along every wall in both rooms. Yuk. When Lisa gets out of the shower, I accidently knock against her in this tiny, crowded room and she brushes up against a side wall. Both of us are grossed out. "I've been slimed. You slimed me!" Lisa screams. At this moment, we look at each other and burst out laughing. We can't stop laughing. I mean the bend-over-and-try-to-breathe kind of laughing. By the time I get out of the shower, we are still laughing so hard we have tears streaming down our faces. It's at this moment we decide we will not shower for the rest of the trip if it means coming back here. We would rather smell. This is truly disgusting.

Hours later, after numerous intermittent bursts of laughter, we are back at the church and ready for bed. When the final light goes out and we are snug in our sleeping bags, I turn to Lisa and say, "What the hell are we doing here?" She looks at me and, once again, we burst into uncontrollable laughter, trying desperately to muffle ourselves.

Someone says, "Be quiet." I mean really, the adults are not the ones that should have to be told to be quiet. This of course, makes us laugh even more.

The bell rings. The older girls are coffee lovers. They immediately jump out of their sleeping bags and run downstairs to the kitchen to find a cup of coffee and bring it up to the room before they change and get ready for breakfast. I ask them to bring me a cup, with cream please. Coffee sounds really good. Almost like comfort food. When they hand me my coffee, they smile and wait. I taste it. It's heaven. They have just introduced me to flavored creamers. This is decadent. "Thanks girls. This is fabulous. What is the flavor?" I blurt out with approval. Even Anna wants a taste. Yum. I don't want to know what it's made of. Chemicals, I'm sure. But, for right now, ignorance is bliss. I am going to give myself some grace.

Over by the window and above the green paper, I stand with my coffee, taking in our surroundings. It's pretty much water starved desert bushes and dirt, sprinkled with lots of garbage. Across the field, I see a few partially built houses and some trees protruding from the landscape. While the hills in the background are dotted with more houses, I am reminded how lucky we are to live in the United States. I hope Anna sees it.

Today we visit the Camalu Indians. It's a two-hour drive through winding roads and we have our two vans and a little car loaded with clothes and quilts. Lisa and I are riding in the small car with our driver, a woman from Hope Lutheran. There are two front seats and a space behind the seats for a third person. It's not pretty. The three of us force ourselves into the car and sit in cramped positions, following the two vans across the desert. We had a little trouble with one of the vans this morning and got a late start on our day. Once we are underway on the open, winding desert roads, I am a wreck. The locals pass on curves, drive like bats out of hell, and basically follow no road rules. Fortunately, we have the walkie-talkies and AJ is telling us when it is safe to pass slow trucks and what is ahead. Thank you, God. I know I have no control, but my plan was not to die in a small compact car on a remote road in Mexico. I keep checking with AJ to make sure they are safe. Anna thinks I'm a nut case. "Is that my mom again?" I hear her irritated voice. Oh, well. Ann did say it would only get worse.

We reach the Camalu Indian Reservation in late afternoon. Not good. We have a program to put on, games to play, and merchandise to distribute. This must all be done before the sun goes down. Apparently, it can get dangerous once the men come in from the fields. We are told they may be intoxicated and can get very aggressive during the distribution of clothing. Our plan is to sing some songs, play games with the kids, and hand out the clothes and quilts we have brought. It's going to be tight. In past years, the mission group had arrived by noon and had all afternoon with the Camalu Indians. We empty the vans and are ready to start our program, after the drivers pull our three vehicles into a tight U shape pattern. This will prevent anyone from getting into our vehicles and will keep us safe in case we have any problems. There is also a table set up at the top of the U, closing the open gap while providing a solid surface to place our clothing. The terrain is flat and brown. It's a perfect setting for a soccer game, which starts up between a few of the local kids and our group. They've been waiting for us.

Lots of smiles, kids, moms and babies, balloons, games and fun fill our first hour. That's about all the time we have for play if we want to make it through our program. The chaperones gather our kids into a group and Jeff pulls out his guitar. We sing kid-friendly songs in Spanish, gathering the voices of the Camalu Indians as they catch onto the rhythm and the words. It's going well. The sun is beginning to fade and we have got to distribute the clothes. The Camalu women start to pour into the area and line up for their turn to pick clothes for their families. One ninety-year-old woman emerges and Lisa escorts her to the front of the line. She gets one of the few quilts we brought. She is very thankful and slowly retreats with her quilt wrapped around her frail body. The rest of the line is very respectful toward the elderly lady and is careful not to get in her path as the excitement escalates with the clothing distribution.

Within forty-five minutes, the sun is almost gone and the crowd is getting very anxious, afraid we will leave without making sure everyone receives some clothing. Lisa is on red alert, beginning to get concerned about the girls. She approaches AJ and tells him it's time to get the girls in the van. AJ agrees and within minutes, the girls are locked in the van. A man tries to skirt the line and approaches the window of one of the vans. Jeff approaches the man and helps him out, avoiding a confrontation. The decision is made to leave the rest of the clothing, in boxes, for the families to distribute to themselves. We quickly load up the boys and drive out of town, exhausted from the day and relieved to be leaving the escalating situation on the Camalu reservation. Now we have to drive back in the dark on these horrible roads. I close my eyes and pray. We are all filthy, but no showers today. That's okay. I just pray we make it back to our little yellow church alive.

The remainder of our trip is very rewarding, even though Anna is pulling further and further away from me. Her desire for independence is growing every day. She's only sixteen. She wants to be twenty-one. Hmm. We have built beds, given away quilts, had a much nicer shower experience, eaten authentic Mexican food, and shopped in Ensenada. When we cross over the border and reenter the United States, I can hear the cheering coming from the van ahead of us, as well as, our own van. We made it. Thank you.

Our plane doesn't leave San Diego until late tonight. Jeff has planned a day at the beach and the kids are hot, tired, dirty, and thrilled. With towels and blankets down, the chaperones are scattered across the sand to keep an eye on the kids. Coincidentally, Greg's Aunt Marilyn lives a few blocks from the beach and I call her to say hello and bring her up to date on where we've been. "Come for a visit," she says. I explain to Aunt Marilyn that we don't look too good and haven't showered regularly, but she still wants us to come. I clear it with the other chaperones, making sure it's okay to leave and take Lisa with me. Anna refuses to go, and sadly, it's okay with me. I don't need any attitude from her right now, especially in front of Aunt Marilyn. Family is rapidly becoming secondary to Anna Brown. Lisa and I figure the house is about a mile from the beach and we think we know where we're going. On the way, we come across a wonderful restaurant which just happens to have a twin in Seattle. We recognize the name immediately and vow to grab a seat on the way back. Maybe we'll have enough time for a quick lunch break. We are one busy road, with no crosswalks, away from Aunt Marilyn's street. It's actually more like a four-lane highway through town. We look at each other and contemplate how to do this safely. Just then, cars start stopping to let us cross. How nice. They must have looked at us, figured we were homeless, and decided to give us a break. Either that or they figured we were ready to run out in front of their cars and they didn't want to run over such unfortunate looking people. In any case, we cross the street. Thank you.

Well, come to find out, Aunt Marilyn is thrilled to hear about our mission trip. She lets us in on a little story of her own.

"When I was younger," she says, "I used to drive across the border and bring back people to work at our house." Who knew? I don't even think Greg's dad knows this. Wow. She wanted to help them. That's a mission on its own.

"But," says Aunt Marilyn, "things have certainly changed since then and I would never be able to do that now." Lisa and I agree.

After a short visit and a tour of her beautiful home, it is time for us to get back to our group. We thank Aunt Marilyn for inviting us and ask if we could quickly use her bathroom. I try not to look in the mirror too long, just a minute to try to pull myself together. Lisa does the same. Hopefully we made a few adjustments that make us look a little more with it, but I'm not sure there is any real hope of that. We leave Aunt Marilyn's, only after she gives me a brightly colored muumuu, and make our way back to the restaurant. People stop to let us cross the highway again. We must be quite the breathtaking pair.

The hostess doesn't seem too appalled by our appearance. She seats us outside under an umbrella with a soft breeze blowing in our direction. "I hope it's not because we smell," I mention to Lisa. We both laugh.

"Do you think we could have a glass of wine?" Lisa asks with raised eyebrows and a sly look in her eyes.

"Yes," I nod my head. When our waitress comes to our table, we order two glasses of Sauvignon Blanc.

"A toast. We made it," smiles Lisa.

Clink-clink is the happy sound of two celebratory glasses of wine being drunk by two women who have experienced shower hell and lived to laugh about it. The whole trip was worth it. I think.

The good news is, no one at the beach has missed us and we return just in time to sit in the sun for fifteen minutes before we load up for the airport. Yay, we're going home!

Chapter Twenty-Seven

"Mom. I'll see you tomorrow and all weekend"
— Max Brown

By the middle of August, life at the Brown house has started to undergo a dramatic change. Max is preparing to leave for Gonzaga at the end of the month and has worked all summer to save money for college. That was our deal if he wanted to go to a private school. He needed to get a scholarship, which he did, and he needed to finance his social life. We would pay for everything else. Max, being a man of his word, held up his end of the bargain and will leave for Gonzaga with a full bank account. He surprised me a little bit when he decided to go to a school none of his friends were going to. Max loves his friends. I thought that might matter to him. I'm glad it didn't. Venturing into the unknown alone shows security and self-confidence. Brad will be at the University of Washington, Riley at Washington State, Marcus in California and Josh in Colorado. They will see each other on breaks. Good enough.

Anna is my concern. The girl is giving me fits. Since our return from Mexico, she has been very difficult. Her attitude is rather disrespectful and rude and it appears to be aimed towards me. Greg isn't on the receiving end of her poor attitude, yet we have spent the better part of this summer locked in conversations and confrontations with her. I'm sad and worried. She started driver education class in June and helped out with Vacation Bible School in July. She finds every excuse to be gone from the house, be it going to the movies or spending the night at her friends. I have actually started noting on my calendar where she is every night because Greg doesn't see her absence as a problem. In my heart and in every cell of my body, I know this is wrong. It has all happened so quickly. I have to convince Greg that her absences are, in part, related to her bad attitude. I am wondering if this is part of her brain injury or if this is who she is right now at the ripe age of sixteen. Either way, it's not working well for me or for our family, and I suspect Anna is in turmoil herself.

Amie and her parents have invited Anna to go to Hawaii the week before Max leaves for Gonzaga. Yes, Hawaii again. This is a tough decision. Part of me wants her to go so we can have a break from the disruption she has created at home. It will also allow her some supervised time away from our family. Hopefully she would adjust her mindset. But, given her attitude, should we let her go? Greg is an emphatic yes. I wonder if she is being catered to and ask myself, "Has she earned it?" This is a difficult decision. I love her so much and have always loved being around my kids, but right now I could really use a break from Anna. She's wreaking havoc on our family. I defer to Greg's decision. She gets to go.

The night before they depart, Anna spends the night at Amie's because their flight leaves before sunup and we agreed it would be easier on everyone if Anna was already at their home and ready to go. The following morning when Greg and I wake up, she is already in flight. That was the first uninterrupted night of sleep we've had in weeks. No late-night phone calls to extend curfew, no last-minute change of plans, no "I've decided to spend the night at Candice's house." No stress. We forgot what it felt like to be well rested. Heaven.

Max and I have a lot to accomplish this week before he leaves. He has a list of what every freshman needs from Gonzaga. It's surprisingly long. This means we will be doing lots of shopping and gathering of items for him. He and Greg order a well-promoted package which includes a laundry bag, sheets, pillow cases, comforter, and assorted other interesting necessities. Max and I shop for almost everything else. He can't stand to shop. Finally, he says, "Mom, will you just pick it out for me. I'm sure it will be fine."

Laughing to myself, I think, "Yep, should have known this was coming." Max chose hunter green and navy for his bedding, so we are working around those colors and building quite a coordinated ensemble of needs. His room is going to look fabulous by the time we're done, or so I tell myself. He could care less. Boys. But, I'm having fun!

Moving day comes faster than I want it to. With Anna back from Hawaii, it's time for us to take Max to college. Unbelievable. We load up the Pilot with all of Max's new needs, his clothes, and a few things he wants to take from his room, and off we go. Sammy is staying with his nanny and Pam graciously agreed to take care of our kitties. This is going to be rough on Jazz. Max is his boy. Jazz slept in Max's room last night and they both cuddled and slept in a heap. I think they'll both be sad. I think all of us will be sad. I am excited for him to start his new life adventure, but going to miss that little boy very much.

Five hours later we are in Spokane. The dorms open tomorrow morning at 9:00 am. Tonight, all four of us will sleep at the home of our wonderful friends, the Whites. Ross is a fraternity brother of Greg's and Jamie is his terrific wife. Ross also happens to be our attorney and has watched our kids grow up. We made many phone calls to Ross after the accident. He's been an incredible support. Greg and I are comforted knowing Ross and Jamie are only fifteen minutes from Max. Spokane is a warm family friendly city with a small-town feel. Perfect for Max. Knowing the Whites are so close by makes Greg and I feel safer. Just in case.

After our long drive, we are hungry and tired. Sitting in the car for five hours is tedious for me. I am not a good passenger and Greg will certainly testify to that. The kids watched a movie and listened to music. They travel better than I do. After we throw our belongings into their house, Ross and Jamie take us out to their favorite family tavern for burgers. The kids love it. We are seated at a huge round table amongst an assortment of old, but very comfortable, padded chairs. It is very casual with TV screens in every corner, all tuned into the most current sports news. The boys can barely focus to order. But, order we do, and after our first bite, we find that the burgers are fabulous. This is exactly what you'd expect at a great tavern.

Tomorrow is a big day for us. Greg, the kids, and I are tired. And, everyone is full from our big, fat, juicy burgers. Jamie takes the kids downstairs to set up their sleeping arrangements. Anna's in the bedroom that one of their four kids used to sleep in, and Max is on the couch. Greg and I are upstairs in the guest room. Before we turn the lights out, we look at each other in shock that our first born will be moving in to his college dorm tomorrow. Both of us shake our heads and need a moment to process. Wow. Good night, honey.

The next morning, the sun is out and we are ready to go! With Starbucks in hand, we pull up close to Max's dorm and start unloading. There are parents, kids, and student volunteers everywhere. It's fun. We find Max's room and start hauling his boxes and bags upstairs. Anna is very helpful, no attitude today. When Greg starts setting up the electronics, he discovers we need additional cords for some of the equipment we brought, so Greg and Max go find whatever it is they need and Anna and I put Max's room together. We unpack everything and hang up his clothes. This is probably the one and only time his clothes will see hangers, so we try to get his room as organized as possible. By the time Anna and I have finished with his room, the boys are back and everything is hooked up, working and in place. Max is ready for us to leave. We drag our feet.

I keep asking him, "Are you going to be okay? Is everything done? Do you need anything else?"

He finally looks at me and says, "I'm okay Mom. You can go. I'm okay." He walks us back to the car and as we drive off, my eyes well up with tears. It's going to be a long ride home.

When we get home, we call him. He had a great day. He didn't say that, but we hear it in his voice. He saw a couple of guys he played against in high school basketball. They all recognized each other and, seeing a familiar face, hung out together and met other boys in their dorm. He said his roommate is a nice guy and even though they don't have much in common, it sounds like it will work out just fine. We say goodbye, relieved all is well with Max Brown.

On Tuesday Anna starts school. Her junior year. Eleven months since the accident. She has been working out with, but not playing with, her soccer team for weeks. She's getting herself ready to play, waiting to be cleared to join in and play contact sports again. We are nearing that dreaded moment. She wants to know, exactly when she can play contact sports. Can I say never? Can I protect her? God knows I'll try, but she has to live and enjoy her life. I have to trust the doctor's decision and not let my own fear get in the way of Anna having a full life. This isn't my strong suit. Fortunately, we have about six weeks before she can see her doctor and she has a busy schedule up until then. I pray.

After a few weeks into the school year things are looking good. Anna was placed in all the classes she wanted and has immersed herself into her school work. Her memory is strong and her classes are hard. Her attitude is good. As for Max, he appears to be very happy at Gonzaga and has met a core group of kids from his dorm. He's obviously having a great time. We just hope he's studying, too. All's well in the Brown home. Thank you.

Before we know it, weeks have passed and the doctor appointment we've all been waiting for, or dreading in my case, is hours away. Monday October 13th. One year and one week after the car accident. I drive Anna to her doctor's office. She is so excited. This is terrifying for me.

We check in and take a seat in the waiting room. We've been coming to this office since Anna and Max were babies. Anna and I relax into our chairs. Minutes later, with chart in hand, the nurse stands near the front desk and calls her name. Anna looks at me and says, "I want to go in alone." Of course she does. I wait. I read. I wait. Finally, I hear my name called. The nurse escorts me back to the examination room where Anna and her doctor stand smiling when I walk in. She's clear. She can play soccer right away and can resume her basketball career this season. She's thrilled and I am thrilled for her. Scared to death, but thrilled. God is working on me, I hope.

Sunday October 19th. She puts on her soccer uniform, shin guards, and soccer shoes. She is coming back for the first district playoff game. The team has done well without her, but is looking for her aggressive skill in defense. Fortunately, her coach Mark Gauger, is a dad first and a coach second. He knows this is an exciting, yet tough moment for all of us. He was at the hospital. He remembers. He will be careful with her. He will not put her in danger.

This team has prayed for, cried for, and waited for Anna to heal. Anna has known half of them since first grade. They are a fabulous group of young women and when they see her suited up and walking toward the team bench, they run out to circle around her and welcome her back to the game. She's ready.

Mark puts her in and she trots out to the field with her teammates. I can barely breathe. It starts to rain. The whistle blows and the game begins. She's ready. It's exciting and scary. Then it starts to pour. Anna doesn't miss a beat. She's back. Mark rotates her in and out, continually checking with her, making sure she feels okay and her head is okay. When the final whistle blows calling the game to a close, it's a victory for the team. Not only a victory for the Jaguars, but a victory for Anna. Mark looks at Greg and me and says, "She was awesome." This has been a huge morning.

Anna is soaking wet and shivering cold when we load her into the car. We have a fleece blanket in the backseat and she immediately wraps it around her shoulders and neck. She just got another part of her life back. It shows. We talk all the way home about the game and how she feels both physically and mentally. She's tired and understandably so. Working out with the team was certainly helpful, but she isn't used to nonstop running and physical exertion. All she wants to do is go home, take a hot shower and sleep. I ask her if her head is okay. She says yes. I remind her that she and Amie have youth group tonight. She remembers. Good.

It's October 23rd. Max's birthday. Even though we are leaving in the morning for Family Weekend at Gonzaga, this is the first time in nineteen years, there's no Maxie, no cake, no candles, and no celebration.

There's just a phone call with a birthday wish. We did send a package to him on Monday, full of cookies, a gift certificate to Safeway, a subscription to ESPN magazine, and a birthday card. He got it this morning and said the cookies are almost gone. Good.

He laughs when I tell him I miss him. "Mom, I'll see you tomorrow and all weekend," he says.

"Yes," I say, "it's true, but you've never been gone on your actual birthday and it's weird." Pause. Okay, he gets that. Tomorrow will be the first time we've seen Max in eight weeks. He's having the time of his life at school and we can't wait to meet his new friends. Max doesn't share much, but we gather he has found his niche at Gonzaga.

Our weekend on campus with Max is fun. On Saturday morning, we pick him up and take him out to breakfast at his new favorite place to eat. Then back to Gonzaga for an extensive tour of campus. He shows us where all of his classes are and where he plays pickup basketball games with random guys. We meet his new friends, hang out, and eat lunch in the cafeteria he eats in every day. We let him take the lead and we go wherever he wants us to go. Anna is fascinated. She sees college life as pure freedom. I can see the wheels turning.

After dinner, we drop him back at his dorm. On Sunday morning, we pick him up for breakfast and say goodbye. Such a short amount of time and a quick trip, but it was great to see him. He's one happy guy and he's hanging out with a good group of guys.

On Monday morning, Coach Mark sends out a schedule for the Jaguars. If they continue to win, their last district championship game will be November 22nd. After that, they will be on their way to the state semi-finals and then the state championship game, which is in December. This means Anna may be playing soccer and basketball at the same time. Basketball practice begins on November 17th. Whew. That's a lot.

On top of Anna's schedule, we are entering an extremely busy time of the year for both Greg and I. I am hosting a neighborhood Bible study at our home on Friday mornings, acting as team mom for Anna's basketball team, organizing the youth Turkey lunch, hosting a table for Advent by Candlelight at church, and doing all the usual other things a mom at home does. Plus, there are only nine weeks until Christmas. That means decorate the house, shop for presents, and get our traditional holiday gatherings booked and on everyone's calendar. No time for bonbons and soap operas here.

Aside from his day job, Greg has volunteered to help with Anna's basketball team and run the scoreboard at home games. I know he'll end up doing a few other things for the team as well, and that's important for him. This season, he is really going to miss watching and being part of Max's life and basketball. This is perfect for him.

Just as we settle into a manageable routine, we acquire a new wrinkle. Anna finds a boyfriend. He's a nice young man and Anna thinks he's the most handsome guy she's ever met. He really is a nice kid. However, he is a car junkie and his car is unacceptable to us. Anna is not allowed to ride in it. He's rebuilding it. He's working on it. No airbags. That's problematic. He comes to Anna's soccer games and is quite the soccer player himself, according to Anna. The girl is smitten. And so is the boy. We let him drive over and take her out on their dates in our Volvo. That may appear to be a little over the top, but when you've been through what we've been through, it is what it is. We will continue to do what we think is best for Anna. The Volvo is the safest car on the road. She rides in the Volvo or they stay home and entertain me. Given the choice, the Volvo looks good to them.

Not soon after we get the boyfriend, Anna starts to pester me about getting her license. It's time, I agree. She's ready. I schedule her driving test to be taken four weeks before her 17th birthday. If she passes this, she gets her driver's license. Will the stress ever end?

Soccer dominates our life right now. The girls are on fire and the last district final game is days away. After all these years of playing together, it's great to see them still having fun and winning at the same time. Throughout good seasons and bad, this team has always had fun. It's because of Mark. He's an incredible coach and manages to keep the girls positive and laughing. We have never seen him yell at any of them, and Heaven knows there have been times when we wanted to scream. Mark just paces. He's put in more miles on that sideline than I can count. That's his stress reliever.

"Nothing is impossible," is the slogan Mark has impressed on this team and these are their final words as they throw their arms up in the air and take their places on the field. The girls will play their hearts out for the next two hours. Nothing has been easy during district finals. Teams that have lost their games all season have rallied to redeem themselves. It's going to be tough.

We start the game strong. It's a hard-fought battle from the beginning. The girls are focused and relentless. Mark has told us many times, "These girls never, ever give up." He's right. Game after game they've continued to take their places on the field and dominate the competition. Today all of their perseverance and strength pay off. When the final whistle blows, Greg and I stand looking at the Jaguars, the new district champs and winner of the District President's Cup. They played hard. Anna played without any problems. Thank you, God.

By Tuesday night Max is home for Thanksgiving. He's looking forward to the privacy and comfort of his own bedroom, as well as, giving some long overdue attention to Jazz. Naturally, Jazz is all over that and attaches himself to Max the minute he walks through the door.

On Thanksgiving Day, we have a big breakfast at our house with the Allens. Max and Brad had spent last night catching up, so this morning is all about food, neighbors, and friends. Pam brings champagne and orange juice, "Mimosa anyone?"

"Yes," is my answer. Since turkey dinner is later this afternoon at Gramma and Grandpa's and I don't have to cook today, why not? This is the second year in a row I've not spent most of Thanksgiving Day in the kitchen. I could get used to this, even though I do love having the family over for turkey and all that goes along with it. But, it's a nice break.

Friday, the day after Thanksgiving, is our traditional neighborhood trek for our Christmas trees. Pam and Brian had been going for years, when the rest of us decided to follow along with kids, dogs and relatives. The farm loves and encourages our four-footed friends to join in the fun. This year, as usual, Sammy starts whining as our car gets closer to the Christmas tree farm. He knows. He's so smart. That dog knows exactly where we are. Greg barely gets the trunk unlatched when Sam barrels out of the Pilot and begins to run amok. He will fly around here for another hour or so until we find the perfect Christmas tree and load it into Brian's trailer. Sammy will be exhausted for the rest of the day and maybe tomorrow. That's the best part.

The kids dart around looking for a tree, in between taking pictures, playing with Sammy, and swapping old Christmas tree stories. Pam and I scour the farm looking for the perfect tree, while the kids scream out, "How about this one?" It starts to pour. We are getting cold and wet. Our final decision comes quickly and the trees are found, cut and loaded in sixty minutes. Let's go home. Oh, wait. We can't go home quite yet. We have one more tradition to uphold. We must stop for a big old-fashioned breakfast before the drive home. Yum.

By Sunday evening, Max is back at Gonzaga, Anna has had soccer and basketball practices, and Greg has managed to drag our ten-foot tree into the toy room. It's undecorated, but it's standing and soaking up tons of cold water. Yes! We did it and everyone is safe at home. Thank you.

About 10:00 pm the phone rings. It's Ann. Dad has been taken to the hospital by ambulance and she's there with him now.

"What happened?" I ask.

Ann explains, "Dad didn't come down for dinner, which is highly unusual, and when the staff went to check on him, he was lying in pain on his bed. They called an ambulance. Gene, Dane, and I are with Dad at the hospital and we're waiting for the doctor who examined him to come back and tell us what's going on."

While I try to digest this information, "Oh, here he comes now. I'll call you back," Ann blurts out and hangs up the phone.

Greg and I are sitting in bed, waiting to hear back from Ann. I have my pen and paper in hand ready to take notes as soon as she calls. I know from experience that doctors don't stay long, so I am trying to wait patiently to hear back from Ann with the details.

It seems like hours before our phone finally rings. It's Ann. I immediately ask, "Hi, what's going on?"

Ann says, "Dad is awake, coherent, and lying comfortably right here next to me. Remember the medical device implanted in him years ago, for a stomach aneurism? It's leaking. The options are to do nothing or to perform surgery with a less than 50% chance of survival. However, the doctor said that with Alzheimer's and Dad's age, there is a very strong possibility he will not make it through the surgery and if he did, he would most likely have severely decreased mental capacities."

My heart drops.

Ann continues, "Dad and I have talked. He says that he has had a good go and doesn't want surgery."

I can hear him in the background and he is laughing and joking with Dane. He gets a big kick out of Dane and they are constantly bantering back and forth. Ann says Dad is telling Dane, "You better make sure that front lawn is mowed properly because I will be flying over to check your work and make sure you're doing a good job."

Ann hands the phone to Dad and he immediately says to me, "I've had a good go, honey." He's very jovial and I don't make the conversation depressing. Dad would not like that.

"Okay, Dad, I'll fly down tomorrow and see you tomorrow afternoon."

"Sounds good," he says and he hands the phone back to Ann.

"Okay, I'll fly in tomorrow," I tell Ann, "I'll call you with my arrival time. What's Teensie's plan?"

Chapter Twenty-Seven

"She doesn't have one yet. Hang on," Ann whispers.

"Lynn, I had to leave the room. They don't know if he will make it through the night. He's leaking a lot of blood," she says. Both of us struggle to hold it together.

"Okay, I'll get there as soon as I can. Keep me posted." I feel so bad for Ann. She is very strong, but this is hard. Thank goodness, she has Gene and Dane there with her.

Greg immediately books me on the first, available flight leaving tomorrow.

Dad manages to make it through the night and has been carefully moved to hospice care. Apparently, the leaking blood has clotted and is buying all of us a little time. I thank God for the opportunity to arrive in time and be with him before he goes to Heaven. I just hope he can hang on until Teensie arrives tomorrow so that we three are here together with him. He's pretty much out of it due to the pain medications, but is resting comfortably, mostly sedated.

Ann asked her mother-in-law, Joan to pick me up from the airport. Joan drives a little Mercedes convertible and we have just enough room to fit my suitcase and my carry-on in the space behind the two front seats. Unbeknownst to me, Joan drives like a bat out of hell and by the time we get to the hospice, I feel like I have died and been reborn a dozen times. I'm fairly confident the people sharing the road with us feel the same way. I do manage to tell Ann I would rather take a cab next time. She knew exactly what I was talking about and we had a moment of laughter over my near-death experience.

Dad looks good but is heavily drugged. The hospice people are truly amazing. They are so supportive and encouraging. We know what the eventual outcome will be, yet, we hang on to hope in a situation that seems unreal. The hospice nurses encourage us to go home and get some rest. They feel very strongly that he has stabilized for the time being and promise to call immediately if Dad seems to be deteriorating. We are very tired and retreat back to Ann's house. By tomorrow night he will be surrounded by his three daughters. Thank you.

No late night or early morning calls about Dad. He is still hanging in there. I think he's waiting. He is somewhat unresponsive and his breathing is labored, but he is alive when Teensie walks into his room. The three of us spend the afternoon by his bedside. Teensie and I are so thankful we were able to get here in time to see and talk to him. Even though he doesn't answer, I am confident he knows we are here.

On Wednesday afternoon, surrounded by his three daughters, Dad died. It was peaceful. I had the privilege of holding his hand while he took his last breath. What a blessing. Ann stood next to him and Teensie sat in a chair close by. So very sad. He is our last parent. He's our dad. We cry.

The arrangements are easy. We are going to have a celebration of life on Sunday, at the assisted living home where Dad has been for the past two years. Greg is flying down and Ann calls close relatives and friends that should be notified. Everything is set. We'll have a little food, a little drink, and a few stories from family and friends about Dad. He would love to see this. He will probably be watching.

Dad was well liked. On Sunday afternoon, we greet all of his friends from business, golf, his neighborhood, as well as, some long-lost cousins we haven't seen in decades. They have come to pay their last respects. Ann's husband Gene and I share stories, while everyone mingles and parties, all in remembrance of Dad. And believe me, everyone here knows Dad liked a good party. Dad would have enjoyed this.

On Sunday night, I am finally able to hear about Anna's weekend. We chose to have her stay home. She tells us about her Saturday morning soccer game in Burlington, sixty miles north of Seattle. It was a semi-final game with eight teams vying for a berth in the state playoffs next weekend. She says the girls fought hard and it was a very physical game. They won. Anna makes sure to tell me they protected her. A part of me is relieved I wasn't there. She also had a basketball game in Darrington that night. Darrington is seventy miles northeast of Seattle. They lost. Sunday morning, she went back up to Burlington for the last semi-final game with her soccer team. They won. They are one of the top two soccer teams in the state in their age group. She is exhausted. I am relieved it's over and she's safe. Next weekend her soccer team goes to state. Thank goodness, its only thirty minutes south of home. I thank God for watching over her.

When Monday morning rolls around, we say goodbye to Ann and her family and thank her for everything she has done. She has taken care of Dad for the last two years. That made our lives easier. Dad became part of her family. He depended on Ann and loved being with them. Even though it was a lot of work for her, primarily due to the Alzheimer's, I know she would say it was worth it.

Teensie and I fly back home to our families to resume our daily lives. I am sad, happy, tired, and relieved. It's so hard to believe both Mom and Dad are gone. Exactly when did everyone grow up and grow old? I guess the best part of all of this is that our parents raised three girls that will forever stay in touch and be friends. That's an accomplishment. That's a blessing. Mom would have loved to see this. She was the glue. She taught the three of us to be the glue. Thank you, Mom. Goodnight Dad.

Chapter Twenty-Eight

"She still forgets parts of movies she's seen many times"
— Candice Whipple

Monday afternoon I pick Anna up from basketball practice. She's visibly upset.

"What's wrong?" I ask her softly as she fastens her seatbelt.

"Coach announced our starting lineup for the game Wednesday night. I'm not in it," she says with tears in her eyes.

"Honey," I look her straight in the eye and say, "you've worked hard to get yourself conditioned for two sports. You're alive and you're still improving. You've only been back in the games six weeks. You were out of basketball for almost two years. It's okay."

She's very sad. I'm sad because she's sad. We both know how hard she's worked since the day she almost died. First, she battled for survival. Second, she worked diligently to regain her physical and mental faculties. And third, she pushed herself just to get her life back. My heart breaks for her. But, one thing has always been for sure with Anna. That girl has more determination than anyone I know. Anyone.

When we get home, she tells Greg and he comforts her. She won't understand until she's a mom that we're just thankful she's alive. It's a quiet evening.

Anna wakes up Wednesday morning with her game face on. She is wearing her game day outfit including sweats and a Cedar Park Eagle sweatshirt. I kiss her goodbye and tell her, "Dad and I will see you at the game." She may not be starting, but this is a very important day for Anna and for us. Tonight, is her first basketball game since the car accident. She's anxious. I'm worried.

I must admit, when the team comes out and the starting lineup is announced, I feel a little sad. I look across the floor and watch Anna. She is okay. Supportive, cheering, clapping, and quite honestly, excited. A few parents around me turn and ask why Anna isn't starting. One dad said, "I've been to the practices and am surprised she isn't in the starting lineup."

I just say, "She's working hard to regain all of her skills." I feel a little sting in my eyes as the referee tosses the ball in the air and the game begins.

It isn't too long before subs are made and out she trots to the floor. It is low key, but it is a beginning. I can tell she is thrilled to be in the game and her strength and determination shows. She is a little rusty in her delivery, but that is expected. Coach doesn't leave her in too long. Coach is a mom. I think both of us have an unspoken and ongoing worry about Anna's head injury. I certainly do. I want her to play, but I don't want her to be touched by another player. How exactly does that work in basketball? Not very well.

When the final buzzer sounds, we are the victors. The girls played a great game. It's a successful night all around. The team won, Anna played and everyone is safe. No injuries. Thank you. Greg and Anna want to stay for the boy's game. That's no surprise, but I'm mentally and physically spent. Sammy is waiting patiently in the back of my car, so he and I drive home alone. Anna and Greg will come home later in the Volvo. It's been a long day.

Anna is tired and calm when she gets home. She was happy to play but not happy to be a sub. She has basketball practice every day for the rest of the week and a state soccer tournament on Saturday. It's also her 17th birthday this Sunday. Thank goodness, she doesn't have soccer practice during the week. That would be way too much. This is nuts.

Greg and I don't go to Friday night's basketball game. It's quite far away and the girls will go and come home late on the bus. Anna's okay with us not being there, and may even be happy about it. Her attitude is a little bent as of late and I'm not sure what's going on. She's busy with sports, school, and her boyfriend. Parents are an annoyance to be ignored. Or, I would say, used.

Saturday afternoon we sit high on the metal bleachers in a huge stadium in Tukwila, far removed from our usual sideline positions, watching the girls prepare for their most important soccer game of the season. Anna has her phone and calls me from the sidelines. "Do I have any water? Oh, never mind, here's some." Well, at least I know I can contact her from the bleachers if I need to!

It's cold out here, but we haven't seen the wet windstorm that was predicted to hit today. There are some pretty dark clouds looming above and I pray they wait a few hours until this game is over before dousing us. And, there is a slight breeze, but nothing like the weatherman predicted. Let's hope his prediction is late or wrong. Anyone who lives here knows it's not fair to hold the weatherman to his word. When you live near the power of the ocean and all of its inlets, you know the weather can change on a dime.

There is a huge turnout of enthusiastic fans. Most of Anna's teammates attend our local public high school, and their friends are here to cheer them on. Anna knows most of these fans because she started kindergarten with them and still socializes with quite a few of them. It's very exciting. I expect it to be very loud. Good. The Jaguars will love it.

The game begins with the shrill blast of a whistle and a loud roar from the fans. We immediately see that this game is going to be aggressive and physical. There is a fine line between aggressive play, and dangerous play, in soccer.

I am constantly worried about Anna's brain injury. It is always in the back of my mind. Deb Fly had told me that the brain injury may heal completely and Anna may never have another problem with it. Or, if she gets hit again, there could be a huge problem. No one knows. The brain is difficult to read. I am constantly judging myself as her parent. Allowing her to play means I am putting my child, who I love more than life itself, at risk. What mother does that? Yet, not allowing her to play steals important pieces of who she is. That in itself changes her ability to become the person God intended her to be. What mother does that? I pray that the league has its best referees on the field.

The teams attack the ball and their opponent's goal. It is scoreless at halftime. We are barely into the second half when our goalie is hit. She is down on the ground rolling in pain. The referee blows his whistle and Mark runs out to help. Every girl on the field takes a knee, lowering themselves to stop the game. Our injured goalie is not getting up. Within a few minutes, we realize something is very wrong. She's conscious, but in a lot of pain. They help her off the field and her parents load her up and leave for the emergency room. They suspect she has torn her ACL. That's not good.

Each team regroups. Mark puts in our replacement goalie and we are ready. Despite being upset by the injury, the Jaguars pull themselves together, girded for action. The whistle blows. It's intense. The game continues to be a physical match with much pushing and shoving. Of course, it's not one-sided. Both teams are handing out their own fair share of aggressive play. There's another whistle. It's Anna. She's down.

Oh Lord, please. She gets up. Mark pulls her out of the game.

Anna immediately sends me a text, "Do you have any ibuprofen?"

"Why? What's wrong?" is my fearful response.

"I have a headache and I have no ibuprofen. Do you have any water?" she wants to know.

"I don't, but Dad will find some and bring it to you."

Greg takes water to her, both of us hoping her headache is due to dehydration. My mind is racing. We wait and watch. Fifteen minutes go by. Thirty minutes. She still has a headache. Mark can't put her back in and she doesn't want to go back in. The fact that this is the state championship game and Anna doesn't want to go back in because of a headache, clearly tells me she is not healed. She knows it and I know it.

The final whistle blows. The Jaguars are the number two team in the state. Greg and I stand at the stadium gate waiting for the team to come out. They slowly stream by, each one processing the loss differently. When Anna approaches, her eyes well up with tears and she folds herself into my arms sobbing. There's a lot going on here. She loves this team. She couldn't help secure a win. Her friend has been taken to the hospital. Anna's head is still broken. She's scared. She's sad. We just had a huge dose of reality. That's a lot for one afternoon.

We pour her into our back seat and get on the freeway just as the rain begins and the wind picks up. The weather forecaster was right, just a few hours off. Thank you for the delay.

The minute we walk in the door, we feed Anna and give her more ibuprofen. She's so tired. She takes a quick shower and lies down for a rest. It's no surprise she is asleep within minutes. She has her lamby pulled up around her neck and her comforter pulled softly around her body. Thank you, God.

Sunday morning, we congratulate Anna on her 17th birthday. She's had an exhausting two weeks and a very big year. Her headache is gone, but I am watching her like a hawk. We encourage Anna to take it easy this afternoon and allow her body to recover. With me gone to Las Vegas for a week, I had no input over her schedule. She had a brutal two weeks and my mommy flag is waving frantically.

Anna's good friend Amie is also celebrating her 17th birthday this week. Three days apart, those two were born at Swedish hospital and most likely, were in the nursery together. Months ago, Amie's mom Julie and I had made the decision to celebrate their birthdays together this year. We have reservations for both families at the Cheesecake Factory in Bellevue.

At 4:30 pm we load our family into the car and make our way to a long awaited, and well-deserved birthday celebration. Anna feels better and I am calmer. Thank you.

Chapter Twenty-Nine

"I hope God wins"
— Lynn Brown

It's Christmas Day. Our home is full. The smell of bacon and coffee travels through the house and ends in the toy room where empty boxes, wrapping paper and ribbons, are scattered across the floor. Max is resting on the couch, Anna is sitting in the overstuffed comfy chair and Sammy is chewing on his new toy with its hidden cookie pouch. Jazz is trying to eat a curly ribbon, which I snatch away from him, Belle just wants Anna to hug her and Moses won't come in for more than two minutes at a time. We are a pack.

I'm not sure why we are so tired after we open presents and eat breakfast. Every year, the kids fall asleep watching a movie, Greg puts some new thing together and then falls asleep, the animals are exhausted and sleeping in various parts of the house, and I rush to make our bed. This is so I don't crawl back in and get comfy. One year I did get back in bed and slept for hours. Needless to say, that made me more tired and dinner was late. That was stressful. So, I'll try not to do that again this year. Try being the key word. Napping is a great invention.

Around 4:00 pm, Gramma and Grandpa arrive for Christmas dinner. By this time, we are cleaned up, well napped, my mom's bread dressing is made, potatoes are peeled, rolls are ready to bake, and Mr. Turkey is stuffed and in the oven. The house is now filled with the wonderful smells of family and food. I pour myself a flute of cranberry juice and champagne to celebrate the fullness of the day and mark the beginning of our Christmas dinner. Ah, traditions.

Christmas dinner is particularly enjoyable for Max. Compared to dorm food, this is Heaven and he knows there will be lots of leftovers to carry him through the week. He keeps rolling his eyes and smiling. I love that boy. We all love the leftovers. Greg's favorite is a basic turkey sandwich with lettuce, sprinkled with salt and pepper. Oh, and Fritos. My favorite is a turkey sandwich with cranberry sauce, mayonnaise, and a little salt, accompanied by a handful of potato chips. Yes, regular old potato chips. No new and exciting flavors, just the usual potato and salt. I know. Not good for me. But, hey, once in a while won't hurt. Right?

We have the same menu every year and we love it. It's a tradition I am not ready to change. We have turkey with dressing and gravy, mashed potatoes with butter, both jellied and whole cranberries, delicious rolls, and a big vegetable dish. This is way too many carbs and not enough fruits and vegetables, but we have a good protein source! To top off the poor food choices, we have dessert. In a few days, we turn around and do it all over again with a full family celebration at Gramma and Grandpa's house. Nice.

Greg sends Gramma and Grandpa home with a bag of turkey and all the trimmings to make a few sandwiches and carry them over for a couple of dinners. Max and Anna are sprawled out on their beds talking to friends, watching movies and resting. It was a relaxing day and I am sure everyone is quite full and ready for a good night's sleep. Well, I am anyway.

We close out the year with lots of basketball. Anna has practices, a game, and a tournament in Port Townsend. And don't forget the boyfriend. She manages to fit him in any possible moment. He's still a nice kid. She still can't ride in his car.

By the middle of January, the Christmas decorations are down, Anna and Max are both back in school, and I am subbing at the preschool for two weeks.

Anna's attitude is fluid. I never know which personality will be greeting me in the morning. Will it be, "Bye Mom, love you," or will it be, "What? Why are you staring at me?" Thus, we continue with constant conversations and reminders of both our family values and our house rules. For some unexplainable reason, these seem to be new concepts to Anna. She has known what our values and house rules are for her entire life, but now, they appear to be new in every sense of the word. Sometimes I want to burst out laughing and say to her "Really?" in hopes she will start laughing too. But I can recognize a challenge when I see one and this is one challenge she will carry through to the end. Whether it's about going to church, staying out late on a school night, or wanting to disappear every weekend, we are thrown into a constant battle of the wills. So, what's the solution? If I had an answer to this question, I would become the first person in the history of parenting to figure out what to do with teenage attitude. Greg and I rely on consistency, honesty, love, discipline, and prayer.

Anna understands right from wrong and she knows our values and rules. What she's trying to do is figure out her own values and rules as they relate to her upbringing. I think. In any case, she's making life very stressful around the old homestead. Nothing we can't handle, even though I do scream into my pillow on occasion, or, maybe daily. Remaining calm and having a poker face is also good, though I have been known to sob uncontrollably while trying to have a conversation with her. I am just trying to do my best, whatever that means.

We are happy Anna is busy with school and sports. This Saturday she takes her first SAT exam. Once we see how she does, we'll see if she needs help in any subject and then we'll schedule her second SAT exam, with her final SAT to be taken in the fall, at the beginning of her senior year. She is starting to think about college and where she may want to go. Her boyfriend is, did I mention, a year older, and planning on going to WSU. From this parent's perspective, at this age, the best boyfriends live hundreds of miles away. I like that.

We don't hear much from Max. What a surprise. We call and check in with him a couple of times a week, faking reasons to ask him something. He's having a great time and getting a terrific education in the mix. Gonzaga is perfect for him and he is succeeding both personally and academically. I do call with a real question once in a while. Today I asked him if he was interested in going with Anna and I, to New Orleans in June on our church mission trip. I already knew the answer, but it was worth a try. He said, "No thanks."

"How about helping with Vacation Bible School?"

Again, "No thanks."

Well, for crying out loud. That kid!

Anna continues to work towards getting back into the starting lineup. She looks better and stronger every game. Her coordination has dramatically improved and she is almost back to her old self. She is slowly clawing her way to the top of the pile and it doesn't appear as though anything will stop her. The therapists at Children's are right. She's unbelievably motivated. I already knew that, but to see her continually battle her way forward is impressive. She has three games this week and the last one is with Cedar Park's biggest rival. She's on pins and needles. She's prepared herself and she's looking for success.

The first game is an easy win for the team. Anna subbed a lot and had a great game. It was a good game for her to rotate in and out of. She had lots of play time.

The second game was also a win, although not quite as easy as the first. Anna got a lot of playing time again and is giving it all she's got.

On Friday morning, Anna leaves for school dressed in her basketball garb. With tomorrow afternoon being a huge game for the team, she's a little preoccupied with getting through school today and preparing for the contest. I go about my morning routine when the phone rings. "Hello?"

Anna's voice is high pitched and she's talking ninety miles an hour. "Mom!" she screams, "I'm starting tomorrow!"

There's a pause. My first concern, given her shrill voice, is that she's okay. I grab my car keys, ready to go. I peel myself off the ceiling, realizing what she said. I put the car keys down and take a breath. She's waited and worked a long time for this and I am ecstatic for her victory.

"Oh, Anna, that's awesome. Congratulations!" I scream back into the phone.

"Tell Dad, I gotta go."

"Drive safe." I manage to blurt out before she hangs up.

When I hang up the phone, I have a rush of mixed feelings. When your children are seriously injured and they live through it, a parent's immediate reaction is to nurture and protect. Well, it's mine anyway and I don't pretend to think these are unique reactions. For the last fifteen and one-half months, I have engaged every part of my body to support and protect Anna. I had no control over keeping her safe playing soccer and I have once again lost control over her playing basketball. Only prayer works. I have to hand it over to God again.

Tomorrow's game is against the toughest team in the league. This is, of course when I ask myself, again, "What kind of parent am I to allow my child to be put in harm's way?" Then I ask myself, "What kind of parent would I be if I placed fear in the heart of my child?" Do I replace living with living in fear? This discussion has no answer. The answer is to pray. I run to Greg's office and give him the good news. He smiles. He knows this is a victory. Anna's knocking on the doorstep of her normal.

The band is playing and the teams are on their respective benches waiting for the announcer to get things started. It's a home game, which is great, because the announcer is well acquainted with every girl on our team and with Anna's struggle to get back to her normal self. He begins his introduction, followed by the national anthem and then a prayer for both teams to have a safe game. Jumping from one team to the other, he announces the starting lineup for tonight's game. When he announces, "Anna Brown", my eyes fill with tears. I can't be too obvious about my excitement, because in reality Anna replaced another girl who also worked hard to make the starting team. Her parents are in the bleachers and they are dealing with a disappointed daughter tonight. However, many parents begin commenting to me that they are glad to see Anna back in the mix. One parent of a senior player grumbled, "About time." But, I must say, at Cedar Park, the philosophy is about much more than winning. It's about supporting, caring about each other, and being a team. It's about right versus wrong, behavior, character, and teaching the girls to be good people. Ultimately, that trumps the position or the win.

Anna plays hard. She's so competitive. Tonight, she is in full throttle. It's a battle, but at the end of the game, the score board doesn't lie. We lose. But, Anna had a victory and for that I am thankful. She's safe. Both teams are safe. It's a basketball game.

Anna remains a starter in game after game. After weeks of regulation play, the team makes it to the league playoffs. Our first game is against our second biggest competitor. It will be tough. One loss and you're out.

On a rainy Tuesday night in the middle of February, we sit in our opponent's gym, full of excitement and school spirit, waiting for our chance to advance towards state. It's all on the line. The competition has one girl that scores most of their points. She's short, she's fast, and she weaves in and out of traffic like a pro. This girl rarely misses when given the chance to shoot. She's their ticket to state.

The girls position themselves on the floor and up the ball goes. The game begins with intensity. Anna is guarding their best player. Yes, their short, fast, point-making machine. Our girls are not intimidated. They fight for the right to advance in the finals. Anna is on fire. She is shutting down her target and our opponent is rapidly losing the ability to score. Time is closing in on the end of this game. At the final buzzer, we are the victors. The entire team worked together to succeed. Anna contributed. The girls are elated.

We have another victory followed by a defeat. We are out. No state for this team. The girls retire their jerseys until next fall. I can stop worrying about injuries for a while. We are done temporarily. My body relaxes.

Wait, not so fast. Now that basketball is over, Anna has lots of time on her hands. This is not necessarily a good thing. Her attitude is still a touch defiant. She wants to spend her time on open afternoons and evenings with her friends and her boyfriend. Max rarely argued with the no going out during the week on a school night rule, yet Anna seems to think it is optional. For Anna, we have to clarify what is meant by going out on a school night. Let's see. School activities are great, evening dates are not, meeting friends for homework or treats is fabulous, staying out past 9:00 pm not happening, and keeping your grades up for college is imperative. Anna delivers a volatile and argumentative response. We must be terrible parents. Where's my pillow? It's time to scream.

Thank goodness mid-winter break arrives. Lisa and I take Anna, Katy, and Amie to Arizona for seven days. No rain. Just a huge dose of sunshine. The girls will most likely sleep all day. They're too young to drive the rental car. This is good and bad, but 99% great. Our first night here, it's late and they want to go out. We are barely in the door when the begging begins. Lisa finally looks at them and says, "Girls, we just got here. We are having dinner here. It's late. We'll go out and play tomorrow night." There's a little mumbling, but that is pretty much the end of the subject for the night. Thank you, Lisa. I don't always have to be the one who sucks the life out of the word fun!

We shop, lie in the sun, watch movies, shop some more, and let the girls sleep most of their days away. We have a few minor issues with attitude, but for the most part, the vacation is nice and relaxing. The minute we arrive home, Anna wants to go out and see her friends. I should have booked a flight that got in at midnight. That would have solved the problem! Hindsight. It's not the saying no I have a problem with. It's the exhaustion of the ensuing argument that wears me out. Both my husband, thank you so much, and Anna have pointed out to me that no is my go-to word. My mom always said maybe. Perhaps we should settle with let me think about it.

Max comes home for his spring break the day after we get back from Arizona. I love that he came home and so does Jazz. He's thrilled to have his boy home and is making sure Max knows how much he misses him. I miss Max, too. He's sort of the stabilizer these days. Max never really causes an uproar in the family and, while he is still a man of few words, just having him home and hanging out is comforting. It's good for Anna to have her brother home and to be able to talk to someone she loves during her downtime. Well, if she will allow herself any downtime! But, they do manage to spend a few late evenings swapping stories and filling each other in on the latest news of their lives. Good. Thank you.

The week flies by quickly. While Max relaxes, eats, sleeps, and visits his friends, Anna spends her days in school and her nights pushing the house rules to their breaking point. The girl is a junior and she is a handful. Now, I must say, this is all relative. For as much pillow screaming and unrest that occurs, we are not in any serious trouble. As far as I know. No life-altering behaviors with a string of poor choices attached to them. As far as I know. But, we're not done and the other shoe hasn't dropped yet. From all accounts, it appears that Anna's behavior is quite normal. As far as I know. Greg and I are new. We are new parents to this new child. We are doing our best to stay on top of it. I'm strict. We have expectations. Kids need guidelines. So far, so good. As far as I know.

When Max heads back to Gonzaga, Jazz and I sit on his bed and chat. Jazz is a great listener. He never talks back to me and purrs through my entire conversation. It's refreshing. When I'm all talked out, I pull the sheets off the bed to wash them and Jazz falls asleep on Max's mattress. It's Sunday, it's quiet. Everyone is just relaxing. So far.

Sunday night I peek at my calendar. The week is filled with commitments. Anna has an appointment with the dermatologist, I have an appointment with the dentist, and the kitties are going in for their shots. Sprinkle all of that with a church dinner on Wednesday night, Bible study Friday morning, a Costco run, Anna's belated soccer team party here on Friday night, cousin Alina's harp recital on Saturday and our bedroom drapes being installed on Sunday. Lots going on.

With just three weeks until Easter break, life is filled with activity while we prepare for our much-needed Hawaiian vacation. We receive Anna's SAT results. They're pretty darn good. This is very exciting. Another indication of how well her brain is healing. She does want to raise her SAT score, so we call the same man that tutored Max, and get him lined up to help Anna when we get back from Hawaii. This week she has the PSAT's at school, followed by the Junior Senior Banquet on Saturday night. She is going with her boyfriend. Let's hope Saturday is a fun, relaxed day. However, these big school events have been known to turn even the nicest, most soft-spoken girl into a crazed beauty queen. One local high school decided these events are so out of control and the kids are so stressed out by the time the event begins, that they declared the party be held after one of their football games, in the gym, with pizza. It was a huge hit with the kids and a great relief to the parents. I like that school. I remind myself to stay calm. I'm not new to this day. After the third entitled plea for a manicure and pedicure, I tell Anna to talk to her dad. Little does she know that Greg and I have already discussed this day. He's not new either. Greg is very generous with Anna and gives in to her more times than I would like. He knows, however, that by the time you get the dress, the accessories, the hair, the shoes, the stockings, and the bill, it is no longer a small event. It's nearing the cost of a weekend vacation. It's nuts and by the end of the day it's not fun for anyone. Well, at least not for the exhausted, stressed out, and might I add, unappreciated mom. Yes, the same mom who said the expensive dress is fabulous and we will splurge this one time. Oh, and those accessories are a little expensive, but okay. And finally, don't you have those shoes at home? I do believe everyday opens with hope. By early afternoon my hopes are quickly dashed and crisis looms like a cloud over the upstairs bathroom as the sound of sobbing making its way down the hall.

I carefully enter the bathroom, look at my red-eyed daughter and ask what's wrong. Between the fits of gasping sobs, I hear the word hair. Yes, at the last minute, the lady that was to do her hair is running late. So late, in fact, that there would not be enough time to get Anna's hair done and get ready for the evening. Tears. Lots and lots of tears. I look at Anna and say, "I may have a solution!" She doesn't believe me, nonetheless, I run down the hall and call Lisa. We need reinforcements. Even though Anna's hair looks so much better when she does it herself, this is not the time to tell her.

Lisa answers the phone and I explain the situation to her. She says, "Tell Anna we will be right there!" Lisa grabs Katy, Anna's new hairdresser, and arrives in minutes, loaded with bobby pins, curling irons, assorted hair products, and a bottle of wine. Katy boldly enters the bathroom. Laughter is soon flowing out of the bathroom while hair is being neatly curled and sprayed. When Katy is finished, Anna's hair looks more beautiful than any other event hairdo she has worn and we agree it looks natural and fabulous. Since everyone is now in a much lighter frame of mind, I recount my own high school hair story, that still horrifies me to this day--good choice. Even Anna laughs. Yes!

I get my own hair done on Monday. For a little over an hour, no one needs anything or says anything stressful to me. Vicky and I laugh and catch up with our latest stories about our kids and lives. It's wonderful. It's therapeutic. It buoys me for the day. Thank you.

Monday was so relaxing, that I manage to ignore conflict all week. This is not like me. But, Hawaii is just a few days away, and I ask myself, "Why leave for vacation upset?" Max gets home on Thursday night and is staying through the weekend. Gonzaga is a Jesuit Catholic school and gives the students Monday and Friday off to spend Easter with their families. Unfortunately, this year, we are leaving tomorrow morning and Max will be home alone for Easter. He's okay though. He just wants to sleep.

On Friday morning, I jump out of bed and take Sammy to his nanny's house for the week. Thank goodness Pam agreed to take care of our kitties once Max goes back to school. That is, admittedly, a frustrating job. Yet, Pam handles it for me and makes sure they are all in at night and safe. She has no idea what a relief it is for me, knowing the kitties are well cared for.

We hug Max goodbye and leave for the airport. Eight hours later we land in Hawaii leaving behind rainy days and wet pavement. It's hot and beautiful here. This is just what we need.

Sunday morning Greg and I stroll along the ocean path, with Anna and friend in tow, to experience Easter's sunrise service on the beach. It's funny how getting up early on vacation is different than getting up early at home. There is no complaining. No attitude. Thank you. We round the corner of the lava path, seeing a small gathering of guests on a little hill accompanied by hula dancers and a trio of musicians playing Hawaiian music. What an incredible setting. Easter service with the backdrop of the Pacific Ocean. It is beautiful. The guests, the dancers, the pastor, and the musicians are swaying in the breeze. We near the gathering and receive a cream-colored paper with the service outline written in both English and Hawaiian. The kids love this. The service is calming and fulfilling. Amazing Grace is the final hymn and we make our way back home. We walk quietly for a moment to take in the beauty and uniqueness of the morning. Of course, silence doesn't last long. Everyone is starving. The conversation turns to breakfast and how soon it will be ready once we reach the villa. Okay, so a moment of reflection is better than nothing and I must admit my stomach is growling, too. Our slow walk home turns into a fast clip and sooner than later we are inhaling eggs, bacon, toast, and coffee! Reality.

Hawaii is a slower pace. It occurs to me that regardless of where you are, vacation or home, it is always a wonderful surprise to have moments of nothingness. They are rare, especially for an active family. Quite frankly, what makes them so special is that there aren't many of them. We are a very active and involved family. Sports, church, work, and school have dominated our lives for years and I wouldn't have it any other way. However, you look up to take a breath in a moment of nothingness and you realize your babies aren't babies anymore and somehow you have shaped these little creatures into young adults. Then you start asking yourself, "Have I missed anything? Have I taught them well? Are there any other tidbits of information I want them to know?" The realization that your daily parenting career is coming to an abrupt halt can be a revelation. There is nothing left except to turn them loose. In my case, loose with strings or, better yet, ropes and a pulley. I give them to God. He takes them. Then, I wrestle to get them back. It's an ongoing discussion. I hope God wins. The girls want to go back to bed after breakfast. However, they inform us, they want an adventure after their morning nap. We decide the pool is our adventure today and as soon as they wake up, they can go for a swim, or in their case, go on a boy watching and tanning adventure. I grab a book and head for the beach. I saw this little Adirondack chair sitting atop the mound of sand where the church service was this morning. It's calling my name. Bye Greg.

Alone time is important to me. When I plunk myself down in that chair, the stress I am carrying seeps right out and drifts off to attach itself elsewhere. For two hours, I watch the turtles, read, watch the turtles, talk to God, watch the turtles, pray, read some more, and watch the turtles. Greg appears at my little oasis and tells me the girls are still asleep. No surprise there. He is going to work out at the gym while I commune with nature a little longer. I ask him to stop by on his way back to the villa and I will walk with him along the winding black lava path. An hour later, he returns to pick me up and I load up my belongings, leaving my little chair sitting quietly in the sand. Yes, I've claimed it. It's mine.

We hear movement when we reach the front door. The girls are up and ready to go to the pool. Wanting nothing to do with parents, they are out the door and off to the pool with towels, flip-flops, cover-ups, tee shirts, phones, keys, tissues, sunscreen, magazines, books, and water. They look like they're going on a weekend hike, except for the bikinis. Well, at least they won't have to come back to the villa for anything. It's not possible they have left anything important behind.

After days at the pool, a trip to the volcanoes, a drive around the island, and many trips to the coffee stand in the golf cart, it's the end of the week. We sit in the warm breeze of the Kona airport and wait to board our flight and fly back home. It was fun. We had a few bumps, but not many. Lots of time was spent walking, reading, turtle watching, sunbathing, and finding our own spot. All in all, a very relaxing vacation. For me, there is truly no place like home. I can't wait to get Sammy home and wake up tomorrow morning in my own bed. That's Heaven on earth to me.

Chapter Thirty

"She has subsequently shown a very good recovery"
— Neuropsychologist at the UW Medical school

Attitude, attitude, attitude. Anna's whole life has been big. She's full of spunk, character, fun, and as a teenager, full of herself. It's tough. She has more wants than Max could ever dream of. But, I find it's not the wants as much as it is the deserves. Her generation may go down in history as the entitled and deserving generation. Somewhere there has to be a silver lining. I think. We did manage to dodge the grunge era. While each generation has its own style, I'll never forget seeing our beautiful little neighbor girl walking up the hill on her way home from junior high school with ripped, torn jeans shredded at the hem from being walked on with filthy black-bottomed bare feet. She looked like she needed to take a bath and wash her clothes. I know that era has its followers, but I'm glad as a mom, that I didn't have to deal with the hygiene and safety issues pursuing the grunge look. Thank you.

Amidst listening and trying to understand what goes on in the mind of a seventeen-year-old girl, the conclusions can be confusing. Thus, I choose to periodically take myself back to my high school years and try to recall how I felt at that time. Mind you this is not done in front of my daughter, but in private conversations with my mom who is looking down on me, laughing I'm sure. I do remember blaming my mom for anything that upset me. If I had problems with friends, I was irritated with Mom. If I woke up with a pimple, I was irritated with Mom. If I was in a bad mood, I was irritated with Mom. So, I get it. As Anna's mom, I'm irritating. My mere presence can be a problem. So, I ask myself how I feel about that. I laugh because actually, I feel fine. Being a mom means you're a teacher and an example. She's not going to get me to perma-nently crumble. Well, not yet anyway! I will stay the course with love, discipline, and prayer. Anna knows I love her. I know Anna loves me. She knows she loves me. At least we are clear on the issue of love. And, as the old saying goes, love conquers all. Right? Let's hope that's the case.

We get a brief reprieve from high school angst when May rolls around. Yay! Max is coming home for the summer. Greg, Anna, and I drive over to Spokane for the weekend and pick him up. Boy has he accumulated a lot of stuff. I can't believe he is already through one year of college. Wow. It will be great to have him home.

Max has his summer job lined up and is excited to get started and make some money. It doesn't start until the middle of June because he is working with kids and sports camps. The camps don't begin until the kids are out of school and that date seems to get later and later every year. In the meantime, we have hired him to help with some projects around the house and Greg is going to have him do some analytical reports for one of his clients. I know Max will save almost every penny of his paycheck. Max is great about finances. He knows what he saves this summer will be his entertainment money for next year. And Heaven knows he and his friends enjoy their entertainment!

When we get back home and unload all of Max's stuff, we find his room isn't equipped to handle all of his belongings. We fill containers with his stuff and stash them under the bed, in the guest room closet, and any place else we can find a nook or a cranny. It's amazing he fit all of this in his dorm room. I'm not really sure how he did that!

After a few days of rest and relaxation, I am ready to get Max started on our home improvement projects. But, committing to doing something and actually doing it can be two different animals. It's interesting how your own child will happily help others with a smile and a thank you, yet, at home we offer money, lunch, and convenience, only to be met with irritation and prolonged procrastination. I love that boy. He hates yard work. But, it's a life lesson. You commit to it, you do it.

Going from two kids living at home, to one, then back to having two kids living at home, is quite the adjustment. Who would have guessed? Max is in and out with his friends. He's really great about checking in with us and making sure we know where he is and if he's safe. The thing about Max is that he's usually home by midnight and he loves to sleep in his own bed. Bonus.

Anna, on the other hand, is not so accommodating. She has one month left in her junior year, still has the same boyfriend, keeps busy with friends, tries to break the weekday curfew time and calls at midnight on weekends to ask for an extension to stay out past midnight. It's exhausting. Literally. Thank goodness, our mission trip is coming up at the end of June. New Orleans can't come fast enough. The Mexico trip was an eye opener and gave Anna an appreciation for her lifestyle and, I think, for her life as an American. New Orleans will be a different experience. It's in the United States. I can't wait to see what this brings to all of us.

We hobble through the next month with Max working for Greg and doing a few projects for me. Anna finishes her school year and is offered a job as a nanny for two young girls from church. They love her and she loves them. It's a perfect fit. This will keep her busy and give her a little extra spending money. Good job Anna.

Max has his first week of working with the kids' sports camps while Anna and I head out for our mission trip. Finally, Greg will get some sleep and a reprieve from the late-night phone calls from his darling daughter. Secretly, I know he's thrilled as he kisses us goodbye and sends us off for seven days.

Arriving in New Orleans with the same group we traveled with to Mexico is easy for the entire group. We get along and are familiar with each other's habits. Hope Lutheran has organized this trip, forgoing Mexico this year due to a sharp increase in danger to outsiders. Personally, I would not have gone back anyway. Staying in the United States is a much better idea, and I believe it's important to help those in need in our own country. The kids are just as happy to be here, and are excited to help those that were devastated by Hurricane Katrina.

The New Orleans sky is half blue and half black. These are really dark clouds. I signed up to be one of our three van drivers. I can't stand to drive in bad weather. I am forced to put my fear aside and play follow the leader as we leave the airport and make our way to our residence for the next week. We no sooner get on the freeway, when off in the distance we see bolts of lightning and sheets of rain pounding the distant horizon. I pray while I drive, wanting to get to our destination before this weather hits us. It's not helping that our lead driver, and mission leader, drives like a bat out of hell. Fortunately, we have walkie-talkies and I radio him to slow down. He does and we eventually arrive simultaneously at our destination, all three vans intact. We barely make it out of the car when the rain begins to pelt us. I smile. Thank you.

We are staying at a Lutheran church that has converted itself into a headquarters for mission teams. After Hurricane Katrina hit New Orleans in 2005, people came from all over the world to help. This church provides a place for organized teams to stay. The facility has large bunk rooms, a huge cafeteria, a fellowship and game area, a huge yard that houses equipment, and a wonderful group of Christian men and women to support the mission volunteers. It's really something. People are amazing.

The girls in our group set out to explore the sleeping areas and decide to take up residence in the second, of two, large bunk rooms available for girls only. It is currently unoccupied. The boys have a huge room of their own at the end of the hall. We each put our bags on a bed and get ourselves acclimated to the area. The girls picked the far corner of the room and tucked our little group into a nice, neat little space. It seems perfect. We're not sure how many other mission teams are coming from around the country, but we are certain we will not be alone by the end of the day.

A large group from the Midwest shows up after dinner and puts their bags on the beds surrounding our little group. Another group arrives and our bunk room is full of kids and adults waiting to venture out tomorrow and help the communities rebuild their lives. It's very exciting. We have a meeting and breakfast at the crack of dawn, to be followed by our assignments. Our hosts suggest lights out at 10:00 pm in order to get enough rest to be up and ready by 7:00 am. That means most of the girls will get up around six in the morning. This will be interesting. It will be a full day.

We turn everything out and off at 10:00 pm. One of the adult leaders of the group next to us doesn't think the suggested bedtime applies to her. She continues to engage her girls in conversation and laughter, keeping the entire room awake. This goes on for about an hour until one of our girls gathers up her sleeping bag and leaves the bunk room. At that point, I politely ask the other group to stop talking, as they are keeping all of us awake and we have a very full day tomorrow. The leader from the Midwest group quiets down. Temporarily. She starts up again, in a more muffled voice, within five minutes. I continue to ask them to be quiet. No go. Rude. Needless to say, we did not have a restful night's sleep.

Our group decides we should move into the first bunk room if they have room. We stop by in between breakfast and our meeting to see if there is space for us. There is. There is also a group of girls in there that are very nice and thrilled to have us. We quickly gather our things and transfer ourselves to the first bunk room. The Midwest leader asks me why we are leaving. I am not surprised that she had no idea given her lack of concern for others. In front of her team leaders and her girls, I tell her there is more space in the other bunk room and quite frankly, her group was too noisy and kept us all from sleeping. The truth is the truth.

We are excited to get our day started. The mission groups are divided into work parties to paint, tile, clean up, or somehow restore selected homes and areas. Each group will load into a designated van and spread out to different locations to work. Anna and I are in different groups. I would love to work with her, but she is simply not in the same mindset as I am. It's okay. That's what part of this trip is for.

We know the South is famous for its combination of heat and humidity. We are dripping wet before we even meet at the shed to collect our tools for our project today. No one is actually perspiring, yet we have moisture dripping from our bodies. It's a whole new experience. The kids are great about it. They just want to work and help. Thank you.

Our first job will be quite an eye opener. We are going to a house that was flooded during Hurricane Katrina and is in need of cleaning, painting, and retiling. The way the rebuild has been set up is great. Home owners are given an account at Home Depot. My understanding is that Home Depot actually built their store to participate in this program. Don't know that for a fact, but that's what we have been told. Then, the homeowner uses their account to purchase what they need to restore their houses. Smart. No direct money to anyone, forcing the finances to go to the rebuilding of property. Volunteers from around the country, and maybe the world, come to work. Sometimes a project can be held up if a home is waiting for a professional, like an electrician or a plumber. But, overall, volunteers clean, paint, tile and do yard work to get the house ready for its family to return. Occasionally the homeowner will work alongside the volunteers, but that may not be possible if they work during the day. In any case, the homeowner has chosen the materials we are working with and when they finally move back in, their house is restored with their own choices.

By the time we get to our job, we have collected tools and been to Home Depot to fill our list of supplies specific to this project. We pile out of the van and are met with a smile and the project coordinator from the facility we are staying in. He's been on this house for a while and is ready for us to finish the final touches. We get lucky. The owner stops by on her lunch hour. She is very thankful and excited to move back in. It's only a matter of weeks now, not years. This is very uplifting for the kids and for the rest of us. The heat and our soaking wet clothes become funny. We roll up our jeans and the girls tie up their tee shirts and gather up their sleeves. On a mission trip, it is important to represent yourself and your church in a modest fashion, so we have been given fairly strict dress codes. Mexico was even more stringent. We could only wear shirts with sleeves and long skirts. So, this is nothing as the kids throw themselves into their projects to finish this house for the family.

We paint three rooms, disinfect and paint the bathroom, and prep the living room floor for tiling. We get a lot done. Before returning to the church, our driver takes us on a tour of the neighborhood. It's quite shocking to see the devastation caused by Katrina. Even though it has been four years, there are still abandoned homes, with plants growing out of the roof and windows, their seeds deposited by the water that swept and retreated across the rooftops. There are missing doors, windows, roofs, and siding. But, most saddening are the crosses, or X's, and notes on the doors. Notes left by separated family members pinned to the empty door frames, looking for each other and leaving contact information. The X's are another story. Almost every house we see has an X. We come to understand that if you read each quadrant clockwise starting from the top, the quadrants tell their own story. The top quadrant starts with the date and maybe the time the house was searched. The right side carries a message left by the searcher of no entry or other. The bottom quadrant gives a count of those found dead in the home and the final quadrant on the left contains the identity of the team that searched the house. So sad. So sobering. It is at this point that the reality of Hurricane Katrina, and its aftermath enters the minds of our team.

People help each other heal. That's the way we are made. Compassion is a human character trait. Not everyone chooses to embrace this trait. Not everyone chooses to help others. That is a human fault. Every one of us has chosen at some point in time to tear another person down. We don't think about others sometimes. But today our little group chooses to lift someone up and hopefully we will remember for the rest of our lives to lift up each other. Whether it's a kind word, a compliment, or simply the holding of one's tongue, it is better to lift up than to pull down. Amen. Thank you.

Our own group meets after dinner. We have choices for the remainder of the week. We can continue to work on homes, help out an old church in downtown New Orleans with Vacation Bible School, or spend some time at our home camp keeping it organized and up to par. Our kids are a wonderful group of human beings. Since we have three groups among us, they want to take one more day to finish what they started in the houses, then branch out and send each group to a different area of need. We will have one full afternoon to sightsee, as well as a few evenings and late afternoons. We plan to capitalize on all of our time in New Orleans with both helping to rebuild homes and being tourists.

However, tonight we are spent. Tomorrow is a full day and we are going to the French Quarter tomorrow night. We put our showered bodies in bed, thankful we switched our sleeping arrangements, and our entire roomful of women is fast asleep soon after the lights go out. What a great day. Thank you.

We clean up and head into town after a full day of tiling, putting up blinds, and finishing our painting jobs. The French Quarter is everything we heard it would be. Shops, nightclubs, back alley parties, skeletons, hints of Voodoo, and beignets. Okay, I had never heard of a beignet before. They're like a full fluffy donut smothered in powdered sugar. And they're served on a round plate with large quantities of them piled on top of each other. We don't have them at home thank goodness. Anna and I both would be in deep trouble. Good heavens. They're deadly. Delicious, but definitely deadly.

Each group wants to see different things along the main drag. We chaperones have our work cut out for us. After all, this in New Orleans and we are in unfamiliar territory. It wouldn't be the first time one of our kids found a way to get into trouble. So, a guiding eye is best as I walk around with a bunch of young women, including Anna. She's been pretty good with me today. So far. An older girl from our church has spent a lot of time with Anna. She told to me Anna would grow out of her attitude towards me. She said she went through the same thing with her mom. She even talked to Anna about it. I think that helped both of us.

We get up early Wednesday morning, eat breakfast, and drive to an inner-city Lutheran Church to help out with Vacation Bible School. This church is old and huge. It's in an area that has become very run down and impoverished. It's obvious the homes were, at one time, a beautiful example of Southern architecture. We see glimpses of original woodwork, leaded windows, huge front porches and large receiving rooms. We come to understand these houses are the homes of most of the VBS students we will be meeting today. As the kids, ranging from elementary age to high school age, stream into the Sanctuary, I see that some are excited, some not so much and others have been forced to come. Just like kids at any other church. It makes me laugh. In front of me sits a group of teenage girls. Years ago, this would have been a daunting group for me to deal with. Not now. I am raising Anna Brown. I have valuable experience. I'm ready.

The church itself used to have over five hundred members. It is led by a very young and eager vicar and his wife. He tells us he started serving a weekly barbeque dinner when he first came, about a year or so ago. At first, no one came. Now, people in the neighborhood come. It sounds like he's helping people through the doors. I hope so. Church changes our Sunday. God changes our lives.

After the church opener, we break into groups. Most of our girls want to work with the middle school and younger kids while our boys take on all ages. I go with the teenage girls. They're tough. But, you know, they're just looking for love. Like every other kid their age, they want to be re-spected and loved. I break into their little circle over against the wall. They're not particularly happy to have me because they really don't want to be here. I sit down with them anyway and let the day unfold.

Hours later, we are exhausted and happy to have spent our day at a beautiful old church full of kids and fun activities. The little ones were thrilled. They had a craft hour, were carried around piggyback style, sang songs, were taught games, and did a little teaching of their own. A couple of the VBS girls showed Anna how to perfect a few of her dance moves. It was hilarious. The bigger kids were outside playing relay games, and at one point the boys played flag football. They did participate in the crafts and singing, though they were much happier outside. It turned out to be a great experience for us and, hopefully, for them too. We want to come back. They have a trip planned on Friday to the aquarium. Some of the kids have never been and since the Vicar is looking for chaperones, we volunteer. It's been a great day again. Thank you.

We see the Mississippi River and some of the surrounding neighbor-hoods on Thursday morning. We see churches, homes, and land that has been flooded by Hurricane Katrina and still carries the scars from the forces of destruction. We include a trip to Chalmette Battlefield where General Andrew Jackson defeated the British during the Battle of New Orleans towards the end of the War of 1812. I think to myself how time does heal most wounds. The United States and Great Britain are strong allies today. It's comforting to think of the possibilities of healing. Thank you.

We make our way to the Lower 9th Ward after lunch. All we see is flat land, weeds, and a few newly constructed homes. This is the area where actor Brad Pitt's Make It Right Foundation is building elevated homes to protect them from the damage caused by rushing waters. We pull the vans over in front of an occupied new home. The homeowner comes out to greet us and he turns out to be one of the pioneers of this project. His stories of loss are heart breaking. His grandchild was swept from the roof of their home while they were waiting to be rescued. I don't know how you survive that. I hope he is a man of faith. When he finishes talking about the losses of both himself and his neighbors, he makes a point of focusing on the rebuilding of the Lower 9th Ward. We are hanging onto his every word and trying to understand what happened. We want to know.

He explains that Hurricane Katrina was so forceful she engorged the Mississippi River and Lake Pontchartrain with walls of water. Levees crumbled and finally gave way, sending surging water into the Industrial Canal. The waves were so powerful, they lifted a tethered barge and threw it across the Lower 9th Ward. The barge basically scraped anything and anyone in its path off the land. We are standing here with tears in our eyes and our mouths open. Speechless. But, this man is a realist and an optimist. He won't be held down. He lifts us back up with his stories of reseeding, rebuilding, and moving back into his neighborhood. He loves the new houses and appreciates the help and gifts that have been given to New Orleans. He insists on leaving us with the feeling of hope and the knowledge that life goes on.

I'm glad we came. I'm glad Anna is here. You can see the wheels turning. We have a new understanding of what these people have been through. I wish Greg and Max could be here to. It's a life changer. We rest our heads on our pillows saying prayers for everyone we met and for those we will never meet.

Well, it's Friday morning, and here we go to the New Orleans Aquarium. We wake up ready to take on the day, and the VBS kids. We load up our vans and drive our crew to the aquarium to meet the arriving carloads of excited VBS kids. It's confusing at first trying to find the kids and locate our entrance into the building. We connect and get ourselves organized into groups with chaperones. In we go. It's immediately engaging. This is a great aquarium. Lot's to see. The VBS kids want their pictures taken in front of the many glass windows while sea creatures swim behind them. It's a privilege to see the smiles on these kids as they wander through this magnificent building, learning and seeing many things for the first time in their lives. Lot's to remember. Thank you.

I am glad to get home to Greg and Max. So is Anna. We're lucky to have us. Max's work is going well and Anna starts her nanny job on Tuesday. We are back to our regular life. We're very fortunate. Thank you.

It doesn't take long for Anna to slide into, yet another, difficult phase. I must have been lulled into a happy place to think this was over. Boy was I wrong. She's disrespectful, confrontational, demanding and not very much fun to be around. Now, I must say, she's only like that when she's not pleasant, happy, kind, caring, and talkative. Apparently, we have two Annas living with us. I much prefer the second Anna. I actually think she does too. It's just that she hasn't figured that out yet. So, we continue to have rules, be parents, and talk to her when the timing is in our favor. She's much more receptive to conversation at night. It may start out with accusations and confrontations, but Greg is a master at getting to the point without emotion. I think a man is best at that, especially if it's a mother-daughter thing. I try to wait my turn to join in. Try. Sometimes she says the weirdest stuff and I am forced to reply. For some reason, her issues with life are my fault. I must be the root of her evil. For all her kicking and screaming, she still tells me she loves me and still confides in me on occasion. I can't wait until the two Annas meld into one, hopefully the second one. She really is a fabulous kid. When I watched her in New Orleans with the kids and the group she was open and fun and lovely to be around. Finally, I write her a poem and put it up on the chalk board.

It is titled "Kipsy Brown." I can't remember why I started calling her Kipsy, but it has stuck for years.

Kipsy Brown
There once was a girl, Kipsy Brown
Who didn't know if to laugh or to frown
Every evening such a surprise
Her parents sure felt their demise
Yet knew at some point she'd come 'round

She vacuumed with power and go
The animals and I watched the toe
For fear we may lose one or two
Have them sucked up in a bag, leaving few
And eventually all gone, have no 'mo

Kips kicked like a cat in a bag
And seemed like a wicked old hag
Then in the wink of an eye
And a sneeze of the nose
Was laughing as if it was a gag

She tortured herself to be wild
Yet knew God's gift made her mild
So she fought and tried true
To be sometimes someone she knew
Was the behavior of some other's child

Eventually her humor does win
She smiles and laughs with a grin
Claiming nothing is funny at all
Though she knows who she is
And is loved by none other than her mom, Lynn

Greg liked it. Max liked it. I thought it was hilarious. Anna, not so much. Oh well. Such is the life of the mother of Anna Brown.

It's not unusual to have a child that requires more of your time and space than another. It seems like Max gets the short end of my attention these days. He may like this. I ask a lot of questions. It hurts me to think he may feel left behind. His sister requires so much mental space that it's hard to give him as much as he deserves. Max is interesting. He rarely complains. When he was little, he was the happiest little boy in the world. He would scooch across the floor laughing. He rarely cried. He woke up every morning with a smile on his face and a twinkle in his eye. One morning I found him standing in his crib smiling with his black and white polka dot lampshade on his head. That was so funny. I was new. I moved the lamp. As he got older, he became more and more interested in basketball. He never had to try hard to get good grades. He was happy with As and Bs. He probably could have neared the 4.0 average. But he liked to round his life out with fun, friends, school, and sports. When he was about eight, I started to lose him as my baby. Greg became the guy for Max. It was hard for me. He didn't want his mom any more. He wanted his sports buddy dad. I ask myself if there was something I could have done, or can do to get that relationship back. When Anna started playing sports and we had to split up, I took Anna most of the time. Greg was Max's coach and had to go with Max. That was another divide. Occasionally I would try to get Max to open up about how he felt about all of this. But, he was tight lipped. Communication was something, and is something, both the men in my life struggle with. They are both rather quiet in nature. Then Max graduated from high school and left for Gonzaga. Time flew by and in the meantime, I didn't get my little boy back.

But, I am so proud of him and who he is. He knows how much I love him because I never stop telling him and I never will. He will always be my Bug.

In the middle of August, Anna and I sit at the station in downtown Seattle, getting ready to board the train from Seattle to Eugene, Oregon. She is starting to look at colleges and wants to visit University of Oregon. Anna is interested in communications and public relations. What a surprise. Now, having graduated from Oregon State University, I must say that having a child attend U of O is not in my dreams. But, they have a good communications program and she wants to check it out. I keep saying "What about University of Washington? They have a great communications program, too. And they're in-state." This tidbit of information falls on deaf ears. Oh, well.

We board the train and are led to our own compartment with sliding doors to close us into this cute little space. Our seats face each other and a tray folds down between us. Cool. Greg did a great job booking this little trip. It is a seven-hour ride and we are very excited about it. No one in our family has ever taken a train ride before. This will be an adventure.

As soon as the wheels begin to roll, the conductor stops by to offer us a glass of champagne. I tell him Anna isn't old enough. He winks and replies, "I'll just give you two then." Anna looks at me and smiles. She's feeling awfully grown up. I let her have a glass of champagne. It's a nice start.

I stare out the window for almost seven hours. It makes me wonder about my mind. Would a normal person look out a window for seven hours? The scenery and the towns are very interesting to me. Even though we did get up for lunch, I still look out the window and watch as we travel through little towns I will never see again. It is mesmerizing.

We find a bus to our hotel and eventually arrive, throwing our bags into the room and freshen up before going to campus. We can walk to the campus and upon leaving the hotel, stumble across a coffee stand. Anna loves the coffee. "This is the best coffee I've ever had," she says with newfound excitement, "We have to come here again tomorrow morning before our campus tour." She's obviously impressed.

We walk past the construction and into the heart of campus. Even though school is out for the summer, there are a few kids on campus for summer session and enough to see that Anna is getting a flavor of U of O. A skateboarder with long flowing blond hair cruises by. I say nothing. Anna, like every kid, is seeing if she fits here. We walk around on our own for about an hour and then go back to the hotel for dinner.

Next morning, we get our coffee at her new favorite coffee stand and find our way to the new student tour and meeting room. Before breaking into the tour groups, the meeting leader gives us a little bit on information about U of O. When he asks if there are questions, Anna raises her hand.

"Is this a liberal or conservative campus? If a student is caught with alcohol on or off campus, what are the consequences?"

Okay, I'm thinking and loving her spunk, but where the hell did that come from? He tells her it's a liberal campus and he doesn't really understand her second question.

After a little time, she raises her hand and asks another question, "Regarding public high school verses private high school admissions here. Are they both looked at equally?"

A mother, apparently with her public high school student from Portland, lets out an irritated groan. I just sit and listen. I guess Portland must have the best public high school system in the country. Really? On to the tour.

At the end of the tour and back at the hotel, Anna confesses, "I am not going to college here."

A sigh of relief passes through my body. I did know this was not a good fit. She had to figure it out herself. Having gone to school at Oregon State with a terrific agricultural program and lots of kids from farming communities in eastern Oregon, I was well aware of the differences between the two universities. OSU was known as the more conservative school and U of O was known as the more liberal school. Enough said.

I spend the week packing Max up for college, taking him in for his physical and round of immunizations, canning peaches, having the roof cleaned, getting the windows washed, clearing the gutters out, and making pesto to freeze for the winter.

Finally, it's Saturday morning. We start with a pre-scheduled appointment in downtown Seattle for Anna. It's not the best timing, but it was the only appointment available. Our insurance company is requiring us to take her for a two-year follow up exam with a neuropsychologist. The doctor will be testing her from 9:00 am until noon. Greg and I sit patiently waiting while Anna undergoes a battery of neurological exams to determine if there are any permanent problems from her brain injury. It's a little nerve wracking.

At 11:30 am she's done. We won't have the results for a few weeks. So, we gather up our reading materials, call Max to tell him we are on our way, and journey back to the house. Anna thinks it was a breeze. She tells us about some of the activities she had to do and laughs. Matching, remembering. It sounds like there were all kinds of activities to stimulate her brain and her memory. Good for her. She even got done early. I hope that's a good sign.

At 12:15 pm we zip into the driveway and pick up Max. Sammy dog is at the nanny's and Pam is taking care of the kitties. The doors are locked and the alarm is set. We are good to go. Gonzaga, here we come.

Max loves his friends, Gonzaga, and his life. There's a new configuration of roommates this year. Like every sophomore college student, you put together a group you met as a freshman, usually from your dorm, and find a new place to live. Life's an adventure. The boys are very excited. Every one of them arrives with furniture and stuff in tow. Hours later, we unload Max's last box and put the final touches on his new digs. He hugs us and says, "Thanks. See you later." Nice. Once again, my job is done. Greg, Anna and I drive over to the Whites to spend the night and will drive back home tomorrow morning. No time to tarry. Anna starts her senior year on Monday. Help!

Chapter Thirty-One

"I had a collision ... we both fell to the ground"
— Anna Brown

The Story of Anna
She's wild, she's crazy, she's full of life,
Her mama loves her — oh, the strife.
Like a cat in a bag, she fights to get out,
Punching, screaming to run about.
Yet her constant demand to be heard by all,
Will be a fabulous advantage — next Fall!
She's ready to go, to fly away soon
Seems just yesterday her nap was at noon.
We will miss her more than she will ever know,
And so proud she created the opportunity to go
Greg will be sad, our house will feel small,
Our Anna at college — he'll miss her and call.
Max already gone to college two years,
He'll have advice for Anna, we hope that she hears.
I will miss my baby girl, her laugh and her smile,
May sit in her room and reminisce for a while,
We love you and pray that your life is a blast,
As your journey begins — your freedom at last!!!

We Love you Anna B.
Love, Dad, Mom, and Max

This is the senior poem I write for Anna. Just like the poem I wrote for
Max, this is written in assorted colors on the chalk board in the downstairs
bathroom. It's a little kick-off to their senior year in high school. In 2007
when I wrote "The Story of Max" on the chalkboard, people stayed in the
bathroom a little longer and always had a comment to make when they

came out. That was fun. There were even a few teary eyes from parents. We all know the joy and sadness of raising children. We want them to leave and we want them to stay. It's a heart breaker no matter how you look at it.

Anna's first week of school is great. I know this is going to be a good year for her. She will play her final season of soccer with friends and teammates she's known most of her life. She will play her final season of basketball as a starting guard with a group of girls and a coach she loves. Her boyfriend is off to college, thank you, and she's going to be a bridesmaid in her cousin's wedding in November. She has signed up for drama as an elective. The drama teacher has been after her for years. He can obviously see she is quite dramatic. Welcome to my world. Yep, this is going to be a busy year. Good.

I am teaching preschool and Greg is working from his home office two days a week and going downtown three days a week. Life is good. Thank you.

Anna goes to her high school retreat for four days. The seniors leave on Tuesday and the underclassmen follow, leaving on Wednesday. Everyone comes home on Friday. It's a time for the students to come together, worship together, build friendships, and even mend broken relationships. It's a great opportunity to pull the school together before the students get too far into the year. This retreat also allows the students a little time to get to know each other. That can head off a lot of issues during the school year. Good thinking.

It's hard to believe that on the third week of school we have a mandatory meeting for parents of seniors It's already time to go over the calendar for the year, sign up to help with activities and get information about graduation obligations and dates. Wow. I have said before and I will say it again; no school does senior year like Cedar Park. Not one. It's a blessing for these kids. It's terrific.

I check with Anna and she agrees to let me chaperone the Senior Sneak at the end of their school year! I sign up to work on the committee and this time I get to go with the class on their surprise outing for one full day. Yay! Do I see a hint of maturity? I better not get carried away.

This year will be fun for Greg and me too. I am team mom again for Anna's basketball team, Greg is helping out with the filming and statistics, and we are involved in many of the school's activities for the senior class. Our last baby. Bittersweet.

Anna has Cap and Gown Day on the last day of September. During her lunch break, she gets measured for these necessities of graduation.

Later in the afternoon when she comes home, I sense this had brought a new reality to her last year in high school. Even though the school year has just started, she is rapidly working her way up to senioritis. Now, if you ask her, she would say, "I can't wait to be on my own." But, what she's really thinking is, "I can't wait to leave the restrictions at home for the freedom of college. I'll be able to do whatever I want!" I understand that. But, there is still a full year ahead, chock full of activities she's participated in since she was in kindergarten. She may not realize that leaving those behind will be a little sad. I know she will be ready when that time comes, but I do feel she needs this one last year to finish cooking before she goes off to college.

Anna casually strolls into the kitchen. When she wants to hang around me, it's usually because she wants to tell me something. I wait.

"Oh," she says, "I got a lead part in our improv skit for drama class. The name of the skit is 'Broadcast News.' My character's name is Lynn Letoya and I will be a newscaster. There will be practices and a show. I'll let you know when it is."

"Well congratulations," I tell her, "that's awesome."

"And," she continues, "I have been asked to represent Cedar Park for a portrait studio interested in offering senior pictures and photo packages."

Apparently one of her soccer teammates had given Anna's name to the studio and they called her. They want her to hand out their cards and, basically, send business their way in exchange for some free and discounted senior pictures. I like it. However, they want an email list of all the seniors in her school. I tell Anna we can't provide them with an email list. That's private information. We decide I should call the studio to make sure we have the whole story before she gets too involved in this.

I call while Anna stands by in case she needs to offer up some info. They are legitimate, but I was clear there will be no email list available to them. They are fine with that and by the end of the conversation all is a go. Anna has a makeup session and a photo shoot scheduled for Friday after school. This will be a fun experience for her. I want to go!

Saturday is Greg's birthday and, thank the Lord, we have nothing planned except a home cooked dinner and yummy dessert. Now, Greg is not much of a dessert eater, so the responsibility falls on the shoulders of Anna and me. Oh well, someone has to eat cake, right? Anna and I manage to choke down a piece of chocolate cake with vanilla ice cream. Let's face it. Can you eat a piece of chocolate cake without vanilla ice cream? I don't think so.

Anna has a 9:00 am select basketball game on Sunday. At 1:00 pm she has a soccer game. It's time for me to put on my worry hat. Here we go again. Tomorrow afternoon we have a conference call with the neurological psychologist about Anna's test results. She seems to be feeling great and mentally doing well. I pray all is well with her test results. I guess we'll know tomorrow.

Monday morning my neighbor Stacey picks me up at 5:30 am to go work out. What was I thinking? This is so early. Way too early for me. I won't be doing this again. It sounded like such a good idea to get my workout in early and have the rest of the day. Stacey does this all the time. She is a better woman than I am. When we call the neuropsychologist at 1:00 pm, I can barely keep my eyes open.

The doctor begins with a review of the accident. Then he fast forwards to the day of testing. The person testing Anna noted she, "showed excellent effort throughout a lengthy day of testing. Fatigue or lack of persistence did not appear to be an issue. She tolerated frustration well although was somewhat anxious at times." Anna's comprehension and vocabulary skills were in the 91st percentile for her age. Great news. Thank you. She is still struggling with similarities and processing speed. The arithmetic, reading, and spelling tests all proved Anna to be above her grade. However, the memory and recognition testing was more of a challenge for her. In summation, the doctor said she appeared to have "minor auditory verbal memory problems" and that these problems will go largely unnoticed unless she is fatigued. Basically, what I heard is that she's perfect. When she goes to college she will have to make sure she lets her brain rest in order to perform at her peak. She will be a little more susceptible to mental fatigue. Let's hope she takes this to heart. After all, this is Anna we are talking about.

The doctor closes with very little concern and only words of encouragement. He feels if there are any noticeable memory issues, they are minor and something only we would be able to detect. It's such great news. Thank you.

When Anna gets home we give her the news. The doctor said she's in great mental shape. Anna is unaffected by this information. We think she simply knows who she is and what she's capable of. She's a proven fighter. To her, the sky's the limit. I agree. You go girl!

Anna and I go to the portrait studio to take a look at her proofs. When we walk through the door, there is a 46" x 32" portrait of Anna on the wall behind the reception desk in the lobby. I look at Anna, Anna looks at me and we look at the receptionist. We all laugh. The picture is one of Anna lying on her stomach, arms bent lifting her upper body, with her knees casually bent up in the air and her chin resting on the palm of her left hand. Her slight smile and the sparkle in her eyes say it all. In her white tee shirt and blue jeans, the portrait is pure Anna. It's an incredible picture. The receptionist says the studio loved it so much they blew it up and framed it on this hard board. The studio will keep it on display until next summer. "Will it be for sale? I want to buy it," I say. She takes note that I want it when they are ready to take it down. I can't wait to tell Greg. How fun is that!

On the way home, Anna gives me some of that temporarily lost attitude. I pull out a pen and a piece of paper to write another poem for her when we get in the house. I have decided the best way to deal with the attitude this year will be with a sense of humor. I'll give it a try anyway.

I post my latest creation smack dab over her sink on the bathroom mirror.

I ALWAYS KNEW YOU WERE A DRAMA QUEEN
To: Anna Brown
Ballet, T-ball and Arts Umbrella,
Definitely girl —not a fella.
She's always been charming, with quite a wit,
Laughing and crying and having a fit.
Her mood sways up and quickly down,
To go back up before shopping in town.
It's only natural, and perhaps it's fitting,
A huge personal portrait after just one sitting.
A late blooming talent, something not seen,
Our family has born the first "Drama Queen!!"
Congratulations on improv!
Love,
Mommy

I get no response. Hopefully it will help to keep her positive and add a little levity to our lives. We'll see. That attitude seems to be making its way back. I could use a little help, please.

Thursday and Friday are wonderful in the attitude department. Thank you. We've made it two days. In the thick of all of this it's hard to make good decisions every day on how to react to a hormonal teenager. Do we reward for good behavior? Quite honestly Anna is a great kid. She stumbles with attitude. I am thankful that's what it is. It's not a life altering behavior. And, it's not like we don't address the attitude situation. I'm not quite sure where to go with this, so I pray. And, I call my sister Ann daily. But, then I make a mom mistake. I have been lulled into the land of rewarding good behavior, however short that behavior may be. Anna announces she is in need of new tops to go with her jeans, dress pants, and skirts. I know if I go to the mall with her it will be expensive and a very unpleasant experience for everyone involved. So, I decide to go to TJ Maxx and pick out a few tops to surprise her. I lay them across her bed, in a fashionista kind of way, pairing them with her assorted bottoms. It gives her a bird's eye view of what everything looks like together. Having been in the fashion industry, I think I know what I'm doing. I also post another poem on her mirror. I'm not sure who these poems are helping the most, but they sure make me feel better!

A SHOPPING FRENZY FOR POO
An assortment, a bevy of tops to be had,
The idea of it all will sure make you glad!
Some may be loved, others may not,
But to the store I went and bought, bought, bought!
So do let us see, perhaps have a view,
A fashion show with accessories and on you!
Waiting, waiting, waiting!
Love,
Mom—me

I hear her drive up and come in the house, I can hardly wait. She goes up to her room and I hear nothing. I creep up the stairs and tiptoe to her room.

She looks at me and says, "Thanks Mom, but I don't like any of them."

Of course you don't, goes through my mind. I say "Okay, I'll take them all back."

As I turn to walk out, she says, "But, thanks anyway Mom." The good news is that she is thankful. The bad news is that she will now want to go to the mall. Help!

I say "You're welcome," and leave the room. It was worth a try. But should I have done it?

I mull over the reason why I bought the tops in the first place, asking myself what my motives were. Of course, saving money was one. Aggravation was two. But, am I trying to please her? This is a question to be dealt with. She has a family who loves her dearly. She has a great life. Why would I try to please her? Many girls would be thankful to have new clothes. They are not entitled to spend their parent's money. What is going on here? I feel like we are walking on eggshells half the time. We've had two days without attitude. Should I really be glad about that? It's like we keep falling off the horse and I'm the one that has to climb back in the saddle. Okay, so the job of the parent is to be the adult. This is truly a balancing act and I am definitely out of balance. Now what?

I decide to focus on what is okay and what is not okay. This is a personal decision within a family. It's different than what is right and what is wrong. We are very clear about that. But what is acceptable and normal versus what is not acceptable and not within the scope of normal teenage behavior is what we need to decide. Here comes the divide. Greg and I have a different take on Anna's attitude right now and how it affects the family. In all fairness, there is a difference in how a girl behaves towards her mom versus her dad. Dad doesn't get the brunt of the attitude. It is reserved specifically for mom. In our case, that is of course, me. Greg thinks I need to relax and let go. This, to me, is man-speak for ignore everything and just try to get along. That doesn't work for me. Parenting is about loving and teaching. But, at what point am I helping her if our encounters become negative? Hmmm. I call Ann.

Ann understands the dilemma. Her husband Gene and Greg are very similar when it comes to parenting their daughters. They want harmony at most any cost. They don't understand the dynamics of the mother and daughter relationship. Who really does? It takes a lot to push either of them into action. Some may say this is a good checks and balance system. Then the lesson dawns on me. Raising kids is hard on a marriage. Really hard. It's not meant for the weak and timid. So, how do we resolve this? Must we be in a constant state of emotional highs and lows? Must Greg and I argue over every difficult encounter we have with Anna?

Ann says, "I hate to tell you this, but until she leaves for college, this is it." I can't take it. I scream into my pillow.

We make it through Homecoming without much hysteria and Max has another birthday at Gonzaga. Aside from these two events, I am ready to lose my mind. Anna's attitude is worsening and dealing with it daily is exhausting. Every day is a roller coaster ride. It really is true that a parent's happiness rests on the shoulders of their children. Why is this?

Ann enlightens me yet again. She has an interesting observation connecting their behavior to their daily life. Their bedroom is the key. "If their room is a mess, they are a mess." Anna's room is a mess. I wonder what is going on in Anna's life that she's not clear about. Is she making poor choices? Is that what is happening? Do I get the short end of the stick even though she's really frustrated with herself? Ann must be right in some strange way. Yet, my room is clean and I feel like I'm the mess. What does that mean? It means Anna has a hold over my heart strings. Where's my pillow?

I can't wait for basketball to officially start. Anna will be practicing every day after school unless she has a game. Maybe she'll be so tired, she'll lose the attitude. Is this wishful thinking? She wants to be so independent. She's responsible, has great grades, and is very nice to everyone except me. There's hope in that. At least she knows how to be nice to other people. My training has not gone unnoticed. Her coaches love her. Her teachers love her. Her friends love her. I love her. She just doesn't like me very much. That's okay. I like me just fine. That makes one of us. Okay, stay strong. Just stay strong.

The funny thing is that we do have moments of clarity. We even have fun on occasion. It seems to be best when it is just the two of us. The minute a friend is brought into the picture I'm the odd man out. I'm gathering that Anna has made me look like a loon to her friends and their parents. Isn't that special? Fortunately, most of them know me and having daughters of their own, understand the insanity is grossly over-exaggerated. For those that don't know me, I can't help them and they'll just have to believe what they believe! Maybe I am a nut and don't know it. Ignorance is bliss.

Greg continues to strive for harmony. I want harmony, but not like an ostrich with her head in the sand. So occasionally we have a discussion and try to understand each other's viewpoint. We do show a united front, and Greg manages to keep us focused and calm. Thus far we have ended up with a little humor and a little understanding of the ongoing problems. Thank you for that.

November appears to be the calm before the storm. I make an effort to reengage our social life and take time to enjoy my own friends. It's refreshing and energizing. I can see why parents prematurely check out of their kid's lives. It's for self-preservation. Not a good choice, but understandable. I know so many women who have been before me, and are coming after me, with teenage daughters. Their stories are ones of either happiness or dread. I am somewhere in the middle. Again, I remind my-self to keep my sense of humor. This calm allows me to appreciate the choices Anna has made at each fork in the road. She's still a great kid. She's testing me into insanity, but a great kid.

I think Anna found a broom in her closet this morning and decided to fly through the house on it. Not good and I have no idea why. Thus, I found my own broom in the garage and flew around behind her. To top off the morning, Greg announces he's going out of town for a week and will be back the day of Advent by Candlelight at church. I am trying to peel myself from the ceiling by the time Anna leaves for school and Greg goes to work. Where is that humor when you need it? Breathe. Better yet, "Hello God, are you there? Mom can you hear me?" I need help here. I sit down in my bathroom and cry. There are lots of tears as Sammy lies down beside me to lend his support. Even Jazz nudges up against me as if to say, "I'm here too."

You know, a good cry is helpful. I miss my mom so much. She would be great in this situation, whatever this situation is. I have no idea what happened this morning. But, I do get an answer to my prayers, "Move on and start anew." Before Anna gets home from school, I write another poem and tape it to her mirror.

It's all tied together
The ups and the downs,
We choose our direction
Let's all lose the frowns.
Today we go postal
We're happy and glad,
To have a great family
Max, me, you, and Dad!
Be happy ... let's start anew

I draw an eyeball, heart, and the letter u to symbolize I love you, and sign it, Mom.

Naturally, I get no response. But, I feel better for having written anoth-er poem. If mom were here, she would say, "Whatever works." I am going to go with that.

By the end of the week, Greg is back home, the house is complete-ly decorated for Christmas, Advent by Candlelight was the comforting evening it was intended to be, and Thanksgiving is days away. Max is coming home on Tuesday. I can't wait to see him. Thank you, God.

Greg picks Max up from the airport. Months ago, I insisted on the plane versus Max catching a ride home. It's the pass and the weather conditions. It is difficult to predict snow, ice, avalanche, or bad traffic. Having been raised in Las Vegas surrounded by desert and heat, snow is something I always loved but was never around. Therefore, it scares the heck out of me to drive in the snow and for my kids to be in cars driving in the snow. Once again, I thought I would be better after the accident. More relaxed. What are the chances of another car accident? But, unfortunately, I'm worse. Will this fear ever go away? I pray about this too. It's so hard to give up control when there's so much love in your heart for your babies.

By 4:00 pm, Max is home. I run out and hug him. Max has a big smile on his face. He's excited to be home too. I would like to think it's because he missed me. But, it's probably because he has a nice comfortable bed to sleep in, every meal is made for him, and his laundry will finally be done. Okay, so there is a huge bag of laundry. Laundry is exactly what I want to do today. How did he know?

Thanksgiving Day is a blast. The kids sleep late and around eleven we have a big breakfast. I am in the kitchen most of the day, but really enjoying myself preparing our Thanksgiving feast. The kids are safely home relaxing, the turkey is in the oven, and the wonderful smells of homemade bread, dressing and turkey are wafting through the house. Everyone is content, even the animals. The rest of the family arrives for the celebration and between the cousins, the brothers, the sisters-in-law, and the grandparents, food and fun is had by all. It's a perfect day. Thank you.

It's Christmas tree day. At 9:30 am, the Allens, the Blackburns, and our family load up and begin the drive to Sylvana for our Christmas trees. Even Sammy knows where we are going and he can hardly wait. He loves the dog party. We have to stop at Starbucks to have a morning treat or it wouldn't be tree day. Hours later when everyone has found their perfect Christmas tree and loaded it up into the Allen's trailer, we begin the trek back home. But not before we stop for breakfast. The tradition continues.

Brian drops each tree off at the respective homes, where we immediately cut a little disc off the bottom of the tree and then stick the tree into a bucket of cold water. It will stay there for a day. This is when it begins to get interesting. Every year is the same. You would think we would have figured this out by now. In my world, Saturday would be the day we haul the tree into the house and decorate it. Since the rest of the house is fully decorated, the tree is the final thing to be put up. Plus, decorating the tree should be done with the family and everyone should be having fun, right? Well, that's not what happens here. First, Greg does not want to deal with the tree until the end of the day on Saturday and often times that is even too soon for him. Then he gets out the chain saw and wants to whack off, what I consider, too much of the tree. So, let the tension begin! By the time we have measured the tallest possible height and marked the cut line at the base, Greg revs up the chain saw and slices the bottom piece off. He drags and pulls the tree into the house through the door that leads from the garage to the toy room. All the while I am trying to protect the millwork around the door. More tension. We have white millwork and it would be nice if it stayed that way. Our carpet is already hunter green. We do not need green millwork. Getting the tree upright and stable is hilarious. Hilarious in a way that only people who have been married for a hundred years can understand. Greg likes to attach it to our large, wide spread Christmas tree stand first and then hoist it up until it is standing by itself.

"Shift it to the left, no right, no back to the left. Okay, tighten the screws. No, it's leaning again."

When we finally agree it is perfect, I hold it and he ties clear fishing line from the top of the tree to the hooks screwed into the various discreet locations on top of the window moldings. We never bring the ladder in first, so I stand holding the tree for, what seems like eternity, collecting sap and debris on my clothes and hands. By the time we stand back and look at our tall straight Christmas tree, it's time to start getting dinner ready. Never mind the fact there are needles and branches all over the carpet that must be cleaned up.

"Would you please get the vacuum?" I ask my lovely husband. He's very grumpy, but he treks upstairs for the vacuum. I pour a glass of champagne and proceed to make dinner. On the positive side, once the tree needles are sucked up, the vacuum will smell like Christmas pine for the rest of the season. That's a great thing! Ahhhh--tradition.

The tree does not get decorated on Saturday night or Sunday night, for that matter. Max goes back to college on Sunday afternoon, Anna is into her full blown busy and testy mode so we wait until Monday. Greg and I put the lights up together, but I can't leave the room or I will find nothing but a weird and vertical stream of lights on the tree. "For Heaven's sake," I am screaming to myself, "lights go around the tree, not up and down!" Shouldn't this be funny by now? Anna comes in to the toy room to see what Greg is doing with the lights. She makes a few jokes about Greg's past lighting experiences. Well, at least she is enjoying a little Christmas humor.

I ask Greg to try to hide the wires as best he can. He has a tough time at the top of the tree.

Greg looks at me and barks, "Do you want to do them yourself?"

I have to laugh. The wife in me wants to say, "Well, I have done everything else myself." but I refrain. "No, that's good," I say, knowing I will take care of this later. I see more green wires than I do tree. Oh well.

We hang ornaments on the long, protruding branches. Not all of them mind you. Greg can only handle so much ornament hanging. Then he's done. One year he decided we were only doing gold and red. It looked pretty. The real reason we only did gold and red was because then he wouldn't have to hang all the ornaments. But, as long as he was doing them and Anna was his assistant, I was happy. She has a very good eye for these things and it worked out beautifully. This year, we have an assortment of ornaments hanging on the branches. At least each branch has one. Well, almost each branch. Greg doesn't want to hang any ornaments on the back third of the tree because it is facing a corner. But, I convince him that since there are three windows behind the tree, it would be nice to see lights and ornaments through the windows. God knows my heart. I am looking at this man thinking, "Really?"

At the end of the evening, we turn out all the lights except the Christmas tree lights. It glows. It looks beautiful. I look at Greg and tell him he's done a great job. Thank you.

Tuesday night is Anna's first basketball game as a senior. She has been elected cocaptain for the season and does not take this responsibility lightly. She knows this is an honor. The girls look good. They win. I think this is going to be an exciting season. Busy, but exciting.

Greg, Anna, and I fly to Las Vegas for my niece, Jordyn's, wedding on Friday night. Thursday is the rehearsal and quite the interesting day with Anna. My sister actually snaps a picture of Anna and me talking to each other. Oh, the body language. My head is drawn forward talking to Anna and that little girl of mine has her nose tilted up and her jaw firmly locked with her chin pushed out. I can see the defiance in the picture. Getting a physical snapshot depicting our relationship is no accident. It's a message to me. This is war and I'm not a quitter. The devil can't have her. He may be trying, but I'm positive even Anna doesn't want to go there. She's my ally in this fight and she doesn't even know it. We need some help. Thank you in advance.

Ann has everything under control and Jordyn's wedding and reception are beautiful. The whole evening is fun. Ann brought Mom and Dad in their urns and set them up at the top of the staircase to watch. I know that may sound a little weird, but it made us feel good having Mom and Dad there. They would have loved to have seen this. I know they're watching.

Early Saturday morning the three of us fly home. With basketball in full swing and college admission deadlines rapidly approaching, our days are full. It's a little crazy. Anna is completely focused on school and basketball. She does, however, manage to maintain a very disagreeable disposition. Not every moment of every day, but many moments of many days.

Tuesday night Anna has her second game of the season. It's fun to see her walk out on the floor with her cocaptain and help lead the girls. The team looks well prepared and we easily take the win.

Thursday night we play our biggest rival. It's on their home turf which is a huge advantage for them. We fight hard. The lead goes back and forth. We are in and out of our seats. In the end, we lose the game. The girls are not happy. They are a good team and want to go to state this season. Wouldn't that be great? Max's team went his senior year and I pray the same for Anna. It's a great way to finish your high school basketball career and take some good memories with you.

Anna has a very busy weekend. She has basketball practice on Saturday morning, a meeting in the afternoon to discuss college options with a counselor, youth group on Sunday night and homework in between all of that. This is all good news. She's very busy. It seems to help her attitude, or at least keep me out of the direct line of fire. I'm good with that.

Greg is leaving Sunday afternoon for business in Las Vegas. Thank goodness, it's only for one day. He will miss a Christmas party Sunday night, but he will make it home in time for Anna's birthday. She will be eighteen years old on Monday. Wow.

Anna wakes up in a positive mood, thank you, and all is good. Greg arrives just in time for cake and ice cream. All is relaxed and calm for one whole day. Yay!

'Tis the Season, and this week is packed with activities and celebrations. It is Anna's last week of school before Christmas break and she has two basketball games, one on Wednesday night and one on Thursday night. And, of course, practice on Friday afternoon after school. Greg and I have a Christmas party on Tuesday night, Max is flying home on Wednesday night, my preschool Christmas program is Thursday morning, and Friday night we have the preschool staff party at our house. We have lots of festive activities, but along with that, there will be lots of fun.

Come Saturday morning everyone sleeps in. Tonight is supposed to be family night. It's easy to plan, but difficult to get both of them to stay home. I remember those Saturday nights in high school and during college breaks. You want to see your friends, play, have fun, and enjoy life. I get that. We'll see. I would love for it to happen, but it probably won't.

We have a life changing situation on Tuesday night. Again. Anna comes into our room and sits down.

She says, "Coach said she was going to call you if I didn't tell you tonight. Last Friday I had a collision with one of my teammates during practice. Our heads hit each other pretty hard and we both fell to the ground. I had to sit out the rest of practice. I haven't felt right since then and she won't let me practice."

We sit in silence for a moment. I ask, "What does that mean, honey, that you don't feel right?"

"I just don't feel like myself and a little like I remember feeling after the accident. Sort of disconnected."

Greg and I let her talk and let everything she is telling us sink in. We already get it. It needs to sink into Anna.

When she leaves the room, I turn to Greg and say, "Okay, that's it. She's done with contact sports forever."

Greg agrees, but says, "She needs to figure it out. It needs to be her decision. Anna has to come to the conclusion that she can't play basketball anymore."

A few minutes later, Anna comes back into our room. "Anna," I offer, "you need to see your doctor. I will call tomorrow and make an appointment." Fortunately, she completely agrees with me and also wants to see her doctor. This has scared her, too. Good.

The next day, I am dialing her pediatrician's office before they open, hoping they will answer. Anna has gone to this doctor for years and likes her so much, we haven't changed Anna to a general practitioner. I get through and there are no appointments available until after Christmas. I ask them to talk to her doctor and get us in. I explain the situation and tell them, "Anna still doesn't feel right."

They call back, "Of course Anna's doctor will see her." I knew she would. It won't be until tomorrow morning, but she'll see us. Okay.

Wednesday night Anna comes back into our room. I've been watching her like a hawk since she told us.

"I don't think I should play basketball anymore." She starts to cry, "I can't take a chance of getting a permanent injury. It's not worth it."

We know. She gets it. Now she knows. "Okay," we respond, "Honey, we think that's the right decision. You have our full support. We agree with you. Nothing is worth permanently damaging your brain." Thank you.

It's the day before Christmas and Anna and I are at her doctor's office. She wants to go in alone. Within twenty minutes, the nurse comes out and gets me. She takes me to the exam room where Anna and her doctor are waiting.

"She has a bad concussion from the hit. The next time could be very dangerous. I've told Anna it's not worth it." She knows Anna had already come to that conclusion, but she wants to emphasize the decision is a good one. I really like her. She's a great doctor for Anna.

When we leave the doctor's office, I can see Anna's wheels turning. She's still putting all of this together. At her young age, she doesn't realize what this truly means. She's got to be vigilant the rest of her life to guard her brain. We don't need to point that out. Not yet, anyway. I ask Anna what she would like for lunch. She says, "Hamburger." Ah, comfort food. Well, if there ever was a time for comfort food, this would be it. We stop and get burgers.

We wake up Christmas morning happy to have this glorious day. We are steeped in tradition at our home. When Anna was little, she even wrote out a list of our Christmas traditions. Her list included receiving a special ornament on Christmas morning, finding a stuffed animal in their stockings, getting a new dress from Max for her birthday, and wearing that new dress to the Santa Breakfast we attend every year with the Allens and anyone else who wants to join us.

Well, the stuffed animal collections got out of control over the years and we no longer do that, the kids outgrew the Santa Breakfast and Anna got very picky about her dresses. We still give them a special ornament every year. It is always an ornament that reflects the past year of their life. Eventually their ornament collections will be on their own trees. When that day comes and they are explaining each ornament to their own babies, it will be a walk through their lives and our family history.

Our Christmas morning always begins the same. We wake up and I go downstairs to see if Santa has come. The kids crawl into our bed and watch TV while Greg and I go downstairs to make coffee, build a fire, turn the Christmas lights on and let the excitement build. Greg finds the video camera and when we are ready, he films the kids coming out of our bedroom, down the stairs, through the house, and into the toy room. From their first birthday and every year after, Greg captures the look on their faces when they walk into the toy room and see that Santa has filled their stockings and added a few presents. This tradition still remains exciting for all of us.

As creatures of habit, this Christmas morning starts with our ritual and ends with a pile of discarded wrappings and a huge breakfast. While the kids lounge around the toy room, I get dressed and begin puttering around in the kitchen. I love today. Not only because of the meaning of Christmas and the joy Christ brings to my family, but because everyone is relaxing and hanging out. No one wants to go anywhere. We are content to be home. Thank you for the gift.

It will be the four of us with Gramma and Grandpa tonight. I think they're coming over around 5:00 pm. We are having the full family get together on Saturday at their house. After that, they are leaving for Arizona. Gramma and Grandpa are snowbirds and enjoy the warm days of the desert when it is cold and wet here. I'm glad they are coming here for dinner tonight. The kids don't get a chance to see them too often anymore.

It's Monday and Anna has a scheduled basketball practice this afternoon. I am going to drive her to the gym, run some errands, and pick her up when practice is over. Today is the day she will tell the team she can no longer play and compete with them. This will be tough for her. It makes me sad for her but proud she has the strength to face this decision. They have a tournament starting tomorrow, so the conversation needs to take place today. Anna has already called her coach and talked with her about the finality of her basketball career. Coach understood completely. She's a mom. She was wonderful with Anna and asked Anna to stay on the bench and help out with the girls. Anna is thrilled to be part of this team and this is a perfect solution considering she can't actually compete. Thank you.

I drop Anna off at the gym and return later to pick her up. I go inside to see the team and let Anna know her chauffeur has arrived. Coach sees me standing at the far end of the gym and walks over to talk to me.

"Hi," she starts, "Just want to let you know how everything went this morning."

She points to the center of the gym floor where the Cedar Park Eagles logo is painted, "At the beginning of practice, the girls sat in a circle in the middle of the floor. I told them that Anna needs to talk to them. Once Anna started talking, they sensed where this was going, and they started crying. They understand, but they're very sad for Anna after all she's been through. The news was really hard on them. When Anna was done, they all stood up and hugged her. I told the girls that Anna is still part of the team and will continue to be cocaptain. She will be at all the practices. She will suit up every game, be on the bench and help the coaches with an extra pair of eyes and moral support. She just won't be on the floor with them."

Tears well up in my eyes and I thank Coach for everything she's done for Anna and for continuing to include her and keep her part of the team. Coach nods and turns back to the team. I look across the gym at this terrific group of young women. They are such a wonderful and supportive group. They didn't cry because their starting forward is out, they cried because their teammate is suffering and they know her history. Everyone is sad. I love the part about the hugging at the end. Girls hug. This is very important.

Out of the corner of my eye, I see the assistant coach, Sherri Staudacher, coming towards me. She is always smiling and very funny. The woman makes me laugh. Sherri has a daughter Rachel who is not only a sophomore, but our starting guard. Sherri is frequently at school and is around the girls all the time. Sherri and I talk about the concussion for a minute before Sherri says, "Anna is a leader and has brought confidence and calm to the team. She has a big personality. Anna has a lot of power at school."

I look at Sherri, a little worried, and ask, "What does that mean?" hoping we are not talking about mean girls.

Sherri laughs, sensing my concern, and relates a story to me.

"There was a small issue between Rachel and another girl. While they were having a conversation, Anna walked up and put her arm around Rachel and said, 'She's my girl.' That was it. That took care of that. Issue over."

Sherri, again, seeing I am thinking Anna is some kind of enforcer, starts laughing. "No," she says, "Anna is an inspirational leader and very protective of her teammates."

Okay, good, not mean, inspirational. Sherri had me going there for a minute! Whew.

Driving home, Anna tells me a much smaller version of today's team meeting. That's okay, I don't want to pry. I'm glad the coaches enlightened me. It's nice to know the child you raised is who you think they are. She's my Schmoo.

Before Max goes back to college, he is able to attend one of Anna's games. It's her debut as an injured support player and she embraces this new roll by calling out to the girls on the floor during play. Max comes to encourage her and brings his high school friends with him. She loves it. The girls win. They look great. On Sunday Max returns to Gonzaga. It's been an emotional and eventful Christmas break. It's always a little sad when Max goes back to school. I miss him, but I am so excited for him to have started his own life adventure. Naturally, I don't miss the mess he makes, but he is loved and missed when he is not home.

It's now the middle of January and our life merges into the rhythm of winter in Seattle. We enjoy rain, basketball, and busy. Greg returns to his regular work routine, preschool is in full swing and Anna is in her last five months of high school. She can't wait for her freedom. My cat in a bag wants out. Ready or not, it's almost time to release her.

Anna's attitude is improving, even though I was forced to tape a few notes on her mirror yesterday. They were simple notes. I thought I would try a new tactic. Her side of the mirror was covered with thought provoking memos like:

Problems only get Big when they are ignored. Speak.
God spoke and said, "Enjoy that child!"
Who am I to argue with God?
Choose Happy.

Finally, a simple drawing of a curved smile on top and a frown drawn below it with the word or nestled in between the two symbols. I thought it was funny. No response. But, she left them on the mirror rather than wad them up and throw them away. Is that a good sign?

After suffering one loss and two wins, the girls continue on their quest. The playoffs are in February with the goal of going to state in March. It's visibly obvious Anna would rather be on the court, but she is handling her new role with dedication and commitment. The parents of the girls have been awesome. They are compassionate and disappointed for Anna, but fully support her continuing with the team.

Amidst all of this, Gramma calls from Arizona and says Grandpa is not feeling well. We knew before they left that Norm had seen his doctor here and he had been concerned about Norm's PSA levels. Norm was supposed to have his blood count monitored while they were in Arizona. He had been given a diagnosis of prostate cancer years ago, and had been treated and cured, so we were all concerned when they decided to go to Arizona for the winter. But, Gramma and Grandpa were not concerned and insisted everything was fine. They wanted to stay warm and play golf.

We have a little break from basketball when the drama department holds The Besties Awards on Saturday night. It's like the Oscars, a night of a thousand stars! Anna is nominated in the category of Best Duo for her portrayal of Lynn Letoya in "Breaking News." Hilarious. Our evening event's ticket says the night begins with delicious desserts, followed by the awards program, and a short improv performance. The actors are excited and it looks to be a truly light-hearted evening. Greg and I take our seats with our plates full of desserts and wait for the program to begin. Anna has to sit in the back row with the award nominees. I can't help but turn my head around and watch her. She smiles. Funny girl.

When the category for Best Duo comes up, we hear the name Anna Brown as the winner. She is so perfect for this. And, I must say, "Breaking News" having been her first show, was very funny. She knew all of her lines and didn't miss a beat. That girl has confidence. I thank God for her, attitude and all.

The next three weeks bring six more games with the final game of the season being Senior Night. This is when, just as with Max, each senior is recognized by the announcer and enters the floor individually to be given that final cheering by the student body. It's Anna's last conference game and the crowd does not disappoint. All the seniors receive the same rally cry and their parents can feel the end of their senior's basketball career is just days away.

The girls make the playoffs. Now they need to make it through the playoffs. Practice continues and Anna comes home the night before the playoffs with a deal. The coach, the girls, and Anna have an idea. They have made it this far and if they make it to state, it would be a shame if she couldn't play for just a few seconds. But, in order to play in state, she has to play in the playoffs.

"What if," Anna says, "Coach puts me in for a few seconds and the girls protect me? Surround me. They don't let anyone come near me. Then Coach pulls me out. If we make it to state, I am eligible and I get to play a few seconds in the state game. The girls will protect me. Then I can say I played at state my senior year in high school. Coach is going to talk to you."

I look at her thinking, "Are you nuts?"

Chapter Thirty-One

Greg looks at her saying, "Oh, that might be okay."

I look at both of them and am thinking about college, marriage, kids, and her future.

Just watching their faces, I can see they are thinking, "And I played in the state game my senior year in high school." What is wrong with this picture? Who is not clear here?

The next day, after our first playoff game, we talk to Coach. I do love Anna's coach, but I think Anna, Greg, and Coach have all gone mad. She assures us, that, "They will not allow anyone to get near Anna. She'll be in for just a few seconds to keep her eligible if the opportunity arises for her to play in the state game. The girls will surround her for a few seconds." Coach makes it sound like they will deck anyone that comes near Anna. She wants us to know how much the girls and Anna want this. Greg is all for it. God?

I can't believe this. Guess who gets to be the bad guy? Again. My heart is so heavy. If I knew she would not be touched, I would let her play in a heartbeat. But, things happen quickly on the court. And this is the playoffs. I agree to pray about this and leave this decision until the final playoff game. If it looks like they are going to state, I will let them know if she can go in.

The playoffs for their district are scattered over a period of eleven days. The girls start out winning and just need to place in the top couple of teams to go to state. As they continue to win, I continue to worry. Greg is not supportive of my no play stance. And it's not even mine alone. What about the doctor? What about Anna's decision in December? Competitive people lose their minds when it comes to sports. Why is this my decision and only mine?

As luck would have it, we are down to the last game and we are winning. Winning by a big margin, I might add. Our opponent is no match for our girls. It's decision time. Greg looks at me, Coach wants the go ahead, the girls turn around and give me the nod and Anna is heartbroken about not playing in the playoffs. Oh yeah, this is just great. Okay, God, what's the answer?

After trying to ignore the heart tugs and listen quietly for the answer to my prayers for the last eleven days, it is time to make a decision. A guided decision nonetheless, but a decision. I give a nod. Yes. I don't need to say it, but coach knows this means just a few seconds. When they announce the sub and that Anna Brown (#33) is going in, I release her to God. She's in, she plays, the girls surround her and she's out. I thank God she's out. Greg is silent. Anna is all smiles. I'm exhausted. Thank you for protecting her.

It's a huge win for the girls and they are ecstatic. We are going to state next week. They hug each other, they hug the coaches, they hug the parents, and then they disappear into the locker room for a meeting. They emerge after fifteen minutes and begin to stream out into the waiting crowd. Anna makes a beeline for us.

"See, it was fine Mom."

Not, "See, it was fine you guys," but, "See, it was fine Mom." I think to myself, "Yes, there you have it."

Coach comes to talk with us. She is checking in. She loves Anna. Coach played basketball herself. She understands playing at a state tournament. She knows this was hard, but she also knew the girls would protect Anna. Fortunately, everything turned out okay. Thank you.

Once we are home from the game, Greg talks to his mom in Arizona. We had been checking in regularly to make sure they were okay and find out how Grandpa was doing. One day he's home, then a few days later he's in the hospital. Right now, he's in the hospital and he doesn't feel good. Greg asks his mom if he could talk to the doctor and for the doctor's phone number. He calls the doctor and leaves a message. By the grace of God, the doctor calls back immediately.

At the end of their phone call, Greg looks at me and tells me what the doctor just told him. We are both stunned. The doctor is going to try one more thing, and if that doesn't work by Monday, there is nothing he can do. The cancer is obstructing Norm's organs and it would be best to move Norm to hospice care. What? What?

Greg calls his brothers. They also are stunned. Greg books a flight for next morning.

Chapter Thirty-Two

"You truly are very blessed"
— Cathalynn Hublou

By Sunday morning things aren't going well with Grandpa. It's a matter of days. This is not only difficult, but so unexpected. As Greg begins making arrangements to move Norm to the hospice, he calls his brothers with the sad news. They need to go and say goodbye to their dad. Within a few hours, they have made flight reservations and will arrive tomorrow afternoon. So sad.

Greg has spent Friday, Saturday, and today with his Mom and Dad. He has gone over all the necessary loose ends with his dad and is in the process of saying goodbye for the last time. Tomorrow when Greg's brothers arrive in Arizona, Greg will be on a plane making his way back home. He made the choice. He loves his dad. He also loves his daughter and wants to be present when she boards the school bus and leaves for state. After everything Anna has fought for, Greg wants to send her off with his support and love. He wants to be there. He wants her to see him caring.

Monday afternoon Greg flies home. Rick and Doug make it safely to Arizona and are able to be with Nancy and see Norm. Nancy needs her boys right now, just as every mom needs their kids. There is no substitute for family. Thank you, God, that all three of Norm's sons will have had the opportunity to say goodbye and that Rick and Doug will be by Nancy's side for the next few days.

Tuesday morning in Arizona, Norm is moved into hospice. Rick, Doug, and Gramma are with him. He's hanging in there.

Tuesday morning in Washington, Greg and I are at Cedar Park. Students are lining the hallway. It's an all high school rally to send the girls off to state. This is new. I've never seen Cedar Park do this before. It's very lively. Great idea. Bill Bettinger announces each player's name as they run through the center of the crowd, arms out, slapping hands with their fans. Bill saves Anna for last. He has been one of her biggest supporters. The thing that is special about all of this is simply, all of this. Every student, parent, teacher, administrator, and person in the hallway knows Anna's story. All of it. From the car accident, the year with no sports, the comeback, and finally, the concussion that ended her career. They know everything.

Bill announces Anna's name. Not just announces her name, he winds up and blasts out, *"Aaaannnaaa Brooowwwnnn!"* Anna runs down the center of the hallway with outstretched hands, slapping palms with supportive classmates. I kid you not, the crowd cheered so loud it was deafening. It was also heartwarming. This school will never know how much I appreciate them and hold them in my heart. All of them. Every single one of them. The grace. The support. Unbelievable. And the smile on Anna's face? That tells a story in itself. Thank you.

The decorated bus slowly pulls out of the driveway with fans cheering and clapping for their success. The girls wave their arms out the window. The whole school is behind them. How great this is for these girls. Especially the seniors.

Norm spends Tuesday with his two youngest sons and Nancy. He's talking, laughing, and having a pretty good day. Greg and I call to check in. Rick says he's drugged but alert and not in too much pain. It gives me an opportunity to talk to Norm on the phone and say goodbye to my father-in-law. It affords Greg a chance to talk to his dad again. Norm knows he's dying and he has accepted his earthly end. Greg and I just pray he has accepted his Heavenly Father. We don't know.

Very early Wednesday morning Greg and I leave for Yakima and the state playoffs. It's a three-hour drive and the first playoff game is this morning at 9:00 am. On the way over we call Rick to check in and see how everybody is doing today. He says they are on their way over to the hospice and will give us a call later this afternoon. Thank goodness for Rick. He's a volunteer fireman and responder. He is acutely aware of what's happening from a technical standpoint and is able to give us the facts, as well as his insight surrounding Norm's condition.

At 8:30 am we pull into the Yakima Valley SunDome. We are early enough to see the girls before they disappear into the locker room. We hug Anna and many of the other girls while belting out words of encouragement. We hike up to our seats and sit with the rest of the parents and fans. At 9:00 am the game starts and it is crazy. Fortunately for me, it's double elimination. That tells me Anna will not play in this game. No need. There will be a second game. I can relax, scream my cheers, and enjoy. Whew. Thank you.

We lose. We really lose. The end score is 61 to 25. Ouch. But, tomorrow holds another game and another opportunity. We will just be in a different bracket. That's all. Greg and I watch as the girls come out of the locker room. They're pretty upset. Understandable. They had a great season and got blown out their first game. The parents just hug them.

I know this loss is huge to the coaches and team. I also know they have a better perspective than most. This isn't a life changing event. It's part of a story. Playing in the state tournament is a fun piece of history for all of us. They will be back tomorrow to play their best. Tomorrow will be a new day for this team. No wallowing in defeat.

A little after lunch, Rick calls. Norm's not doing as well today. He's not talking although Rick thinks he understands everything that is being said. The nurses gave him additional pain medications last night. Apparently, he was very uncomfortable. Nancy is on automatic pilot. We think she is in shock. There's nothing anyone can do now. Greg is relieved his brothers are there. It gives him peace. He knows his mom needs them as much as they needed to go down there.

We have dinner with the girls Wednesday night, give them a dose of encouragement and send them back to their rooms. Coach wants them completely rested and mentally ready for their game tomorrow morning at 9:00 am. We venture back to our room, too. Not only are we tired, but this is Yakima. Not a big nightlife here. We probably wouldn't participate even if there was something to do. Too much going on right now.

We close our eyes. Tomorrow is a new day. We have no control.

Chapter Thirty-Three

"Thank you"
— Lynn Brown

The phone rings. It's Rick. Norm died at the hospice in the middle of the night. It was peaceful.

Rick says he will handle the immediate arrangements and we will figure out the rest of the plan later. Greg talks to his mom for a few minutes. He needs to know that she is okay. With this sadness weighing heavily on our minds, we leave for Anna's game. On the way to the SunDome, we call Max and let him know Grandpa has died. However, our decision to tell Anna is a little different. We are not going to deliver this news to her until after the game.

At 9:00 am the second game begins. We are seated in the SunDome surrounded by Cedar Park parents, administrators, a few teachers, and even a couple of students that have driven over to see the girls play. Greg is on my right and Sue Halvorson is on my left. Sue's daughter Erin is one of Anna's friends and a forward on the team. We have known the Halvorsons for years through our church and sports. Great family.

The game begins. The girls have sloughed off yesterday's loss and are full of energy and hope. A win today will keep them alive in the playoffs. They know a loss is the end of their quest for a state title. This is immediately a physical game. It is too physical for Anna. I start to worry about the plan to put her in so she can say she played at state. Not worth it. By the end of the first quarter, it is apparent we are in trouble.

The second quarter is no better. Anna is on the sidelines. I can see her barking her support to her teammates. She wants to participate. I know her. She wants to help. She wants to play.

I sit in my seat anxiously awaiting the inevitable. We are getting clobbered. One thing I do believe is that God always has a plan. This is a brutal game. Maybe Anna got a concussion in December because this playoff game would have been the game that permanently injured her. I do believe things happen for a reason. Perhaps they are all part of a bigger picture. Bigger than the one I see in my little world.

The half time buzzer goes off. Thank you. While the girls run off the court to the locker room, I turn to Sue and tell her that Greg's dad died this morning. It is quite unbelievable actually. Her eyes well with tears. No doubt, this morning has been tough. Here we sit in our seats watching Anna's playoff game while a thousand miles away, Greg's mom and brothers are mourning the loss of Norm and making the arrangements to get Norm home.

Greg can't sit still. He knows we not only had to, but wanted to be here. Nonetheless, the timing is difficult. His mind is working overtime. I can see it.

The girls fly back onto the court. The third quarter begins. Greg stands up and asks one of the other team parents if he can borrow their video camera. Our video camera broke yesterday and he wants to film part of the second half. No problem. He secures the video camera and walks down the flight of stairs, planting himself on the outside corner of the basketball court. This is where he is comfortable. Good.

By the time the fourth quarter starts, it is evident we will not win this game. This means Coach is going to try to put Anna in for a little play time. For the memories. Good memories for her, a nightmare for me. Our opponent continues to be relentless and the physically aggressive game continues, despite the huge gap in the score. Our players are having a tough enough time defending themselves, let alone having the responsibility to take care of Anna on the court. Fear is bubbling up from the depths of my soul.

With three minutes left in the game, there's a break. Anna subs in and the play resumes. The girls know they must guard her. Anna hits the floor running. Within one minute she has forced two turnovers and taken a charge from her opponent. I can't breathe. She's unharmed, but Coach pulls her out. I begin to breathe again.

Anna barely gets seated on the bench when I see the coach talking to one of her assistants and looking at Anna. Her assistant gets up and walks down to Anna. The little smile on her face tells me she knows exactly what he is going to say. I can't hear him, but during his brief conversation with her, he points down to the end of the court where Anna took the charge. He walks back to his seat. She knows. What was she thinking?

Done. I sit back relaxed in my seat and breathe in a deep sigh of relief. It's over and she's safe. Anna has played in her state tournament in her senior year in high school. Just like Max. Thank you. This was my wish for her and a memory I hoped she would have.

With one minute left in the game, the clock is ticking and the play continues to be physical and constant. The score is 61 to 26. I am thinking that even though we will go home without a win, we will go home in the knowledge that we made it to state and we played our best. That is something to be proud of. This is, of course, what a mom would say. Thank you.

We are down to twenty seconds left in the game. Relaxing in my seat, I see Coach sending Anna to the center clock and check-in table. I bolt upright. What? I don't understand. She's been in. She has the memory. Why?

Anna is crouched down, ready to go in if there is an opportunity to sub. The clock ticks off ... 19 seconds ... 18 seconds ... 17 seconds ... 16 seconds ... 15 seconds — and then the referee's whistle blows. There's a foul. It's against our opponent. Cedar Park gets the ball. There's a buzzer. Anna flies onto the court. My heart is in my throat. This isn't the plan. My mind is racing. It's like the stories about the person who has one final day at work before they retire and they never make it through that day. This is dangerous for her. What is going on? Why are we taking this risk? God? Help me.

Another buzzer. We resume play ... 14 seconds ... 13 seconds ... 12 seconds — Anna breaks out and races to the corner of the court where Greg stands filming her. The ball is passed to Anna. She catches it with ease. Her teammates position themselves to protect her. Our opponent is trying desperately to get to Anna and the ball. They are so far ahead, I can't figure out why they are so physical. They haven't even taken out all of their starters. Anna's teammates stay close to her. The clock continues ticking ... 11 seconds ... 10 seconds ... 9 seconds ... 8 seconds — Anna launches the ball. Oh--I see. Coach set up the final play and a special memory just for Anna. With all she has been through, from the accident and the determination to climb back on top and get herself back, to the concussion that altered her final season, Anna is given one final blessing. The arc is perfect. The ball sails through the air and curves toward the hoop. It slams right through the basket. The buzzer goes off. She made it.

A perfect plan. Three points. Nothing but net, baby girl. Thank you.

Our girls go wild! They swarm the floor. Judging from their behavior, you would have thought they won the game. They rush to Anna and hug her and each other. Wow. Parents are crying. I am crying. Greg is on the perimeter of the floor watching the team and continuing to film the excitement. It's simply an unbelievable reaction to the end of this game. It's a testament to the character of this team. It's a win of another nature.

One of the tournament officials is so baffled by the team's reaction, considering we suffered such a huge loss, he tracks down Bill Bettinger to find out why we are so happy. After hearing Anna's story, he awards her an unofficial medal for Shot of the Week. This is only the second day of the tournament, but he places that medal around her neck fully convinced she is the only one that deserves it.

The following week when The Yakima Herald-Republic recapped the tournament in an article titled "Oscars Schmoscars, here are the Dribblies" Anna won for "Best Documentary Short Story."

At the end of the season, the coach gives Anna the award for most inspirational player. I certainly cannot argue with that. Finally, after two and a half years, I take a deep breath and thank God it is over.

That three-point shot represented the hard work and miracle of Anna's recovery. She made it. Through the grace of God, she conquered her physical and mental injuries. She had been prayed through her trauma. It was the final sign that ended my doubts about her becoming herself again. Thank you.

While agreeing to let her play contact sports one year after the accident or in the final state game, I will never know how I would have lived with myself if something had happened to her. There is no doubt that there was and always will be varied opinions and responses to our decisions. One thing I do know is that we can only do our best to make decisions with our parenting responsibilities. At some point, we have to choose not to pass on unhealthy fears to our children. I used prayer and hope in trying to figure out what was best for Anna.

Through all of this I am thankful. I have seen my children wrapped in the arms of angels and held tight in their safe hug. I have talked to God. He has answered. Thank you.

Today

Max: He chose to study in Florence, Italy for the first half of his junior year at Gonzaga and had the time of his life. He graduated from Gonzaga on time, in four years. Thank you for that! He is working for an advertising agency in downtown Seattle. We are very proud of Max. He's an awesome guy. He continues to tell us he's, "Livin' the dream."

Anna: She graduated from Washington State University with honors, also in four years. She works in downtown Seattle in public relations and loves her job. She's very happy, has a terrific attitude, and is having a great life. She is completely healed. Oh, and she likes her mom!

Greg and I: When Anna left for college, we took a three-week vacation to recuperate from the stress of the last three years. Both the kids missed us. Funny.

Sampson and Moses are alive and well.

Our beloved Jazz died peacefully at the age of sixteen in August of 2012. Greg, Max, and I were with him, petting him and loving him until the very last moment.

Anna's wonderful Belle died at the age of nineteen in November of 2015. She was surrounded by Greg, Anna, and me.

Those two cats were loved and cherished. They will never know how much I appreciated what they did for our family.

When you write a book, the first thing people ask you is what your title is going to be. *Three* has been the title of this book from the moment it was born.

- There were three beings in the car on the day of the accident. Two were human.

- From the day of the car accident until Anna went back to school three weeks had passed.

- Anna's three-point shot at State was a culmination of her determination and success to regain her normal self.

- I started writing this book three years after the car accident.

- It took three years to write the book.

- *Three* is a story of Faith, Hope, and Prayer

It's proven to be a worthy title and for good reason, both apparent and not so apparent from beginning to end.

About the Author

Lynn Brown lives in Kirkland, Washington with her husband Greg. After having two wonderful careers in retail buying and sales, she decided to retire and enjoy every moment of her young family's life. This allowed Lynn to volunteer as room mom, team mom, and chaperone as long as Max and Anna would let her. Lynn is also a church volunteer, gardener and caretaker of her cottage, as well as, the author of her first book *Three*.

Visit:

www.threethebook.com

Made in the USA
San Bernardino, CA
15 September 2017